Securities Arbitration for Brokers, Attorneys, and Investors

Securities Arbitration for Brokers, Attorneys, and Investors

J. KIRKLAND GRANT

Q

QUORUM BOOKS
Westport, Connecticut • London

Library of Congress Cataloging-in-Publication Data

Grant, J. Kirkland.
Securities arbitration for brokers, attorneys, and investors / J. Kirkland Grant.
p. cm.
Includes index.
ISBN 0–89930–682–9 (alk. paper)
1. Securities—United States. 2. Arbitration and award—United States. I. Title.
KF1070.G73 1994
346.73'066'0269—dc20
[347.306660269] 94–2992

British Library Cataloguing in Publication Data is available.

Library of Congress Catalog Card Number: 94–2992
ISBN: 0–89930–682–9

First published in 1994

Quorum Books, 88 Post Road West, Westport, CT 06881
An imprint of Greenwood Publishing Group, Inc.

Printed in the United States of America

The paper used in this book complies with the Permanent Paper Standard issued by the National Information Standards Organization (Z39.48–1984).

10 9 8 7 6 5 4 3 2 1

This Book Is Dedicated to N.P.G.
And I.F.G.,
Both Of Whom Have Been My Strength And Inspiration.

CONTENTS

LIST OF ABBREVIATIONS

1933 Act	The Securities Act of 1933
1934 Act	The Securities and Exchange Act of 1934
AAA	American Arbitration Association
AMEX	The American Stock Exchange
C.B.O.E.	The Chicago Board Options Exchange
CPLR	New York Civil Practice Law and Rules (McKinney's 1993 Supp.)
de Quijas	*Rodriguez de Quijas v. Shearson/American Express, Inc.*
Exchange Act	Securities and Exchange Act of 1934
FAA	Federal Arbitration Act
Federal Arbitration Act	The Federal Arbitration Act of 1925
Federal Securities Laws	The 1933 and 1934 Securities Acts, Trust Indenture Act of 1939, Investment Company Act of 1940, and other federal statutes enforced under the auspices of the Securities and Exchange Commission.
F.R.C.P.	Federal Rules of Civil Procedure

McMahon	*Shearson/American Express Inc. v. McMahon*
N.A.S.D.	National Association of Securities Dealers, Inc.
N.F.A.	National Futures Association, Inc.
N.Y. CPLR	See CPLR
N.Y.S.E.	The New York Stock Exchange, Inc.
RICO	Rocketeer Influenced Corrupt Organizations Act
Rodriguez	*Rodriguez de Quijas v. Shearson/American Express, Inc.*
SEC	The Securities and Exchange Commission
Securities Act	The Securities Act of 1993
S.I.C.A.	Securities Industry Conference on Arbitration
SRO	Self-Regulatory Organization. Under the 1934 Act, a securities industry organization that regulates conduct of members to ensure compliance with fair and equitable principles.
U.S.C.	United States Code
Uniform Act	The Uniform Arbitration Act
Uniform Code	The Securities Industry Conference on Arbitration Uniform Code of Arbitration
Wilko	*Wilko v. Swan*

PREFACE

Arbitration is a method whereby two or more persons have a dispute between them resolved by impartial persons, called arbitrators. Typically, the persons resolving the dispute have some expertise in the subject area of the controversy.[1] Processing cases in forums other than the courts has become popular in recent years. One of the hallmarks of Warren Burger's tenure as Chief Justice of the U.S. Supreme Court, was his advocacy of alternative dispute resolution as a way to relieve the perceived heavy burden of cases and expense in the court system.

Securities arbitration has existed for over 175 years and is now the primary method used to resolve disputes in the securities industry. It is an attractive alternative to expensive and time-consuming litigation in the courts, permitting resolution of conflict in an orderly and timely manner. This book, directed at securities industry members, customers, and lawyers, teaches how to take a potential securities claim and evaluate, commence, prosecute, and resolve it through the use of securities arbitration. The key for success in securities arbitration is: (1) knowledge of law and procedure, and (2) mastery of the facts in dispute. This book will discuss the former; the latter is the responsibility of the person bringing a securities arbitration claim. By knowing the facts, the law will fall into place and the claim can be evaluated and prosecuted successfully.

This book concerns methods by which a lawyer, customer, or broker can utilize the process of securities arbitration to settle disputes arising in connection with the brokerage industry. It is oriented to the unsophisticated lawyer or customer, either a business or individual, who might confront problems in the manner in which the brokerage firm and its employees, including the customer's registered representative, have dealt with the customer and her account. Discussed briefly are various theories of brokerage firm liability, such as churning, the "know your customer" rule, suitability, and the like. These issues of liability are then developed through examination of the viability of the claim and probable successful arbitration. Included are materials for settlement and mediation of securities disputes.

Securities industry arbitration began principally as a means of resolving disputes among brokers and those connected with the securities business. Today, "industry arbitration" still describes arbitration between those engaged in the securities industry, but arbitration has progressed to where conflicts between industry persons and those not affiliated with the brokerage industry, principally customers,use this process.

1987 AS A SEISMIC YEAR

In a 1987 case, the U.S. Supreme Court found that customers were bound to arbitrate even when there were alleged violations of federal securities law, a matter previously felt to be properly decided in the federal courts. This case and another 1987 event had an impact on the resolution of disputes arising between brokerage firms and their customers that might be compared to an earthquake--both shook the foundations of the prior methods used by the securities industry to resolve disputes, and since that time, the growth in securities arbitration has been exponential. The June U.S. Supreme Court ruling in the case *Shearson/American Express, Inc. v. McMahon*,[2] expanded in 1989 by *Rodriguez de Quijas v. Shearson/American Express, Inc.*,[3] held that securities industry customers who have signed standard contracts opening brokerage accounts, most of which contain standard clauses selecting arbitration forums for resolution of disputes *before* the occurrence of a dispute,[4] were relegated to the alternative dispute resolution process in the event of a dispute and could not apply to the courts for judicial relief. *McMahon* concerned claims under both the federal securities laws[5] and the Racketeer Influenced and Corrupt Organizations Act (RICO),[6] all of which were held arbitrable in a securities industry forum.

Prior to *McMahon*, the law permitted brokerage customers alleging violations of the federal securities laws to select either the federal courts or arbitration to resolve the issues. The arbitration decision had to be made *after* the dispute arose; not *before*. Since these cases, securities arbitration, rather than judicial action, has been the appropriate manner for resolution of most investor-broker disputes, as a result of *predispute* arbitration clauses in the standard, form-pad brokerage customer agreements. It no longer matters that investor claims are made for violation of the securities or other federal or state statutes; arbitration will decide all the issues presented.

The second event that has had a far-reaching effect on the arbitration process in the securities industry occurred less than five months later--the October 19, 1987, "Black Monday"--when in one day the stock market declined over 500 points on the Dow-Jones' averages,[7] or over 22 percent of the Dow value. The value of all outstanding U.S. stocks decreased by almost one trillion dollars.

A flood of legal claims was filed by customers for losses associated with the stock market plunge that day. The very size and volume of trading on Black Monday caused confusion. Brokers have a fiduciary duty to execute trades for their customers at the best possible price. Included in Black Monday's aftermath were disputes regarding improper executions, inaccurate quotes, non-execution of trades ordered, poor price executions, as well as precipitous liquidation of margin accounts without notification and ability to cover margin calls. Under the *McMahon* and *Rodriguez* precedents, most of these claims were resolved by industry arbitration pursuant to the customer's predispute arbitration agreement.

Due to the mass of arbitration filings for 1987 activities and the more than doubling in cases submitted for arbitration since then, arbitration facilities in securities were strained. Public pressure called for the introduction of new rules, procedures, and responses. As a result, increased attention has been given to securities arbitration dispute resolution.

MATTERS TO BE EXAMINED

This book will examine the common law view of arbitration, its advantages and disadvantages, both before and after its change by state statutes and the Federal Arbitration Act of 1925.[8] The interaction of the federal securities laws and arbitration will be examined in regard to caselaw, including the 1953 landmark case of *Wilko v. Swan*,[9] which held claims under § 12(2) of the Securities Act of 1933 not to be arbitrable. It will then consider the development through *Wilko's* progeny, up to its reversal in the *McMahon* and *Rodriguez* cases. The arbitration process and forums within the securities industry and the American Arbitration Association (AAA) securities industry arbitration, including evaluation of the claim, the typical procedure to begin and present a securities case in arbitration, and possible review of the arbitration award by a court will be reviewed. Throughout, the book will examine whether arbitration adequately protects the investor in today's securities markets.

For the reference of the readers, included are the arbitration rules of the different forums hearing securities disputes; model submission agreements, which initiate securities arbitrations; the Federal Arbitration Act (see Appendix A) and references to state arbitration statutes, including New York's arbitration law (see Appendix B), which was the model for the Federal Act. Forms have been included to meet general requirements and provide assistance to the drafter, including a form for submission of a claim in securities arbitration, examples of discovery requests, subpoenas, and other forms that the lawyer or the parties will find helpful in contemplating prosecution of a claim in securities arbitration. Also included is basic information about the types of violations that a customer might experience in his or her dealings with a brokerage firm. Industry claims are also briefly covered.

Thus the goal of this book is to provide information to the lawyer and layman about the grounds for and procedures of securities arbitration and, to a lesser extent, securities mediation. Using this volume, a claim can be evaluated and the process can be begun and taken to the final stages in resolution of the conflict.

ACKNOWLEDGMENTS

This book is an expansion of an article written for *The New England Law Review*,[10] and parts are reprinted with permission of *The New England Law Review* but not otherwise acknowledged in the text. Research assistance on this book has been generously provided by President Bernard Lander and Dean Howard A. Glickstein of Touro College Law Center. I thank my research assistants Hillel Goldman, Michael DeSantis, Robert Saldarelli, Susan Coyle and Eugene Petrone, and for preparation of this manuscript, the late Carolyn Popielarski, Amelia Wilson, Marj Daniels, Lorraine Winch, and particularly the significant contribution of M. Karen Lall in preparing this printed copy. The materials have also benefited from my experience as a member of the arbitration panels of the New York Stock Exchange, American Stock Exchange, National Association of Securities Dealers, and the American Arbitration Association, and in representing parties involved in securities disputes resolved through arbitration. Much of the practical advice in this book comes from such experience. I am also indebted to Christopher Marley, Esq., who prepared the material on discovery, and together with Peter D. Grant, Lawrence Steckman, Esq., and Barry Warren, Esq., reviewed this manuscript, making many valuable suggestions on form and content. However, the author remains responsible for any and all errors and omissions.

I hope that this book will be a valuable and practical aid to those interested in the resolution of securities industry disputes through arbitration and mediation.

Huntington, New York J. Kirkland Grant

NOTES

1 *See* ARBITRATION PROCEDURES 3, a pamphlet prepared by the Securities Industry Conference on Arbitration (S.I.C.A.) (May, 1991 ed.), which is contained in Appendix C.

2 482 U.S. 220 (1987).

3 490 U.S. 477, 109 S. Ct. 1917 (1989).

4 *See* chapter 6 which discusses the content of a customer's agreement and the clause providing for predispute arbitration.

5 The term "securities laws" as used herein refers to the Securities Act of 1933, 15 U.S.C. §§ 77a-77m (1982) (1933 Act), and the Securities and Exchange Act of 1934, 15 U.S.C. §§ 78a-78kk (1982 and 1988 Supp.) (Exchange Act or 1934 Act). *McMahon* raised issues under § 10 of the Exchange Act, and *Rodriguez* under § 12(2) of the 1933 Act. *Wilko v. Swan*, overruled by *McMahon* and *Rodriguez*, is discussed in detail in chapter 8.

6 19 U.S.C. §§ 1961-1968 (1982 and Supp. II 1988) (RICO). Section 1961 of RICO provides a private right of action for violation of the statute, triggered if the plaintiff can show that a defendant conducted an "enterprise" engaging in a "pattern of racketeering activity." Section 1961 defines a "pattern" as two or more violations of certain criminal offenses (including fraud in the sale of securities violative of the federal securities laws, and federal mail and wire fraud along with murder and robbery) within ten years. Of major import is the penalty recovery permitted--treble damages and attorney's fees if a violation is proved.

7 From 2,200 to 1,734 in a record turnover of 245 million shares. The Dow had hit a high of 2,722 on Aug. 25, 1987. Stocks had, however, begun the decline earlier--235.48 points on Friday, Oct. 16, 1987. On Friday, Oct. 23, 1987, the Dow regained some of its loss and closed at 1950.76. Other markets also had precipitous declines on Black Monday.

8 Federal Arbitration Act of 1925, P. L. No. 68-401, 43 Stat. 883, codified as amended at 9 U.S.C. §§ 1-14, 201-208 (1982) (reproduced in Appendix A).

9 346 U.S. 427 (1953).

10 J. Kirkland Grant, *Securities Arbitration: Is Required Arbitration Fair to Investors?*, 24 NEW ENG. L. REV. 389 (1989).

Chapter 1

DISPUTE RESOLUTION METHODS

Conflict resolution is the underlying issue in arbitration, but it can occur using many different processes. This chapter briefly examines the alternative procedures available to resolve conflicts arising between parties in a private relationship--as opposed to conflicts between a person and the public order that result in violation of some duty or law and must be resolved in the judicial system.

1) GENERALLY

Conflict seems to be on the rise in an increasingly complex economic, political, and social order. The resolution of disputes that have arisen among parties can take place in many venues and utilize the efforts of many types of institutions. The rules governing the procedure and practice of these different types of conflict resolution derive from many sources, including common law, statutes, and custom. Ultimately, force can also be used to resolve conflict--whether it be public (nation to nation, e.g., wars; or nation to individual, e.g., criminal acts) or private (a duel or punch in the nose)--but civilization has continually tried to eliminate the use of force and encouraged the substitution of reasoning to resolve a dispute with a minimum of disruption to the fabric of society.

There is nothing in the definition of conflict to indicate that, in itself, conflict is evil. While some conflicts are evil, such as one resulting in murder or war atrocities, it should be the goal of society and all members of the human race to minimize its bad results. One way to do this is through dispute resolution without the use of force or might.

2) LITIGATION TO RESOLVE DISPUTES

One of the reasons for the existence of government is to resolve the disputes that arise affecting its citizens and to protect the populace from incursions due to conflicts with outsiders. As a result, governments will typically provide conflict resolution procedures in order to satisfy this need and justify their existence. In our system, courts have been established by the governmental entity (whether federal or state) and are designed to meet this need. The determination of the court is normally referred to as a judgment or decision.

The judicial system that has developed is bound by rules and regulations, both external governing laws adopted by the legislative organs of government and regulations set by the executive and judiciary. It is as a result of these strictures bound by an increasingly complex hierarchy of courts, that trial courts, or courts of first impression, hear the dispute through taking evidence and listening to the arguments of the parties. Appellate courts, sometimes of several levels, review the lower court actions in terms of the proper application of procedures and legal rules in such a way as to maintain a system of order, and within that legal system a degree of uniformity in application of legal rules, so that there is some degree of certainty and predictability in governing the relations of the state and its citizens.

Of course, a major feature of litigation is that one party can force the other party to have the conflict resolved by a court having jurisdiction over the issue or person of the other party. This coercive nature of litigation suggests that the parties might be unwilling to participate at all in settlement of the conflict, and the positions of the parties will certainly harden. The result is a loss of flexibility and further coercion in order to force acquiescence in the decision imposed by the court upon the losing side. However, the result in the judicial decision may not be the most meaningful; the parties may have been able to resolve their differences in a more meaningful and socially useful manner, but for their inability to resolve the conflict between themselves.

3) DESIRE FOR NON-JUDICIAL DISPUTE RESOLUTION

As a result, for any number of reasons, parties to a dispute may want to resort to the judicial system established by the state for the resolution of their disputes. Of course, many disputes will not be permitted to be resolved outside the state system--criminal actions and other violations of society's required standards of minimal behavior. But with purely civil matters, which do not affect the state or society and are only disputes between private parties, there is every reason to use a process outside the parameters of state sponsorship and control. Of course, the major reason for using these alternatives to judicial determination is the fact that they differ from the court system--radically in some cases. There has been a dramatic increase in the use of alternatives to the court process in the last half century. Arbitration is only one of these methods. It is these different sources of dispute resolution that this chapter examines. The next chapter will examine the arbitration procedure in greater detail, and the remainder of this book will then dissect the process of arbitration of securities disputes.

4) ARBITRATION AS A METHOD OF DISPUTE RESOLUTION CREATED BY CONTRACT

Arbitration is one of the methods whereby the parties select an alternative to conflict resolution in the court system. It is the reference of a dispute through voluntary agreement of the parties to an impartial person who will resolve the conflict by determination on the basis of submission of evidence and, in most cases, argument by the parties. Because it is the creature of contract agreement between the parties, arbitration is a matter of contract.[1] The parties normally agree to be bound by the arbitrator's determination in advance of a submission to arbitration.[2] In a more informal setting, arbitration can be an unofficial person's investigation and determination of a disputed matter submitted by the contending parties for decision.[3] It is only a form of procedure for settling differences, not a definition of rights and wrongs out of which the dispute has arisen.[4] The decision of the arbitrator(s) is normally referred to as an award, rather than a judicial decision or judgment.

A) Forms of Arbitration

There are at least three forms of arbitration. The first, used in securities and most other arbitrations, is binding arbitration under which the parties agree to accept the decision of the arbitrator with no appeal. The second is the high/low arbitration, where the parties agree to accept a minimum and pay a maximum and any amount set by the arbitrator within those ranges is binding. The parameters are not revealed to the arbitrator, and if the figure is outside the range, the claimant receives the minimum amount agreed to by the respondent. Third is "baseball" arbitration, where each party submits a figure to the arbitrator who is bound to accept one or the other but no other amount. It is so named because of its use in baseball player contract disputes.

B) What is Arbitrable?

Because the arbitration of disputes is a matter of contract, the parties can agree by private negotiation to submit almost any conflict for resolution by use of the arbitration process. Under the arbitration statutes,[5] there is clear preference for arbitrability, provided that the agreement to arbitrate is unambiguous. Consequently, almost any dispute connected, however tenuously, to those for which arbitration is provided will be arbitrable. Reference to arbitration will be permitted even when the contract is very general, for example providing that all disputes are arbitrable, regardless of the fact that the parties did not even contemplate a particular conflict ever arising.[6] If there is some reason to question the parties voluntary agreement to arbitrate the dispute, however, a court will stay the arbitration proceeding.

Clearly, the parties to private treaties can also exclude matters from arbitration. In such cases, the arbitrator will find that the submission is improper, or one party can go into court and seek a stay of the arbitration proceeding.

5) OTHER DISPUTE RESOLUTION PROCEDURES

In addition to the use of the judicial system (in litigation) and arbitration, other methods of conflict resolution between private parties have developed over the years. Arbitration coexists with the judicial process (litigation) and these other private dispute resolution procedures. Sometimes all of these non-judicial dispute resolution methods are referred to as Alternative Dispute Resolution (ADR). The major difference between arbitration and these other forms of dispute resolution is that most other methods do not provide a binding determination.[7] Among these other ADR procedures are:

A) Mediation

Mediation is the process of persuasion. A neutral third party, the mediator, intermediates between the parties to a dispute for the purpose of making suggestions, forcing the parties to listen to the facts, and to avoid emotionalism, all of which will lead the parties to reconciliation and settlement of the dispute through the mediator's conciliation, accommodative recommendations, clarifications, interpretations, and advice. The process is voluntary. Either party can reject further action by the mediator. The mediator has no power to make a final determination of the conflict--unlike arbitration where the arbitrator is authorized by the parties to make a decision based on the evidence and arguments presented by the parties.[8]

Parties choose mediation to have more control over the process than with either the court or arbitration resolution of the dispute. The parties ultimately must decide to continue with mediation and whether or not to accept the suggestions of the mediator that will lead them to mutually agree as to a resolution of the conflict. The process is felt to be speedier than the judicial process, and more fair and open to a result reflecting the parties views. Moreover, it leads to a lessening of hostilities, especially when the parties must continue to work with one another, by not polarizing the positions of the parties; further, it is seen as being less expensive than both arbitration or litigation, focusing on the causes of the disagreement and resulting in more creative solutions in accommodative problem solving by the parties.

Case appraisal is a type of mediation in which the parties agree that they will not be bound by the decision of the mediator and can proceed to bring the action in court. Statistics show that this form of mediation-arbitration is successful in resolving the dispute in 90 percent of the cases. Typically, the mediator is not connected to the parties, unbiased by either financial or personal relationships (unless both parties consent). There are professional associations of mediators, and these organizations have established ethical standards of responsibility for those acting in the field.[9] The mediator may have joint and separate meetings with the parties; obtain expert advice; and generally conducts the mediation within very broad ground rules established by the parties at the time of the submission to mediation. Normally there is one mediator, although the parties can select more if it is a complicated matter or for other reasons. There is no stenographic record, and the mediation can not affect the rights or position of either party in later litigation, arbitration, or other proceedings. The American Arbitration Association encourages mediation.[10]

Sometimes the parties will agree to Med-Arb, a process where the issues not resolved in mediation will be submitted to arbitration for final determination. This process gives parties more control over the resolution of issues, but results in binding determination of those issues they are unable to resolve.

B) Summary Jury Trial

Summary jury trials have each side present their case, in an abbreviated form, to a mock jury before a judge or magistrate in a courtroom. Witnesses are typically not examined, but their testimony is offered by each side. The jury renders an advisory verdict, which may not be used in later action if the parties refuse to be bound by it, but often gives the parties an idea of the probable result in an actual jury trial and leads to more directed settlement discussions. If the "advisory verdict" is not accepted, the case will be put on the trial calendar.

C) Mini-Trial

A mini-trial may also be held. Under this procedure, the rules of evidence are relaxed and evidence is presented much like the summary jury trial. The trial, however, is before an attorney-mediator who establishes the rules of procedure. It is a fact finding process, and often results in stipulation of the facts upon trial and settlement.

D) Conciliation

In conciliation, a neutral third party reduces the parties hostility, bringing them together to discuss and resolve the conflict at issue. The conciliator does not participate in the process, nor does the conciliator have the power to compel attendance, take evidence, or decide the issue. It is, therefore, a much less compulsory process than either litigation or arbitration, and it is even less intrusive than mediation.

E) Reference

Reference is the act of referring a case to a referee, auditor, or master by a court. The referee (which includes master or auditor in this discussion) is an impartial party who by appointment becomes an officer of the court for a specific purpose--usually only that which he was appointed to hear. The referee has the powers of a judicial officer, including the powers to take evidence, hear testimony, hear arguments of the parties, and find facts that are in dispute. The factual findings determined by the referee are submitted to the referring court, usually in a written report of the referee, and normally adopted by the court.

The parties can agree to submit the dispute to final decision by the referee, in which case the findings in the report will be final. The report will so indicate and become conclusive unless tainted by a material error of law. If the parties do not agree to the referee making a final decision, the report can be treated only as *prima facie* evidence by the judge.[11] In appropriate cases, usually when there is an error of law, the report can be resubmitted through a motion to recommit. Basically, since the referee process is instigated by the court, it is subject to judicial supervision even when the parties agree the report is to be final. It is contrasted with arbitration, where the arbitrator's award is final and hardly ever subject to judicial review.[12]

The use of the referee depends to some extent on local practice and state or federal law that must be examined to determine if the matter can be subject to reference. In New York, for example, it is relatively easy to get a reference--either by the court or by stipulation of the parties. In that state, a referee might well be preferable to arbitration--because the decisions of the referee are advisory to the court, the court's action on the referee's recommendation is fully appealable in the judicial system--it has all the advantages of arbitration with appealability.[13]

F) Fact Finding

Fact finding is the process whereby an impartial third party is asked by the parties to a dispute to investigate the facts and issues. The fact finder is normally asked only to report findings, but sometimes will also make recommendations regarding settlement of the dispute. The recommendations and report of findings are not binding on the parties in most cases.[14]

Fact finding is non-judicial and not binding on the parties, much the same as mediation and conciliation. The parties may stipulate to be bound by the findings and then return to negotiations or other dispute resolution methods to finally resolve the conflict.[15]

G) Negotiation

Where the parties to a dispute meet in an effort to resolve their differences and settle the conflict, a negotiation process is undertaken. This is the best possible resolution of the dispute, since the parties themselves reach the solution. A mutuality of commitment results, which is probably better than even acceptance of settlements proposed by fact finders, mediators, or conciliators; and, certainly more apt to have the agreement of the parties than imposed settlements resulting from litigation or arbitration reached by non-parties.

Negotiations often begin by conferences, discussions, and bargaining by attorneys for the parties to a dispute. Normally they are resolved through bargaining: the submission of offers by each side until an agreeable offer is made and accepted.[16]

H) Settlement as the Best Alternative

Settlement of the dispute is probably the best solution. Both parties will probably be somewhat dissatisfied; but the mutual agreement will lead to easy enforcement, as the parties will perform as agreed in most cases. The problem is that by the time lawyers are involved, the parties have reached the conclusion that they will be unable to settle the dispute themselves. Consequently, one advantage of the lawyer's involvement is that he or she may look at the dispute differently than the involved parties and come up with creative solutions that will lead to settlement--the best of all worlds since it can be prompt and efficient. Other similar techniques are the neutral evaluation (or non-binding mediation) mini trial, or summary jury trial. Often a lawyer will be able to link these different methods to result in an acceptable compromise prior to litigation or arbitration.[17]

Most disputes are undoubtedly settled through negotiations between the parties. It is only the most severe conflict that will lead the parties to engage others to assist them in settling it. Litigation and arbitration obviously are the least attractive forms of settlement, since the parties have little to say about the determination of the outcome. Whether by jury trial, judicial determination, or arbitration award, the ultimate decision is out of the hands of the parties and in the hands of neutral, impartial persons who, in many cases, haven't the vaguest idea about the matters in controversy and must be educated as to the business as well as the facts of the dispute. To the extent that the trier of the conflict is not informed, and perhaps does not care, the outcome is subject to question.

6) CONCLUSION

There are many different alternative dispute resolution methods from which to select. In some cases, such as under brokerage firm customer agreements, binding arbitration will be expressly provided for. In other cases (and in securities cases as well), the parties can opt for another method in the hope of resolving the dispute out of court quickly and economically.

Mediation achieves the goals of low cost, high speed, and the possibility of maintaining or improving the relationship of the parties while offering somewhat greater privacy. If vindication is desired by a party, litigation is the best, but will be lengthy and expensive; arbitration, especially now with the release of award information in the securities industry, may also serve this goal. A binding precedent will be created only in litigation.

Possibly the biggest impediment to mediation and settlement, however, is that for most securities claims the parties have severed their relationship. There is little to gain in compromise, unlike in business situations when the prospect of future business may help make up more give-and-take in negotiations.

Undoubtedly, the best arbitration is no arbitration.[18] The parties will be best served by deciding the conflict themselves. It is to this end that ADR has developed. The essence of ADR, other than arbitration, is compromise voluntarily reached by both the parties. These solutions to disputes will bear the imprimatur of both sides to a dispute and thus be observed in compliance with the result agreed upon without need for involvement of others in enforcement. But ADR procedures are not always available, and in those cases where the parties are unable or unwilling to resolve the dispute themselves, arbitration and litigation procedures suffice to resolve the dispute for them.

NOTES

1 *See* the discussion in chapter 2 regarding the contract basis of arbitration generally.

2 *See* C.J.S. ARBITRATION § 5 (1975).

3 *Id.* § 14.

4 *See* R. RODMAN, COMMERCIAL ARBITRATION § 1.1 (1984 and 1987 Supp.).

5 *See* chapter 4.

6 *See* RODMAN, *supra* note 4, at § 5.2.

7 *See* the finality of the arbitration award discussion in chapter 6.

8 *See* RODMAN, *supra* note 4, at § 2.21; N. ROGERS & C. MCEWEN, MEDIATION: LAW, POLICY, PRACTICE (1989).

9 *See* Ethical Standards of Professional Responsibility for the Society of Professions in Dispute Resolution (adopted 1986); The American Bar Association's Standards of Practice for Lawyer Mediators in Family Disputes (adopted by the House of Delegates in 1984).

10 *See* the discussion of the AMEX Pilot Mediation Program and AAA mediation under AAA Securities Arbitration Rule § 10 in chapter 10. *See* 3 SEC. ARB. COMM., discussing securities mediation.

11 *See* RODMAN, *supra* note 4, at § 2.51.

12 *See* chapters 5 and 16 for discussion of the overturning of arbitration awards.

13 *See* N.Y. CPLR 7500 *et seq.* (McKinney 1980); J. KIRKLAND GRANT & E. SCHULMAN, USE OF A REFEREE : ALL THE ADVANTAGES OF ARBITRATION *PLUS* THE RIGHT OF APPEAL MANUSCRIPT (1994).

14 *See* RODMAN, *supra* note 4, at § 2.71.

15 *See* Abramson, A PRIMER ON RESOLVING DISPUTES: LESSONS FROM ALTERNATIVE DISPUTE RESOLUTION, N.Y. ST. B. J. 51 (1992).

16 *See* RODMAN, *supra* note 4, at § 2.61.

17 *See* Sander and Goldberg, MAKING THE RIGHT CHOICE, 79 A.B.A. J. 66 (1993).

18 W. BAER, ARBITRATION FOR THE PRACTITIONER xi (1988).

Chapter 2

THE HISTORY OF ARBITRATION

In order to understand the present process of securities dispute arbitration, it is necessary to have some background in how arbitration developed.

1) ARBITRATION AS A CREATURE OF CONTRACT

A general principle of contract law is that parties may agree to make any arrangement that they desire.[1] Absent a public policy against such an arrangement, the contractual agreement will be enforced by the courts within the intent of the parties. Consequently, predispute arbitration clauses selecting a forum for dispute resolution are supported by the courts under concepts of freedom of contract.[2] The agreement to arbitrate is perceived primarily as a forum-selection clause, but also governs procedures to be applied. As long as there is no fraud involved in the parties' determination of the arbitration forum and procedures, this intention regarding resolution of disputes will be recognized and arbitration enforced, even if in some cases there may be a loss of the proper judicial forum which also carries with it the loss of substantial rights.[3]

Basically, the obligation to arbitrate derives from the agreement between the parties.[4] An intent to avoid the judicial process can easily be stated: the contract should simply and clearly state that arbitration applies to all disputes arising under the contract, including the question of whether arbitration is available. It must be in writing. The arbitration clauses in contracts usually fall into three categories. A broad clause, providing for arbitration of "any dispute arising out of or relating to this contract,"[5] is, for example, felt to intend to submit almost any dispute to arbitration. A more narrow clause, for example, to submit any dispute "relating to the calculation of insurance coverage," would, of course, indicate intent to reserve disputes in all other areas than such coverage calculations to the court rather than the arbitrator. The middle ground is a clause that is ambiguous as to the parties' desire to submit the type of dispute that has arisen to arbitration. As with other contracts, the court must then consider the tone of the clause within the contract as a whole in determining whether the dispute falls within the type that requires arbitration. Once again, there is no excuse for drafting a clause that is not clear--unless the intent is to permit judicial review.[6] But this will defeat the major advantages of arbitration: quick and cost efficient resolution of disputes.

A) Tests For Arbitration

A four part test has developed to determine whether disputes should be arbitrated under common law:[7]

1. Did the parties agree to arbitrate?[8]
2. Is the dispute within the scope of the written arbitration agreement?
3. If statutory claims are asserted, did the legislative body intend those claims to be non-arbitrable? and
4. If the court concludes that some, but not all, of the claims in the case are arbitrable, it must then determine whether to stay the balance of the proceedings pending arbitration.

B) Effect of Arbitration

Once the parties lawfully submit to arbitration and a final decision is reached, the result is binding.[9] Furthermore, if one of the parties tried to relitigate the issues decided in that arbitration, the doctrine of *res judicata* applies[10] and, in appropriate cases, sanctions are imposed, such as recovery of attorney's fees and costs under Rule 11 of the Federal Rules of Civil Procedure or Rule 38 of the Federal Rules of Appellate Procedure.[11] Under the Federal Rules of Civil Procedure 8(c), collateral estoppel will also bar a subsequent proceeding even on a different cause of action and in another court (federal or state) because an arbitration award can be pled as an affirmative defense.[12]

C) Securities Arbitration: Predispute Arbitration Agreements

If the parties have indicated their agreement to arbitration of a dispute *after* it has arisen, the courts are uniform in enforcing such arbitration.[13] A predispute arbitration agreement is limited, however, to disputes arising after its execution, and prior disputes are not arbitrable.[14] Because arbitration in the securities industry refers a dispute to an impartial person or persons chosen by the parties, its jurisdiction arises from and is based on voluntary agreement of the parties, or their contract.[15]

Not all brokerage house customer agreements contain mandatory predispute arbitration clauses. Of those that do not, securities arbitration will still be available after the dispute arises. The language used in brokerage firm agreements is reviewed in chapter 6. An agreement to submit an existing dispute to arbitration is binding.

D) Goal of Predispute Arbitration Agreements

Since the intent of the parties in predispute arbitration agreements is to achieve a final disposition of a future dispute in an easier, more expeditious and less expensive manner than litigating such a dispute, its goal is to avoid the formalities, delay, and expense of the judicial dispute resolution process. The parties' intent in a contract containing a predispute arbitration clause, as a result, should result in very limited judicial review of the arbitration process and award.

2) HISTORY OF ARBITRATION

Arbitration has been called the "oldest known method of settlement of disputes."[16] King Solomon used arbitration;[17] Roman law recognized arbitration agreements;[18] and mythology evidences arbitration precedents.[19] The preference for arbitration centers on the "ancient concepts of freedom of contract."[20]

International arbitration and negotiation have also been used to settle differences between nations, resolving issues which might lead, or did lead to, armed conflict.[21]

The English tradition developed from Roman practices as interpreted by the ecclesiastical courts and application of canon law from the 7th century.[22] The medieval British craft and merchant guilds established arbitration as a means of resolution of disputes among guild members by the 14th century. Thus the development of merchant law included provisions for private dispute resolution by arbitration. By the mid 19th century, arbitration was tolerated by the English courts, but prior to that time there was a generally hostile attitude toward the arbitration process and determinations.

Early English courts were not interested in the way guilds enforced what they considered purely private matters, including submissions to arbitration. Consequently, arbitration within the guild membership and even among different guilds became the rule. Of course, one of the major questions was how to enforce an arbitration award. This was accomplished within the guild, with the ultimate penalty being ouster from membership with its attendant loss of livelihood: a drastic result for not observing an arbitration award. Some guilds enacted regulations that forbade members from litigating in the courts, but a 1504 statute prohibited the guilds from barring actions at law.[23]

The common law of England at the time of the revolutionary war and the formation of a separate common law in the United States was hostile to arbitration. But the early state statutes permitting arbitration applied to already existing disputes and permitted court enforcement of an award without further court procedure.[24] Thus English arbitration was applicable to both pre- and post-dispute arbitrations, while American arbitrations were enforced only as to agreements to arbitrate arising *after* the dispute had arisen.

By the middle of the 19th century, even the U.S. Supreme Court had held that an arbitrator's "honest decision" should not be set aside even for mistakes of law or fact.[25] But both state and federal courts were not disposed to permit predispute arbitration agreements that would "oust the courts of jurisdiction conferred by law"[26] and "allow the parties to deprive themselves of their right of resort to the courts."[27]

3) COMMON LAW DISFAVOR OF ARBITRATION

Nevertheless, the courts were hesitant to deny themselves jurisdiction over otherwise judicial actions. They were reluctant to enforce predispute arbitration agreements if there was any way the court could find to do so.[28]

The common law therefore adopted the approach that parties could revoke their agreement to submit to arbitration and request judicial resolution of disputes, even up to the point in time immediately before the arbitrator's award was rendered. Typically, this came in a judicial action for a stay of arbitration. It was always more difficult for the courts to overturn an already rendered decision to which the parties had submitted themselves and in which process they had participated. To overturn an award, common law required that it fall into certain well-defined grounds: statutes that forbade arbitration of this type of dispute; or judicially created grounds such as manifest disregard of the law, capriciousness, arbitrariness, or a result against the weight of the evidence. Another argument against arbitration, especially of statutory claims, was that the arbitrators are not bound by *stare decisis* and need not justify nor explain their decisions. The courts also found that arbitration was inapplicable because of legislative intent to allow redress only by judicial process, especially in claims involving violation of a statute which provided a judicial remedy.

The courts, therefore, were not responsive to arbitration agreements. When one party to such a predispute agreement desired, that party needed only to bring an action in a judicial forum seeking judicial redress instead. In the early days, one explanation advanced for the courts' hostility was related to the judges salaries, which came from fees of the cases before them. Naturally, the judges were unwilling to countenance a process that would reduce their incomes, and arbitration resulted in no fees to the court. Perhaps a more highbrow explanation may be that the judges simply wanted to obtain jurisdiction over as much dispute resolution as possible, and they had the power of the state, as opposed to mere contract, at their disposal.[29]

A) Venue

Another reason for this judicial attitude was the development of venue concepts. While parties cannot normally select judicial venue, or the place where the dispute will be determined, in arbitration the situs of the determining forum is controlled by the terms of the arbitration agreement. The purpose of venue requirements is to serve the convenience of the parties and witnesses, and thus promote efficient litigation. One of the concerns of venue is the due process rights of defendants. For example, the defendant's procedural rights are guaranteed under the Fifth Amendment of the U.S. Constitution, which applies in both litigation and arbitration. There are many similarities to the justifications for arbitration. In the securities area, this was evidenced by plaintiffs "forum shopping," or

> purposely selecting a distant forum with the intent of coercing a weaker defendant into settlement. Unfortunately for brokerage house defendants, the . . . actions are almost universally instituted by "weak" investors and defended by "strong" brokerage houses. Consequently, allowing the plaintiff to chose his forum would actually *help* promote the consumer protection theme espoused by the securities acts.[30]

But if the predispute arbitration clause permits only the selection by the investor between two or more mutually inconvenient forums that are convenient to the broker instead, it seems obvious that the investor will not be well protected. The forums for dispute resolution should not only be convenient for the investor, but also not require an investor to believe that the only available location be in New York City. Most of the industry arbitrations are located in New York or the paperwork is generated there. Even though arbitrations are held in many forums in many cities throughout the nation, a perception of bias is created, especially in the minds of the small investor, by the centralized structure of the arbitration divisions of the marketplaces or the N.A.S.D.

B) Judicial Attitudes

The aforementioned reasons resulted in early judicial intolerance toward arbitration. Once a dispute had developed, either party could choose to revoke the predispute agreement and go to court if that was felt to be more advantageous, for whatever reason, by that party. In arbitration, on the other hand, the parties fashioned their own remedial process, but it took both sides to decide to go into arbitration, even with a predispute agreement.[31]

In 1925 the House of Representatives Report accompanying the Federal Arbitration Act, noted the federal courts reluctance to compel compliance with terms of arbitration agreements, stating:

> The need for the law arises from an anachronism of our American law. Some centuries ago, because of the jealousy of the English courts for their own jurisdiction, they refused to enforce specific agreements to arbitrate upon the ground that the courts were thereby ousted from their jurisdiction. This jealousy survived for so long a period that the principle became firmly embedded in the English common law and was adopted with it by the American courts. The courts have felt that the precedent was too strongly fixed to be overturned without legislative enactment, although they have frequently criticized the rule and recognized its illogical nature and the injustice which results from it. [The Federal Arbitration Act] declares simply that such agreements for arbitration shall be enforced, and provides a procedure in the Federal courts for their enforcement.[32]

The reasons for arbitration in 1925 were similar to those proffered for arbitration today: reduction of court congestion, less expense, quicker resolution, and industry expertise of the arbitrators. Judicial enforcement of arbitration awards was necessary to make securities arbitration an effective procedure in cases involving investors. Otherwise, arbitration would only be duplicative: one would have to relitigate the same issues in court. A major advantage in securities arbitrations, however, was that the industry could itself enforce arbitration awards through its own process. Obviously, the enforcement sanctions in the securities industry, such as firing an employee or making a firm withdraw from membership on an exchange in the event the award was not met voluntarily, were of little help in dealing with customers over whom the industry had no effective means of policing an award. So for intra-industry disputes, the Federal Arbitration Act was of no great significance to the already existing securities industry arbitrations. The real issue was due process for those not involved in the industry. Courts felt due process was only ensured by judicial proceedings, and the industry could not be relied upon to protect those non-industry members.

Accordingly, in order to overcome this predisposition of both the federal and state courts regarding the propriety of arbitration generally (not just in securities industry matters),[33] it became necessary to have legislation authorizing such arbitration. Such statutes normally included a provision regarding judicial enforcement of an arbitration award. This permitted enforcement of securities industry panel awards through the judicial system.

4) ENGLISH ARBITRATION STATUTES AS PRECEDENT FOR ARBITRATION IN THE UNITED STATES

As noted above, the English common law was changed by arbitration statutes.[34] As a result, by the turn of the century certain provisions could be waived by contract. This included the resolution of disputes in courts. Arbitration was permitted under freedom of contract notions. One court, however, held waivers into arbitration enforceable as long as they were not too "tricky."

The English Companies Act of 1900[35] compelled full disclosure of matters in the sales of securities in a prospectus, and waivers of this right were not permitted as a means of evasion of the statutory requirement in favor of investor full disclosure. Consequently, the English precedent indicated that a predispute arbitration agreement would not be recognized despite freedom of contract, as it was against the Companies Act provision of an exclusive judicial forum for resolution of securities disputes.

However, in the United States, because the Federal Arbitration Act was adopted before the 1933 and 1934 securities laws, the precise scope of non-waiver in securities actions was unclear. Is arbitration a "waiver?" The English precedent is of little help due to the fundamental differences in their arbitration and companies law. (See discussion of the waiver defense in chapter 3.)

5) A CHANGE IN ATTITUDES: STATE STATUTES AND THE FEDERAL ARBITRATION ACT OF 1925[36]

Because the courts were hostile to arbitration, and because of the economic needs of the developing American business world, court dockets became crowded and delays in resolution of business disputes were not unusual. The problem of court burden continues despite increasing use of arbitration, but it cannot be doubted that in many respects the tolerance of judges for arbitration has changed considerably over the last 65 years.[37]

In 1915 a federal district court judge in the Southern District of New York found that there was no authority in law to permit the parties to "permit any other body of men to even partially perform judicial work,"[38] and therefore "complete ouster of jurisdiction as is shown by the clause [providing for arbitration of later arising disputes] . . . is void in a federal forum,"[39] and the arbitration agreement unenforceable. This case resulted in the 1920 adoption of the New York Arbitration Act that permitted predispute arbitration agreements. This statute also validated once and for all the principle that once a submission was made to arbitration, it was not subject to revocation as a matter of right, and that stay of judicial proceedings would be appropriate if arbitration was agreed upon between the parties, even in advance of a dispute arising.

In 1914, prior to the case cited above, the New York State Bar Association had already created a committee on dispute prevention. This committee's work and the response to the case resulted in the first modern arbitration statute in 1920.[40] As noted above, this act provided for binding arbitration under predispute or post-dispute agreements. In 1920 the American Bar Association began drafting the statute that ultimately became the 1925 Federal Arbitration Act. As noted above, businessmen were the major impetus for adoption of the Act. They were alarmed at the cost and delays in resolving disputes through the judicial process before 1920. At the time the Act was passed, the American Arbitration Association was not yet in existence. It was formed in 1926 from the merger of two existing arbitration societies. One, the Arbitration Society of America, had been organized in 1922. Some businessmen then, as today, felt it desirable to avoid lawyers and resolve disputes on the basis of a common understanding of right and wrong. On the other hand, lawyers were reluctant, like judges, to permit a method of resolving disputes outside the law. But "once it became clear to lawyers that they would have a substantial voice in the operation of the new dispute-processing system [the AAA], [the lawyers'] opposition vanished and modern commercial arbitration was born."[41]

Lawyers and businessmen felt arbitration was desirous because of speed and efficiency. Further, businessmen desired not only potentially lower legal fees, but also the privacy involved with arbitration--typically arbitration awards and proceedings are not made public, as is the case with the judicial process.

One important thing to bear in mind is that the Federal Arbitration Act predates the Federal securities laws. The 1933 Act and its progeny, including the Securities and Exchange Act of 1934, the Trust Indenture Act of 1939,[42] the Investment Company Act of 1940,[43] and the Investment Advisor's Act of 1940,[44] were all adopted *after* the Federal Arbitration Act. This later adoption of the securities laws is one reason for many of the problems found in securities arbitration over the last 60 years.

There is no subject matter jurisdiction specified in the Federal Arbitration Act, but there is no question that securities transactions are governed by federal law, including the Federal Arbitration Act, under the commerce clause, because they involve interstate and international commerce and utilize the medium of the national securities exchanges or traders contacted through facilities of interstate commerce, such as the mails, telephone, or telegraph. As a result, such transactions clearly fall under the Federal Arbitration Act's provision applicable to any "written provision in . . . a contract evidencing a transaction involving Commerce."[45] The Federal Arbitration Act requirement of a writing, however, is not a statute of frauds provision. As long as it is in writing, arbitration is enforceable. This is the case even if the party against whom arbitration is to be compelled has not signed the arbitration provision.[46]

The Federal Arbitration Act provides for the enforcement of predispute agreements in commercial or maritime transactions, providing,

> A written provision in . . . a contract evidencing a transaction involving commerce to settle by arbitration a controversy thereafter arising out of such contract or transaction . . . shall be valid, irrevocable, and enforceable, save upon such grounds as exist at law or in equity for the revocation of any contract.[47]
>
> * * *
>
> If any suit or proceeding be brought in any of the courts of the United States upon any issue referable to arbitration under an agreement in writing for such arbitration, the court in which such suit is pending, upon being satisfied that the issue involved in such suit or proceeding is referable to arbitration under such an agreement, shall on application of one of the parties stay the trial of the action until such arbitration has been had in accordance with the terms of the agreement, providing the applicant for the stay is not in default in proceeding with such arbitration.[48]
>
> * * *
>
> The court shall hear the parties, and upon being satisfied that the making of the agreement for arbitration or the failure to comply therewith is not in issue, the court shall make an order directing the parties to proceed to arbitration.[49]

Therefore, the Federal Arbitration Act first validates predispute arbitration agreements as forum selection provisions and then proceeds to allow the court to determine the validity of such an agreement. Once it is determined to have been validly entered into, the court cannot act further and must order the matter submitted to arbitration, including compelling the recalcitrant party to submit to such arbitration. Nevertheless, the common law bias still exists. The courts will not compel a party to arbitrate an issue that he or she did not agree to arbitrate,[50] but federal courts must enforce valid arbitration awards under the Federal Arbitration Act.[51]

One of the advantages to arbitration is the lack of ability to appeal a decision.[52] In arbitration, there is no appellate process; judicial review is very limited. Such review is subject to the exceptions noted above for manifest disregard of facts or law, prejudice and so forth. Such standards for review of an arbitration award are so stringent that most parties will not have an incentive to do so. But it also reflects a reason many persons want to arbitrate--the private nature of the proceeding.

The role of the courts in cases with arbitration agreements is, therefore, limited to (1) determining if the requisite intent is present to show agreement to arbitrate and, assuming such intent is found, (2) determining if the dispute is arbitrable. With statutory claims, the court must also (3) determine if the legislative body, Congress in the federal case, intended only to allow the claim to be litigated in the courts or if it intended to permit arbitration.[53] "[B]y agreeing to arbitrate a statutory claim, a party does not forego the substantive rights afforded by the statute, it only submits to their resolution in an arbitrable, rather than judicial, forum."[54] The court retains its equitable power to overturn an arbitrable award if it is found to be arbitrary or capricious, such as against the weight of the evidence presented, or not in accord with the law.

6) JURISDICTIONAL ASPECTS OF FEDERAL ARBITRATION ACT

As noted above, the Federal Arbitration Act does not in itself establish jurisdiction. For example, a federal district court denied a brokerage firm's petition for a confirmation of an arbitration award of $46,181, finding that it lacked jurisdiction under the $50,000 jurisdictional floor for civil actions, and diversity jurisdiction did not exist.[55]

7) CONCLUSION

The history of arbitration has progressed from judicial hostility to the point where the courts are encouraged by statutes to permit alternatives to judicial dispute resolution. Both the Federal Arbitration Act and state statutes mandate arbitration agreements be observed by the courts as well as the parties to those agreements. In large measure this has been a result of delays in the courts and the expense of litigation. For a speedy and cost effective resolution of disputes, arbitration is an attractive method of final dispute resolution.

NOTES

1 *See* 17 AM. JUR. 2D CONTRACTS § 149 (1964).

2 *See* Scherk v. Alberto-Culver Co., 417 U.S. 506, 511, 94 S. Ct. 2449, 41 L. Ed. 2d 270 (1974).

3 *See Id.* at 532 (Douglas, J., dissenting). Douglas, with White and Marshall concurring, noted that the international arbitration forum did not carry with it protections such as development of a record; judicial review for arbitrariness or capriciousness; federal rules for pretrial discovery; and wide choice of venue. As to the majority's observation that the contracting parties were sophisticated businessmen "surrounded and protected by lawyers and experts," Douglas discussed the rights of parties under the Federal securities laws. "The Act does not speak in terms of 'sophisticated' as opposed to 'unsophisticated' people dealing in securities. The rules when the giants play are the same as when the pygmies enter the market." *Id.* at 526.

4 *See generally* R. RODMAN, COMMERCIAL ARBITRATION 1-6 (1984 and 1987 Supp.).

5 This is the American Arbitration Association's suggested language for inclusion in a contract. It is usually advisable to also put in the location where the arbitration will take place.

6 Of course, this presupposes that the parties can anticipate and thus provide for all of the potential pitfalls that can develop. This, as any drafter probably will confirm, is virtually an impossible task to accomplish in today's rapidly changing business and social environment.

7 Genesco, Inc. v. T. Kakiuchi & Co., 815 F.2d 840, 844 (2d Cir. 1987).

8 Mitsubishi Motors Corp. v. Soler Chrysler-Plymouth, Inc., 473 U.S. 614, 105 S. Ct. 3346, 87 L. Ed. 2d 444, (1985).

9 Sayre, *Development of Commercial Arbitration Law*, 37 YALE L. J. at 1139 (1928).

10 This common law doctrine bars the readjudication of a matter already decided because there should be an end to litigation.

11 States are also adopting similar rules relating to the filing of frivolous actions and motions. *See, e.g.*, the New York provision in Part 30 of the Rules of the Chief Administrator, Office of Court Administration, effective January 1, 1989 (347 N.Y. ST. L. DIG. 1 [Nov. 1988]). *See also* First Investor's Corp. v. American Capital Fin. Serv., Inc., 823 F.2d 307 (9th Cir. 1987) (permitting attorney's fees and double costs under Rule 38 for an appeal that the Court found had ignored the law and the announced federal policy preference for arbitration and was, therefore, totally frivolous).

12 *See also* similar provisions under the Uniform Act, N.Y. CPLR 3018(b) (McKinney 1988 Supp.).

13 *See* Moran v. Paine, Webber, Jackson & Curtis, 389 F.2d 242 (3d Cir. 1968); Gardner v. Shearson, Hammil & Co., 433 F.2d 367 (5th Cir. 1970), *cert. denied*, 401 U.S. 978, 91 S. Ct. 1209, 28 L. Ed. 2d 329 (1971).

14 Energy Factors Inc. v. Nuevo Energy Co., 1993 WL 454125 (S.D.N.Y. 1993).

15 The language of a predispute arbitration agreement used in the securities industry is discussed in chapter 6.

16 *See* Emerson, *History of Arbitration Practice and Law*, 19 CLEV. ST. L. REV. 155 (1970); Sayre, *supra* note 9, at 595; F. KELLOR, AMERICAN ARBITRATION, ITS HISTORY, FUNCTIONS AND ACHIEVEMENTS (1948).

17 *See* I Kings 3:16-28.

18 5 R. POUND, JURISPRUDENCE 360 (1959).

19 *See* Emerson, *supra* note 15, at 156.

20 Breman v. Zapata Off-Shore Co., 407 U.S. 1, 11, 92 S. Ct. 1907, 32 L. Ed. 2d 513 (1972). The question is whether putting one of the parties to arbitration will be "an unreasonable disadvantage and thereby subvert the interest of justice."

21 For example, President Theodore Roosevelt negotiated the end to the Russian-Japanese War in 1904--for which he received the Nobel Peace Prize. Throughout history various rulers (temporal and spiritual) have arbitrated conflicts among vassal as well as sovereign states.

22 *See* KELLER, ARBITRATION AND THE LEGAL PROFESSION (1952); Sayre, *supra* note 9, at 597.

23 19 Henry VII, c.7.

24 *See* Pirsig, *Some Comments on Arbitration Legislation and the Uniform Act*, 10 VAND. L. REV. 685, 687 (1957).

25 Burchell v. Marsh, 58 U.S. 344, 350 (1855).

26 Home Ins. Co. v. Morse, 87 U.S. 445, 451 (1874).

27 Calif. Annual Conf. of the Methodist Episcopal Church v. Seitz, 74 Cal. 287, 291, 15 P. 839, 841 (1887).

28 *See, e.g.*, Nute v. Hamilton Mutual Ins. Co., 72 Mass. 174 (1856); Nashua River Paper Co. v. Hammermill Paper Co., 223 Mass. 8, 111 N.E. 678 (1916); W. H. Blodgett Co. v. Bebe Co., 190 Cal. 665, 667, 214 P. 38, 39 (1923); Cocalis v. Naxlides, 308 Ill. 152, 159-60, 139 N.E. 95, 98-99 (1923).

29 *See* Jones, *Historical Development of Commercial Arbitration in the United States*, 12 MINN. L. REV. 240 (1928); and Note, *Effect of the United States Federal Arbitration Act*, 25 GEO. L. J. 443, 445 (1937). For example, the defendant's procedural rights are guaranteed under the Fifth Amendment of the U.S. Constitution, which applies in both litigation and arbitration.

30 *See* Comment, *Statutory Proposal to Determine Arbitral Forums for*

10(b) Disputes, 28 SANTA CLARA L. REV. 389, 407 (1988) (emphasis in original).

31 Kulukundis Shipping Co. v. S/A Amtorg Trading Corp., 126 F.2d 978, 989 (2d. Cir. 1942) distinguished this proposition from Radiator Specialty Co. v. Cannon Mills, Inc., 97 F.2d 318 (4th Cir. 1938), where the defendant after a long pretrial period moved for compulsory arbitration. The trial court correctly determined there was a waiver of the right by the defendant who was in default.

32 H.R. Rep. No. 96, 68th Cong., 1st Sess. 1-2 (1924), *cited in* Dean Witter Reynolds Inc. v. Byrd, 470 U.S. 213, 105 S. Ct. 1238, 84 L. Ed. 2d 158 (1985).

33 An example of this predisposition occurred in Stroh Container Co. v. Delphi Indus., Inc., 783 F.2d 743, 751 n.12 (8th Cir. 1986), *cert. denied*, 476 U.S. 1141, where Chief Judge Lay indicated that the initial attractiveness of arbitration has waned with recent experiences finding that arbitration often is not simple, inexpensive, and expeditious, but rather "complex, expensive and time consuming," and the results "by private and untrained 'judges' are distantly remote from the fair process procedurally followed and application of the law in judicial proceedings."

34 The Federal Arbitration Act of 1889, 52 & 53 Vict., ch. 49 (1899), provided that predispute and after dispute arbitration agreements were irrevocable, thus reversing earlier common law. The distinction between pre- and post-dispute arbitration agreements is uniquely American. *See* Sayre, *supra* note 9, at 605.

35 Companies Act of 1900, 57 & 58 Vict., ch. 58, repealed by Companies (Consolidation) Act of 1908, 8 Edw. VII, ch. 69.

36 For a more detailed discussion of the Federal Arbitration Act of 1925, see chapter 4 and the Act in Appendix A.

37 *See* Shearson/American Express, Inc. v. McMahon, 482 U.S. 202, 226 (1987) ("'[W]e are well past the time when judicial suspicion of the desirability of arbitration and of the competence of arbitral tribunals' should inhibit enforcement of the [Arbitration] Act 'in controversies based on statutes.'" (citing *Mitsubishi Motors Corp. v. Soler Chrysler Plymouth Inc.*, and *Wilko v. Swan*).

38 U.S. Asphalt Refining Co. v. Trinidad Lake Petroleum Co., 222 F. 1006, 1010 (S.D.N.Y. 1915).

39 *Id.* at 1012.

40 England, for example, passed its first Federal Arbitration Act in 1698, but that act allowed for revocation of submission. By the turn of the century, English law had been revised so that predispute arbitration agreements were enforceable. *See* discussion in chapter 4.

41 J. AUERBACH, JUSTICE WITHOUT LAW? 104-5 (1983).

42 15 U.S.C. §§ 77aaa-77bbb (1982 and 1988 Supp.).

43 15 U.S.C. §§ 80a-1-80a-52 (1982 and 1988 Supp.).

44 15 U.S.C. §§ 80b-1-80b-21 (1982 and 1988 Supp.).

45 *See* 9 U.S.C. § 2 (1982 and 1988 Supp.).

46 This argument is usually not made with customers who will sign the account agreement containing the waiver provision. But it does apply to brokerage employees, who indicate in their employment agreements to be bound by the applicable exchange constitution or rules. *See* discussion of intra-industry arbitration in chapter 10. The N.Y.S.E. Constitution Article XI, § 1 provides, for example, that any controversy between a member and any other person arising out of the business of the member shall be submitted for arbitration upon submission of the member. Not all customer agreements provide for arbitration. In such a case, N.Y.S.E. Rule 600(a) provides that a dispute between a customer or non-member and member shall be arbitrated under the Constitution and Rules as provided by any "duly written agreement or demand" of the customer or non-member.

47 9 U.S.C. § 2 (1982).

48 *See* 9 U.S.C. at § 3.

49 *See* 9 U.S.C. § 4.

50 *See* Williams v. E.F. Hutton & Co., 753 F.2d 117 (D.C. Cir. 1985); C. D. Anderson & Co. v. Lemos, 832 F.2d 1097 (9th Cir. 1987) (arbitration award had preclusive effect because brokerage firm had waived its right to litigate federal securities law and RICO claims in federal court by submitting those claims to arbitration).

51 Under Federal Arbitration Act §9, the federal court "must grant an order" confining the arbitration award. *See* chapter 15 discussion on the award.

52 *See* 9 U.S.C. § 10 and discussion of judicial review of arbitration awards in chapters 5 and 16.

53 This is really a question of the intent of the framers of legislation regarding the forum or forums in which they wished claims of the statute's violation to be resolved. Of course, the problem is that in many statutes such legislative intent is lacking. For example, in Section 27 of the Securities and Exchange Act of 1934, exclusive jurisdiction for violations of the Act is in the federal courts, but arbitration is clearly not precluded after *McMahon*.

Another dimension of this issue is federal preemption of state law regarding the arbitrable process. *See* General Motors Corp. v. Abrams, 703 F. Supp. 1103 (S.D.N.Y. 1989), 897 F.2d 34 (2d Cir. 1990), where a Federal Trade Commission consent order requiring a manufacturer to implement a nationwide arbitration program was found not to preempt the New York

Lemon Law. The arbitration program provided the consumer broader remedies and required that the arbitrators be specially trained in the Lemon Law's provisions. New York's law was found not to "work such significant changes upon the manner in which arbitrators arrive at their decisions as to be preempted by the federal agency consent decree because the consent decree was afforded due regard under the more stringent New York law's requirements." But *see* the dissent of Judge Winter.

54 *Mitsubishi*, 473 U.S. at 628.

55 Quick & Reilly, Inc. v. Aaglio, 717 F. Supp. 822 (S.D. Fla. 1991) ($44,181 claim on margin account dismissed); Giangrande v. Shearson Lehman/E.F. Hutton, 803 F. Supp. 464 (Mass. 1992) (no federal jurisdiction where only $24,000 claim). For all civil actions after May 18, 1989, the diversity dollar limit is $50,000 (Judicial Improvements and Access to Justice Act, Pub. L. No. 100-702, § 201, 102 Stat. 4642, 4646 (1988), codified as amended at 29 U.S.C. § 1332 [1988]).

Chapter 3

THE LAW OF ARBITRATION GENERALLY

This chapter discusses the common law development of arbitration as a method of dispute resolution.

1) COMMON LAW ARBITRATION

Because arbitration in the securities industry involves referral of a dispute to an impartial person or persons chosen by the parties in advance of the dispute arising, its jurisdiction arises from and is based upon voluntary agreement of the parties--their contract.[1] The intent of the parties is to achieve a final disposition of a future dispute in an easier, more expeditious and less expensive manner than litigation. The goal is to avoid the formalities, delay, and expense of the judicial dispute resolution process, with the result that there should be little judicial review.

Contracts are interpreted applying a "plain meaning" to the language the parties chose to express their intent. For example, the typical commodities customer agreement that clearly specifies that arbitration "applies to all disputes arising between the parties" will extend the application of such contract beyond those pertaining to the account's activities. Thus, the options agreement would include, under its arbitration provisions, regular cash account trading for the same customer under a different contract without an arbitration clause. But under normal rules on construction of contracts, a customer should be able to choose not to arbitrate when some of his accounts have predispute arbitration clauses and others do not. The contract clauses will be construed against the broker who drafted the various customer agreements.[2]

Due to the contractual basis of arbitration, its enforceability in any given case gives rise to the question of whether the clause was agreed to voluntarily.

If not, the courts will not find a meeting of the minds of the parties, and consequently the arbitration clause will be void. Others who are not parties to the contract can not be forced to arbitrate a dispute any more than parties who have not unequivocally consented to do so. So, for example, if the party that has been compelled to accept an arbitration clause in an agreement is acting under a disability or is incapacitated, the entire contract can be void or voidable under general principles of contract law.[3] Further, if there is controversy regarding the capacity of a party or to the intent of the parties regarding a contract containing an arbitration clause, these issues can be resolved by the judicial process. If the requisite intent is present and the party had the capacity to enter into the contract, the court will find the voluntary agreement to arbitrate mandates submission to arbitration (as such process is defined in the contract).[4]

Not all brokerage house customer agreements contain mandatory predispute arbitration clauses. Of those that do not, securities arbitration will still be available after the dispute arises. Clearly, an agreement between the parties to submit an existing dispute to arbitration is binding.[5]

2) DEFENSES AGAINST ARBITRATION OF DISPUTES

If a party seeks to avoid arbitration, the easiest way is not to agree to arbitrate disputes that might result from the parties relationship. But generally, if an agreement has been entered into, either before or after the dispute has arisen, arbitration will be mandated. If the contract is defective, however, and can not be said to require it, arbitration will not be permitted. This, of course, is on the grounds that any arbitration is an abridgment of the right to resort to the judicial system and must be part of the parties' express agreement.

The usual grounds for not permitting arbitration are that a valid agreement to arbitrate has not been made, or that the subject matter can not be settled by arbitration due to statutory preemption or public policy.[6] But the agreement to arbitrate itself can be subject to all defenses that would justify the finding that the contract or arbitration clause is itself unenforceable under legal or equitable contract law principles. The following is a brief discussion of the arguments that may be made to invalidate what otherwise appear to be contracts to arbitrate. These general defenses are available in all jurisdictions; however, some arbitration statutes provide a very limited time to raise such defenses. New York, for example, provides that there is only 20 days after service of a notice of intent to arbitrate for the other side to raise challenges against arbitration.[7]

A) Contract of Adhesion Defense

One of the major areas of defense to the mandatory arbitrations provisions in contracts relates to the "contract of adhesion" argument.[8] Under this defense, it is asserted that the courts should not enforce a predispute agreement to submit to arbitration because of public policy. The public policy argument centers on fairness[9] and unconscionability.[10] Finding a contract one of adhesion is, however, not determinative. This will only permit the court to examine the fairness of its terms. If found to be oppressive applying this standard, the arbitration provision will be invalidated.

The RESTATEMENT (SECOND) OF CONTRACTS § 208 takes the position that contracts of adhesion are not unenforceable unless they are unconscionable. Courts have consistently taken the position that arbitration agreements are not, as a matter of law, unconscionable as long as the arbitration clause is commercially reasonable, and plaintiffs have a reasonable opportunity to understand it.

The courts have developed the adhesion theory to ameliorate the harsh consequences resulting from enforcement of contracts that contain oppressive or unexpected terms. Adhesion contracts have two elements: first, they are drafted by a stronger party and the weaker party, or "adhering" party, has no opportunity to negotiate any of the substantive terms. Second, the adhering party has no realistic opportunity to look elsewhere for the goods or services needed. In essence, due to the nature of the marketplace, there is no freedom of contract as far as the adhering party is concerned. Business realities require adherence to the standard-form contract required by the stronger party.

In broker's customer agreements, there may be an ability to negotiate some of the minor terms of the agreement, but the substance of the transaction is set and non-negotiable as far as the adhering party is concerned. Since most brokerage firms incorporate an arbitration agreement as one of many clauses within an overall "client's" or "customer" agreement, the argument is made that a customer cannot maintain an account with a firm without executing such an agreement, and therefore the agreement is an unenforceable contract of adhesion.

The courts have allowed this defense to protect the weaker party who is unable to protect himself. The issue presented in securities arbitration is whether there is another way to protect the consumer, especially the small investor, who lacks bargaining ability. Clearly, due to competition among brokers for its business, the larger, institutional investor has the bargaining power to omit predispute arbitration clauses from their brokerage agreements. The small investor, on the other hand, does not have this competitive advantage. In fact, many firms maintain that the small investor is not economical anyway. Consequently, in this oligopolistic industry, the small investor is clearly at a disadvantage in negotiating the terms under which he or she will find access to the securities markets--through the brokerage firms. One commentator feels "in predispute arbitration clauses . . . no true freedom of contract exists; securities customers must unilaterally waive a portion of their rights in order to be able to enter into a brokerage agreement [or transaction purchasing or selling almost any trading security]."[11]

The courts have been reluctant to find adhesion clauses enforceable, particularly if it is also against public policy as too overreaching. Consequently, they are an important ally of the investor-customers in brokerage cases and may find the clause unenforceable. The rest of the agreement is nevertheless enforceable. The courts base this exception to freedom of contract on public policy grounds.[12]

There are also cases where the adhesive nature of the contract does not go to the question of arbitrability, and mere inequality in bargaining power between the parties is not enough to preclude arbitration.[13] Thus the strong public policy favoring arbitration and economies of standardized contracts requires a heavy burden (similar to a summary judgment) of the one seeking to avoid it by establishing unconscionability. This can be done by a clear showing that arbitration did not fall within the reasonable expectations of the parties, a difficult claim in securities cases because after *McMahon* and *de Quijas*, it can hardly be said that arbitration is not the industry standard, and thus it is not a "surprise."

In a recent Nevada case concerning a medical clinic's mandatory predispute arbitration agreement from patients, the Nevada Supreme Court found a contract of adhesion. There was no informed consent because when the patient signed the agreement she was informed that otherwise there would be no treatment given, and there was no ability to modify any of its terms, including the waiver of right to trial.[14] This same rationale can, of course, be applied to a case of a securities firm customer told that the only course is to acquiesce to the customer agreement, without the ability to modify its terms, including that he or she must accept arbitration and waive the right to litigate both securities and other claims that might arise.

But the general argument that a predispute arbitration clause is void as an adhesion contract has been uniformly rejected.[15] This is so because to be unenforceable an adhesion contract must be unduly oppressive, unconscionable, or violative of public policy. Arbitration agreements cannot be cast in these terms because the U.S. Supreme Court has established a strong national policy favoring arbitration and has expressly approved Self-Regulatory Organization (SRO) arbitral forums as fair and impartial. The courts have consistently held that arbitration agreements are not unconscionable as a matter of law.[16] There is a heavy burden on the one seeking to establish the invalidity.[17]

But the small investor has two important allies: the Securities and Exchange Commission (SEC) and consumer protection groups that might influence Congress, the SEC, or the SROs. If these groups can use their forces to protect the small investor's interests, then freedom of contract notions should be applicable and judicial activism unnecessary. If the investor-consumer lacks the resources or ability to organize, however, the situation cries out for adhering party protection--there is a defect in the contract's formation. Judicial or other intervention to correct this defect is required. "It also comes close to speaking nonsense to argue that the kinds of legal changes herein suggested are beyond the proper constitutional authority of the judiciary. The legal doctrines concerning the determination of what is a contract and of contract damages were created by judiciaries."[18]

The RESTATEMENT (SECOND) OF CONTRACTS § 211, entitled "Standardized Contracts," provides that if the writing is reasonable and applies equally to all those similarly situated it will be valid, but "[w]here [a party] has reason to know the party manifesting . . . assent would not do so if he knew that the writing contained a particular term, the term is *not* part of the agreement. So if the language used is unreasonable, indecent, or oppressive, the courts will look at the relationship of the parties and the customs and usages of the business to determine if the adhesive term is a "sound particularization of the deal" or "bizarre" or "clauses of oppression or outrage."[19] The courts will also look to see if the clause is unconscionable;[20] the business is affected with a public interest;[21] the negotiations or transactions are tainted by economic duress; or the superior bargaining power of one of the parties has been exercised to oppressive subjection of the other.[22] If such situations are found to exist, the courts will override the terms of the agreement, finding a lack of voluntary assent to the adhesive terms, resulting in a lack of mutuality.

A Massachusetts court has held; "Customers who adhere to standardized contractual terms ordinarily 'understand that they are assenting to the terms not read or not understood, subject to such limitations as the law may impose.'"[23]

In fashioning the rule of public policy on adhesion contracts, one commentator suggests that the court should consider "what the applicant might reasonably expect; [this is] just as relevant [as] the courts' own sense of what is fair."[24] It is really a question of what the "public has a right to expect,"[25] especially in contracts which deal with industries affected with the public interest, such as the securities markets. In a purely economic analysis, the trading costs on securities markets have become price competitive only since the "Big Bang" of 1975,[26] when the SEC and Congress required the abolition of century-old industry fixed commission rates in favor of negotiated commissions.

If the investor is forced to agree to a predispute arbitration agreement as a condition to access to the securities markets, freedom of contract is, of course, reduced.[27] If other securities accounts were treated like commodity accounts that permit the customer to "opt out" of the predispute arbitration clause, there would be no argument of adhesion. In reality, to enter the non-commodity securities market the public investor can not mutually negotiate her customer agreement with the firm, but must accept the standardized contract without deviation. Moreover, in many cases the stronger party will insert terms that are clearly overreaching.[28]

Because arbitration clauses usually specify the arbitral forum as well, there are two other dimensions to the perception of overreaching by the party writing the contract. First, where the tribunals are industry-sponsored and there is a lack of common interest or shared commercial interests between the parties, such as between brokers and their customers, enforcement may be less desirable unless the panels are deemed fair by both sides.

Second, if the industry is able to impose forum selection by virtue of limiting the choices of arbitration facilities available, while seemingly permitting choice there is, in reality, none. The consumer can be forced to choose between forums that are selected in the brokerage agreement principally due to their convenience to the broker. This has been amply demonstrated in several cases where the brokerage firm seeks a judicial stay of proceedings because the arbitration clause calls for resolution in a forum distant from the customer. If the customer, whether plaintiff seeking redress for a wrongful execution or churning or defendant being sued for a margin balance due, is required to arbitrate in a distant place, it will frustrate due process.[29] Of course, if the securities investor is permitted to opt out of arbitration, which is permitted in some cash and option accounts, this question of adhesion becomes moot.

B) Public Policy Defense

The contract of adhesion defense is one of the public policy defenses and was raised in the *Wilko, McMahon*, and *Rodriguez* cases. It was one justification for SEC Rule 15c2-2, which provided that there could be no arbitration agreement for federal securities law claims in broker's customer's agreements.[30] The Supreme Court has recently held that "refusal to enforce an award for contravention of public policy is only justified when such policy is well defined and dominant, as ascertained by reference to laws and legal precedents, rather than general considerations of supposed public interests."[31]

C) Unconscionability Defense

The concept of unconscionability is another judicially created doctrine to permit avoidance of contracts that are harsh, oppressive, "shock the conscience,"[32] or affront the sense of the dignity of contract."[33] While there is a distinction between procedural unconscionability, which is directed at defects in the bargaining process (and may include adhesive behavior), and substantive unconscionability, which is directed at the content of a contract, the distinction is in enforcement. One which is procedurally unconscionable is normally enforceable if bargained for, but substantive unconscionability will make the contract unenforceable whatever the bargaining context. Freedom of contract will permit procedures to be bargained away, but not allow the enforcement of offensive agreements. As noted in the discussion on adhesion, unconscionability and adhesion may go hand-in-hand as possible defenses against enforcement of the contract, or in this case the arbitration clause.

In a California case concerned with union arbitration in the entertainment field, the court denied enforcement on the grounds of unconscionability because there was a lack of "minimum levels of integrity" in the dispute resolution arrangement set forth in the contract, which was found to "smack of adhesion."[34] This was an important extension of the role of unconscionability, because it found that procedural grounds permitted a court to find the entire contract unenforceable as a matter of substantive law. The courts thus are to "police provisions and contracts for substantive abuses rather than encouraging them to search for procedural flaws on which to base their decisions."[35] Finding the adhesive nature of the procedural aspects of dispute resolution gave credence to the arguments of substantive unfairness under the adhesion theory, all of which permit the courts to take an active role in striking harsh terms to protect the weaker party. This same judicial activism might apply, however, even in freely negotiated arbitration agreements.

But in *Cohen v. Wedbush, Noble, Cooke, Inc.*,[36] the Ninth Circuit used *McMahon* to deny a customer's claim that the rules of arbitration were unconscionable because they were drafted by the securities industry. Holding that this argument, if upheld, would frustrate a "carefully crafted regulatory scheme," the Court found the arbitration agreement enforceable as a matter of law. It did not matter that the customer had not read the contract before signing it; the court found "state law adhesion contract principles may not be invoked to bar arbitrability" under the Federal Arbitration Act, and there was no unfairness evident from a rule "expecting parties to read contracts before they sign them." This is in accord with common law. A person will be presumed to have intended the results of his agreement. His negligence in not reading the signed agreement will not allow for his disaffirmance.

In one case considering a one year statue of limitations,[37] the Sixth Circuit Court of Appeals found that there is nothing contrary to either state law or federal securities law in the parties agreeing to a lesser statute of limitations. Further, since neither the 1934 Act § 10 (b) nor Rule 10b-5 provide a statute of limitations period,[38] and because the three year provision of Exchange Act

§ 18(c)[39] is not uniformly applicable to securities claims, the court looked to Michigan law. Michigan law allows private contracts to set time limitations within which a suit must be brought, although the courts will limit the time to a reasonable period.

D) Fraud in the Inducement

When looking at the underlying contract to determine the enforceability of the arbitration clause, a party may assert that the contract itself came about due to fraud. In what is known as fraud in the factum, the entire agreement is unenforceable for lack of a meeting of the minds at its inception. Fraud in the inducement can be contrasted to fraud in the factum. Some courts have held it improper to submit the issue of fraud in the factum to arbitration; however, a different result will occur where fraud is alleged only in connection with a misrepresentation that induced a party to sign the contract.[40] Fraud in factum goes to the validity of the contract--assent itself is at issue. In fraud in the inducement, assent is not at issue, misrepresentation is the essential question is whether the fraud permeates both the principal agreement and the arbitration clause: if it does, the court should determine the matter; if not, the arbitrators can do so. In either fraud case, the party seeking relief must not ask for damages, which would be enforcing the contract, but must seek rescission.[41]

There are many cases treating execution of the customer agreement in securities accounts as having been compelled by fraud and undue influence. For example, a customer will argue that the broker "distracted his attention from the clause by treating the [entire] agreement's execution as a mere formality."[42] Such a situation will prohibit arbitration, until resolution of the issue of meaningful waiver is decided by the courts.

The Court in *Prima Paint*[43] considered the fraud in the inducement question in conjunction with the Federal Arbitration Act. It was, however, limited to consideration of the arbitration clause alone. A doctrine of separability resulted, where a court could hear contract defenses regarding the clause, but not on the underlying contract. The general attack of fraud was thus decided by the arbitrators. In 1963, in *Mosley v. Electronic & Missile Facilities, Inc.*,[44] the Supreme Court held that an illegal contract results from fraud in the inducement. Therefore, the *Prima Paint* court found that only the arbitration clause could be struck; in *Mosley*, the entire contract including the arbitration clause was invalid.

But the fraud in the inducement must be separate from the conduct for which the customer is suing the firm.[45] For example, in *Western Hospitals Fed. Credit Union v. E.F. Hutton & Company, Inc.*,[46] the court held that by churning the account the broker did not breach its fiduciary duty in a manner that would "boot-strap" as a separate reason for voiding the arbitration clause.

State courts have reached differing conclusions when confronted with fraud in the inducement claims: some permit both issues to be resolved by the arbitrator, others permit court involvement only on the issue of the validity of the arbitration clause.[47]

When pleading fraud which will defeat the arbitration agreement, the burden of proof is on the plaintiff who must submit evidence to support this defense.[48]

E) Waiver of Right to Arbitrate

In many cases, persons who do not want to have the dispute resolved in arbitration will argue that the party seeking to compel arbitration has waived that contract right, either through express waiver or, more usually, by action that would now make it inequitable to require the complaining party to submit to arbitration. While permissible under freedom of contract notions, the waiver must not be unconscionable.

A normal ground justifying waiver is that the parties have proceeded with the litigation. The courts will examine the facts carefully, but are bound to resolve any doubt in favor of arbitration.[49] Given the Federal Arbitration Act's preference, this requires a "heavy burden" on the party claiming waiver of arbitration.

The prejudice to justify waiver may come in a variety of ways. Included are: (1) the defendant's use of discovery that would not be permitted in arbitration,[50] for example, taking depositions in litigation before moving to compel arbitration can be a waiver of the right to arbitrate;[51] (2) incurring substantial legal costs in pretrial, motion practice, including filing for summary judgment,[52] and aborted trial; (3) time and expense in defending against cross-claims and counterclaims of defendant; and (4) the time spent in litigation versus arbitration.[53] However, if prejudice to the other party is found, for example through participation in discovery, waiver is sometimes found.[54]

F) Signatures

Because arbitration requires consent, the absence of a signature may be enough to preclude enforcement of a predispute arbitration clause. In some cases, however, the courts have held that as long as the documents sent the party referred to arbitration, it will be enforced under the Federal Arbitration Act's mandate.[55] The Federal Arbitration Act requires a written agreement, but does not require that it be signed.

Forgery, or absence of a genuine signature, is also a common defense against the enforcement of the entire agreement, including the arbitration clause.[56] In securities cases, for example, often a customer will maintain that he or she never saw, let alone signed, the customer agreement containing the arbitration clause. Clearly, the parties do not have to explain the contract under present law.[57] But see the questions raised in light of the broker's fiduciary duty, discussed in chapter 11.

G) Failure to Read

Courts routinely hold that the failure of a customer to read the account opening agreement containing a predispute arbitration clause is not a good defense. Persons signing a contract can not avoid obligations under it by claiming that they did not read what was signed.[58] On the other hand, some brokerage customers have been successful on the ground that under the fiduciary duty, the broker owed them an explanation of the terms of this complex contract, including the arbitration clause.[59] The question is if the customer's reliance on the representations made (or failure to explain) by the registered representative are in violation of this fiduciary duty. There is normally no duty to orally highlight, disclose, or explain the terms of an agreement, including the existence of an arbitration clause.[60]

H) Rescission of Arbitration Agreement

A customer may have attempted to rescind the agreement to arbitrate they signed, usually by writing the broker. These are normally felt to be attempts at unilateral rescission and do not render the arbitration clause unenforceable.[61] A question may arise if the activity complained of arose before or after the notice.

I) Other Contract Defenses

In addition to the defenses of adhesion and unconscionable contract, and fraud in the inducement, other typical contractual defenses can be raised against the enforceability of the entire broker-investor agreement (which may contain an arbitration clause). These defenses would include incapacity, such as minority, mental infirmity, disability; other breach of fiduciary duty (which may include the broker's fiduciary duties owed to the customer); self-dealing; duress; undue influence; misrepresentation and non-disclosure; mistake; and the like.

It is, of course, beyond the scope of this book to review the law of contracts extensively. Other sources are available for this purpose. But the above does examine those defenses of particular use in securities litigation. The issue is one of enforceability: can the contract stand despite the defense? If so, the next inquiry is to the arbitration clause. Can it be enforced?

3) WHO DECIDES IF A MATTER IS ARBITRABLE?

Common law is split on the question of whether a court or the arbitrator should determine if the dispute is arbitrable. Under *Prima Paint's* doctrine of separability developed in the question of fraud in the inducement under § 4 of the Federal Arbitration Act, if the making of the arbitration agreement is at issue, the federal court is required to proceed summarily to the trial of that issue through an evidentiary hearing. The court will, therefore, hold the motion to compel arbitration in abeyance as long as there is an unequivocal denial that an agreement has been made and some evidence in support thereof. But if the agreement to arbitrate is clear, the arbitrator will be charged with the determination of the validity of the contract itself or the legitimacy of these contract defenses. Sometimes the clause will be read as not including determination of some of these defenses, especially when the allegation goes to determination of the basis of the arbitration clause itself, that is, the entire agreement.[62]

Consequently, as long as the arbitration clause is clear that all disputes are to be resolved in arbitration, court review of the clause and the underlying contract will be unavailable in federal and most state actions.

Under in-house interpretations of the rules of some arbitral forums, the Director of Arbitration may decide if a matter is eligible for arbitration under the forum's rules. As a result, some claims may be includable and others excluded. See the discussion of eligibility for arbitration in chapter 9, and chapter 12 which discusses the function of the arbitration forum personnel in more detail.

4) RESULT AT COMMON LAW

An agreement to arbitrate was permitted at common law. Usually, it was found as a condition precedent to defeat the right of a party to bring suit; but the general rule remains that either party may revoke a submission to arbitration under contract at any time before an award has been made. Such party will be liable, however, for damages for breach of contract. Under common law arbitration, then, an arbitration award was enforceable if the parties had agreed to such submission, the submission and award were within the scope of the agreement, and the submission was completely decided.

NOTES

1 *See generally* R. RODMAN, COMMERCIAL ARBITRATION 1-6 (1984).

2 Gilmore v. Shearson/American Express, Inc., 668 F. Supp. 314, 320 (S.D.N.Y. 1987). Again, this is the permissive reading of the Federal Arbitration Act at work. *But see* Azriliant v. Shearson Lehman American Express, Inc., FED. SEC. L. REP. (CCH) ¶ 93,393 (S.D.N.Y. 1987).

3 It is interesting to note that the differences between federal and state law will apply here. For example, the claim that an arbitration agreement clause was fraudulently induced may be determined by the court, but if the court determines it was not so induced, the question whether the entire contract was induced by fraud is one for the arbitrator's determination. *See* Prima Paint Corp. v. Flood & Conklin Mfg., 388 U.S. 395, 87 S. Ct. 1801, 18 L. Ed. 2d 1270 (1967).

4 The question under Federal Arbitration Act § 4 relates to the entire contract, not the issue of arbitration.

5 Moran v. Paine, Webber, Jackson & Curtis, 389 F.2d 242 (3d Cir. 1968); Gardner v. Shearson, Hammil & Co., 433 F.2d 367 (5th Cir. 1970), *cert. denied*, 401 U.S. 978, 91 S. Ct. 1209, 28 L. Ed. 2d 329 (1971).

6 *See* chapter 1 discussion.

7 N.Y. CPLR 7503(c) (McKinney 1990).

8 *See* Note, *Keating v. Superior Court: Oppressive Arbitration Clauses in Adhesion Contracts*, 71 CAL. L. REV. 1239, 1247 (1983), noting that the term was introduced into the American legal vocabulary by Patterson, *The Delivery of a Life-Insurance Policy*, 33 HARV. L. REV. 198, 222 (1919). *See also*, Kessler, *Contracts of Adhesion--Some Thoughts About Freedom of Contract,* 43 COLUM. L. REV. 629, 631-32 (1943); Rakoff, *Contracts of Adhesion: An Essay in Reconstruction*, 96 HARV. L. REV. 1174 (1983); DiFiore, *Problems in Alternative Dispute Resolution: Arbitration Agreements as Contracts of Adhesion in Consumer Securities Disputes*, 93 COM. L. J. 259 (1988).

9 *See* CORBIN, CONTRACTS (1960 and 1980 Supp.): Finding a contract to be one of adhesion means nothing more than the court must review its terms for fairness. (§ 559C at 327 [1980 Supp.]). To be fair, a contract of adhesion must not give one party all the benefits while giving the other party all of the burdens of the contract. (*Id.* § 559F at 331).

10 *See* Finkle and Ross v. A. G. Becker Paribas, Inc., 622 F. Supp. 1505, 1511 (S.D.N.Y. 1985) (although the contract of adhesion existed, the agreement was enforceable because it was not unconscionable or violative of public policy); Pierson v. Dean Witter Reynolds, Inc., 742 F.2d 334, 339 (7th Cir. 1984).

11 Sanchez, *Should Claims Involving Public Customers Arising Under*

the Securities Exchange Act of 1934 Be Subject to Compulsory Arbitration?, 10 HARV. J. L. & PUB. POL'Y 1, 187 (1987).

12 One need only remember the provisions of Uniform Commercial Code § 1-203 setting forth the principle that in commercial transactions good faith is required in performance and *enforcement*. Official Comment (emphasis supplied). Also relevant is UCC § 2-302, allowing the courts to refuse to enforce a contract clause that is found to be unconscionable. This determination of unconscionability is one of law to prevent oppression and enforce a contract or clause that is "contrary to public policy or to the dominant purpose of the contract." Official Comment 1 to § 2-302.

Most brokerage firms did not permit a customer to open an account (particularly a margin or options account) without agreeing to mandatory arbitration provisions.

This situation is somewhat changed by the larger type and highlighting notice of arbitration clauses now common in customer agreements. *See* chapter 6.

13 *See* Nessman, *The State of the Law*, *in* SECURITIES ARBITRATION 446-458 (D. Robbins ed., 1993).

14 Obstetrics & Gynecologists Wixted v. Pepper, 101 Nev. 105, 693 P.2d 1259 (1985), *reported in* 71 A.B.A. J. 123 (May 1985).

15 *See* Adams v. Merrill Lynch, Pierce, Fenner & Smith, Inc., 888 F.2d 696 (10th Cir. 1993) (boilerplate or form contract not sufficient to dissolve the contractural terms); Coleman v. Prudential Bache Securities, Inc., 802 F.2d 1350, 1351 (11th Cir. 1986); Pierson v. Dean Witter Reynolds, Inc., 742 F.2d 334, 339-40 (7th Cir. 1984); Surman v. Merrill Lynch, Pierce, Fenner & Smith, 733 F.2d 59, 61 n.1, (8th Cir. 1984); Finkle and Ross, 622 F. Supp. at 1511-12; Ilan v. Shearson/American Express, 632 F. Supp. 886, 891-892 (1986); Speck v. Oppenheimer & Co., 583 F. Supp. 325, 328 n.4 (W.D. Miss. 1984); Preston v. Kruezer, 641 F. Supp. 1163, 1172-73 (N.D. Ill. 1986); Brener v. Becker Paribas, Inc., 628 F. Supp. 442, 446 n.3 (S.D.N.Y. 1985).

16 *See, e.g.*, Sablosky v. Edward S. Gordon, Inc., 73 N.Y. 2d 133, 538 N.Y.S. 2d 513, 538 (1989) ("There is no general test for measuring the reasonableness of a transaction but we have recently provided this guidance: [a]n unconscionable contract is one which 'is so grossly unreasonable in the light of mores and business practices of the time and place as to be unenforceable.'"); Cohen v. Wedbush, Noble, Cooke, Inc., 841 F.2d 282, 286 (9th Cir. 1988); Pierson v. Dean Witter Reynolds, Inc., 742 F.2d 334, 339 (7th Cir. 1984); Surman v. Merrill Lynch, Pierce, Fenner & Smith, Inc., 733 F.2d 59, 61 n.2 (8th Cir. 1984); Hurlbut v. Ganshar, 674 F. Supp. 385, 392 (D. Mass. 1987).

17 Brown v. Merrill Lynch, Pierce, Fenner & Smith, Inc., 664 F. Supp. 969 (E.D. Pa. 1987).

18 *See* Slawson, *Mass Contracts: Lawful Fraud in California*, 48 S. CAL. L. REV. 1, 50 (1974).

19 *See* K. Llewellyn, THE COMMON LAW TRADITION: DECIDING APPEALS 366 (1960).

20 *See* UCC § 2-302 (Unconscionable Contract or Clause) and § 1-203 (Obligation of Good Faith).

21 Where the nature of the business requires access to the industry by anyone and there is no discretion in the firms in the industry as to with whom they can deal under applicable regulation calling for non-discrimination.

22 *See* Henningsen v. Bloomfield Motors, Inc., 32 N.J. 358, 161 A.2d 69 (1960).

23 *See* Carpenter v. Suffolk Franklin Savings Bank, 370 Mass. 314, 346 N.E. 892 (1976), citing the RESTATEMENT (SECOND) OF CONTRACTS § 237 cmt. b (Drafts Nos. 1-7, 1973), in a case construing a customer-bank agreement on mortgage escrow funds for taxes; Rakoff, *supra* note 8, at 1280 notes that the Judge in Carpenter was the Reporter for the RESTATEMENT (SECOND) OF CONTRACTS.

24 Rakoff, *supra* note 8, at 1269. *See* David L. Threkeld & Co. v. Metallgesellschraft Ltd., 923 F.2d 245 (2d Cir. 1991).

25 Rakoff, *id.*

26 *See* Gordon v. New York Stock Exch., Inc., 433 U.S. 659, 662, 673, 680, 682 (1975). The Court in *Gordon*, however, ultimately held that the actual fixing of commission rates by the SEC was immune to any attack under the antitrust laws. *Id.* at 685-86, 689.

27 *See* Katsoris, *Securities Arbitration After McMahon*, 41 FORDHAM URB. L. J. 361, 374 (1988).

28 For example, one broker inserted a one year statute of limitations in his customer agreement, despite the Uniform Code § 4 six year rule for bringing actions in arbitration. *Id.* at 375. *See* the discussion of time limitations on actions in chapters 6 and 11.

29 *See* Comment, *Statutory Proposal to Determine Arbitral Forums for 10(b) Disputes*, 28 SANTA CLARA L. REV. 389, 404 (1988).

30 *See* discussion in chapter 6.

31 *See* HOELLERING, ARBITRAL FINALITY, ARBITRATION & THE LAW 1987-88 32, 37 (AAA Office of the General Counsel ed., 1988).

32 *See* Jacklich v. Baer, 57 Cal. App. 2d 684, 693, 135 P.2d 179, 183 (3d Dist. 1943).

33 *See* J. CALAMARI & J. PERILLO, THE LAW OF CONTRACTS 316-328, 325 (1977).

34 Graham v. Scissor-Tail, Inc., 28 Cal. 3d 807, 623 P.2d 165, 171 Cal. Rptr. 604 (1981).

35 *Id.*

36 841 F.2d 282 (9th Cir. 1988).

37 Roney & Co. v. Goren, 875 F.2d 1218, FED. SEC. L. REP. (CCH) ¶ 94,438 (6th Cir. 1989).

38 In 1991 the U.S. Supreme Court found a uniform one year from discovery or three years from violation time limitation on Rule 10b-5 actions. This period was implied from examination of common law and state statutes on securities fraud actions. *See* Lampf, Plera, Lipkind, Frupis & Petigrow v. Gilbertson, 111 S. Ct. 2773, *reh'g denied*, 112 S. Ct. 27 (1991).

39 15 U.S.C. § 78r(c) (1982).

40 *See* Kupperman and Freeman, *Selected Topics in Securities Arbitration*, 65 TULANE L. REV. 1547, 1568-71 (1991).

41 Atcas v. Credit Clearing Corp. of Am., 292 Minn. 334, 197 N.W.2d 448 (Minn. 1972). California courts have taken the view that judicial determination is required where the fraud is alleged to permeate the entire agreement.

42 Jeppsen v. Piper, Jaffray & Hopwood, Inc., FED. SEC. L. REP. (CCH) ¶ 93,996 (D.C. Utah 1988).

43 Prima Paint Corp. v. Flood & Conklin Mfg. Co., 388 U.S. 395, 87 S. Ct. 1801, 18 L. Ed. 2d 1270 (1967).

44 374 U.S. 167 (1963).

45 United Paperworkers International Union, AFC-CIO v. Misco, Inc., 484 U.S. 29, 108 S. Ct. 364, 98 L. Ed. 2d 286 (1987).

46 700 F. Supp. 1039 (N.D. Cal. 1988).

47 Bayscene Resident Negotiators v. Bayscene Mobilhome Park, 15 Cal. App. 4th 119 (1993); Main v. Merrill Lynch, Pierce, Fenner & Smith, Inc., 136 Cal. Rptr. 378, 67 Cal. Ct. App. 3d 19 (1977).

48 Holloway v. Gruntal & Co., Inc. 1993 WL 36170 (S.D.N.Y. 1993).

49 *See* Nesslage v. York Securities, Inc., 823 F.2d 231, 234 (8th Cir. 1987) (citing Moses H. Cone Memorial Hospital v. Mercury Construction Corp., to the effect of preference for arbitration in a situation where there was a two year delay in moving for arbitration and participation in discovery, but this was justified in light of the retroactive application of *Byrd*). *Accord*, Kronfeld v. Advest, Inc., 675 F. Supp. 1449 (S.D.N.Y. 1987) (some purchasers of Washington Public Power System bonds had signed arbitration clauses with the broker underwriter from whom they purchased the bonds, others had not; "the prospect that different plaintiffs with like claims may have to litigate in two different forums is unpersuasive . . . No cognizable prejudice will result." *Id.* at 1453); Rush v. Oppenheimer & Co., Inc., 779 F.2d 885 (2d

Cir. 1985) (defendant delayed eight months before moving to stay for arbitration; had moved to dismiss; filed an answer; and participated in discovery); Gilmore v. Shearson/American Express, Inc., 668 F. Supp. 314, 317 (S.D.N.Y. 1987) (claims previously determined to be non-arbitrable and motion to compel arbitration previously withdrawn at request of federal judge were properly subject to a later motion to compel arbitration after *McMahon* decision and addition of RICO claim by plaintiff because "[If] before a case in a district court has proceeded to final judgment, a decision of the Supreme Court demonstrates that a ruling on which the judgment would depend was in error, no principal of 'the law of the case' would want a failure on our part to correct the ruling" [citing Zdanok v. Glidden Co., 327 F.2d 944, 951 (2d Cir.), *cert. denied*, 377 U.S. 934 (1964)].

50 A distinction must be made of the cases considering discovery under the previous securities arbitration rules and the new rules. The new rules provide for much more extensive discovery. As a result, prejudice will probably not exist. *See* discovery discussion in chapter 12 and Russo v. Simmons, 723 F. Supp. 220 (S.D.N.Y. 1989).

51 ABN Int'l Capital Markets Corp. v. ZwitserLeven, 996 F.2d 1478 (2d Cir. 1993), where taking six depositions in a Netherlands proceedings over six months unfairly prejudiced the party sought to be held to a later arbitration under federal law. The *Rush* principle was extended to foreign litigation. In Hibbard Brown & Co., Inc. v. ABC Family Trust, 959 F.2d 231 (4th Cir. 1992), the arbitration sought ten months after venue was transferred did not prejudice the parties since there had been no discovery. Further, disqualification of counsel would interfere with the arbitration and justified a deferral by the lower court.

52 Under the Federal Rules, a Rule 12(b)(6) motion to dismiss can be converted into a Rule 56 motion for summary judgment by the court, with the result that the party making the motion to dismiss will be held to have waived the right to arbitrate. *See* Sweater Bee by Banff, Ltd. v. Manhattan Indus., Inc., 754 F.2d 457 (2d Cir.), *cert. denied*, 474 U.S. 819 (1985).

53 *See* Stone v. E.F. Hutton & Co., 898 F.2d 1542, 1543-44 (11th Cir. 1990); Frye v. Paine, Webber, Jackson & Curtis, Inc., 877 F.2d 396, 399 (5th Cir. 1989).

54 *Rush* 779 F.2d at 887-89. In Ketchum v. Prudential-Bache Sec., Inc., 710 F. Supp. 300 (D. Kan. 1988), the court held that the plaintiff's claims of prejudice were ill-founded on the grounds of expenses and attorney's fees incurred responding to production requests, interrogatories, and requests for admissions. "Plaintiff's complaint is rather ironic, considering he chose to litigate . . . [I]ncurring expenses . . . in preparation for trial has not prejudiced [him] in such a way or to such an extent as to warrant a finding of waiver . . .

[P]laintiff has not met his heavy burden of proof."

55 For example, see Pearce v. E.F. Hutton Group, Inc., 828 F.2d 826 (D.C. Cir. 1987).

56 The issue of validity of the entire agreement is affected by forgery. Chastain v. Robinson-Humphrey Co., Inc., 957 F.2d 851 (11th Cir. 1992), held that a party seeking to avoid arbitration on the grounds of forgery must provide (1) an "unequivocal denial" that an agreement was ever made, and (2) there must be "some evidence" supporting the denial. Otherwise the issue will be decided by the arbitrators due to the signed agreement under *Prima Paint's* doctrine. *See also* Donato v. Merrill, Lynch, Pierce, Fenner & Smith, 663 F. Supp. 669 (N.D. Ill. 1987); Gilmore v. Shearson/American Express, Inc., 668 F. Supp. 314 (S.D.N.Y. 1987) (plaintiff had no recollection of seeing customer's agreement, let alone signing it, but did not contend that the signature was obtained by forgery or fraud; therefore, plaintiff could not avoid the rule that a person of ordinary understanding and competence will be bound by contract provisions whether or not he has read them).

57 "Brokers *are not* required as a matter of law to disclose or explain arbitration clauses to the customer." *Rush*, 779 F.2d at 1052 (citing Pierson v. Dean Witter Reynolds, Inc., 742 F.2d 334 [7th Cir. 1984]); Rush v. Oppenheimer & Co., Inc., 638 F. Supp. 872 (S.D.N.Y. 1986); Adams v. Merrill Lynch, Pierce, Fenner & Smith, Inc., FED. SEC. L. REP. (CCH) ¶ 92,328 (W.D. Okla. 1985); Pelzman v. Paine, Webber, Jackson & Curtis, Inc., FED. SEC. L. REP. (CCH) ¶ 99,408 (D. D.C. 1983).

58 Coleman v. Prudential Bache Securities, 802 F.2d 1352 (11th Cir. 1986).

59 Plaintiff's failure to read a contract containing arbitration clauses "may be excusable in light of allegations of a fiduciary relationship and defendant's misrepresentations." State v. Dean Witter Reynolds, Inc., 272 Cal. Rptr. 680 (Cal. Ct. App. 1990), *cert. denied*, 111 S. Ct. 1417 (1991).

60 *See Cohen*, 841 F.2d at 288; Gershman v. Goldman, Sachs & Co., 1992 LEXIS 19193, FED. SEC. L. REP. (CCH) ¶ 97,438 (E.D. Pa. 1992).

61 New York Gen. Obligations Law § 5-1103 permits a contract modification to be enforceable without a new consideration, but it must be in writing signed by the party to be charged. It is highly unlikely that the brokerage firm will have signed or acknowledged the purported rejection of arbitration.

62 *See* C.B.S. Fed. Credit Union v. Donaldson, Lufkin & Jenerette Sec. Corp., FED. SEC. L. REP. (CCH) ¶ 94,385 (W.D. Tenn. 1989).

Chapter 4

STATUTORY ARBITRATION

Due to the reluctance of the courts to enforce predispute arbitration agreements between parties to a contract, and the limitations on the validity of common law arbitrations discussed in the preceding chapter, various statutes have been enacted by the states and federal government providing for enforceability of arbitration agreements.[1] In those situations where the statute does not specify procedures, common law arbitration rules will still apply and revocability will be permitted.[2] This chapter will discuss these statutes.

The major thrust of such statutes is that an agreement to arbitrate an existing dispute is not revocable at any time prior to the award (as was the case at common law). Under the typical statute, the party seeking judicial review is not liable only for breach of the agreement to arbitrate. If a party refuses to appoint an arbitrator, the appointment may be made by the court. If a party institutes a judicial action, an order may be entered staying its prosecution. An order may also be entered compelling a defaulting party to perform the arbitration agreement, and, perhaps most importantly, these statutes provide that an award can be enforced through judicial means, typically an execution on a judgment entered on the basis of the arbitration award. The statutes also provide somewhat for arbitration procedure, that is, issuance of subpoenas; discovery, including taking of depositions, administration of oaths; and the like.

Between 1980 and 1984 more than 17 states enacted more than 19 arbitration and mediation laws. This explosion in legislation is also reflected in the development of private firms specializing in alternative dispute resolution.[3] There is support from business, lawyers, and the community at large for such programs in diverse areas including family and divorce, automobile "Lemon Laws," voting rights, and many other disputes. Mediation and arbitration are being used in all sorts of fields, for all manner of disputes. The statutes "break down institutional barriers to mediation by establishing methods for courts and other entities to refer cases. They also provide guidelines for mediators on important ethical and legal issues."[4] Many have received governmental funding, in addition to credibility from this legislative support, due to the perceived "public" function of this type of dispute resolution.

Under most arbitration statutes there is still judicial review. As noted above, those statutes invoking voluntary arbitration between the parties still permit a court to review the formation of the contract to be sure that it is an enforceable one. All the contract defenses will be permitted to show the lack of requisite agreement, including that regarding arbitration.[5] Most statutes also provide for the right of the court to review the award, as well as modify, correct, or confirm it. The usual reasons for review are manifest disregard of the law or facts presented, public policy, or other abuse of the process of arbitration.

There are few laws that require mandatory arbitration of disputes.[6]

1) UNIFORM ARBITRATION ACT

The Uniform Arbitration Act was approved by the National Conference of Commissioners on Uniform State Laws and the American Bar Association in 1955.[7] The Uniform Act, like the Federal Arbitration Act, first validates arbitration agreements and finds them "valid, enforceable and irrevocable, save upon such grounds as exist at law or in equity for the revocation of any contract."[8] It then sets forth the procedures to compel or stay arbitration;[9] provides for court appointment of arbitrators in the absence or with a failure of the agreement to so provide;[10] provides for the hearing;[11] witnesses, subpoenas, depositions;[12] fees and expenses;[13] provides for exercise of power by a majority of arbitrators;[14] and has several provisions regarding the award and its modification and correction, including judicial review and enforcement.[15]

Forty-five states have adopted some variation of the modern arbitration law embodied in the Uniform Arbitration Act.[16]

A) Recent State Arbitration Enactments

Businesses are resorting more and more to arbitration as an alternative to litigation in resolving civil disputes. New Jersey, for example, has enacted an entirely new arbitration statute in response to complaints about existing arbitration procedures.[17] This statute provides for discovery, including exchange of documents and depositions; appeal of various procedural issues; requires the award to be in writing and state findings of fact and conclusions of law used by the arbitrators; and provides that arbitration is fully reviewable for legal error by a court.

B) The New York Arbitration Act

The New York statute contained in the Appendix is the most widely used of the uniform state statutes. This is due to the governing law provision in brokerage agreements that normally chooses New York no matter where the account is opened, customer resides, or the local brokerage firm office is located.

2) UNITED STATES FEDERAL ARBITRATION ACT

As noted above, Congress passed the Federal Arbitration Act in 1925. This was done as an exercise of the commerce power. It creates a substantive federal right.[18] Both the Federal Arbitration Act and the Uniform Arbitration Act were derived from the earlier New York law.[19]

While the two statutes are similar, there are some differences. The Federal statute will apply in matters of interstate or foreign commerce[20] and applies in federal and state courts. One of the major differences is the power of the federal courts to remove a case from state courts and thereafter place it in arbitration.[21] But there can be no federal jurisdiction created for claims less than jurisdictional amount.[22]

The text of the Federal Arbitration Act of 1925, as amended, is reproduced in the Appendix.

3) RESULT FAVORS ARBITRATION

These federal and state statutory and judicial developments encourage arbitration of disputes and permit the enforceability of predispute agreements. The courts have consistently found a legislative approval, and even encouragement, of parties submitting disputes to a non-judicial forum. While the arguments are that such process is less expensive and quicker than judicial action, one major advantage is that an increasing number of cases are being referred to arbitration with the result that the court system is relieved of an even larger caseload.

NOTES

1 The major statutes in the United States are the Federal Arbitration Act of 1925 and the state adoptions of the Uniform Act. *See* the Federal Arbitration Act and New York statutes reproduced in Appendixes A and B, respectively.

2 England, for example, passed its first arbitration act in 1698, but that act allowed for revocation of submission. By the turn of the century, English law had been revised so that predispute arbitration agreements were enforceable. New York adopted the first modern U.S. arbitration statute in 1920, which provided for binding arbitration under predispute agreements.

3 *See* Wiehl, *Private Justice for a Fee: Profits and Problems*, N.Y. Times, Feb. 17, 1989, at B5, col. 3. This article notes that there are more than 50 such companies specializing in resolving corporate disputes.

4 Freedman, *Legislation on Dispute Resolution*, 1984 A.B.A. Special Committee on Dispute Resolution, ii.

5 *See* the discussion of contract defenses in chapter 3.

6 *See, e.g.*, New York CPLR 3405 which permits court-annexed arbitration of cases too big for small claims treatment but at the low end of the scale (applying to cases claiming as much as $10,000 in civil court, but $6,000 in other courts); Anderson v. Elliott, 555 A.2d 1042 (Me. 1989) (bar rules requiring submission of fee disputes to binding arbitration upheld).

7 The Uniform Act of 1955 has been amended. It succeeded the prior 1925 Uniform Act, which was withdrawn by the Commissioners in 1943. The 1955 Act follows the arbitration laws of New York and some fifteen other states. The only states that do not have arbitration statutes are Alabama, Montana, Nebraska, North Dakota, West Virginia. Vermont and Georgia have modern law only for construction disputes. The 1955 Uniform Arbitration Act is similar to the Federal Arbitration Act of 1925. R. RODMAN, COMMERCIAL ARBITRATION 1-6 (1984 and 1987 Supp.)

8 Uniform Arbitration Act § 1.

9 Uniform Arbitration Act § 2.

10 Uniform Arbitration Act § 3.

11 Uniform Arbitration Act § 5.

12 Uniform Arbitration Act § 7.

13 Uniform Arbitration Act § 10.

14 Uniform Arbitration Act § 4.

15 *See* Uniform Arbitration Act §§ 8, 9, 11, 12, 13, 14, 16, 17, 18, and 19.

16 The state arbitration statute citations are:

Alabama. ALA. CODE Tit 7, Chap 19, § 6-6-1 *et seq*.

Alaska. ALASKA STAT. § 09.43.010 *et seq*.

Arizona. ARIZ. REV. STAT. ANN. § 12-1501 *et seq.*
Arkansas. ARK. CODE ANN. § 34-511.
California. CAL. CIV. PROC. CODE § 1280 *et seq.*
Colorado. COLO. REV. STAT. § 13-22-201 *et seq.*
Connecticut. CONN. GEN. STAT. ANN. § 52-408 *et seq.*
Delaware. DEL. CODE. ANN. tit. 10, § 5701 *et seq.*
District of Columbia. D.C. CODE ANN. tit. 16, § 16-4301 *et seq.*
Florida. FLA. STAT. ANN. § 682.01 *et seq.*
Georgia. GA. CODE ANN. §§ 7-101, 7-105, 7-301 *et seq.*
Hawaii. HAWAII REV. STAT. § 658-1 *et seq.*
Idaho. IDAHO CODE § 7-901 *et seq.*
Illinois. ILL. REV. STAT. ch. 10, para. 101 *et seq.*
Indiana. IND. CODE ANN. § 34-4-2-1 *et seq.*
Iowa. IOWA CODE ANN. §§ 679A.1 to 679A.18.
Kansas. KAN. STAT. ANN. § 401 *et seq.*
Kentucky. KY. REV. STAT. ANN. §§ 417.010 to 417.040.
Louisiana. LA. REV. STAT. ANN. § 9:4201 *et seq.*
Maine. ME. REV. STAT. ANN. tit. 14, § 5927 *et seq.*
Maryland. MD. CODE ANN., Cts. & Jud. Proc. § 3-201 *et seq.*
Massachusetts. MASS. GEN. L. ch. 251, § 1 *et seq.*
Michigan. MICH. COMP. LAWS § 600.5001 *et seq.*
Minnesota. MINN. STAT. ANN. § 572.08 *et seq.*
Mississippi. MISS. CODE ANN. §§ 11-15-101 to 11-15-143.
Missouri. MO. REV. STAT. § 435.350 *et seq.*
Montana. MONT. CODE ANN. § 27-5-101 *et seq.*
Nebraska. NEB. REV. STAT. §§ 25-2103 to 25-2120.
Nevada. NEV. REV. STAT. § 38.015 *et seq.*
New Hampshire. N.H. REV. STAT. ANN. § 542:1 *et seq.*
New Jersey. N.J. REV. STAT. § 2A:24-1 *et seq.*
New Mexico. N.M. STAT. ANN. § 44-7-1 *et seq.*
New York. N.Y. CPLR 7501 *et seq.*
North Carolina. N.C. GEN. STAT. § 1-567.1 *et seq.*
North Dakota. N.D. CENT. CODE §§ 32-29-1 to 32-29-21.
Ohio. OHIO REV. CODE ANN. § 2711.01 *et seq.*
Oklahoma. OKLA. STAT. tit. 15, § 801 *et seq.*
Oregon. OR. REV. STAT. § 33.210 *et seq.*
Pennsylvania. PA. STAT. ANN. § 7301 *et seq.*
Puerto Rico. P.R. LAWS ANN. tit. 32, § 3201 *et seq.*
Rhode Island. R.I. GEN. LAWS § 10-3-1 *et seq.*
South Carolina. S.C. CODE ANN. § 15-48-10 *et seq.*
South Dakota. S.D. CODIFIED LAWS § 21-25A-1 *et seq.*

Tennessee. TENN. CODE ANN. §§ 23-501 to 23-519.

Texas. TEXAS REV. CIV. STAT. ANN. art. 224 *et seq.*

Utah. UTAH CODE ANN. §§ 78-31-1 to 78-31-22.

Vermont. VT. STAT. ANN. § 521 *et seq.*

Virginia. VA. CODE ANN. § 8.01.577 *et seq.*

Washington. WASH. REV. CODE § 7.04.010 *et seq.*

West Virginia. W. VA. CODE §§ 55-1-0 to 55-10-8.

Wisconsin. WIS. STAT. ANN. § 788.01 *et seq.*.

Wyoming. WYO. STAT. § 1-36-101 *et seq.*.

17 N.J. Rev. Stat. § 2A:23A-1 to 19 (1987). *See* Comment, *The New Jersey Alternative Procedure For Dispute Resolution Act: Vanguard of a "Better Way,"* U. PA. L. REV. 1723 (1988).

18 *See* Merrill Lynch, Pierce, Fenner & Smith, Inc. v. Haydu, 482 F. Supp. 788 (S.D. Fla. 1980), (citing C. WRIGHT, A. MILLER & E. COOPER, FEDERAL PRACTICE AND PROCEDURE, Jurisdiction §3569), *rev'd on other grounds*, 637 F.2d 391 (5th Cir. 1981), *appeal after remand*, 675 F.2d 1169 (11th Cir. 1982).

19 *See* the discussion of the historical development of the arbitration laws in chapter 2.

20 Varley v. Tarrytown Assoc., Inc., 477 F.2d 208 (2d Cir. 1973).

21 9 U.S.C. § 205.

22 Quick & Reilly, Inc. v. Aaglio, 717 F. Supp. 822 (S.D. Fla. 1991) ($44,181 claim on margin account dismissed); Giangrande v. Shearson Lehman/E.F. Hutton, 803 F. Supp. 464 (Mass. 1992) (no federal jurisdiction where only $24,000 claim).

Chapter 5

FINALITY OF ARBITRATION

This chapter discusses the difficulties encountered in appealing decisions of arbitrators. Under both the Federal Arbitration Act and Uniform Act, any party can be forced to arbitrate through a motion for a stay of litigation compelling arbitration.[1] This chapter will discuss the ways by which the parties will attempt to seek arbitration rather than litigation. These subjects are also discussed in more detail in chapter 12, containing materials on responses to the filing of a securities claim in arbitration, and chapter 16, which deals with the appeal from securities arbitration awards.

1) APPEAL OF COURT ORDERS ON ARBITRABILITY

Normally, only final judgments are appealable. Many courts have concluded that arbitration orders constitute interlocutory and not final decisions, but there is not complete agreement.[2] Under § 3 of the Federal Arbitration Act, an appeal is immediate for denial of arbitrability orders.[3] So a stay pending arbitration will permit appellate review. But a denial of arbitration is probably *immediately* appealable, because orders that grant or deny injunctions and orders that have the practical effect of granting or denying injunctions and have "serious, perhaps irreparable, consequences"[4] are appealable at once. This is true regardless of the fact that a final judgment will be appealable under the Supreme Court's finality rule.

In 1988 a new section was added to the Federal Arbitration Act providing that an appeal may not be taken from an interlocutory order "(1) granting a stay of any action under § 3 . . .; (2) directing arbitration to proceed under § 4 . . .; (3) compelling arbitration under § 206 of the Federal Arbitration Act; or (4) refusing to enjoin an arbitration that is subject to this title."[5] As a result, the courts in a number of securities cases have found orders to compel arbitration unreviewable, even retroactively.[6] This law reversed the Enelow-Ettelson doctrine, which made the grant or denial of a stay of an action at law pending arbitration automatically appealable.[7]

For example, *Perrera v. Siegal Trading Co.*,[8] held that an order compelling arbitration is final "when it results from a proceeding in which the sole issue before the court is the arbitrability of the dispute" and is not subject to appellate review under § 16 of the Federal Arbitration Act. Thus an order directing an entire case to arbitration in response to a motion of defendant's to dismiss is an "embedded proceeding," one in which the arbitrability issue arose in an action on the underlying substantive dispute and not as an independent matter.[9]

Under federal law, an appeal of an order dismissing a case due to another pending state action was dismissed as interlocutory since it does not end the litigation but ensures that it will continue. It failed to satisfy the requirement that the decision would be "conclusive" because it is inherently tentative and not the final determination on the subject.[10] Federal Arbitration Act Section 15 does not permit appeal of a motion to compel arbitration, as Congress favors arbitration. But from a denial of a motion to compel arbitration, Section 15 does nothing to change prior state law that this is an interlocutory order which permits 42 days to appeal under Rule 4 of the Alabama Rules of Appellate Procedure, rather than the 14 day period for filing an appeal from interlocutory orders involving injunctions.[11]

2) FINALITY OF ARBITRATION

The decision in arbitration can have *res judicata* effect, even where federal issues are involved.[12] There are few grounds under the typical arbitration statute for a court to disregard the decisions of the arbitration forum. These are usually fraud, misconduct, denial of due process including manifest disregard of the law or facts,[13] and that the arbitrators have exceeded their powers or failed to render a final and definite award that the courts can be called upon to enforce. In these instances, the court will review the process itself.[14]

Sections 10 and 11 of the Federal Arbitration Act specify the following grounds for vacating or modifying an award:

1. Procurement of the award through fraud, corruption, or undue means;
2. Partiality of the arbitrators;[15]
3. Misconduct of the arbitrators including the refusal to hear evidence or to postpone the hearing upon sufficient cause shown;
4. The arbitrators exceeded their powers;[16]
5. The award was made upon a matter not submitted to arbitration; and

6. The award was arrived at through a material miscalculation or other mistake.

Errors of law or fact will not permit setting aside an award. "Once an arbitration award is entered, the finality that courts should afford the arbitration process weighs heavily in favor of the award, and courts must exercise great caution when asked to set aside an award."[17] Therefore, absent exclusion of pertinent and material evidence, the award normally will not be subject to review because the arbitrator failed to consider particular arguments, especially if the parties themselves participated in the arbitration and could have, or should have, brought all relevant facts to the attention of the arbitrator. The standard of manifest disregard is a high one: it does not include the arbitrator's decision when presented with conflicting facts or legal theories, but applies when there is little likelihood that a reasonable person would have decided the way the arbitrator did given the law or facts presented. There can be no appeal on the merits of the arbitrator's decision, only on the basis of the process.

As a result of *McMahon's* holding that § 10(b) and RICO claims are both arbitrable, and the *Rodriguez* determination that § 12(2) claims are also arbitrable, "almost all" securities lawsuits dealing with customer and brokerage accounts will be submitted to arbitration, including securities fraud actions. There is no question but that the result of these cases will be a tremendous increase in the arbitration caseloads of the SROs and the AAA.

Two procedural problems, however, have been created by the Supreme Court's bifurcation of similar factual issues to both arbitration and litigation depending on what type of claims have been asserted. One problem is the question of the effect that awards should be given in later or simultaneous litigation. Another problem is the question of the proper order of the two sets of dispute resolution--which should take place first, or should both be addressed together?

A) Collateral Estoppel

The Supreme Court has not ruled on the collateral estoppel effect of arbitration awards.[18] Based on the principle that relitigation is unfair and a waste of resources, the common law doctrine of collateral estoppel prohibits duplicate resolution of the same issue in a subsequent proceeding as a principle of *res judicata*. Three requirements must be met by the party seeking to apply collateral estoppel:[19] (1) the issue must be identical to one already litigated; (2) these parties must have litigated it in another proceeding;[20] and (3) the determination of the issue must have been essential to the decision in the earlier proceeding. New York adds a requirement that must be applied by federal courts construing New York law: that there is a "full and fair opportunity" to present the issue in the prior case.[21]

B) Order of Dispute Resolution

Upon application of one of the parties, the courts will consider the question of prioritizing litigation or arbitration. This ordering of the proceedings is important in several respects. First, the preference for the Federal Arbitration Act requires an automatic bifurcation, making possible disposition of arbitrable and non-arbitrable claims separately and simultaneously, with the possibility of greater delay and inefficiency.

With arbitration and litigation simultaneously proceeding, or one stayed pending determination of the other, confusion may well reign. In addition, such bifurcated proceedings are perhaps to the great disadvantage of the one the securities laws and public policy should be protecting--the customer/consumer. Since many customers seeking redress will be doing so because of financial chaos and possible bankruptcy,[22] it seems dual proceedings can have a very unfair result.

The significance of governing law provisions of customer agreements in securities cases is thus controlling. The result is finality of arbitration,[23] with the concomitant judgment on award, requiring the parties to act in accordance with the decision rendered.[24]

> In ordering arbitration to take place despite the risk of preclusion, the [*Byrd*] Court apparently agreed with those courts that had taken the position that the threat of collateral estoppel "does not justify denying arbitration of otherwise arbitrable intertwined state law claims." In his concurrence, Justice White made this point explicitly, stating that fears of collateral estoppel should not cause a district court to stay or refuse to compel the arbitration of arbitrable claims.[25]

In order for collateral estoppel to apply, the subsequent trier must be made aware of the determination of the issues presented. In present arbitration practice, this is virtually impossible because arbitrators only give the "bottom line" result. While in single-issue disputes this will not create a problem, in the case of several sometimes inconsistent claims on the same facts, which may well arise due to the intertwining nature of the facts and law in securities cases (including what now are RICO claims), it may be more difficult to give the determination collateral estoppel effect: it is not clear which claim's determination the "bottom-line" remedy was decided. Requiring the arbitrator to make separate specific findings of fact as to each issue presented is the result of recently adopted SRO procedures.[26]

Collateral estoppel is a decision within the judge's discretion. As long as the right of the parties to full and fair review is protected, collateral estoppel can result from arbitration. Factual findings are particularly within the authority and expertise of a securities panel. The Eleventh Circuit stated that:

> [A] federal court should be hesitant to preclude the litigation of the federal claim based on the collateral estoppel effects of a prior arbitration award. These cases indicate a case-by-case approach focusing on the federal interests in insuring a federal court determination of the federal claim, the expertise of the arbitrator and his scope of authority under the arbitration agreement, and the procedural adequacy of the arbitration proceeding.[27]

C) Vacating an Award

"[A]lthough arbitrators may properly render a lump sum award without disclosing their rationale where the award has no factual support [a] Court may properly vacate the award."[28] In *Tinaway v. Merrill Lynch and Co., Inc., et al.*[29] for example, the arbitrator had given an award of only five percent of the amount an investor allegedly lost due to the claimed wrongdoing of the broker-defendants, but the Court found that there was no manifest disregard of the law, nor were the arbitrators partial to the defendants. The plaintiff had been unable to show any evidence of direct pecuniary, business, or personal relationship, and although the small award may suggest influence by the arbitrators general professional interests, this was a "general" versus reversible bias. There was no showing of direct, demonstrable bias and remote, uncertain, or speculative bias is not sufficient. The judge noted that the appearance of bias that might disqualify a judge is not sufficient to disqualify an arbitrator. Further, the Court felt that to give reasons for an award, while it would help to uncover failure to apply the law in such a manner that the award could be reversed, would undermine the quick, efficient, and non-appealable attributes of this alternative and private dispute resolution process. This rationale seems to beg the question: if the goal of the securities regulation process is to protect the investor and the integrity of the marketplace, it seems obvious that a written explanation of the findings would be called for in these quasi-judicial proceedings. To have one misapplication of the law is to leave the investor out in the cold, without recovery (or full recovery as in this case). This result can hardly be said to comport with Congressional intent, it seems, as expressed in the securities laws or, for that matter, in the Federal Arbitration Act.

Another reason, of course, for the finality of the award is also the fact that the arbitrator does not have to give reasons for his decision. Even under the new SRO award criteria, the arbitrator does not have to give a "legal opinion" justifying the decision. The court "need not speculate on the arbitrator's reasoning process or his analysis of the issues, and indeed, his grasp of even the rudiments of the controversy, are of no moment to the court."[30] For this reason, the courts will not require an arbitrator to be deposed as such discovery is a fishing expedition and would negate arbitration as a quick means to resolve disputes and mean inordinate delay.[31]

The finality of an award favors both the investor and the brokerage firm in most cases. For the investor who prevails, the award will be enforced by the SRO's internal mechanisms and sanctions, and in AAA and other arbitrations, the investor will obtain confirmation of the award in court. In litigation, however, the possibility of appeal exists for the losing party, with the attendant delay and expense. To the extent that the small customer prevails, arbitration will permit more actions.

3) SANCTIONS

Sanctions have been imposed when a court finds that the objections to arbitration (discussed in chapter 3) have been frivolous.

Also a risk of sanctions pursuant to Federal Rule of Civil Procedure 11 exists when an attorney brings an action to vacate an arbitration award. Where the brokerage firm brought an action to vacate a $1,850,170 award, the court found the "zeal of an attorney who lost the arbitration proceeding cannot overcome the lack of merit in the claims and the fact that objective counsel should have recognized the futility of the [appeal]." Finding the "challenge will not lie and indeed is antithetical to the very nature and purpose of arbitration--to obtain an expeditious, efficient and definitive resolution of controversies," the judge imposed $25,000 in Rule 11 sanctions against the brokerage firm's counsel.[32]

In a continuation of the *McMahon* case, the McMahon's attorney asked a New York court to enjoin arbitration before the N.Y.S.E. and compel it before the AAA instead. Shearson was granted an option to compel arbitration and further state action was enjoined by the Southern District of New York on the grounds that the rationale of McMahon's attorney was frivolous and flaunted the agreement, the Federal Arbitration Act, and the Supreme Court mandate. The filing of the first action did not defeat Shearson's right under the contract to demand N.Y.S.E. arbitration if McMahon did not do so within the contractual time period. McMahon did not, and Shearson prevailed in selection of forum. Finding the action a "blatant evasion" of the court's ongoing jurisdiction and a misleading interpretation of the order, the court concluded the counsel's tactics "unreasonably, vexatiously, and frivolously multiplied these proceedings," justifying an award of sanctions.[33] This case was, however, reversed on appeal, the Second Circuit finding:

> Although other goals for the imposition of sanctions under Rule 11 may exist, for example, punishment for violation of the Rule, compensation for victim of the violation, and deterrence of others, focus should be on the drafters' aim of discouraging dilatory and abusive litigation tactics and eliminating frivolous claims and defenses, thereby speeding up and reducing the costs of the litigation process. Sanctions are the deterrent threat by which a district court judge may deal with counsel who ignore their broadened responsibility under the amended Rule to forward the effective administration of justice.[34]

Imposition of sanctions must be based on a pleading, motion, or other paper signed and filed in the federal court. The standard is whether the actions are "objectively unreasonable." It is not intended to

> . . . chill an attorney's creative, imaginative or enthusiastic advocacy on his client's behalf. So long as his pleadings meet the test of reasonableness and are not interposed for what the amendment identifies as improper purposes--that is to say, counsel's actions are not a dilatory or abusive tactic designed simply to delay, harass or cause his adversary needless expense--sanctions are not warranted.[35]

Sanctions can also be imposed under a "clear showing of bad faith" standard under 29 U.S.C. § 1927, which provides "[a]ny attorney who so multiplies the proceedings in any case unreasonable and vexatiously may be required by the court to satisfy personally the excess costs, expenses, and attorneys' fees reasonably incurred because of such conduct."

4) JUDICIAL REVIEW OF ARBITRATION AWARDS[36]

One corollary to the strong federal policy favoring arbitration is that "arbitration awards are peculiarly insulated from judicial review."[37] The scope of such review is "extraordinarily narrow:"

> Because the parties have contracted to have disputes settled by an arbitrator chosen by them rather than by a judge, it is the arbitrator's view of the facts and of the meaning of the contract that they have agreed to accept. [A]s long as the arbitrator is even arguably construing or applying the contract and acting within the scope of his authority, that a court is convinced he committed serious error does not suffice to overturn his decision.[38]

Any challenge that concerns the merits of an award "must be considered presumptively unjustified."[39] Hence, the burden on the party seeking to vacate or modify an arbitration award is very heavy indeed.[40]

These general standards govern a district court's order confirming or vacating an arbitration award. Whether the same standards apply to an appellate court's review of such an order is unclear. The Eleventh Circuit applies an abuse of discretion standard in reviewing a district court's ruling.[41] The Fifth Circuit applies a *de novo* standard,[42] reasoning:

> In the arbitration context, granting the deference ordinarily due the district court risks forgetting the prior and critical deference due the findings of the arbitration panel. *De novo* review . . . enables us to assess whether the district court accorded sufficient deference in the first instance, an assessment that a more restrictive appellate review would cripple.[43]

Federal Arbitration Act § 15 permits interlocutory appeals of orders favoring litigation over arbitration but not vice-versa. More specifically, it permits interlocutory appeals of orders denying motions to compel arbitration and motions to stay litigation pending arbitration but forbids interlocutory appeals of orders granting motions to compel and motions to stay.[44]

A) Procedure for Obtaining Judicial Review

Following the issuance of an arbitration award, any party may petition the court for relief. A party seeking to enforce an award may move to confirm it under Federal Arbitration Act § 9. A motion to confirm must be filed within one year from the date the award was issued. A party seeking to overturn or correct an award, in whole or in part, may petition the court pursuant to Federal Arbitration Act § 10 or § 11. Section 10 sets out the grounds for vacating an award, and §11 sets out the grounds for modifying an award. In contrast to a party seeking confirmation, a party seeking to vacate or modify an award must file within three months following receipt of the award under § 12. Failure to file within that time results in a waiver of the right to seek such relief.[45]

An interesting problem arises when a party files a timely motion to vacate an arbitration award and then, outside the three month period, moves to amend to raise additional grounds for vacation. The Eleventh Circuit recently held that the solution to this problem is to be found in the Federal Rules of Civil Procedure. The court concluded that since "the papers filed by a party seeking to confirm or vacate an arbitration award function as the initial pleadings in post-arbitration proceedings in the district court, . . . Rule 15, which governs amended and supplemental pleadings in a civil action, should also apply to amended motions to vacate arbitration awards."[46]

When the relief sought is vacation or modification of an award, the party seeking it may file a motion in the district where the award was made.[47] When the relief sought is confirmation of an award, the party seeking it may file a motion in the district were the award was made or in any other district where the parties have agreed. Notably, though, to file in federal court, whether the relief sought be confirmation, vacation, or modification, "[t]here must be an independent basis of jurisdiction."[48] As the Supreme Court recently observed: "The Federal Arbitration Act is something of an anomaly in the field of federal-court jurisdiction. It creates a body of federal substantive law establishing and regulating the duty to honor an agreement to arbitrate, yet it does not create any independent federal-question jurisdiction."[49] When the party seeking to confirm properly files in one district and the party seeking to vacate properly files in another, the courts are likely to determine which venue is more appropriate by analyzing the issue under 28 U.S.C. § 1404(a).[50]

B) Confirming an Award

The process of confirming an arbitration award is designed to be quick, easy, and inexpensive. It is a summary procedure that simply makes the final arbitration award a judgment of the court. "[C]onfirmation can only be denied if an award has been corrected, vacated, or modified in accordance with the Federal Arbitration Act."[51] "[O]nly clear evidence of impropriety . . . justifies the denial of summary confirmation of an arbitration award."[52]

C) Vacating an Award

Section 10 of the Federal Arbitration Act provides the statutory basis for vacating an arbitration award. The statutory grounds set forth above are very narrow. In summary, an award may be vacated if:

1. the award was procured by corruption, fraud, or undue influence;
2. there is evidence of bias on the part of an arbitrator;
3. an arbitrator was guilty of misconduct that prejudiced the rights of a party; or
4. the arbitrators exceeded their powers.

Many courts have also held that, independently of these stautory grounds, an arbitration award may be vacated if:

5. the arbitrators "manifest[ly] disregard . . . the law,"
6. the award is arbitrary and capricious, or
7. enforcement of the award would violate public policy.

The law is clear that, absent a contractual provision to the contrary, arbitrators need not follow any particular form or format in making their award. "It has long been settled that arbitrators are not required to disclose or explain the reasons underlying an award."[53] Lump-sum awards, which simply state whether the request for relief is being granted or denied and, if granted, the amount of the award, are commonplace and permissible. Not only are the grounds for vacating an arbitration award very narrow, but courts also "have repeatedly condemned efforts to depose members of an arbitration panel to impeach or clarify their awards." The policy behind such a rule is clear. If arbitrators were required to issue an opinion or otherwise detail the reasons underlying an arbitration award, the very purpose of arbitration--the provision of a relatively quick, efficient, and informal means of private dispute settlement--would be markedly undermined.[54] Hence, absent extraordinary circumstances, a district court need not and will not conduct a hearing on a motion to confirm or vacate an award. A district court properly remands an award for clarification of its meaning.[55] The court will base its decision on the written submissions of the parties and, possibly, on the oral argument of counsel.

5) CHALLENGING AN AWARD UNDER § 10(a)

Under Federal Arbitration Act § 10(a), a court may vacate an arbitration award "[w]here the award was procured by corruption, fraud, or undue means." To prevail under this section, a party seeking to vacate must prove three things:

1. The movant must establish the fraud by clear and convincing evidence;
2. The fraud must not have been discoverable upon the exercise of due diligence prior to or during the arbitration; and
3. The person seeking to vacate the award must demonstrate that the fraud materially related to an issue in the arbitration.[56]

The standard for determining whether an award should be vacated under § 10(a) is "nearly identical" to the standard for determining whether a party should be relieved from a final judgment under rule 60(b)(3) of the Federal Rules of Civil Procedure.[57]

6) CHALLENGING AN AWARD UNDER § 10(b)

Section 10(b) permits a party to challenge an arbitration award by evidence of "evident partiality or corruption in the arbitrators, or either of them." As a general rule, a party seeking to vacate an award on this ground must object at or before the start of the arbitration hearing. Failure to object at that time ordinarily results in a waiver. No waiver will be found, however, unless "[a]ll the facts now argued as to [the] alleged bias were known . . . at the time the [arbitration panel] heard [the case]."[58] However, arbitrator bias is determined only after the decision is rendered.[59]

Assuming bias is asserted in a timely fashion, the party asserting it bears the burden of proving it. Most courts agree that the applicable standard for establishing bias falls somewhere between the lesser standard of an "appearance of bias" and the more exacting standard of "proof of actual bias." Most courts have held that bias or "evident partiality" exists only "where a reasonable person would *have* to conclude that an arbitrator was partial to one party to the arbitration." An arbitrator's alleged bias may not be the basis for vacating an award (or, initially, for disqualification) unless the bias is "direct, definite, and capable of demonstration rather than remote, uncertain, or speculative."[60]

To satisfy this standard, the party seeking to vacate an award ordinarily "must show that an arbitrator had some sort of personal interest whether pecuniary or otherwise in the matter before him or her that would have biased or prejudiced his or her judgment." Bias based on race, religion, sex, or national origin may also provide a sound basis for vacating an arbitration award under § 10(b).[61]

Arbitrator bias is reviewed in detail in Chapter 10. It goes without saying that "[a]n unfavorable decision is not in and of itself evidence of partiality" and that, except in highly unusual circumstances, the "[s]ize of an award alone is not a sufficient basis for a finding that the arbitrators are partial toward the winner." To a large extent, these and similar rules are nothing more than an expression of the longstanding doctrine that actionable bias "must result from an extra judicial source."[62] To date, no reported decision shows a court vacating or modifying an arbitration award in the securities context on the ground of "evident partiality."

7) CHALLENGING AN AWARD UNDER § 10(c)

A court may vacate an arbitration award under Federal Arbitration Act § 10(c) "[w]here the arbitrators were guilty of misconduct in refusing to postpone the hearing . . . or in refusing to hear evidence . . . or of any other misbehavior by which the rights of any party have been prejudiced." Not every failure by an arbitrator to admit relevant evidence or to continue a hearing, however, constitutes misconduct requiring vacatur of an arbitrator's award. . . . In fact, an award may be vacated under § 10(c) only when the exclusion of relevant evidence results in a party being "denied a fundamentally fair hearing."[63] This is hardly surprising since appellate courts apply virtually the same rule when reviewing a lower court's decision to exclude material evidence at trial. Courts have likewise held that only an arbitrary refusal to grant a reasonable request for a continuance constitutes misconduct under § 10(c).

8) CHALLENGING AN AWARD UNDER § 10(d)

Under Federal Arbitration Act § 10(d), a court may vacate an arbitration award when an arbitrator exceeded his authority "or so imperfectly executed [it] that a mutual, final and definite award . . . was not made." An arbitrator's authority is defined by the agreement to arbitrate and by the canons of construction that apply to such agreements. Most courts accord the "narrowest of readings" to § 10(d)'s authorization for a court to vacate an award when an arbitrator has exceeded his authority.[64] A court may "not interfere with an arbitrator's decision unless it can be said with positive assurance that the contract is not susceptible to the arbitrator's interpretation." The courts will also not reformulate remedies. In light of the federal policy favoring arbitration, the court's resolves all doubt in favor of the arbitrator's authority to award a particular remedy.

Some courts have narrowed the scope of permissible inquiry under § 10(d) by concluding that "a court's ability to vacate an award under [that] section . . . depends not on the outcome of a particular legal decision but rather on whether the arbitrators were requested to make the decision at all."[65] Under this view, an arbitrator exceeds her authority only if a court must conclude that the parties did not agree for her to resolve the matter in dispute. Other courts have construed § 10(d) more broadly and concluded, at least implicitly, that an arbitrator exceeds her authority whenever she renders a decision that either is irrational or manifestly disregards the law.[66] This broader interpretation is discussed in the following section.

9) CHALLENGING AN AWARD UNDER THE "MANIFEST DISREGARD" DOCTRINE

Arguably, an arbitration award entered under the Federal Arbitration Act may only be vacated pursuant to § 10 of the Act.[67] Parties often seek to vacate or modify an arbitration award on the grounds that the award evidences a "manifest disregard of the law" by the arbitrators. Whether the "manifest disregard" doctrine may properly be applied in the securities context is debatable. In any event, the doctrine appears to have originated in *Wilko v. Swan*, in which the Supreme Court declared in dicta:

> While it may be true . . . that a failure of the arbitrators to decide in accordance with [applicable law] would "constitute grounds for vacating the award pursuant to § 10 of the Federal Arbitration Act," that failure would need to be made clearly to appear. . . . [T]he interpretations of the law by the arbitrators in contrast to manifest disregard are not subject, in the federal courts, to judicial review for error in interpretation.[68]

The leading case to date on the subject of "manifest disregard" in the securities context is *Merrill Lynch, Pierce, Fenner & Smith Inc. v. Bobker.*[69] There, after plaintiffs prevailed in arbitration, Merrill Lynch moved to vacate on the ground that the award was in "manifest disregard" of the law.[70] The dispute concerned the applicability of Rule 10b-4 to short sales in connection with tender offers. Shortly after tendering all of his 4,000 shares of Phillips Petroleum Company (Phillips) in response to a tender offer by Phillips, the plaintiff instructed one of his Merrill Lynch brokers to sell short 2,000 shares of Phillips. The broker did so but, immediately thereafter, Merrill Lynch canceled the sale on the ground that it violated the firm's policy, as well as Rule 10b-4, which requires a shareholder to have a "net long" position in a security both on the date the security is tendered and on the date the tender offer expires. The arbitration panel found for the plaintiff.

In response to Merrill Lynch's motion to vacate, the district court asked the SEC to file an amicus brief. The SEC submitted a brief in support of Merrill Lynch. The district court agreed with Merrill Lynch and the SEC, and ruled:

> The arbitrators were aware of the Rule and its purpose yet proceeded to ignore it, despite the fact that the illegality of the proposed transaction was pressed by Merrill Lynch. Permitting this award to stand would have the unacceptable result of penalizing Merrill Lynch for acting in accordance with the law. Accordingly, the Court finds that the award . . . was in manifest disregard of the law and is hereby vacated.[71]

On appeal, the Second Circuit reversed the district court and articulated the following definition of the "manifest disregard" doctrine:

> "Manifest disregard of the law" by arbitrators is a judicially-created ground for vacating their arbitration award. It is not to be found in the federal arbitration law. Although the bounds of this ground have never been defined, it clearly means more than error or misunderstanding with respect to the law. The error must have been obvious and capable of being readily and instantly perceived by the average person qualified to serve as an arbitrator. Moreover, the term "disregard" implies that the arbitrator appreciates the existence of a clearly governing legal principle but decides to ignore or pay no attention to it. To adopt a less strict standard of judicial review would be to undermine our well established deference to arbitration as a favored method of settling disputes when agreed to by the parties. Judicial inquiry under the "manifest disregard" standard is therefore extremely limited. The governing law alleged to have been ignored by the arbitrators must be well defined, explicit, and clearly applicable. We are not at liberty to set aside an arbitration panel's award because of an arguable difference regarding the meaning or applicability of laws urged upon it.[72]

Applying this standard to the facts in *Bobker*, the Second Circuit found that the arbitrators had considered the relevant rule of law, which is neither well-defined nor explicit, and applied it as they saw fit. The court concluded that this was not a matter of the arbitrators disregarding the law, but rather of interpreting or misinterpreting the law, but that decision was not subject to *vacatur*. Courts should "refrain from commenting on the correctness or incorrectness of the arbitrator's factual findings and legal conclusions. That is not the court's function."[73]

In the overwhelming majority of reported cases, courts have refused to vacate a securities arbitration on the ground that the arbitrators "manifestly disregarded the law." In fact, there is only one reported decision, *Ainsworth v. Skurnick*,[74] in which a court has vacated an award in a securities arbitration on this ground.

The arbitrators' failure to explain their disposition of a statutory claim which was required by the forum rules did not permit vacation of those portions of the award. The rules do not have the force of law, and a rule violation is not one of the grounds for vacatur mentioned in the statute and can not be, by itself, "manifest disregard" of state or federal law.[75]

Further, in vacating an award on the basis of a claim that there was a manifest disregard of the law, the courts are limited to review of the facts from a transcript of the arbitration proceedings. Without the transcript to review, the motion to vacate on this ground will be denied.[76]

10) CHALLENGING AN AWARD UNDER THE "ARBITRARY AND CAPRICIOUS" STANDARD

Some courts have held that an arbitration award may be vacated if the award is arbitrary or capricious.[77] The First Circuit recently discussed this basis for vacating and award, declaring that:

> [While] [c]ourts . . . retain a very limited power to review arbitration awards outside of § 10, . . . [there are] two classes of cases where an arbitral award is subject to [such] review. One category, usually involving labor arbitration, is where an award is contrary to the plain language of the collective bargaining agreement. The second category embraces instances where it is clear from the record that the arbitrator recognized the applicable law--and then ignored it.[78]
>
> While we understand the temptation to recognize a third, residual category for cases, which are "completely irrational," "arbitrary and capricious," or "unfounded in reason and fact," we resist it. In our view, any case which purports to fall into this residual category involves an award made contrary to the plain meaning of the contract authorizing arbitration or one made in manifest disregard of the law.[79]

This conclusion is debatable. Suppose two parties stipulate that the defendant did not convey material information to the plaintiff, and that the plaintiff did not otherwise have the information. As a result of not having it, the plaintiff decided to hold his stock rather than sell it and lost $25,000. The dispute between the parties turned on whether the defendant had a duty to disclose the information to the plaintiff. The law on the subject is unclear. The arbitrators concluded that the defendant owed a duty to disclose and breached it, but declined to award damages, finding that the plaintiff actually had the information and thus that no causal connection existed between the failure to disclose and the damages sustained. In this situation, the arbitrators' decision is "unfounded in . . . fact," and hence arbitrary and capricious, but the error arguably does not fit into either of the two categories identified by the First Circuit.

Setting this issue aside, however, there appears to be only one reported decision, *Clemons v. Dean Witter Reynolds, Inc.*,[80] in which a court has declined to confirm a securities arbitration award pursuant to the "arbitrary and capricious" standard. The *Clemons* court concluded that it could not vacate the award pursuant to the "manifest disregard" doctrine. The court nonetheless concluded that, since there were "no facts in the record which would support the award of $50,000," the award should be remanded to the arbitrators for them to explain how they calculated the plaintiffs' damages. In so doing, the court noted that "it may be that the arbitrators had a factual basis for the award which they have not adequately expressed."

11) CHALLENGING AN AWARD UNDER THE "PUBLIC POLICY" EXCEPTION

Another objection to confirming an arbitration award is that confirmation would violate public policy. The contours of the "public policy" exception were first outlined by the Supreme Court in *W.R. Grace & Co. v. Local 759, International Union of United Rubber, Cork, Linoleum & Plastic Workers.*[81] There, the Court held that, for an asserted public policy to be sufficient to preclude enforcement of an arbitration award, the policy has to be "explicit" and both "well defined and dominant." The Court further held that such a policy may be established only "by reference to the laws and legal precedents" and may not be the product of the parties' or the courts' "general considerations of supposed public interests."[82] Rarely will an arbitrator's award be so egregious that enforcement of it would violate public policy under the *Grace* test.

12) CONCLUSION

Due to the statutory preference for resolution of disputes through arbitration, courts will look warily at attempts by parties to have judicial review of the arbitration process, as well as the resulting decisions or awards. As a result of the very narrow grounds for appeal, most arbitration awards are, for all intents and purposes, final and non-appealable.

NOTES

1 *See* Federal Arbitration Act §§ 3 and 4, and Uniform Arbitration Act § 2; N. Y. CPLR 7503.

2 Perrera v. Siegel Trading Company, Inc., 951 F.2d 780 (7th Cir. 1992).

3 Under 28 U.S.C. § 1292(a)(1).

4 Gulfstream Aerospace Corp. v. Mayacamas Corp., 485 U.S. 271, 108 S. Ct. 1133, 99 L. Ed. 2d 296 (1988), superseded by a 1988 amendment adding a second § 15 to the Federal Arbitration Act that permitted appeal of an order denying arbitration/litigation under state law, as stated in H.G. Edwards & Sons, Inc. v. Clark, 558 So. 2d 358 (Ala. 1990) and Sierra Rutile, Ltd. v. Katz, 937 F.2d 743 (2d Cir. 1991); 937 F.2d 743 [2d Cir. 1991]).

5 Judicial Improvements and Access to Justice Act, Pub. L. 100-702, § 1019, 102 Stat. 4642, 4670-71 (1988).

6 *See* Campbell v. Dominick & Dominick, Inc., 872 F.2d 358 (11th Cir. 1989) (Act meant to apply to appeals in cases pending on date of its enactment); Jeske v. Brooks, 875 F.2d 71 (4th Cir. 1989); C.B.S. Employees Fed. Credit Union v. Donaldson, Lufkin & Jenrette Sec. Corp., FED. SEC. L. REP. (CCH) ¶ 94,385 (W.D. Tenn. 1989) (fraud went to the very nature of the contract, so it was for the court, not the arbitrator, to determine); Rauscher Pierce Refsnes, Inc. v. Birenbaum, 860 F.2d 169 (5th Cir. 1988) (denial of stay pending arbitration not appealable under collateral order doctrine because judgment could be set aside with claims referred to arbitration and no serious or potentially irreparable consequences); Turboff v. Merrill Lynch, Pierce, Fenner & Smith, Inc., 867 F.2d 1518 (5th Cir. 1989); Purdy v. Monex Intl., Ltd., 867 F.2d 1521 (5th Cir. 1989). *But see* Delmay v. Paine Webber, 872 F.2d 356 (11th Cir. 1989) (retrospective application conferring appellate jurisdiction applies to pending cases); McCowan v. Sears, Roebuck and Co., 722 F. Supp. 1069, 1076 (S.D.N.Y. 1989) (claims under state law involved different elements so that the outcome of one proceeding not determinative of the other; whether to stay arbitration "is a decision left to the district court as a matter of its discretion to control its docket").

7 28 U.S.C. § 1292(a)(1). *See* Thompson McKinnon Sec., Inc. v.

Salter, 873 F.2d 1397 (11th Cir. 1989) (order final and appealable as it resolves only issue before District Court). *See also Rauscher*, 860 F.2d at 170-71.

8 951 F.2d 780 (7th Cir. 1992).

9 Humphrey v. Prudential Securities Inc., 4 F.3d 313 (4th Cir. 1993).

10 Gulfstream Aerospace Corp. v. Mayacamas Corp., 458 U.S. 271 (1987).

11 A.G. Edwards & Sons, Inc. v. Clark, 558 So. 2d 358 (Ala. 1990).

12 *See* Dean Witter Reynolds Inc. v. Byrd, 470 U.S. 213, 223 (1985).

13 Of course, in both *Wilko* and *McMahon*, the Supreme Court indicated a failure of arbitrators to decide in accordance with the provisions of the securities laws would constitute grounds for vacating the award under the Federal Arbitration Act. Wilko v. Swan, 346 U.S. 427, 436 (1953). Justice Frankfurter commented all the Justices agreed that "arbitrators may not disregard the law." *Id.*, at 440 (Frankfurter, J., dissenting).

In *McMahon*, Justice O'Connor indicated that the possibility of judicial review under the securities laws "is sufficient to ensure that arbitrators comply with the requirements of the [Federal Arbitration Act]" and not disregard the law. McMahon v. Shearson/American Express, Inc., 107 S. Ct. at 2340.

14 *See* Annotations, *What Constitutes Corruption, Fraud, or Undue Means in Obtaining Arbitration Award Justifying Avoidance of Award Under State Law*, 22 A.L.R. 4th 366 (1983); *Refusal of Arbitrators to Receive Evidence, or Peimo Briefs or Arguments, on Particular Issue, as Grounds for Relief from Award*, 75 A.L.R. 3d 132 (1977); *Setting Aside Arbitration Award on Grounds of Interest Bias of Arbitrators*, 56 A.L.R. 3rd 815 (1974); *Liability of Parties to Arbitration for Costs, Fees, and Expenses*, 57 A.L.R. 3d 633 (1974); *Attorney's Fees or Other Expenses of Litigation as Elements in Measuring Exemplary or Punitive Damages*, 30 A.L.R. 3d 1443 (1970).

15 In Tinaway v. Merrill Lynch & Co., 658 F. Supp. 576 (S.D.N.Y. 1987), the court was "unable to infer a ground for the arbitrators' decision from the facts of the case" and vacated the award on the basis of the "evident partiality" of the arbitrators.

16 As the court stated in David v. Chevy Chase Fin. Ltd., 667 F.2d 160, 165 (D.C. Cir. 1981), with respect to the scope of the arbitrators' powers:

> "In sum, the genesis of arbitral authority is the contract, and arbitrators are permitted to decide only the issues that lie within the contractual award regarding a matter not within the scope of the governing arbitration clause is one made in excess of authority, and a Court is precluded from giving effect to such an award".

17 Foster v. Turley, 808 F.2d 38 (10th Cir. 1986).

18 "The question of what preclusive effect, if any, the arbitration

proceedings might have is not yet before us, however, and we do not decide it." *Byrd*, 470 U.S. at 233.

19 *See* RESTATEMENT (SECOND) OF JUDGMENTS § 27, Cmt. D (1980).

20 Occasionally a third party who is not a party to the litigation will invoke collateral estoppel to preclude relitigation of an issue completely resolved even to him by the prior proceeding. This result is possible because the prior "mutuality doctrine" was rejected in Parklane Hosiery Co. v. Shore, 439 U.S. 322, 99 S. Ct. 645, 58 L. Ed. 2d 552 (1979).

21 Maidman v. O'Brien, 473 F. Supp. 25 (S.D.N.Y. 1979); Schwartz v. Public Administration, 24 N.Y. 2d 65, 298 N.Y.S. 2d 955 (1969).

22 In many cases, the customer is being sued by the broker as a result of a margin call after his or her account has been sold out and there remains a balance due; or due to churning or other misconduct, the customer is suing a broker with little or no assets left.

23 The litigation aspect of the collateral estoppel doctrine has raised the question if it should be applied in arbitrations. Of course efficiency and economy will result from such an application of the doctrine, but the question has seldom been addressed. Mobilia, *Offensive Use of Collateral Estoppel Arising Out of Non-Judicial Proceedings*, 50 ALB. L. REV. 305, 321 (1986).

24 In some jurisdictions, the award must have been entered as a judgment. Ufheil Constr. Co. v. Town of New Windsor, 478 F. Supp. 766 (S.D.N.Y. 1979), *aff'd without op.*, 636 F.2d 1204 (2d Cir. 1980). But this is not always the case. *See* City of Gainesville v. Island Creek Coal Sales Co., 618 F. Supp. 513, (N.D. Fla. 1984) (collateral estoppel applied to issue of damage award without requiring entry of judgment).

25 Ginger, *Managing Securities Disputes After McMahon: A Call for Consolidation and Arbitration*, 33 VILL. L. REV. 515, 541 (1988).

26 *See* discussion of the content of awards in chapter 14.

27 Greenblatt v. Drexel Burnham Lambert, Inc., 763 F.2d 1352 (11th Cir. 1985).

28 *Id.*, at 1361.

29 692 F. Supp. 220 (S.D.N.Y. July 28, 1988).

30 Guetta v. Raxon Fabrics Corp., 123 A.D. 2d 40, 510 N.Y.S. 2d 576, 579 (1st Dept. 1987).

31 Hunt v. Mobil Oil Corp., 654 F. Supp. 1487, 1495-96 (S.D.N.Y. 1987).

32 Quick & Reilly, Inc. v. Jacobson, 21 SEC. REG. & L. REP. (BNA) 850 (S.D.N.Y. May 25, 1989).

33 McMahon v. Shearson/American Express, Inc., 709 F. Supp. 369, 374-75, (S.D.N.Y. 1989), *rev'd*, 896 F.2d 17 (2d Cir. 1990). *See also* Robinson v. Dean Witter Reynolds, Inc., 129 F.R.D. 15 (D.C. Mass. 1989)

(attorney did not make "reasonable inquiry" regarding law on compelling arbitration).

34 McMahon v. Shearson/American Express, Inc., 896 F.2d 17, 21 (2d Cir. 1990).

35 *Id.*, at 22.

36 This section is quoted from Kupperman & Freeman, *Selected Topics in Securities Arbitration*, 65 TUL. L. REV. 1603-28 (1991). Materials have been edited, slightly reorganized, and footnotes renumbered, eliminated and/or edited without notation, so the reader should consult the original source for the complete, unedited text and footnotes. Reprinted by permission of TUL L. REV.

37 Container Prod., Inc. v. United Steelworkers Local 5651, 873 F.2d 818, 819 (5th Cir. 1989). *See Appealability of Order Staying, or Refusing to Stay, Proceeding in Federal District Court Pending Arbitration Proceeding*, 110 A.L.R. 148 (1993).

38 United Paperworks Int'l Union v. Misco, Inc., 484 U.S. 29, 30-31, 37-38 (1987); *see also* Local 59, Int'l Bhd. of Elec. Workers v. Green Corp., 725 F.2d 264, 268 (5th Cir.), *cert. denied*, 469 U.S. 833 (1984) (Courts are to "refrain from commenting on the correctness or incorrectness of the arbitrator's factual findings and legal conclusions. . . [because it] is not [a court's] function" and "the violation of [public] policy must be clearly shown [if the award is not to be enforced]."). Courts customarily treat the jurisprudence on the scope of review of arbitration awards as a unified body of law, citing securities cases, labor cases, and other cases freely and interchangeably. *E.g.*, Jenkins v. Prudential-Bache Sec., 847 F.2d 631, 634 (10th Cir. 1988); *see also United Paperworkers Int'l*, 484 U.S. at 40 n.9. *But see* Raytheon Company v. Automated Business Systems, Inc., 882 F.2d 6, 10 (1st Cir. 1989) (discussing rationale for allowing arbitrators to award punitive damages in commercial disputes but not labor disputes, unless parties expressly so provide).

39 United Food & Commercial Workers Local 400 v. Marval Poultry Co., 876 F.2d 346, 351 (4th Cir. 1989) (citing International Ass'n of Machinists v. Texas Steel Co., 639 F.2d 279, 284 (5th Cir. 1981)); *see also* Booth v. Hume Publishing, Inc., 902 F.2d 925, 932 (11th Cir. 1990); Office & Professional Employees Int'l Union Local 2 v. Washington Metro. Area Transit Auth., 724 F.2d 133, 137 (D.C. Cir. 1983).

40 *See* O.R. Sec. v. Professional Planning Assoc., 857 F.2d 742, 748 (11th Cir. 1988).

41 *E.g.*, Raiford v. Merrill Lynch, Pierce, Fenner & Smith, Inc., 903 F.2d 1410, 1412 n.2 (11th Cir. 1990); Bonar v. Dean Witter Reynolds, Inc., 835 F.2d 1378, 1383 (11th Cir. 1988).

42 *E.g.*, Anderman/Smith Operating Co. v. Tennessee Gas Pipeline Co., 918 F.2d 1215, 1218 n.2 (5th Cir. 1990); Forsythe Int'l, S.A. v. Gibbs Oil Co., 915 F.2d 1017, 1020-21 (5th Cir. 1990); Delta Queen Steamboat Co. v. District 2, Marine Eng'r Beneficial Ass'n, 889 F.2d 599, 602 (5th Cir. 1989), *cert. denied*, 111 S. Ct. 148 (1990).

43 *Forsythe Int'l*, 915 F.2d at 1021.

44 *E.g.*, Arnold v. Arnold Corp., 920 F.2d 1269, 1274-76 (6th Cir. 1990); Jolley v. Paine Webber, Jackson & Curtis, Inc., 867 F.2d 891, 891-92 (5th Cir. 1989), *cert. denied*, 111 S. Ct. 762 (1991).

45 Drexel Burnham Lambert, Inc. v. Pyles, 701 F. Supp. 217, 219 (N.D. Ga. 1988) ("once the three month period for filing a motion to vacate . . . has expired, an attempt to vacate an arbitration award cannot be made even in opposition to a later motion to confirm") (citing International Bhd. of Elec. Workers Local 969 v. Babcock & Wilcox, 826 F.2d 962, 965 [10th Cir. 1987]; Taylor v. Nelson, 788 F.2d 220, 225 [4th Cir. 1986]; Florasynth, Inc. v. Pickholz, 750 F.2d 171, 175 [2d Cir. 1984]); *see also* Cullen v. Paine, Webber, Jackson & Curtis, Inc., 863 F.2d 851, 853 (11th Cir.), *cert. denied*, 109 S. Ct. 3159 (1989); Professional Adm'rs Ltd. v. Kopper-Glo Fuel, Inc., 819 F.2d 639, 642 (6th Cir. 1987). By the same token, failure to timely object to a late filing of a motion to modify or vacate results in a waiver of the right to object to the late filing. *See* Foster v. Turley, 808 F.2d 38, 41 (10th Cir. 1986).

46 In Bonar v. Dean Witter Reynolds, Inc., 835 F.2d 1378 (11th Cir. 1988), the court stated at 1382:

> The Federal Rules of Civil Procedure "govern the procedure in the United States district courts in all suits of a civil nature whether cognizable as cases at law or in equity or in admiralty, with the exceptions stated in Rule 81." Fed. R. Civ. P. Rule 81(a)(3) provides that in proceedings under the Federal Arbitration Act, the rules apply only to the extent that matters of procedure are not provided for in the Federal Arbitration Act. Since the Federal Arbitration Act provides only that notice of a motion to vacate, modify or correct an award must be served upon the adverse party or his attorney within three months after the award is filed or delivered, *see* 9 U.S.C. § 12, and contains no provisions governing amendments to timely motions, the Federal Rules apply to this issue.

47 9 U.S.C. §§ 10-11 (1988); *see also* §§ 6, 13. "The statutes and rules do not permit a party to initiate a challenge to an arbitration award by filing a complaint or an Application [to Vacate Arbitration Award]." O.R. Sec. v. Professional Planning Ass'n, Inc., 857 F.2d 742, 745 (11th Cir. 1988) (quoting Interior Finish Contractors Ass'n v. Drywall Finishers Local 1955, 625 F. Supp. 1233, 1240 [E.D. Pa. 1985]). The proper procedure is for a party to file a motion to vacate or modify as provided in Rule 6 of the Federal

Arbitration Act and Rule 7(b) of the Federal Rules of Civil Procedure. *Id.*

48 Harry Hoffman Printing, Inc. v. Graphic Communications Int'l Union Local 261, 912 F.2d 608, 611 (2d Cir. 1990).

49 Moses H. Cone Memorial Hosp. v. Mercury Constr. Corp., 460 U.S. 1, 25 n.32 (1983); *see also* Mesa Operating Ltd. Partnership v. Louisiana Intrastate Gas Corp., 797 F.2d 238, 240 (5th Cir. 1986); 13B C. WRIGHT, A. MILLER, & E. COOPER, FEDERAL PRACTICE AND PROCEDURE § 3569 (2d ed. 1984).

50 *See, e.g.*, Fahnestock & Co. v. Waltman, 1990 U.S. Dist. LEXIS 11024 (S.D.N.Y. 1990). 28 U.S.C. § 1404(a) (1988) provides: "For the convenience of parties and witnesses, in the interest of justice, a district court may transfer any civil action to any other district or division where it might have been brought."

51 Taylor v. Nelson, 788 F.2d 220, 225 (4th Cir. 1986); *see also* Booth v. Hume Publishing, Inc., 902 F.2d 925, 932 (11th Cir. 1990); Cullen v. Paine Webber, Jackson & Curtis, Inc., 863 F.2d 851, 854 (11th Cir.), *cert. denied*, 109 S. Ct. 3159 (1989); Ottley v. Schwartzberg, 819 F.2d 373, 377 (2d Cir. 1987).

52 Ormsbee Dev. Co. v. Grace, 668 F.2d 1140, 1147 (10th Cir.), *cert. denied*, 459 U.S. 838 (1982).

53 Antwine v. Prudential-Bache Sec., 899 F.2d 410, 412 (5th Cir. 1990) (citing United Steel Workers v. Enterprise Wheel & Car Corp., 363 U.S. 593, 598 [1960]).

54 *Antwine*, 899 F.2d at 412 (citing Sobel v. Hertz, Warner & Co., 469 F.2d 1211, 1214 [2d Cir. 1972]).

55 *See, e.g.*, San Antonio Newspaper Guild Local 25 v. San Antonio Light Div., 481 F.2d 821, 824-25 (5th Cir. 1973) (when arbitration award may be construed in more than one way, award may be remanded to panel for clarification); Galt v. Libbey-Owens-Ford Glass Co., 397 F.2d 439, 442-43 (7th Cir.), *cert. denied*, 393 U.S. 925 (1968) (approving remand to determine whether arbitrators treated specific contract clauses as being within purview of arbitration provision), .

56 Bonar v. Dean Witter Reynolds, Inc., 835 F.2d 1378, 1383 (11th Cir. 1988) (The last element--that the fraud materially relate to an issue in the arbitration--"does not require the movant to establish that the result of the proceedings would have been different had the fraud not occurred.") (citations omitted); *see also* LaFarge Conseils et Etudes, S.A. v. Kaiser Cement & Gypsum Corp., 791 F.2d 1334, 1339 (9th Cir. 1986).

57 Bonar, *Id.*, n.8; *see also* Harre v. A.H. Robins, 750 F.2d 1501, 1503 (11th Cir. 1985) *vacated*, 866 F.2d 1303 (1989) (standard arising under F.R.C.P. 60(b)(3)).

58 Apperson v. Fleet Carrier Corp., 879 F.2d 1344, 1359 (6th Cir. 1989), *cert. denied*, 110 S. Ct. 2206 (1990) (quoting Early v. Eastern Transfer, 699 F.2d 552, 558 [1st Cir. 1983]); *see also* United Steelworkers Local 1913 v. Union R.R., 648 F.2d 905, 913 (3d Cir. 1981).

59 Shearson Lehman Brothers, Inc., v. MacDowell, 5 SEC. ARB. COMM. 9 at 15 (Albany Cty. Sup. Ct. 1993).

60 Tamari v. Bache Halsey Stuart, Inc., 619 F.2d 1196, 1200 (7th Cir.) *cert. denied*, 449 U.S. 873 (1980); *cf.* Fertilizantes Fosfatados Mexicanos, S.A. v. Chemical Carriers, Inc., 751 F. Supp. 467, 468-69 (S.D.N.Y. 1990) (rejecting vague and unsubstantiated allegations of bias on the ground that "there is nothing more to the extraordinary charges leveled by the dissent[ing arbitrator] than frustration in failing to convince the majority of his position").

61 Hotel, Motel & Restaurant Employees Union Local 471 v. P. & J.G. Enter., Inc., 731 F. Supp. 88, 91 (N.D.N.Y. 1990).

62 Toyota of Berkeley v. Automobile Salesman's Union, Local 1095, United Food and Commercial Workers Union, 834 F.2d 751, 757 (9th Cir. 1987); *see also* United States v. Studley, 783 F.2d 934, 939-40 (9th Cir. 1986). Toyota of Berkeley .

63 *See* Hoteles Condado Beach, La Concha & Convention Center v. Union de Tronquistas Local 901, 763 F.2d 34, 40 (1st Cir. 1985) (vacatur is appropriate only when the exclusion of relevant evidence deprives the party of a fair hearing). An arbitrator's decision not to take further evidence is not grounds for vacation of the award. Coppola v. Charles Schwab & Co., 969 F.2d 1042 (2nd Cir.) (unless there is clear evidence that the award was prejudiced by the arbitrators conduct or Respondent's evidence was perjured, the Award will not be disturbed); Robbins v. Day, 954 F.2d 679 (11th Cir. 1992) (brokers who invoked the fifth amendment due to concurrent indictments for securities fraud could not be compelled to testify; arbitrators failure to force testimony did not constitute misconduct warranting vacatur of award).

64 *E.g.*, Kerr-McGee Refining Corp. v. M/T TRIUMPH, 924 F.2d 467, 471 (2d Cir. 1991); *see also* Davis v. Chevy Chase Fin., Ltd., 667 F.2d 160, 164-65 (D.C. Cir. 1981).

65 J.A. Jones Constr. Co. v. Flakt, Inc., 731 F. Supp. 1061, 1064 (N.D. Ga. 1990).

66 *See, e.g.*, Federated Dep't Stores v. J.V.B. Indus., Inc. 894 F.2d 862, 866 (6th Cir. 1990) (arbitrators exceed their authority when "they display a manifest disregard of the law"); National Post Office Mailhandlers v. United States Postal Serv., 751 F.2d 834, 843 (6th Cir. 1985); Andros Compania Maritima v. Marc Rich & Co., A.G., 579 F.2d 691, 703-704; Electronics Corp. of Am. v. International Union of Elec., Radio & Mach. Workers, 492 F.2d 1255, 1257 (1st Cir. 1974).

67 Rostad & Rostad Corp. v. Investment Management & Research, Inc., 923 F.2d 694, 697 (9th Cir. 1991) ("In light of *Rodriguez de Quijas v. Shearson/American Express, Inc.*, there is some doubt as to whether a federal court will overrule arbitrators even when they act in 'manifest disregard for the law.'") (citations omitted); Rainford v. Merrill Lynch, Pierce, Fenner & Smith, Inc., 903 F.2d 1410, 1413 (11th Cir. 1990) ("This court has never adopted the manifest-disregard-of-the-law-standard; indeed, we have expressed some doubt as to whether it should be adopted since the standard would likely never be met when the arbitrator provides no reasons for its award [which is typically the case]."); O.R. Sec. v. Professional Planning Assoc., Inc., 857 F.2d 742, 747 (11th Cir. 1988) ("This circuit has never adopted manifest disregard of the law as a ground for vacating an arbitration award."); Mosely, Hallgarten, Estabrook & Weeden, Inc. v. Ellis, 849 F.2d 264, 267 n.7 (7th Cir. 1988) (declining to adopt, albeit not rejecting, the "manifest disregard" rule); Jenkins v. Prudential-Bache Sec., 847 F.2d 631, 634 (10th Cir. 1988).

68 346 U.S. 427, 436-37 (1953), *overruled on other grounds*, Rodriguez de Quijas v. Shearson American Express, Inc., 490 U.S. 477 (1989). *See* discussion of *Wilko* and *de Quijas* in chapter 8.

69 808 F.2d 930 (2d Cir. 1986).

70 Merrill Lynch, Pierce, Fenner & Smith Inc. v. Bobker, 636 F. Supp. 444, 445 (S.D.N.Y. 1986).

71 *Id.* at 447-48 (footnotes omitted).

72 808 F.2d at 933-34 (citations omitted); *see also* Government of India v. Cargill, Inc., 867 F.2d 130, 133 (2d Cir. 1989) ("though recognizing the correct rule, [the panel] must have nonetheless chosen to ignore [it]"); Jenkins v. Prudential-Bache Sec., 847 F.2d 631, 634 (10th Cir. 1988) (manifest disregard occurs when a panel is "willful[ly] inattentive to the governing law").

73 Local 59, Int'l Bhd. of Elec. Workers v. Green Corp., 725 F.2d 264, 268 (5th Cir.), *cert. denied*, 469 U.S. 833 (1984).

74 909 F.2d 456 (11th Cir. 1990).

75 Ketchum v. Prudential-Bache Securities, Inc., 710 F. Supp. 300 (D.C. Kan. 1989).

76 Pyle v. Securities U.S.A., Inc., 758 F. Supp. 638 (D. Colo. 1991).

77 *E.g.*, Raiford v. Merrill Lynch, Pierce, Fenner & Smith, Inc., 903 F.2d 1410, 1412 (11th Cir. 1990); French v. Merrill Lynch, Pierce, Fenner & Smith, Inc., 784 F.2d 902, 906-907 (9th Cir. 1986) (award should be upheld because it was not "completely irrational"); Local 1445, United Food & Commercial Workers v. Stop & Shop Cos., 776 F.2d 19, 21-22 (1st Cir. 1985); Safeway Stores v. American Bakery & Confectionery Workers, 390 F.2d 79, 82 (5th Cir. 1968) ("if no judge, or group of judges, could ever

conceivably have made such a ruling"); *see also* Gunther v. San Diego & Ariz. E. Ry., 382 U.S. 257, 261 (1965) ("wholly baseless and completely without reason").

78 Advest, Inc. v. McCarthy, 914 F.2d 6, 8-9 (2d Cir. 1990) (citations omitted).

79 *Id.*, at 9 n.6 (citations omitted).

80 708 F. Supp. 62 (S.D.N.Y. 1989).

81 461 U.S. 757 (1983). This was reaffirmed in *United Paperworkers Int'l*, *supra* note 35.

82 *Id.*, at 766.

Chapter 6

AGREEMENT TO ARBITRATE SECURITIES DISPUTES

Since the agreement to arbitrate is a creature of contract, the arbitration agreement or clause to arbitrate is of major importance. This chapter will examine the language used in the resolution of securities disputes by arbitration.

If the customer agreement contains a clause specifying that disputes between the firm and customer will be resolved by binding arbitration, examination of the customer agreement is the first step in analyzing a customer claim. The agreement will tell how, when, and where arbitration must be used, if at all, to resolve disputes. This chapter will also examine the waiver of the contract right to arbitrate and arbitration within the securities industry.

1) LANGUAGE TO CREATE AN AGREEMENT TO ARBITRATE

A) Current Securities Industry Language

The language of the customer agreement typically includes a provision concerning arbitration. The Securities Industries Conference on Arbitration (S.I.C.A.) proposed the following five rules regarding arbitration language in customer agreements, as contained in § 31 of its Uniform Code of Arbitration, which has been approved by the SEC,[1] and adopted by the SROs, including the N.A.S.D., N.Y.S.E., and AMEX:

Requirements Concerning Predispute Arbitration Agreements with Customers

> No member shall execute an agreement with a customer containing a predispute arbitration clause unless such clause is:
>
> 1. highlighted and is immediately preceded by the following disclosure language (printed in outline form as set forth herein) which shall also be highlighted:
>   (i) Arbitration is final and binding on the parties.
>   (ii) The parties are waiving their right to seek remedies in court, including the right to jury trial.
>   (iii) Prearbitration discovery is generally more limited than and different from court proceeding.
>   (iv) The arbitrators' award is not required to include factual findings or legal reasoning and any party's right to appeal or to seek modification of ruling by the arbitrators is strictly limited.
>   (v) The panel of arbitrators will typically include a minority of arbitrators who were or are affiliated with the securities industry.
> 2. Immediately preceding the signature line, there shall be a statement, which shall be highlighted, that the agreement contains a predispute arbitration clause. The statement shall also indicate at what page and paragraph the arbitration clause is located.
> 3. A copy of the agreement containing any such clause shall be given to the customer who shall acknowledge receipt thereof on the agreement or on a separate document.
> 4. No agreement shall include any condition which limits or contradicts the rules of any self-regulatory organization or limits the ability of the arbitrators to make any award.
> 5. The requirements of this subsection (5) shall apply only to new agreements signed by an existing or new customer of a member after [insert date].

This clause is not required to appear in a separate writing. As a result, the clause is included in brokerage firm customer agreements.

The actual effect of a violation of the new rule on the validity of the predispute arbitration clause will probably have to be tested in court, since the new rule does not state that a failure to comply with it automatically invalidates the agreement containing an arbitration clause. Unfortunately, the rule is not retroactive and a person who wants to invalidate a particular customer agreement because it does not contain the required language should review the rules of the applicable SROs to determine if grounds for challenge of the arbitration clause might be due to violation of a SRO rule regarding the content of such clauses.

In 1989 the Securities Industry Association (SIA) proposed that the customer must acknowledge receiving a copy of the agreement containing the arbitration clause on either the agreement or a separate document. The SIA also would not permit the customer agreement (drafted, remember, by the brokerage firm) to contain any condition that limits or contradicts the rules of any SRO, limits a party's ability to file any claim in arbitration, or limits the arbitrators ability to make any award.

Much of the content of the form is prescribed by the SEC, N.A.S.D., or exchange regulations, but the use of the SIA suggested arbitration language is not required. Therefore, arbitration clauses will still vary among firms.

B) Language in *McMahon*

The United States Supreme Court ruling in *Shearson/American Express, Inc. v. McMahon*[2] held that securities industry customers who have signed standard contracts opening brokerage accounts, most of which contain standard clauses selecting predispute arbitration forums for resolution of disputes, are relegated to the alternative dispute resolution process in the event of a dispute and cannot apply to courts for judicial relief.

Most such clauses were similar to the Shearson Client Agreement in *McMahon*:

> ARBITRATION AND GOVERNING LAW. This agreement shall be governed by the laws of the State of New York without giving effect to the choice of law or conflict of laws provisions thereof. Any controversy arising out of or relating to any of my accounts, to transactions with you, your officers, directors, agents and/or employees for me, or to this agreement, or the breach thereof, or relating to transactions or accounts maintained by me with any of your predecessor firms by merger, acquisition or other business combination from the inception of such accounts, shall be settled by arbitration, in accordance with the rules then in effect of the N.A.S.D. [National Association of Securities Dealers], or the Boards of Directors of the N.Y.S.E. [New York Stock Exchange] or the American Stock Exchange, Inc., as I may elect. If I do not make such election by registered mail addressed to you at your main office within 5 days after demand by you that I make such an election, then you will have the right to elect the arbitration tribunal of your choice. Judgment upon any award rendered by the arbitrators may be entered in any court having jurisdiction thereof. (Form 8025 (2/88).

C) Historical Development of the Arbitration Clause

The clause at issue in *Wilko v. Swan*[3] in 1953 was different in many respects from today's language. It provided:

> Any controversy arising between us under this contract shall be determined by arbitration pursuant to the Arbitration Law of the State of New York, and under the rules of either the Arbitration Committee of the Chamber of Commerce of the State of New York, or of the American Arbitration Association, or of the Arbitration Committee of the New York Stock Exchange or such other Exchange as may have jurisdiction over the matter in dispute, as I may elect. Any arbitration here under shall be before at least three arbitrators.

D) SEC Rule 15c2-2 Language

Prior to the *McMahon* decision, it was common for firms to include a sentence to the following effect in the arbitration clause of the customer's contract: "It is understood that such arbitration does not operate as a waiver of my right to bring a judicial action for claims under the securities laws." This provision was required under a 1983 Securities and Exchange Commission Release[4] that was repealed, after the SEC's *amicus* brief in *McMahon*, by Release No. 34-25034 (Oct. 21, 1987).

The SEC's underlying reason for promulgating Rule 15c2-2 was to inform public investors that they cannot be compelled to arbitrate federal securities law claims that have been judicially deemed non-arbitrable, notwithstanding their agreements to arbitrate "any controversy" that exists between the customer and his brokerage firm. In other words, Rule 15c2-2 required a procedural notice clause that does not create any substantive rights.[5]

Older customer contracts may still exist that contain the 15c2-2 non-waiver language. With respect to such agreements, it may be argued that if the customer's claim is based on a securities law violation, arbitration can be avoided.[6] As a result, several firms sent new agreements to customers, asking them to sign and return the "new" agreement telling them that the process is to "update" records and not disclosing this substantial change: clearly this is a deceptive practice.

E) Commodities Industry Language

Under the Commodity Exchange Act[7] and Commodities Future Trading Commission rules,[8] a customer must be warned about predispute arbitration clauses in an agreement. Such an agreement clause is enforceable only if the customer separately signs the arbitration clause after being given warning that he or she surrenders substantive rights that could be asserted in litigation. Executing the arbitration clause cannot be a condition for access to the commodities markets. As a result, commodity customers are less likely to have signed arbitration clauses in their agreements.

F) Arbitration in Other Documents

Arbitration may also be required in brokerage firm documents other than the customer agreement. For example, customer confirmations of trades, monthly statements, and other communications may indicate that arbitration is the means to resolve disputes with the brokerage firm.[9] Since the Federal Arbitration Act only requires a writing, there is no requirement that the customer sign a predispute arbitration agreement, and these communications can be evidence either of acceptance of their terms from inception or later ratification.

2) IMPORTANCE OF EXAMINING CONTRACT

The important thing to remember is that there are still customers whose accounts are regulated by these old customer contracts, which will permit the customer much greater power to select both whether arbitration shall take place, as well as the forum for arbitration. In determining arbitrability, one should first look to the agreement. The arbitrators derive their authority to resolve disputes from the agreement between the parties, not other sources.[10]

A) Absence of Arbitration Clause

In some instances, the brokerage firm will not have an effective arbitration clause. Cash customers, for example, often will not have any agreement with the firm. Commodity investors may not have adopted the arbitration clause as part of their customer agreement. The customer also may be of such a size as to have negotiated out of this provision, or perhaps just crossed it out of the printed form. An investment advisor was not bound to arbitrate under an agreement between the investor and brokerage firm which administered the investments, since the contract did not mention others than the investor/customer and brokerage firm.[11]

Normally, the compliance department of the brokerage firm will find the latter situations on review of the contracts, but if not the customer is not bound. This can be to the customers advantage, for if the agreement does not provide for arbitration, a customer can still mandate the arbitration of a dispute with a broker; because under exchange and N.A.S.D. regulations, a member must submit to arbitration even without a separate agreement to do so. Under SRO rules, the customer can require arbitration of disputes even when he has not signed an arbitration agreement.[12]

B) Conflicting Agreements

If the brokerage firm has not carefully drafted its customer agreements, ambiguities may be found. For example, in a recent case the customer's options account agreement provided for arbitration only with the New York Stock Exchange but cash account agreement allowed the customer to elect between arbitration at the N.Y.S.E., AAA, N.A.S.D. or other exchange forum. The options language explicitly stated it did not "abrogate any diminish" any rights under the cash account agreement, and the court found the right to elect any forum for options trading disputes due to this ambiguity.[13]

C) Other Actions

Even actions *before* execution of the brokerage account agreement can be covered under the language of the customer agreement.[14] The courts construe the Federal Arbitration Act broadly to include even agreements arising out of the contractual performance, but prior to the contract's existence. All the Act requires is "an agreement in writing to submit to arbitration an existing controversy arising out of a . . . contract [or] transaction [involving commerce]."[15]

3) SAMPLE CUSTOMER AGREEMENT WITH BROKERAGE FIRMS

The following form is used by a brokerage firm for customer accounts both for cash and margin trading.[16] Note that the language regarding arbitration and class actions (paragraphs above the signature at end) are made more prominent than the other text.

ORIGINAL

Please read carefully, sign and return

Client Agreement

In consideration of accepting my account and agreeing to act as my broker. I agree to the following with respect to any of my accounts with you for extensions of credit and the purchase and sale of securities, put & call options, and other property. This agreement shall not become effective until accepted by you in your New York office. Acceptance may be evidenced by internal records maintained by you. Throughout this agreement, "I," "me," "my," "we," and "us" refer to the client and all others who are legally obligated on my accounts. "You" and "your" refer to its subsidiaries and parents and any and all divisions or other entities, their officers, directors, agents and/or employees.

1 MY REPRESENTATIONS. I represent that I am of the age of majority according to the laws of my place of residence. I further represent that I am not an employee of any exchange or of a member firm of any exchange or of a member of the National Association of Securities Dealers, Inc. ("NASD"), or of a bank, trust company, or insurance company unless I have notified you to that effect. If I become so employed, I agree to notify you promptly. I also represent that no persons other than those signing this agreement have an interest in my account.

2 DEFINITION OF "PROPERTY". The word "property" is used herein to mean securities of all kinds, monies, options, commodities, and contracts for the future delivery of, or otherwise relating to, commodities or securities and all other property usually and customarily dealt in by brokerage firms.

3 ORDERS, EXECUTIONS, DELIVERIES, SETTLEMENTS AND ORAL AUTHORIZATIONS. I agree that, in giving orders to sell, all "short" sales orders will be designated as "short" and all "long" sales orders will be designated as "long". "Short sale" means any sale of a security not owned by the seller or any sale that is consummated by delivery of a borrowed security. I also agree that you may at your discretion immediately cover any short sales in my account. The designation on a sale order as "long" is a representation on my part that I own the security, and if the security is not in your possession at the time of the contract for sale, I agree to deliver the security to you by settlement date. In case of non-delivery of a security, you are authorized to purchase the security to cover my position and charge any loss, commissions and fees to my account. I agree that if you fail to receive payment for securities purchased you may, without prior demand or notice, sell securities or other property held by you in any of my accounts and any loss resulting therefrom will be charged to my account. By accepting my limit order for transactions in securities in the NASDAQ or over-the-counter market, you undertake to monitor the interdealer market and to seek to execute my order only if the inside bid (in the case of a limit order to sell, the highest price at which a dealer is being quoted as willing to buy securities) or the inside asked (in the case of a limit order to buy, the lowest price at which a dealer is being quoted as willing to sell securities) reaches my limit price. You reserve the right, while my limit order remains unexecuted, to trade for your own market-maker account at prices equal to or better than my limit order price and not to execute my order against incoming orders from other customers. For example, if the inside market is 10 bid, $10\frac{1}{4}$ asked and I place a limit order to sell securities at $10\frac{1}{8}$, you will seek to execute my order only if the inside bid reaches my limit price of $10\frac{1}{8}$ (exclusive of any markdown or commission equivalent that you may charge in connection with the transaction) and, while my order remains unexecuted, you may continue to sell securities for your market-maker account at prices at or above $10\frac{1}{8}$. Unless I have directed that the order be executed on a specified exchange or market and you have agreed to such execution, you will, at your sole discretion and without prior notification to me, execute any order to purchase or sell securities on the over-the-counter market in any location or on any exchange, including a foreign exchange where such security is traded, either on a principal or agency basis. I agree that you shall incur no liability in acting upon oral instructions given to you concerning my account.

4 OPTION POSITIONS. I agree not to enter into any purchase or sale of equity, debt, foreign currency or index put & call options or Index Participations without having read and fully understood the terms, conditions and risks, as set forth in the Characteristics and Risks of Standardized Options booklet and/or Index Participations booklet, and applicable supplements which you agree to furnish me prior to such transactions. I understand clients' short option positions are assigned on a random selection method pursuant to an automated system. All short option positions can be assigned at any time including the day written.

5 NOTICE TO EXERCISE OPTIONS. If I purchase any listed option, I will notify you of my intention to exercise such option no later than two hours before the expiration time of the option (one hour in the case of an over-the-counter option). Failure to give such notice will constitute an abandonment of the option, in which event it may be exercised for my account if it would be profitable to do so. Except as required by the Options Clearing Corporation Rules, you have no obligation to exercise any option absent specific instructions from me to that effect. If it would not be profitable for my account due to commission expenses, it may be permitted to expire or, at your discretion, sold or acquired by you for some equitable payment to me based on your expenses and risk, without any liability or responsibility on your part to me.

6 IMPARTIAL LOTTERY ALLOCATION SYSTEM. When you hold on my behalf bonds or preferred stocks in street or bearer form which are callable in part, I agree to participate in the impartial lottery allocation system of the called securities in accordance with the provisions of the New York Stock Exchange, Inc. ("NYSE") rules. Further, I understand when the call is favorable, no allocation will be made to any account in which you, your officers, or employees, have a financial interest until all other clients' positions in such securities are satisfied on an impartial lottery basis.

7 RESTRICTIONS ON TRADING, TERMINATION. I understand that you may in your sole discretion prohibit or restrict trading of securities or substitution of securities in any of my accounts. You have the right to terminate any of my accounts (including multiple owner accounts) at any time by notice to me.

8 TRANSFER OF FUNDS BY WIRE. By giving you instructions to transfer funds by wire from my accounts to any bank or other entity, I agree to provide you with an accurate account number designating the account to receive such funds. I acknowledge that the bank or other receiving entity may be under no obligation to verify the identity of the beneficiary of the funds transfer and may rely exclusively upon the account number provided by me. I agree to indemnify and hold you harmless from and against all liabilities arising from the provision by me of an inaccurate account number.

9 TRANSFER OF EXCESS FUNDS, EXCHANGE RATE FLUCTUATIONS. You may transfer excess funds between any of my accounts (including commodity accounts) for any reason not in conflict with the Commodity Exchange Act or any other applicable law. If any transactions are effected on an exchange in which a foreign currency is used, any profit or loss as a result of a fluctuation in the exchange rate will be charged or credited to my account.

10 TEMPORARY INVESTMENT OF FREE CREDIT BALANCES, BOND PRINCIPAL AND INTEREST PAYMENTS. I authorize, but do not require, you to automatically invest on a periodic basis the free credit balances in my accounts, including interest and dividends paid to me, in mutually selected money market funds or, in the absence of such selection, in money market funds of your designation. You are not required to remit interest or dividends to me on a daily basis. With respect to bond principal and interest payments, you may credit my account with principal and interest due on the payment dates and are entitled to recover any such payments from me if the same are not actually received by you from the trustee or paying agent. With respect to debits arising from bond principal and interest payments or any other debits, you may redeem my money market fund shares, without notice, to the extent necessary to satisfy any debits arising in any of my accounts. I acknowledge that interest will not be paid to me on credit balances in any of my accounts unless specifically agreed to by you in writing.

11 FEES AND CHARGES. I understand that you may impose various service charges and other fees relating to my account as well as charge commissions and other fees for execution of transactions to purchase and sell securities, put & call options or other property, and I agree to pay such charges, commissions and fees at your then prevailing rates. I also understand that such charges, commissions and fees may be changed from time to time without notice to me and I agree to be bound thereby. I may be subject to an administrative fee on any of my accounts which produce insufficient commission revenue for any calendar year and you will notify me prior to applying this fee. I agree to pay a late charge, to the extent permitted by law, if I purchase securities on a cash basis and fail to pay for such securities by settlement date. Any late charge you may impose will be at the maximum rate of interest set forth in your disclosure statement and may be charged from the settlement date to the date of payment.

12. ACCURACY OF REPORTS, COMMUNICATIONS. Confirmation of orders and statements of my accounts shall be conclusive if not objected to in writing within ten days after mailing by you to me. In the event I fail to receive a confirmation within ten days from the date of a transaction in my account, I agree to notify you immediately in writing. Communications mailed to me at the address specified by me shall, until you have received notice in writing from me of a different address, be deemed to have been personally delivered to me and I agree to waive all claims resulting from failure to receive such communications.

13. INTRODUCED ACCOUNTS. If my account has been introduced to you and is carried by you only as a clearing broker, I agree that you are not responsible for the conduct of the introducing broker and your only responsibilities to me relate to the execution, clearing and bookkeeping of transactions in my accounts.

14 SECURITY INTEREST. As security for the payment of all liabilities or indebtedness presently outstanding or to be incurred under this or any other agreement between us, and for all liabilities or indebtedness I may have to you now or in the future, I grant you a security interest in any and all property belonging to me or in which I may have an interest, held by you or carried in any of my accounts including individual, multiple owner or commodity accounts. All property shall be subject to such security interest as collateral for the discharge of my obligations to you, wherever or however arising and without regard to whether or not you have made loans with respect to such property. You are hereby authorized to sell and/or purchase any and all property in any of my accounts or to liquidate any open commodity futures or forward contracts in any of my accounts without notice in order to satisfy such obligations. In enforcing your security interest, you shall have the discretion to determine which property is to be sold and the order in which it is to be sold and shall have all the rights and remedies available to a secured party under the New York Uniform Commercial Code. Without your prior written consent, I will not cause or allow any of the collateral held in my account, whether now owned or hereafter acquired, to be or become subject to any liens, security interests, mortgages or encumbrances of any nature other than your security interest.

15 LIQUIDATION OF COLLATERAL OR ACCOUNT. You may sell any or all property held in any of my accounts and cancel any open orders for the purchase or sale of any property without notice in the event of my death or whenever in your discretion you consider it necessary for your protection. In such events you also may borrow or buy-in all property required to make delivery against any sale, including a short sale, effected for me. Such sale or purchase may be public or private and may be made without advertising or notice to me and in such manner as you may in your discretion determine. No demands, calls, tenders or notices which you may make or give in any one or more instances shall invalidate the foregoing waiver on my part. At any such sale you may purchase the property free of any right of redemption and I shall be liable for any deficiency in my accounts.

16. LOANS. From time to time you may, at your discretion, make loans to me for any purpose, including the purpose of purchasing, carrying or trading in securities ("Margin Loans") or for a purpose other than purchasing, carrying or trading in securities ("Express Credit Loans"). Pursuant to Regulation T, Margin Loans will be made in a Margin Account and Express Credit Loans will be made in a nonsecurities credit account ("Express Credit Account"). The minimum and maximum amount of any particular loan may be established by you in your discretion regardless of the amount of collateral delivered to you and you may change such minimum and maximum amounts from time to time.

17 EXPRESS CREDIT. I agree not to use the proceeds of any Express Credit Loan to purchase, carry or trade in securities. I also agree not to use Express Credit Loan proceeds directly or indirectly to repay other debt that I incur for the purpose of purchasing, carrying or trading in securities.

18 PAYMENT OF LOANS ON DEMAND. I agree to pay ON DEMAND any balance owing with respect to any of my accounts, including interest and commissions and any costs of collection (including attorneys' fees, if incurred by you). I understand that you may demand full payment of the balance due in my accounts plus any interest charges accrued thereon, at your sole option, at any time without cause and whether or not such demand is made for your protection. I understand that all loans made are not for any specific term or duration but are due and payable at your discretion upon a demand for payment made to me. I agree that all payments received for my accounts including interest, dividends, premiums, principal or other payments may be applied by you to any balances due in my accounts.

19. MAINTENANCE OF COLLATERAL. I understand that the properties in my Margin Account and/or Express Credit Account may be carried as general loans and may be pledged or hypothecated by you separately or in common with other properties. The pledge or hypothecation by you may secure your indebtedness equal to or greater than the amount owed to you by me. I agree to deposit additional collateral, as you may in your discretion require from time to time, in the form of cash or securities in accordance with the rules and regulations of the Federal Reserve Board, the NYSE, the American Stock Exchange, Inc. ("AMEX"), other national securities exchanges, associations or regulatory agencies under whose jurisdiction you are subject and your own minimum house margin maintenance requirements. In the event I no longer maintain a debit balance or an indebtedness to you, it is understood that you will fully segregate all securities in my accounts

in your safekeeping or control (directly or through a clearing house) and/or deliver them to me upon my request.

20. INTEREST CHARGES AND PAYMENTS. I agree to pay interest, to the extent not prohibited by the laws of the State of New York, upon all amounts advanced and other balances due in my accounts in accordance with your usual custom, which may include the compounding of interest. Your custom, which may change from time to time, is set forth in your disclosure statement, which by this reference is herein specifically incorporated. By entering into any transactions with you after I receive your disclosure statement, I acknowledge that I have read and agreed to its terms for all past and future transactions in my account. I understand that interest on all debit balances shall be payable ON DEMAND and that in the absence of any demand interest shall be due on the first business day of each interest period. My daily net debit balance will include accrued interest I have not paid from prior interest periods, if any. I understand that to the extent permitted by applicable law you may charge me interest on the unpaid interest previously added to my debit balance; that is, you may charge me compound interest. Payments of interest and principal and all other payments made by me under this agreement shall be made to your main office in New York, New York. You may, in your discretion, not deem any check or other remittance to constitute payment until it has been paid by the drawee and the funds representing such payment have become available to you.

21. CREDIT AND BUSINESS CONDUCT INFORMATION AND INVESTIGATION. I authorize you at your discretion to obtain reports and to provide information to others concerning my credit standing and my business conduct. You may ask credit reporting agencies for consumer reports of my credit history. Upon my request you will inform me whether you have obtained any such consumer reports and if you have, you will inform me of the name and address of the consumer reporting agency that furnished the reports to you.

22. JOINT ACCOUNTS:

a. If this is a Joint Account, we agree that each of us shall have the authority on behalf of the account to buy, sell (including short sales), and otherwise deal in, through you as brokers, securities, options or other property on margin or otherwise; to receive for the account, confirmations, statements and communications of every kind; to receive for the account and to dispose of money, securities and other property; to make, terminate, or modify for the account, agreements relating to these matters or waive any of the provisions of such agreements; and generally to deal with you as if each of us alone were the account owner, all without notice to the other account owners. We agree that notice to any account owner shall be deemed to be notice to all account owners. Each account owner shall be jointly and severally liable for this account.

b. You may follow the instructions of any of us concerning this account and make deliveries to any of us, of any or all securities or other property in this account, and make payments to any of us, of any or all monies in this account as any of us may order and direct, even if such deliveries and/or payments shall be made to one of us personally or to third parties. You shall be under no obligation to inquire into the purpose of any such demand for delivery of securities, property, or payment of monies, and you shall not be bound to see to the application or disposition of the said securities, property and/or monies so delivered or paid to any of us. Notwithstanding the foregoing, you are authorized, in your discretion, to require joint action by the joint tenants with respect to any matter concerning the joint account, including the giving or cancellation of orders and the withdrawal of monies, securities or other property.

c. In the event of the death of any of us, the survivor(s) shall immediately give you written notice thereof, and you may, before or after receiving such notice, take such proceedings, require such documents, retain such portion of the account and/or restrict transactions in the account as you may deem advisable to protect you against any tax, liability, penalty or loss under any present or future laws or otherwise. The estate of any of us who shall have died shall be liable and each survivor will be liable, jointly and severally, to you for any debt or loss in this account resulting from the completion of transactions initiated prior to your receipt of a written notice of such death or incurred in the liquidation of the account or the adjustment of the interests of the respective parties.

d. Any taxes or other expenses becoming a lien against or being payable out of the account as the result of the death of any of us, or through the exercise by his or her estate or representatives of any rights in the account shall be chargeable against the interest of the survivor(s) as well as against the interest of the estate of the decedent. This provision shall not release the decedent's estate from any liability provided for in this agreement.

e. DESIGNATION OF TENANCY *(This paragraph "22(e)" is not applicable in the State of Texas, where form no. 3882 "Texas Joint Account Supplement . . ." must be executed and returned with this agreement to you.)* You may presume that it is the express intention of us to create an estate or account as joint tenants with rights of survivorship and not as tenants-in-common, unless otherwise provided by striking this paragraph and executing a separate Tenancy-in-Common form and returning it to you. In the event of the death of either or any of us, the entire interest in the joint account shall be vested in the survivor(s) on the same terms and conditions as theretofore held, without in any manner releasing the decedent's estate from the liability.

23. ARBITRATION

- **ARBITRATION IS FINAL AND BINDING ON THE PARTIES.**
- **THE PARTIES ARE WAIVING THEIR RIGHT TO SEEK REMEDIES IN COURT, INCLUDING THE RIGHT TO A JURY TRIAL.**
- **PRE-ARBITRATION DISCOVERY IS GENERALLY MORE LIMITED THAN AND DIFFERENT FROM COURT PROCEEDINGS.**
- **THE ARBITRATORS' AWARD IS NOT REQUIRED TO INCLUDE FACTUAL FINDINGS OR LEGAL REASONING AND ANY PARTY'S RIGHT TO APPEAL OR TO SEEK MODIFICATION OF RULINGS BY THE ARBITRATORS IS STRICTLY LIMITED.**
- **THE PANEL OF ARBITRATORS WILL TYPICALLY INCLUDE A MINORITY OF ARBITRATORS WHO WERE OR ARE AFFILIATED WITH THE SECURITIES INDUSTRY.**

Any controversy: (1) arising out of or relating to any of my accounts maintained individually or jointly with any other party, in any capacity, with you; or (2) relating to my transactions or accounts with any of your predecessor firms by merger, acquisition or other business combination from the inception of such accounts; or (3) with respect to transactions of any kind executed by, through or with you, your officers, directors, agents and/or employees; or (4) with respect to this agreement or any other agreements entered into with you relating to my accounts, or the breach thereof, shall be resolved by arbitration conducted only at the NYSE, NASD, or AMEX or any self-regulatory organization ("SRO") subject to the jurisdiction of the Securities and Exchange Commission and pursuant to the arbitration procedures then in effect of any such exchange or SRO as I may elect. If I do not make such election by registered mail addressed to you at your main office within 5 days after demand by you that I make such election, then you will have the right to elect the arbitration tribunal of your choice. Judgment upon any award rendered by the arbitrators may be entered in any court having jurisdiction thereof.

24. GOVERNING LAW AND APPLICABLE REGULATIONS. This agreement, including the arbitration provisions contained herein, shall be governed by the laws of the State of New York without giving effect to the choice of law or conflict of laws provisions thereof. All transactions for my accounts shall be subject to the regulations of all applicable federal, state and self-regulatory agencies including but not limited to the Securities and Exchange Commission, the various securities and commodity exchanges, the Municipal Securities Rulemaking Board, the NASD, the Board of Governors of the Federal Reserve System and the constitution, rules and customs of the exchange or market (and its clearing house, if any) where executed. Actual deliveries are intended on all transactions. I agree not to exceed the exercise limits and/or position limits set by the option exchanges, for my own account, acting alone or in concert with others.

25. BINDING EFFECT. This agreement and its terms shall be binding upon my heirs, executors, successors, administrators, assigns, committee and/or conservators ("successors"). In the event of my death, incompetency, or disability, whether or not any successors of my estate and property shall have qualified or been appointed, you may continue to operate as though I were alive and competent and you may liquidate my account as described in Paragraph 15 above without prior notice to or demand upon my successors. This agreement shall inure to the benefit of your assigns and successors, by merger, consolidation or otherwise (and you may transfer my accounts to any such successors and assigns at your discretion).

26. WAIVER NOT IMPLIED. Your failure to insist at any time upon strict compliance with this agreement or with any of its terms or any continued course of such conduct on your part shall not constitute or be considered a waiver by you of any of your rights.

27. SEVERABILITY. If any provision of this agreement is or becomes inconsistent with any applicable present or future law, rule or regulation, that provision will be deemed rescinded or modified in order to comply with the relevant law, rule or regulation. All other provisions of this agreement will continue and remain in full force and effect.

28. NO ORAL MODIFICATION; AFFECT ON PRIOR AGREEMENTS. No modification of this agreement shall be effective unless in writing and executed by you and me. This agreement is not subject to any oral modification; the signing of this agreement supersedes any prior Customer's or Client's Agreement (except those governing transactions in my commodity accounts) made with you or any of your predecessors or assignors. To the extent this agreement is inconsistent with any other agreement governing my account, the provisions of this agreement shall govern.

Tax Certification: Under penalties of perjury, I certify that the number shown below on this form is my correct taxpayer identification number or if not, then the number I have entered below per instructions is my correct taxpayer identification number, and that I am not subject to backup withholding because: (a) I have not been notified by the Internal Revenue Service (IRS) that I am subject to backup withholding as a result of a failure to report all interest or dividends, or (b) the IRS has notified me that I am no longer subject to backup withholding (see below), or (c) I am exempt from backup withholding (see below). Note: You must cross out (b) above if you are currently subject to backup withholding because of underreporting interest or dividends on your tax return. For Those Exempt From Backup Withholding (see instructions), write the word "Exempt" here:________________ .

Unless I strike this paragraph and initial the same, you are hereby specifically authorized to lend, either separately or with other securities, to either yourself as broker or to others, any securities held by you on margin or as collateral for a __________ Loan for my/our accounts or as collateral therefor. This agreement shall continue until signed notice of revocation is received by or from me and, in case of such revocation, it shall continue in effect as to transactions entered into prior thereto. By signing this agreement I acknowledge that my securities may be loaned to you or loaned out to others. I understand that if I decline to accept this provision, you may refuse to extend margin or other loans in relation to my accounts. Init. ____

NOTICE: Any person, whether married, unmarried or separated, may apply for a separate account.
NOTICE: By signing this agreement, I acknowledge receipt of a copy of this agreement.

CAUTION TO CLIENT:
IT IS IMPORTANT THAT YOU THOROUGHLY READ THIS AGREEMENT BEFORE YOU SIGN IT.

Account Number: Branch | Account | T | C | FC

NOTICE: This agreement contains a pre-dispute arbitration clause, which is located on this page at paragraph 23.

Client's Signature	X	Date	*This Client's social security or tax identification number on SLB's records is:*
Other Clients Signatures	X	Date	*The social security number of this account is the number of the client whose name appears first.* ***Do not*** *enter the number of any other account owner.*
(ALL account owners must sign this agreement)	X	Date	*The social security or tax identification number shown above is incorrect. The CORRECT number is:*
	X	Date	

4) CLEARING AND INTRODUCING BROKERAGE FIRMS

Often a small brokerage firm will either have another firm do its paperwork, for example, send out confirmations of trades and monthly statements, or even act as the broker to transact the securities purchase or sale because the smaller firm is not a member of the exchange where the securities are traded. The brokerage firm that is used as the agent of the brokerage firm with which the customer deals is known as the clearing broker, because it is through this firm that the trading takes place. The customer's firm is knows as the "introducing" broker or firm. The clearing broker normally will require that the customer execute an account agreement with them. Typically, that agreement contains predispute arbitration disclosures and a clause similar to the one contained in the customer agreement reproduced above.

In several cases,[17] however, an introducing broker was found not a third-party beneficiary of the customer's agreement with the clearing broker it selected to execute the customer's trades. The courts find the parties did not intend to confer a benefit on the introducing broker, but dealt for their own interests instead. In most cases, the introducing broker is not mentioned in the customer agreement nor was there an intent to make the introducing broker an agent of the clearing broker or visa versa. The introducing broker was not allowed to require arbitration under the clearing broker's predispute arbitration agreement. The courts find the introducing broker must be assumed to have some sophistication regarding its rights.[18]

5) WAIVER OF RIGHT TO ARBITRATE

The defense of waiver of the right to arbitration is briefly discussed in chapter 3. Like any contract right, the right to arbitrate can be waived. There is no rule as to what will constitute a waiver. It can occur by express agreement of the parties, whether written or oral, as well as by acts of the parties that will result in an implied waiver. There is often a question of fact as to whether waiver has occurred, requiring adjudication by the trier of facts.[19] The burden is on the party resisting arbitration.[20] Consequently, the validity of a defense raising waiver will normally be determined by the arbitrator in the federal system; in the state courts there is still judicial involvement.

If the parties are clear that they do not wish the arbitration to proceed, their wishes will be respected. As long as the intent to waive is manifested, with both knowledge of its existence and intention to relinquish the right, it will be recognized. The waiver, however, must be clearly established from either the express terms of the parties agreement. The burden will be on the party asserting waiver.

Waiver can come about in several ways:

A) Failure to Comply with Time Requirements; Statutes of Limitations

If the party seeking arbitration has made an untimely demand, arbitration can be precluded.[21] If there is a time limitation on the right to seek redress in arbitration expressly agreed to by the parties, this may act as a type of private statute of limitations. Failure to demand arbitration within the time specified will preclude the claimant from adjudication in arbitration or later at law.[22] For example, in a brokerage agreement requiring service of written notice of intent to arbitrate "within one year after the cause of action accrued," the court held it was up to the arbitrator to determine if the request for arbitration was timely.[23]

In some cases, the failure to meet the arbitration time schedule will result in the court being able to determine the issues; but often the court will prohibit litigation as well on the theory that the parties have agreed to these time limits. In such cases the courts will require that the time limitations agreed upon are reasonable, not unconscionable nor unfair.

Occasionally the rules of the arbitration forum will preclude use of that forum when a time limit has been exceeded. For example, SRO rules provide that arbitration must be commenced within six years.[24] These forum "eligibility" provisions are discussed in detail in chapter 9. More often, statutory time limits will preclude any action on the issues. The New York statute of limitations on arbitration actions is six years, the same as the period for enforcement of contracts.[25]

The time limitation dispute is further complicated with regard to the SRO limitation rules because there are three groups that can, potentially, make decisions concerning whether the period of six (6) years has elapsed. These three groups are: (1) the judiciary; (2) the particular arbitration panel appointed to the hearing; and (3) the director of arbitration of the SRO. Recent case decisions are split regarding the propriety of the action's continuance resting with the courts; some courts have held that the director of arbitration is empowered to determine those cases that are "eligible" for arbitration. If the issue is eligibility, rather than a statute of limitations, this must be decided before any issues, including the limitations period, can be submitted to a panel. If the parties have agreed on arbitration to settle disputes, to preclude arbitration at a particular forum due to an eligibility requirement has the same effect precluding an action as a statute of limitations bar.

Another issue regarding time limitations concerns the occurrence or event that is operative in determining when the period begins to run.

> The Director of Arbitration (of the N.A.S.D.) has demonstrated a willingness to recognize exceptions to the general rule and permit arbitral consideration of transactions more than six years old. The administrative ruling, which is described in a staff letter written in late July 1991, denies a motion to dismiss under § 15 of N.A.S.D.'s Code of Arbitration Procedure, stating "that the purchase date is not the event or occurrence that gave rise to this dispute. Also § 15 does not refer specifically to the purchase date as the time that the six year limitation begins to run. Therefore, it is equally appropriate that the discovery by the claimant be treated as the occurrence or event giving rise to the dispute.[26]

B) Laches

The right to arbitration can also be waived by failure to assert or delay in asserting the right, but usually also requires some prejudice to the other party due to such delay. The doctrine of laches is equitable.

C) Estoppel

A party seeking estoppel must demonstrate: (1) a representation, or conduct which can be implied as a representation, that is intended to induce conduct by the person to whom the representation or conduct is directed; (2) action or reliance on such representation or conduct by the party to whom it is directed; and (3) detriment to the relying party. The undue advantage resulting from such representation or conduct will be enough to find that the wrongdoing party has relinquished his right to arbitrate the dispute, also in equity.

Estoppel differs from waiver because it is not a voluntary, intentional giving up of a known right. Estoppel in the arbitration sense would in all likelihood be the act of not serving notice of intent to arbitrate a dispute, knowing that the other party is relying on the failure and taking action that would be detrimental in the event an arbitration were to be pursued.[27]

D) Participation in Litigation

Most waivers of the right to arbitrate involve participation in litigation. Waiver has been found where the parties file a lawsuit or counterclaim in a court action, participate in a court action by the filing of an answer which defends on grounds other than an agreement to arbitrate, and proceeding in discovery and to trial of the issues, or to judgment. If a party does not consent to arbitration, sufficient "consent" may be found through letters and answering papers.[28] The court will normally determine if actions amounting to an abandonment of the right to arbitrate have occurred. The issue is focused when the party who has participated or instigated the lawsuit seeks a stay pending arbitration.

The courts will normally look to the nature and extent of participation, as well as prejudice to the other party in determining if a waiver has occurred or if arbitration should be permitted. Sometimes the actions taken in the lawsuit are undertaken without knowledge of the right to arbitrate, in which case waiver is not found. Usually the requirement for waiver in such cases is that the investor is prejudiced by the failure to make a timely demand for arbitration. Participation in discovery, particularly taking depositions by the attorneys for the broker, and making substantive motions such as for summary judgment constitute grounds for waiver.[29]

For example, in *Hurlbut v. Gantshar*,[30] the plaintiff claimed a waiver of arbitration by the broker's five month failure to move for a stay of proceedings pending arbitration. The Court found that despite policies favoring arbitration, waiver can be express or implied, depending on the circumstances. An examination will normally look to: (1) whether the party has actually participated in the lawsuit, such as filing a counterclaim, or taken other action inconsistent with his arbitration rights; (2) if the litigation machinery has been substantially invoked and is well under way;[31] (3) if the question of arbitration is brought up when the trial is near;[32] or (4) if the other party is affected, misled, or prejudiced by the delay in seeking a stay; and (5) whether the two lawsuits and arbitration action arise out of the same transactional nucleus of facts. The last of these criteria is the most important. The *Hurlbut* Court concluded:

> Unquestionably, the right to trial by jury is an important constitutional right, fundamental to the preservation of our system of individual rights and liberties. But the right, however significant, is not of such a nature that it cannot be knowingly and intelligently waived in favor of an arbitration process that places either party under an unreasonable burden or gives either party an unreasonable advantage.[33]

"Prejudice is the touchstone for determining whether the right to arbitrate has been waived . . ."[34] A determination of prejudice ". . . incorporates not only the timeliness or lack thereof of a motion to arbitrate but also the degree to which the party seeking to compel arbitration has contested the merits of its opponents' claims; . . . whether that party has informed its adversary of the intention to seek arbitration even if it has not yet filed a motion to stay the district court proceedings; . . . the extent of its non-merits motion practice; . . . its assent to the . . . court's pretrial orders; . . . and the extent to which both parties have engaged in discovery.[35]

Response to discovery requests, however, may not be deemed a waiver of arbitration because the party seeking arbitration is not thereby taking advantage of judicial procedures. Rather, it is to their disadvantage, since such discovery might not be available in arbitration.[36]

E) Who Decides If There Is A Waiver?

Estoppel, laches, and waiver that are implied by the conduct of the parties are essentially equitable in nature. As a result, courts have held that later requests to arbitrate are similar to actions for specific performance of a contract and thus questions for the court and not an arbitrator.[37]

For example, a panel found that the plaintiffs had been substantially prejudiced by the firms failure to seek arbitration promptly where there were numerous pretrial proceedings, depositions of each named plaintiff, and a lengthy memorandum in opposition to class certification of plaintiffs filed.[38]

6) SANCTIONS FOR NOT USING ARBITRATION

Sanctions may be imposed due to the inception of a lawsuit or if an improper appeal is brought.[39]

In keeping with the law's preference for arbitration, the courts are applying sanctions against parties who attempt to avoid legitimate arbitration of disputes. For example, in a recent case, the Seventh Circuit imposed Federal Rule of Civil Procedure 11 sanctions on a brokerage firm for trying to evade arbitration by litigating in the courts.[40] Brokers will not be permitted to, on the one hand, force arbitration on its customers, and on the other, choose litigation when it might be possible to wear down the customer through delays or costs.

In another case,[41] the attorneys for the brokerage firm did not make a reasonable inquiry into the possibility that the broker had forged the customer agreement and nevertheless filed a motion to stay proceedings based on the arbitration clause. The federal court reserved its right to determine sanctions under Rule 11, but "suggested" to the brokerage firm and its attorneys that "further failure to comply with Rule 11 will not be tolerated. Thus, . . . defendants should only proceed . . . on the issue of forgery as their position is 'well grounded in fact.'" In another case,[42] an attorney for customers was personally sanctioned in the amount of $1,000 for misinterpreting a federal judge's stipulated order directing arbitration.

7) INDUSTRY ARBITRATION

From the earliest times, securities arbitration has been the norm for disputes between firms. These disputes are decided by panels of only industry members and consider trading matters such as executions, clearing trades, delivery of securities, and the like. Employment issues, discussed in chapter

11, are a more recent arbitration subject.

A) General Industry Disputes

As part of the SRO rules, the normal procedure to resolve disputes, including employment disputes,[43] is by arbitration. Intra-industry claims are arbitrable. For example, the N.A.S.D. Code of Arbitration Procedures requires:

> (a) Any dispute, claim or controversy eligible for submission under Part I of this Code between or among members and/or associated persons, and/or certain others, arising in connection with the business of such member(s) or in connection with the activities of such associated person(s), shall be arbitrated under this Code, at the instance of:
> (1) a member against another member;
> (2) a member against a person associated with a member or a person associated with a member against a member, and,
> (3) a person associated with a member against a person associated with a member.

Part I of the N.A.S.D. Code provides for:

> [A]rbitration of any dispute, claim or controversy arising out of or in connection with the business of any member . . .
>
> 1. between or among members;
> 2. between or among members and public customers, or others; and,
> 3. between or among members, registered clearing agencies with which the [N.A.S.D.] has entered into an agreement to utilize the [N.A.S.D.]'s arbitration facilities and procedures, and participants, pledgees or other persons using the facilities of a registered clearing agency.

For example, even though the trading of American Depository Receipts (ADRs) was not on the New York Stock Exchange, a broker-dealer in such securities was bound to arbitrate issues regarding interest payment credits due to the broad N.Y.S.E. clause requiring arbitration of an issue connected "with the business of such member."[44]

B) Employee Disputes

The U-4 Form, used when a registered representative becomes associated with a brokerage firm, contains the following language: "I agree to arbitrate any dispute, claim or controversy that may arise between me and my firm, or a customer, or any other person, that is required to be arbitrated under the rules, constitutions, or by-laws of the organizations with which I register."

For example, arbitration of a civil claim by a former employee of a securities firm was governed by federal, rather than New York law, even in a New York court. The fact that the relevant act was related to a crime did not preclude a finding that the act arose out of the "business" of a member of the N.A.S.D. Therefore, the N.A.S.D. rules required arbitration of claims arising from the criminal act.[45]

8) CONCLUSION

The right to arbitrate arises by contract. Normally, this occurs in a predispute arbitration clause in the agreement opening an account with a broker. Sometimes there will be no written agreement, and the parties will elect to submit the existing dispute to arbitration by a submission agreement.

This contract right to resolve disputes, however, can be lost through actions of a party that are found to constitute a waiver.

NOTES

1 SEC Release No. 34-26,805 (May 15, 1989).

2 482 U.S. 220 (1987).

3 346 U.S. 410 (1953), discussed in chapter 8.

4 No. 34-20, 397 (Nov. 28, 1983). *See* Release No. 34-19813, File No. 57-976, 17 C.F.R. Part 240, SEC Slip Op. (May 26, 1983) proposing adoption of Rule 15c2-2, 17 C.F.R. 240.15c2-2. This Release indicated that the SEC had taken the position that less than full disclosure and use of provisions in customer agreements was of doubtful validity and had, since 1951, been considered to be a false and misleading practice, since ". . . all statutes administered by the Commission provide that any condition, stipulation or provision which binds any person to waive compliance with their requirements shall be void [and] [t]he question arises, therefore, whether the result, if not the purpose, of such a [provision] is to create in the mind of the investor a belief that he has given up legal rights and is foreclosed from a remedy which he might otherwise have . . . under the SEC statutes." *Id.* citing Release No. 58 (April 10, 1951). Interestingly, the economic cost of this regulation was felt by the SEC to be minimal--having a printer change two or three lines on a customer's account agreement. *Id.*

Initially, the SEC's underlying reason for promulgating Rule 15c2-2 was to disclose to public investors that they cannot be compelled to arbitrate federal securities law claims that have been judicially deemed non-arbitrable notwithstanding their agreement to arbitrate "any controversy" that exists between the customer and his brokerage firm. In other words, Rule 15c2-2 required a procedural notice clause that does not create any substantive rights.

See Finkle and Ross v. A. G. Becker Paribas, Inc., 622 F. Supp. 1505, 1510 (S.D.N.Y. 1985); Steinberg v. The Illinois Company, 635 F. Supp. 615 (N.D. Ill. 1986); Fisher v. Prudential-Bache Securities, 635 F. Supp. 234 (D. Md. 1986), *aff'd without op., in part, rev'd, in part*, 831 F.2d 290 (4th Cir. Md. 1987); Shotto v. Laub, 632 F. Supp. 516 (D. Md. 1986); Rhoades v. Powell, 644 F. Supp. 645 (E.D. Cal. 1986); Boyd v. Merrill Lynch, Pierce, Fenner & Smith, Inc., 614 F. Supp. 940 (S.D. Fla. 1985).

5 *Id.*

6 *See* the discussion of Rule 15c2-2 in chapter 4; Chang v. Lin, 824 F.2d 219 (2d Cir. 1987).

7 7 U.S.C. §§ 1 *et seq.* (1982).

8 Regulation 180.3, 17 C.F.R. § 180.3(b).

9 *See* Middlebrooks v. Merrill Lynch, Pierce, Fenner & Smith, Inc., FED. SEC. L. REP. (CCH) ¶ 94,399 (N.D. Ala. Apr. 5, 1989), where the court found account statements, confirmation slips, and even checks received by plaintiffs over a period of years provided for arbitration of "[a]ny controversy between us arising out of the transactions in this account or in this agreement."

10 Southside Internists Group PC Money Purchase Pension Plan v. Janus Capital Corp., 741 F. Supp. 1536 (N.D. Ala. 1990).

11 Asset Allocation and Management Company v. Western Employers Insurance Company, 892 F.2d 566 (7th Cir. 1989).

12 *See* N.Y.S.E. Constitution, Article XI, § 1. *See* Mowbiay v. Mosley, Hallgarten, Esterbrook & Weeden, 795 F.2d 1111 (1st Cir. 1986); Okcuoglu v. Hess, Grant & Co., Inc., 580 F. Supp. 749 (E.D. Pa. 1984).

13 Oscar Gross & Son Inc., v. Rosendorf, 183 A.D. 2d 595, 584 N.Y.S. 2d 790 (1st Dept. 1992).

14 *Zink v. Merrill Lynch, Pierce, Fenner & Smith, Inc.*, 13 F.3d 330 (10th Cir. 1993).

15 *Id.* at 333.

16 Margin trading is a fertile ground for claims. *See* the discussion in chapter 11.

17 McPheeters v. McGinn, Smith and Co., Inc., 953 F.2d 771 (2d Cir. 1992); Wilson v. D.H. Blair & Company Inc., 731 F. Supp. 1359 (N.D. Ind. 1992); Curtis v. Newherd Cook, & Co., 725 F. Supp. 1072 (E.D. Mo. 1987); C.B.S. Employees Fed. Credit Union v. Donaldson, Lufkin & Jenrette Securities Corp., (W.D. Tenn. 1991).

18 Shaffer v. Stratton Oakmont, Inc., 766 F. Supp. 365 (N.D. Ill. 1991) ("an investor's 'constructive' consent would not be implied based solely upon the relationship between the introducing and clearing brokers").

19 *See* R. RODMAN, COMMERCIAL ARBITRATION § 6.1 (1984 and 1987

Supp.); Southside Internists Group PC Money Purchase Pension Plan v. Janus Capital Corporation, FED. SEC. L. REP. (CCH) ¶ 96,079 (N.D. Ala. 1990).

20 Merrill Lynch, Pierce, Fenner & Smith, Inc. v. Haydu, 637 F.2d 391, 398 n.12 (5th Cir. 1981).

21 *See* chapter 12 discussion.

22 *See* C. PETERSON & C. MCCARTHY, ARBITRATION STRATEGY AND TECHNIQUE 34-40 (1986).

23 Belke v. Merrill Lynch, Pierce, Fenner & Smith, 693 F.2d 1023 (11th Cir. 1982).

24 N.Y.S.E. Rule 606; N.A.S.D. § 6; AMEX Rule 605.

25 N.Y. CPLR 213 (McKinney 1982).

26 4 SECURITIES ARBITRATION COMMENTATOR 7 (1992).

27 *See* RODMAN, *supra* note 14, at § 6.4.

28 Rubashkin v. Philips, Appel and Waldren Inc., 722 F. Supp. 1135 (S.D.N.Y. 1989) (motion to dismiss).

29 See Cotton v. Slone, 4 F.3d 176 (2d Cir. 1993).

30 674 F. Supp. 385 (D. Mass. 1987).

31 Such as the use of judicial discovery that would not be as extensive in arbitration. *See* chapter 13.

32 *See* Singer v. Dean Witter Reynolds Inc., 614 F. Supp. 1141 (D. Mass. 1985).

33 The Gantshar Court quoted Jones Motor Co., Inc. v. Chauffeurs, Teamsters and Helpers Local 633, 671 F.2d 38, 44 (1st Cir. 1982) in outlining these factors to determine justified waiver, but the criteria were essentially established in Costantini v. TWA, 681 F.2d 1199, 1201-1202 (9th Cir. 1982), *cert. denied*, 459 U.S. 1087 (1982).

34 Gavlik Constr. Co. v. H.F. Campbell Co., 526 F.2d 777 (3d Cir. 1975).

35 Hoxwotht v. Blinder, Robinson & Co., Inc., 980 F.2d 912 (3rd Cir. 1992).

36 Steinberg & Lyman v. Takacs, 774 F. Supp. 885 (S.D.N.Y. 1991).

37 *See* PETERSON and MCCARTHY, *supra* note 17, at 44 and the discussion in chapter 3.

38 Hoxworth v. Blinder, Robinson & Co., Inc., FED. SEC. L. REP. (CCH) ¶ 97,216 (3d Cir. 1992).

39 Chapter 5.

40 *See* Paine Webber, Inc. v. Farnam, 843 F.2d 1050 (7th Cir. 1988). The Court observed: "The securities industry insists that its customer sign arbitration agreements, which the Supreme Court has sustained in part on the premise that it is desirable to have a cheap, quick method to deal with the disputes (many too small to justify full scale litigation) this industry produces."

Id. at 1052. *See also* Herzel & Harris, *An Ambiguous Victory for the Small Brokerage Client*, FINANCIAL TIMES, June 30, 1988, § I, at 9, col. 1.

41 Donato v. Merrill Lynch, Pierce, Fenner & Smith, Inc., 663 F. Supp. 669 (N.D. Ill. 1987).

42 McMahon v. Shearson/American Express, Inc., FED. SEC. L. REP. (CCH) ¶ 94,327 (S.D.N.Y. 1989) (AMEX window arbitration proceedings before the AAA versus N.Y.S.E. arbitration).

43 *See* discussion of intra-industry and employment claims in chapter 11.

44 See *Nomura Securities Int'l, Inc. v. Citibank, N.A.*, 81 N.Y. 2d 614, 601 N.Y.S. 2d 448 (1993), which distinguished *Paine, Webber et al v. Chase Manhattan Bank*, 728 F.2d 577 (2d Cir. 1984), where the conduct complained of did not relate to the member's business and arbitration was not compelled.

45 Singer v. Jeffries & Co., 78 N.Y. 2d 76, 575 N.E. 2d 98, 571 N.Y.S. 2d 680 (1991).

Chapter 7

THE PROBLEM OF ARBITRATION AND THE SECURITIES LAWS

Examined in this chapter are some of the reasons why arbitration is desirable, both for the industry and the investor.

Arbitration has existed to govern dispute resolution within the securities industry for over a century. Early arbitration was between members of the exchanges; not investors and members of the exchange. While there is little question that industry members can opt for arbitration rather than litigation, on the grounds that this can be legitimately one of the "costs" of being a member, when arbitration is sought against a non-industry person, usually an investor,[1] substantial question exists as to whether arbitration serves the goal of investor protection.

One of the basic issues in securities arbitration is the question of arbitrability of the rights of investors established by the securities laws in the aftermath of the market crash of 1929. Both recognized the injury to the economic interests of the nation in the imbalance between investors and those in the industry. Both promote the same policy of investor protection by requiring disclosure and fair and equitable dealings in the marketplace. A recurring theme is the question of investor protection in light of required arbitration clauses contained in most customer agreements. The securities laws were enacted to protect investors from sophisticated and perhaps unethical brokerage firms. "There is a strong argument, however, that one of the purposes behind the enactment of the securities acts was to prevent securities dealers from requiring investors to enter into agreements which purport to waive rights granted the investor under the securities laws."[2]

There is a difference between arbitration and litigation. As the Supreme Court stated in *Bernhardt v. Polygraphic Co. of America*,

> [A]rbitration, whatever its perils or shortcomings, substantially affects the cause of action created. . . . The nature of the tribunal where suits are tried is an important part of the parcel of rights behind a cause of action. The change from a court of law to an arbitration panel may make a radical difference in ultimate result.[3]

This chapter will discuss the development of arbitration in the securities industry.

1) HISTORY OF SECURITIES ARBITRATION

Since the beginning of trading in stocks and bonds, arbitration was provided among members of the exchanges, similar to the private dispute resolution methods used in the guilds in England. The N.Y.S.E. Constitution of 1817 provided that: "All Questions of dispute in the purchase of stocks shall be decided by a majority of the Board [of Directors]." By 1872 the N.Y.S.E. Constitution permitted investors ("non-members") to arbitrate and bound members to observe this dispute resolution process. Later amendments provided for arbitration of all disputes between members (1935) and permitted arbitrations to take place outside New York (1939).

Eventually, the impact of the adoption of state arbitration statutes and the Federal Arbitration Act in 1925, the stock market crash of 1929, and the adoption of the Securities Act of 1933 and the Securities Exchange Act of 1934, resulted in increasing interest in arbitration as a dispute resolution method in the securities industry. The SEC's involvement began in 1935 when it recommended "the Exchange should encourage its members to offer customers a standard arbitration agreement," but this did not occur until 1989.[4]

In 1968 the exchanges and N.A.S.D. adopted arbitration for intra-industry conflicts including employment matters, as well as for investor-member disputes. Standard form-pad customer and employment agreements typically provided for the resolution of any dispute in arbitration. But under the *Wilko* holding, a predispute agreement to arbitrate federal securities law questions could not force arbitration by a non-industry member, such as an investor. This, of course, was changed by *McMahon* and *Rodriguez*.

In 1976 the SEC requested comment on the development of a uniform system to resolve small claims. The industry formed a task force to formulate a response. The task force evolved into the Securities Industry Conference on Arbitration (S.I.C.A.), composed of ten self-regulating organizations from the securities industry (SRO) which maintain arbitration facilities, the Securities Industry Association (SIA), and later three public members. The S.I.C.A.

prepared a small claims procedure rule and later developed the Uniform Code of Arbitration (UCA), which is now in use by all SRO forums.

The procedures of the arbitration process today are a result of this historical development. Thousands of awards have been entered in cases involving industry and non-industry adversaries. Much of the impetus for developing arbitration as a dispute resolution method has come from the securities industry. But the economy markets, as well as statutes and recent court decisions, have greatly enhanced arbitration's role as far as investors are concerned.

2) THE NUMBERS

In a 1987 study by the Division of Market Regulation of the Securities and Exchange Commission of 65 firms, which accounted for over 90 percent of brokerage customer accounts, arbitration clauses were required in 89 percent of firm margin account agreements; 83 percent in option agreements; but in only 40 percent of cash accounts.[5] A 1988 Securities and Exchange Commission staff survey found that there were an estimated 13 million cash accounts held by individual investors, of which 39 percent included arbitration clauses. The same survey estimated 5.5 million margin and option accounts, of which 99.5 to 99.6 percent provided for mandatory predispute arbitration.[6]

Arbitrations have taken a growing number of disputes in recent years. The American Arbitration Association (AAA) reported 1,750 arbitrations in 1950, of which fewer than 500 were commercial. In 1985 the number of arbitrations had increased more than 25 times to 45,000, with 8,000 commercial.[7] This explosion is replicated in the securities industry forums. In the year ending March 31, 1987, there were 3,050 cases dealing with securities, commodities, and exchange claims filed in the federal district courts.

With the impact of the *McMahon* holding and disputes from the October 1987 Black Monday trading, there has been an explosion in industry-sponsored forum (SRO) arbitrations. One SRO forum, the National Association of Securities Dealers (N.A.S.D.), reported that its caseload increased on an average of 31 percent per year from 1980 to 1986, and the number of arbitration cases filed in 1987 was up 82 percent over 1986. In 1988, the increase was 32 percent, with 3,990 cases filed versus 2,886 in 1987 and 1,589 in 1986 (151 percent increase from 1986 to 1988). The N.Y.S.E. experienced a 67 percent increase in filings in 1988. Adding the non-SRO tribunals, such as the AAA, the number of arbitral disputes may have equaled those filed and resolved in federal courts. The numbers have decreased approximately 6 percent at the N.Y.S.E. in the first quarter of 1991, probably a result of the large influx of cases after Black Monday being filed by this time. The N.A.S.D., however, reported a ten percent increase in filings for the same period. This was attributed to overall factors including increased share ownership (N.Y.S.E. surveys indicated 25.3 million shareholders in 1975 and 47 million in 1985); the increase in market volume (N.Y.S.E. average daily trading was $65 million in 1982 and $189 million in 1987); increased number of financial products in the industry (variable annuities, zero coupon bonds, cash and asset management accounts, etc.); increased awareness and use of arbitration; increasing employment cases within the securities industry; and the increasing tendency of society to resort to litigation, especially with industry firms perceived as a "deep pocket."[8]

The SEC received 10,392 complaints regarding securities matters in 1987, up 121 percent from 1982.[9] Of course, the SEC does not adjudicate disputes itself. It informs brokerage customers to seek remedies through other channels. The National Association of Securities Act Administrators (NASAA) estimates over 4,100 claims were filed in 1987, up from 800 in 1980.[10] By 1990, 5,332 cases and by 1991, 5,869 cases were received by all SRO forums.[11] The AAA reported 306 cases filed in the first eight months of 1993, compared to 586 securities cases filed in 1992, 381 in 1990, 440 in 1989, and 495 in 1988.[12]

3) THE ECONOMICS

Delay in the courts and the expense of litigation justify examining all alternatives for speedy and cost-effective dispute resolution, not only in the securities area.

A) Cost Savings as a Justification for Arbitration

The claim that arbitration produces cost savings versus litigation is often made to support arbitration. Significant differences are shown to exist that should lead the brokerage firms to induce customers to enter into such dispute resolution agreements. In fact, however, the inducement for customers may be a benefit to the general customers of brokerage firms, regardless of whether they agree to predispute arbitration. Usually the major inducements to use a particular firm center on its commission structure and other services, such as investment advice, custodial services for securities, and the like. Most people do not enter customer-broker contracts expecting to have a dispute requiring an outside adjudicator.[13]

Several reports deal with the savings in utilizing arbitration rather than judicial dispute resolution.[14] A report of Deloitte Haskins & Sells for the New York Stock Exchange (Deloitte Study) indicated that for the period October 1, 1987 to June 30, 1988, the average legal costs are $12,000 less in arbitration than for litigation. To require litigation would, therefore, add substantially to the legal fees of brokerage firms. In *Securities Industry Association v.*

Connolly, the District Court noted that the Massachusetts regulations forbidding arbitration without voluntary consent could add between one-quarter to one-half a million dollars annually to the legal fees of the Massachusetts brokerage firms that were joined with the SIA as plaintiffs in that case. It further said that, "[c]ustomer legal expenses are likely to mirror broker legal expenses; the finding of the . . . study that broker-dealer legal expenses are significantly less in arbitration than in court litigation may accordingly also be interpreted as predicting relative economic benefit favoring arbitration for the customer."[15]

A major portion of this saving comes from elimination of pretrial discovery. Often no depositions or interrogatories are permitted or, if allowed, are limited in scope by agreement of the parties. Further, motion practice is generally not available, and the arbitrators have freedom to hear anything that can be tied to the dispute, regardless of the rules of evidence.

Of course, these all tie to the normally contemplated savings in time as compared to litigation, especially with the limited right of appeal from an arbitrator's award. The other attributes of the arbitral process--minimization of time spent by the parties in the hearing and discovery process; the lack of publicity and public record; the fact that arbitration tends to be less adversarial in tone--also relate in potential legal and business savings, direct and indirect.

There is more sentiment for arbitration of claims in margin, commodities, and options accounts than when the investor uses the broker only for the purchase and sale of securities. When the investor margins securities, he or she is borrowing funds from the broker to finance securities transactions. Much the same situation exists with the typical commodities and options customer--he or she is also working with the credit of the brokerage firm in buying and selling the commodity or option contracts. It may be that these increased risks created through the use of the brokerage firm's credit led to the conclusion that the broker's ability to recover should be enhanced by the speedy and efficient arbitration process.

This extension of credit can be analogized to bank lending arrangements, many of which also contain arbitration provisions. However, this argument will mitigate against imposing such arbitration on the cash account customer, who simply buys and sells securities and pays or delivers without using any service other than the pure agency of the stock brokerage firm. There is little risk put on the broker in these cash accounts. Hence, the question of whether mandatory arbitration is appropriate in cash accounts is a major issue in the debate on enforceability of these clauses.[16]

The Deloitte Study also indicated that customers receive a higher percentage of their original claims in arbitration (19.57 percent of claims were recovered) than in litigation (2.60 percent).[17] The District Court in *Connolly* concluded:

> In short, on the evidence before me it appears that court litigation affords customers the opportunity to pay more in legal costs to get less in recovery. Moreover, this opportunity will apparently be preserved only after paying for brokerage services at the higher level [if the two-tier commission scheme to reflect these higher industry costs is adopted as is likely as a response to regulations mandating customer waiver of litigation].[18]

A 1989 study by the SEC Division of Market Regulation of N.Y.S.E. data on claim recoveries from litigation versus arbitration in a limited number of cases indicated that there were no significant differences in percentage of claims recovered in one forum over the other. The study concluded that litigated cases take longer and cost more than those arbitrated, but noted that litigation may have a greater number of complex cases. The average amount recovered in litigation ($5,750) was higher than that in arbitration ($3,325).[19] This was not the result, however, in the 1992 study comparing securities litigation and arbitration at several forums.[20]

Since 1989, SRO arbitration results have been made public. In a 1990 survey of 2,279 SRO awards, 1,325, or 58 percent, resulted in customer recovery. With claims over $100,000, the ratio was 64 percent and with claims under $10,000, 58.8 percent. In AAA arbitrations, 57.6 percent resulted in customer recovery. The impact of forum thus appears inconclusive.[21]

Another reason for the lower cost of SRO arbitration is that the forum is subsidized by the SRO members. For example, in 1992 the N.Y.S.E. Arbitration Division employed 17 persons (8 attorneys and 9 staff), had expenditures of $3,279,000, and revenues of $2,016,000. The N.A.S.D. had a 78 person staff (21 attorneys, 17 legal assistants, 36 staff), expenses of $9.8 million, and revenues of $5,880,000.[22]

In 1990 the SROs hired Coopers and Lybrand to study the feasibility of a central or one unified industry arbitration forum. The results of the study led the SROs to conclude that there would be no significant economies of scale in combining forums.

B) Two-Tier Pricing

The economic argument supporting arbitration of disputes in the securities area justifies different prices being charged to the customer who agrees and who does not agree to arbitration. However, this is not the case. Instead, institutional investors, who have the greater bargaining power on negotiated commissions, are those with whom the brokerage firm will continue to deal, despite their refusal to sign an arbitration agreement. The small investor, on the other hand, is the one stuck with firm established commissions, which are non-negotiable due to the volume and revenues his or her trading (or lack thereof) brings to the firm. This is true despite the 1975 SEC regulations prohibiting fixed commissions within the industry. Today there are negotiated commissions and discount brokers, but the small customer is certainly not going to be able to negotiate the commissions charged on a trade of a few hundred shares of the typical stock, small number of bonds, or in limited options or commodity trading. Consequently, the specter of a two-tier commission system depending on whether the customer has agreed to predispute arbitration is purely speculative and probably unmarketable.

Arbitration may well be the only available means of dispute resolution for the small investor--usually one with a cash account. In fact, these investors are faced with increased charges for mailing of the brokerage firms, whether in the form of higher commissions or service charges for preparing statements, custodial fees, or account maintenance charges. Even with these fees, the small investor is probably not economic to the brokerage firm in many cases. Only a minority of brokerage firms, however, require any agreement from customers purchasing on a cash basis; thus the customer purchasing, paying cash, and not leaving his or her securities on deposit with the firm may never agree to arbitrate disputes.[23]

One must bear in mind, however, that not only can a small investor utilize a broker who does not require a predispute arbitration clause, but he or she probably invests (or has invested by others) much more of their capital invested in mutual funds or pensions. Mutual funds accounts are not subject to arbitration clauses. Institutions managing pension investments are normally not bound by arbitration agreements either, as noted above.

C) Advantages of Standardized Contracts

The brokerage firms have created standard form contracts for several purposes. The standard contract will reduce administrative and transaction costs. This may result in lower prices for the consumer. Standardization also promotes efficiency within the large organization and promotes efficient use of managerial and legal resources, as well as acting as a check on wayward behavior. The use of standard forms for drafting party-protective purposes is suspect, but is clearly another reason they are used.[24]

One industry spokesman indicates that the lower cost of dispute resolution through arbitration may even enable "[a]merican financial service companies to control costs and therefore compete more effectively with foreign rivals" since arbitration costs are significantly lower than the cost of litigating in the american court system.[25]

In oligopolistic industries, where there are several large organizations selling goods or providing services, the freedom of contract notions have pretty well disappeared. Monopolies clearly would like complete control over all aspects of the market and can require it. With oligopolistic markets, much the same result will occur for those matters that the firms can agree on, or which are not important to the consumer.[26] The public policy defense in the contract of adhesion argument thus becomes the law's way of policing industry behavior.[27] This is especially necessary when regulation of the industry no longer exists. While the securities industry today is still highly regulated by laws, the SEC, and other regulations, much of the regulation is self-imposed by the SROs and, as one might assume, form-pad agreements have resulted that are similar in most respects, and certainly similar in broker-protective terms.

One industry spokesman stated:

> [t]he brokerage industry is not a public utility. Basically, society decides that in a case where an entity enjoys a "natural monopoly" in the provision of some good or service judged to be essential (*e.g.*, electricity, water, some forms of transportation, etc.) that entity should be treated as a public utility. Of course, none of these criteria are present in the case of brokerage services. But the [SEC] Division [of Market Regulation]'s radical proposal would in large measure institute just such a regulatory approach. The Division has apparently decided that public customers must be offered access to the capital markets on terms that the Division regards as reasonable, and as a result, the Division would undertake to have the SEC decide what substantive provisions may be contained in contracts with the public.
>
> Precisely because the provision of brokerage services is not an instance of "natural monopoly," there is a great deal of consumer choice available. For instance, customers have a choice not only of trading or not trading in the securities market, they also have the choice of trading either on a cash or margin basis. They may also choose to trade options, again either on a cash or margin basis and they can also choose the broker with whom they wish to do business. But simply because a person chooses a particular broker does not mean that the broker in turn wishes to do business with that person. When opening an account a broker may request that the customer sign an agreement which contains a clause to arbitrate disputes. The customer is free at this point to sign or not to sign. The customer is also free to attempt to negotiate and amend the contract if the customer is not pleased with the terms of the contract. The broker is also free in turn to either accept the amendment suggested by the customer or refuse to do business with the customer on the terms suggested by the customer. This is how the free market works.

> It has been suggested that the customer has been deprived of his freedom of choice, if a broker requests a customer to sign an agreement containing an arbitration clause and the customer decides not to do so. This is clearly not so. The customer has exercised his choice by not signing and now is free to approach any and all brokers to determine if he can convince one of them to do business on his terms. In the unlikely situation in which such a customer cannot find any broker in the whole country to do business with him on this basis, he can turn to mutual funds. Even if he cannot find anyone in the whole world to do business with him, the customer has exercised his freedom of choices. Choice is a "two way street." Some appear to define choice to mean the ability to mandate that a broker do business on a customer's terms. This is not a choice.
>
> Again, the securities industry is not a public utility. There is no obligation on broker-dealers to provide a service to anyone who walks in the door. Our industry is not a monopoly; it is free access industry. There is no societal reason to force broker-dealer in its business judgment does not deem appropriate. Absent an agreement that contains a clause which would be void against public policy, in a free market economy, the government ought to enforce agreements between citizens. The government should not seek to intervene in the formation of such agreements.[28]

Nevertheless, the influence of state regulation on arbitration has resulted in one court finding that the probable "influence the . . . regulations will have on commission rate structure suggests insinuation by local Blue Sky[29] authorities into brokerage commission rate making, an area in which the SEC exercises full authority."[30] This supported its finding that a two-tiered rate structure might not be of benefit to consumers, as commission rates might be raised for all to absorb the increased costs resulting from non-mandatory arbitration that will lead to litigation.

The economic savings resulting from mandatory arbitration is, however, open to question. One of the basic conclusions is that there will be little effort to settle the dispute when the costs of submission to arbitration are involved, rather than the larger costs of discovery and the litigation process. It may be for this reason that the percentage of claim recoveries is skewed in favor of arbitration: there are few reports of settled cases included in the surveys.[31]

4) OTHER ADVANTAGES OF ARBITRATION

This section summarizes the advantages of arbitration. Some advantages are discussed above in more detail, but its strengths and weakness can be contrasted to litigation as alternative methods of dispute resolution in the areas as follows.

A) Speed

The average time from commencement of a case to releasing the award or decision is significantly higher in litigation than in arbitration. In 1989, the time was 11.5 months at the N.A.S.D.; 9.4 months at N.Y.S.E.; and 280 days at the AAA. In 1988, the average was 168 days[32] versus the 1988 Deloitte Study finding litigation of securities disputes averaged 599 days. The AAA reported that the 1991 median processing time was 8.7 months versus 9.1 months in 1990. Litigation time is absorbed through motion practice, discovery, and the need to accommodate the court's trial calendar, which has a distinct preference for criminal over civil matters. Arbitration, on the other hand, has limited discovery, virtually no motion practice, and the parties set mutually convenient times for hearings. One disadvantage of arbitration is that in the longer case, hearings may not be scheduled to run on consecutive days and later hearings may have to be scheduled much later due to schedule conflicts of the parties--which might affect the dynamics of a presentation of evidence and arguments. In litigation, the case is normally presented all at once, from beginning to end.

B) Expense

As noted above, expense is a major reason for preferring arbitration to litigation. Due to its speed and the lack of motion practice, simplified discovery, briefs and appeal, costs in arbitration are less. To the extent, however, that there are a number of hearings spread over a long time, legal costs may be higher in arbitration than in a trial.

In arbitration, a lawyer is not required. A party can be represented by themselves *(pro se)*, a lawyer, or another party who is not a lawyer. Small claims lend themselves to *pro se* preparation and presentment. Due to the relaxed evidence rules in arbitration, the party acting *pro se* or with a non-lawyer will not be at as great a disadvantage as in litigation. Brokerage firms will normally be represented by in-house lawyers, keeping legal costs lower than when outside legal firms are hired.

The Deloitte Study referred to above found that it cost an average of $8,000 for a brokerage firm to arbitrate a case versus $20,000 for litigation. Arbitration thus costs 40 percent of litigation. The Deliotte Study found it cost less to arbitrate 142 cases than to litigate 66 cases. This implies another advantage of litigation as far as the customer is concerned: in litigation, a broker may be more willing to offer a higher settlement because of higher costs.

C) Industry Expertise

Because of the nature of the makeup of arbitration panels, the arbitrators selected to hear a case will normally have a much higher level of understanding of the industry than either a judge or jury. As a result, there is no requirement to educate regarding the industry, nor as great a possibility of misunderstanding by the trier of fact. In litigation, both the judge and jury will possibly need such education. As a result, time will be saved: and time is money. But expertise may work against arousing sympathy for the investor.

It may be possible due to the expertise of the arbitrator to eliminate the use of expert witnesses to explain the conflict, with attendant cost savings. [33]

D) Discovery

In litigation, discovery is often abused. The late Judge Irving J. Kaufman of the Court of Appeals for the Second Circuit has noted that the "twin demons of expense and delay" plague parties in litigation in the federal courts. He felt that the liberal discovery rules are used by the parties to make onerous demands on their adversaries and release only the most limited information in response to legitimate requests, while they simultaneously stifle discovery by "swamping opponents with papers when only a few documents are necessary." This is possible but less likely in arbitration.

Discovery in arbitration is discussed in detail in chapter 13.

E) Settlement

Since expenses are reduced in arbitration, as opposed to litigation, there may be a reluctance to negotiate a settlement. As indicated above, however, litigation is much more expensive than arbitration. In addition, the active involvement of judges in the discovery and pretrial process often results in their encouraging the parties to settle. It is estimated that a 95 percent of cases in litigation never reach trial, ending in settlement or other pretrial dispositions.[34] Because there are few prehearing meetings and no ability to evaluate through discovery, the arbitrators are less likely to encourage the parties to settle the dispute privately, and the parties are less likely to see the potential outcome in advance of a hearing.

With the increasing in arbitration discovery and prehearing or preliminary hearings in complex cases,[35] settlements should increase in arbitration.

F) Adverse Publicity

With the rules regarding public release of summaries of the arbitration award, there is little ability to keep securities arbitration awards confidential.

This will result in adverse publicity, which brokerage firms want to avoid as another factor for customers to consider in this highly competitive industry; especially when allegations of negligence or fraud are the grounds for the award. The award will be of little precedent value, however, as the summaries are only that and will be of little help in determining the arbitrators justifications for the award.

The customer may also want to have confidentiality of award, for example, when sued for a margin balance due. The N.Y.S.E. permits a customer to have his or her name omitted from the summary;[36] the AAA omits names of all the parties;[37] but the N.A.S.D. makes all award information public.[38]

G) Rules of Evidence versus Informal Procedure

Rules of evidence are not applied in arbitration because the arbitrators sophistication is supposed to enable them to properly determine the materiality and relevance of the evidence presented, unlike a jury which might be influenced by the irrelevant and immaterial. Most evidence is admitted with the caveat that it is "taken for what it's worth."

H) Bias of Trier of Fact

Because the arbitration panel is selected of securities industry and non-industry personnel and most arbitrations take place in an industry-subsidized SRO forum, there is a problem with respect to the public's perception of bias in favor of the brokerage firm. (See chapter 10 which discusses arbitrator bias and composition of panels.) Of course, AAA arbitrations appear more impartial since the AAA does not have industry persons on the panels and has no connection to the securities business.

I) Type of Decision

The decision process is more informal in arbitration than litigation since the trier of facts must only determine what the evidence shows and is not bound by precedent to adhere to a particular damage calculation. Arbitration is equitable, within the limits of the law. The awards are normally in terms of money damages, but specific performance and other remedies are allowed.

Until the recent SRO rules on the content of an award (discussed in chapter 15), the award did not need to contain findings of facts or conclusions on specific claims. As a result, the awards did not create precedent. In addition, many practitioners believe that arbitration may result in a decision that truly does not determine the claim for one side or another but rather "splits the baby," giving a bit to each side of the argument. This tendency should be reduced by the SRO rules regarding disclosure.

J) Enforcement of Decision

As discussed in chapter 16, an appeal of the award of the arbitrators is limited to those grounds that the statutes permit. This is contrasted to litigation, in which decisions of the court or jury are freely subject to appeal.

Enforcement of a securities arbitration award is relatively easy. When the award is in favor of the broker, the firm under the relevant state statute or Federal Arbitration Act will ask for court confirmation and judgment. Enforcement is easier against a broker because the customer will be able to use the SRO exchange as an enforcement mechanism, with the ultimate sanction that the broker will be suspended from membership for failure to meet the terms of the award.

5) BROKERS PREFER ARBITRATION

Brokers prefer arbitration as clearly expedient and less expensive than trial by jury and other litigation. But arbitration clauses are still in fine print, and in most cases are explained by the account representative inadequately or not at all to the customer filling out all the forms necessary to open his or her brokerage account. Much of the transaction is considered "boilerplate," by both the customer and broker.

There does not seem to be measurable preference for arbitration based on awards. There are no statistics that examine the results of cases in litigation versus arbitration, but the uniform reports of the SROs indicate that in 1980, there were 686 cases concluded of which 205 were decided in favor of the public (30 percent); in 1985 the numbers were 2,190 and 530 (24 percent); by 1990, 5,837 and 1,169 (20 percent) and by 1991, 5,857 cases with 1,033 awards to the public (17 percent). Of course, with increasing numbers of large and complex claims (those over $100,000), the number of cases may be insignificant in terms of the amounts of recoveries.[39]

6) SHOULD INVESTORS PREFER ARBITRATION?

There is no reason to suppose that the arguments regarding arbitration's cost effectiveness and speed would not also lead a customer to want to utilize this forum of dispute resolution. In fact, under SRO rules, the customer can require arbitration of disputes even when he has not signed an arbitration agreement.[40] Of course, if the customer already has this option, the question arises why he or she should ever sign an agreement to arbitrate.

NOTES

1 Several cases raise the question of institutional bias of the arbitration panels, but there is no substantial evidence to support institutional bias claims. *See* Heily v. Superior Court, 202 Cal. App. 3d 255, 248 Cal. Rptr. 673 (1st Dist. 1989), *cert. denied*, 109 S. Ct. 1123 (1989).

2 Malcolm & Segall, T*he Arbitrability of Claims Arising Under § 10(b) of the Securities Exchange Act: Should Wilko be Extended?*, 50 ALA. L. REV. 725, 727 n.14 (1986).

3 350 U.S. 198, 203 (1956).

4 SEC Release No. 34-131 (1935). *See* discussion of predisputes securities arbitration clauses in chapter 6.

5 *See* SEC, Summary of Staff Findings with Respect to the Use of Predispute Arbitration Clauses, David S. Ruder, Statement Before the Subcommittee on Telecommunications and Finance of the House Committee on Energy and Commerce Concerning the Securities Arbitration Process and the Voluntariness of Agreements to Arbitrate Broker-Dealer/Investor Disputes (July 12, 1988). Of the firms surveyed, 30 percent indicated a plan to expand the number of accounts for which arbitration would be required. In Blodgett, *Churning Your Broker*, A.B.A. J. 32 (Oct. 1988), it was noted that, "since *Shearson*, brokerage firms have been sending new agreements to investors with cash accounts asking that they, too, agree to submit any disputes to arbitration." SEC Chairman Ruder indicated his concern with this trend.

In Securities Industry Association v. Connolly, 703 F. Supp. 146 (D. Mass. 1988), *aff'd* 883 F.2d 1114 (1st Cir. 1989), *cert. denied*, 110 S. Ct. 2559 (1990) (*Connolly*), the District Court of Massachusetts found that a significant number of commodities customers preferred not to enter into arbitration agreements; more than 34 percent fewer for Shearson Lehman Hutton and 58 percent for Paine Webber than other securities customers. Of course, in the commodities area, the CFTC has mandated disclosure to the customer as a prerequisite election for enforcement of predispute arbitration agreements and that opening an account can not be conditioned on agreeing to a predispute arbitration clause.

6 BNA DAILY REPORT FOR EXECUTIVES, July 8, 1988, DRE no. 131. The staff said that the decision not to use arbitration clauses had lessened because the brokerage firms indicated earlier that they would add such clauses in cash accounts after *McMahon*. Some regional firms were competing for customers on the basis that they did not require such clauses.

7 *See* Ginger, *Managing Securities Disputes After McMahon: A Call for Consolidation and Arbitration*, 33 VILL. L. REV. 515, 520 n.30 (1988), citing Hirshman, *The Second Arbitration Trilogy: The Federalization of Arbitration Law*, 71 VA. L. REV. 1305, p. 1305 n.7 (1985); Furnish,

Commercial Arbitration Agreements and the Uniform Commercial Code, 67 CAL. L. REV. 317, 317-18 n.1 (1979).

Professor Fletcher notes that AAA arbitration in commercial and labor cases more than doubled from 1975 to 1985. Fletcher, *Privatizing Securities Disputes Through The Enforcement of Arbitration Agreements*, 71 MINN. L. REV. 393, 394 nn.7-9 (1987).

8 *See* E. MORRIS and D. MASUCCI, *Securities Arbitration at Self-Regulatory Organizations*, SECURITIES ARBITRATION 226-228 (D.E. Robbins ed., 1991).

9 Ingersoll, *Sleepy Watchdogs: Regulation of Brokers by Securities Industry Seems to be Faltering*, WALL STREET JOURNAL July 21, 1987, at 1, col. 6. The biggest surge involves unauthorized trading, high-pressure sales tactics, and churning.

10 *See* NASAA Briefing Report: Oversight of Securities Arbitration.

11 *See* SECURITIES ARBITRATION 1991 at 226; SECURITIES ARBITRATION 1992 at 144; SECURITIES ARBITRATION 1993 at 121 (all D.E. Robbins ed.). These sources reviewed the numbers:

COMPOSITE ARBITRATION FIGURES
Self-Regulatory Organizations Using Uniform Code

Year	Cases *Received*	Cases Concluded Including *Settlements*	Public Cases *Decided*	Awards *to Public*
1980	830	686	410	205
1985	2,796	2,190	961	530
1990	5,332	5,837	2,187	1,169
1991	5,869	5,857	1,994	1,033
1992	5,451	5,779	1,964	1,001

12 DISPUTE RESOLUTION TIMES (AAA Fall for 1993) for 1993; G. FREEMAN, SECURITIES ARBITRATION 363, 375 (D.E. Robbins, ed., 1992) for other periods.

13 *See* Rakoff, *Contracts of Adhesion: An Essay in Reconstruction*, 96 HARV. L. REV. 1173, 1220-30 which states that: "the parties will rely to a large extent on each other's good faith in the event of a dispute. But the assumption is that the law will stand as a backup should good faith fail, and that the existence of this sanction will encourage good faith in the first place." *Id.* at 1228 n.196.

14 *See, e.g.*, Moulin, *Review of Legislation and Regulatory Issues*, 650 SECURITIES ARBITRATION 313, 396 (D. Robbins ed., 1989) and Exhibits 0

(Dean Witter Reynolds, Inc. letter); R (letter of Beryl W. Sprinkel, Chairman, Council of Economic Advisors) (brokers will charge customers a premium to cover the exposure to greater costs if they must resolve to litigation rather than arbitration); BNA DAILY REPORT FOR EXECUTIVES, July 26, 1988, DRE No. 143c-6, interview with SEC General Counsel Daniel Goeizer, Pgs. C9-C11 (the SEC would be concerned with changes in commissions to reflect cost of litigation versus arbitration).

15 *Connolly*, 703 F. Supp. at 159.

16 Margin accounts are a particularly fertile ground for arbitration claims. *See* a discussion of claims in chapter 11.

17 *Connolly*, 703 F. Supp. at 159. AAA statistics for 1986 show that of 40 AAA cases against securities firms, 68 percent (27) resulted in awards for customers, averaging in excess of $26,000. Four awards of punitive damages ranging from $50,000 to $150,000 were also reported. N.A.S.D. 1985 statistics showed 55 percent of public cases arbitrated to the award stage went to the customer. *See* Bedell, Harrison & Harvey, *The McMahon Mandate: Compulsory Arbitration of Securities and RICO Claims*, 19 LOY. U. CHI. L. J. 1, 9 (1987).

18 *Connolly*, 703 F. Supp. at 160.

19 2 SEC. ARBIT. COMM., No. 4, at 1 (April 1989).

20 *See* discussion of the GAO Report in chapter 10.

21 *See* 4 SEC. ARBIT. COMM., No. 5 (Sept. 1991).

22 E. MORRIS, D. MASUCCI and ROBERT S. CLEMENTE, *Securities Arbitration at Self-Regulatory Organizations*, SECURITIES ARBITRATION 152 (D.E. Robbins ed., 1992).

23 78 percent of cash account customers do not have agreements. *See Massachusetts Proposal Barring Mandatory Arbitration Clauses Debated*, 20 SEC. REG. & L. REP. (BNA) 1219 (July 29, 1988).

24 This is combined with the small investor's feeling of helplessness and obligation to accept the take-it-or-leave-it terms imposed on him by the broker if he wants the product or service. This justifies, to him at least, the requirement of disclosure of terms of an adhesive nature.

25 Statement of Stephen L. Hammerman Before the Subcommittee on Telecommunications and Finance of the House Committee on Energy and Commerce.

26 "The ideal [contracting party] who would read, understand, and compare several forms is unheard of in the legal literature and, I warrant, in life as well." *Rakoff*, *supra* note 13, at 1229.

27 Contract defenses, including adhesion, are discussed in chapter 3.

28 *See* FITZPATRICK, *The Choice Issue*, in SECURITIES ARBITRATION UPDATE 254, 299-301 (M. Fitterman & T. Krebsbach eds., 1989).

29 The term "Blue Sky Law" refers to state regulation of the securities industry and comes from the 1916 Kansas legislation aimed at promoters who "would sell building lots in the blue sky in fee simple. [T]hey became known as blue sky merchants." Mulvey, *Blue Sky Law*, 36 CAN. L. T. 37 (1916). *See also* Hall v. Geiger-Jones Co., 242 U.S. 539, 550 (1917). Thus, state securities regulation, licensing and legislation have become known as Blue Sky Law.

30 *Connolly*, 703 F. Supp. at 159.

31 *See* Kronstein, *Business Arbitration-Instrument of Private Government*, 54 YALE L. J. 36 (1944); Kritzer & Anderson, *The Arbitration Alternative: A Comparative Analysis of Case Processing Time, Disposition Mode, and Cost in the American Arbitration Association and the Courts*, 8 JUST. SYS. J. 6 (1983).

32 2 SEC. ARB. COMM. No. 2 (Feb. 1989).

33 *See* AAA Rule 34; N.Y. CPLR 7502(c) permits a party to seek a temporary restraining order in court prior to commencement of the arbitration.

34 *See* D. Robbins, SECURITIES ARBITRATION PROCEDURE MANUAL 5 (1991).

35 *See* for example, AAA Securities Arbitration Rule 10 providing for preliminary hearings, which may be conducted by telephone conference call, dealing with discovery and other matters.

36 N.Y.S.E. Rule 627(e).

37 AAA Rule 42(f).

38 N.A.S.D. Code of Arbitration Procedure § 41(e).

39 As of March 1992, 44 percent of the N.A.S.D. docket was cases with over $100,000 in controversy, a 7 percent increase in that category from the prior year. *See* SECURITIES ARBITRATION 147 (D.E. Robbins ed., 1992).

40 *See* the discussion of absence of arbitration agreement in chapter 6. Mowbiay v. Mosley, Hallgarten, Esterbrook & Weeden, 795 F.2d 1111 (1st Cir. 1986); Okcuoglu v. Hess, Grant & Co., Inc., 580 F. Supp. 749 (E.D. Pa. 1984).

Chapter 8

INTERPRETATIONS OF FEDERAL ARBITRATION ACT IN SECURITIES CASES

The Supreme Court of the United States has chosen to review the Federal Arbitration Act often since *Wilko* was decided in 1953. The result has been an unprecedented expansion of the scope of arbitration. This chapter will review these developments.

In the 1984 case of *Southland Corp. v. Keating*,[1] the Supreme Court found the Federal Arbitration Act part of the substantive law of the United States, enacted under the interstate commerce clause of the U.S. Constitution.[2] As a result, the Federal Arbitration Act is the law to be applied in both federal and state courts to any agreement within the coverage of the Federal Arbitration Act. Consequently, the federal preemption doctrine applies and if proper federal jurisdiction is present, state laws relating to arbitration, or non-arbitration, will not invalidate an arbitration agreement. Two years later, a week after *McMahon*, in *Perry v. Thomas*,[3] the Court found Congressional intent "to provide for the enforcement of arbitration agreements within the full reach of the Commerce Clause" and declared that the Federal Arbitration Act created a body of federal substantive law of arbitrability even if there is state law or policy to the contrary. The Court thus transformed "a procedural statute that applied only in certain federal cases into a national charter for alternative dispute resolution."[4]

Because Congress adopted the securities laws after the Federal Arbitration Act, the question was presented if Congress intended the Federal Arbitration Act to apply to and permit the enforcement of predispute agreements to arbitrate disputes for violations of these laws. Consequently, the Federal Arbitration Act must be read in light of the later enactment and perhaps conflicting goals of the securities laws: "Whereas the Federal Arbitration Act was designed to recognize freedom of contract in the area of arbitration agreements, the federal securities laws were designed to protect investors from sophisticated securities dealers."[5]

But the real question remains: why has Congress remained silent regarding the arbitration of securities disputes despite this explosion in litigation? Other federal statutes encourage of arbitration of disputes arising under them.[6]

Actually, as *McMahon* notes, in 1975 Congress did refer to arbitration in the adoption of amendments to the Exchange Act, which added to SEC jurisdiction the supervision of industry arbitration procedures.[7] In language strikingly relevant today, this Conference Report indicated that the securities markets are a major national asset and have flourished under the federal regulation established in the 1930s to provide a share in the profits of the free enterprise system to millions of Americans and a means of raising capital for new and growing business. But the statutory and regulatory structure did not keep pace with economic and technological changes and shifts in investment patterns, with the result

> that there have been operational breakdowns and economic distortions which have impaired public confidence in the securities markets [which] . . . at times have posed threats to the viability of our entire equity investment system . . . Unless [the securities markets] adapt and respond to the demands placed upon them, there is a danger that America will lose ground as an international financial center and that the economic, financial and commercial interests of the Nation will suffer.[8]

Finding the basic goals of the Exchange Act to be providing fair and honest mechanisms for the pricing of traded securities; assuring dealing is fair and without undue preferences or advantages among investors; ensuring efficient transaction costs; and providing maximum openness and orderliness in the markets, the bill was primarily directed at creation of a national securities market. It also modified the position of the exchanges and SROs, created a Municipal Securities Rulemaking Board, coordinated membership in the Securities Investor Protection Corporation, and codified the SEC's authority to eliminate fixed commission rates, among other things. At the end, the Conference Report also noted that the amendment to § 28 of the Exchange Act with respect to arbitration proceedings between self-regulatory organizations and their participants, members, and persons dealing with members or participants, was with "the clear understanding of the conferees that this amendment did not change existing law, as articulated in *Wilko v. Swan* . . . concerning the effect of arbitration proceeding provisions in agreements entered into by persons dealing with members and participants of self-regulatory organizations."[9]

Consequently, 1975 Congressional policy on arbitration was consistent with the holding in *Wilko* regarding non-arbitrability of claims arising under § 12(2) of the 1933 Act and, by implication at least, to claims alleging violation of other provisions of the 1933 Act and the Exchange Act as well. The SEC recognized this prior position in the adoption of Rule 15c2-2, which it alluded to in its *amicus* brief in *McMahon*.[10] But in *McMahon*, the SEC changed its position and supported arbitration.

1) *WILKO V. SWAN*

Before the Supreme Court decided *Wilko* in 1953, there had been no cases interpreting the Congressional intent of the securities laws and arbitration of dispute claiming violation of such investor-protective provisions.

In *Wilko* a customer brought action for violation of § 12(2) of the 1933 Act for alleged misrepresentations and omissions, claiming the brokerage firm account representative had falsely led him to purchase common stock by misrepresenting its value. The false representation was that the stock would be valued at $6.00 per share over the then current market price pursuant to a soon to be announced merger agreement, and that sophisticated investors were then buying the stock for speculative profit. The brokerage firm did not even file an answer to the complaint, but moved for stay of litigation in the Federal courts under the margin agreement arbitration clause the customer had signed in opening the account and under the Federal Arbitration Act.[11]

The Supreme Court held that the 1933 Act reflected congressional intent in favor of judicial enforcement in Federal court.[12] Since § 12(2) changed the prior common law principle of *caveat emptor*, the Court found a "special right" was created in the purchasers of securities under the statute, and that it was drafted "with an eye to the disadvantages under which buyers labor." The statute was found to expressly give a securities buyer a judicial remedy for his protection. Thus the 1933 Act prevailed over the 1925 Federal Arbitration Act because under § 14 of the 1933 Act, any "condition, stipulation, or provision binding any person to waive compliance with [the 1933 Act] . . . shall be void,"[13] and an arbitration clause was construed as a "stipulation" under the statute.

The Supreme Court in *Wilko* expressed concern about securities industry arbitration procedures at that time. First, they found arbitrators had no judicial instruction from a judge regarding the law they were to apply in the arbitration cases they heard. The Court specifically mentioned the lack of instruction and possible misconception with the "legal meaning of such statutory requirements as 'burden of proof, 'reasonable care,' and 'material fact.'"[14] The Court felt this particularly significant since the securities laws provisions are not the same as "[d]etermination of a quality of a commodity or the amount of money due under a contract." Issues such as "material fact," or "reasonable care" were being determined without the securities laws' meaning being applied by the arbitrators.[15] Second, because of a lack of a record being made of the proceedings, questions regarding burden of proof, admissibility of evidence, and the like were difficult for the courts to supervise. Third, judicial power to vacate an award was limited by the Federal Arbitration Act.[16] And, fourth, some awards were never subject to court review.

But the basic premise of § 12(2) of the 1933 Act was that a person is liable to a buyer of securities if he sells or offers through any means of interstate commerce, makes an untrue statement or fails to state a material fact, and the purchaser is unaware of the omission or untruth. Further, the 1933 Act also specifies that the investor-buyer need only prove the omission or untruth, and thereafter the burden of establishing that the buyer did not know or, in the exercise of reasonable care, should have known of such omission or misstatement, falls on the seller of the security.

This shift of the difficult burden was one of the major reasons the Congressional intent in *Wilko* was determined by the Court to support non-arbitration. Another was the nationwide venue and service provision under § 12(2). A third was the reasoning that arbitration is ill-suited to protect unsophisticated buyers from unscrupulous sellers. Moreover, the *Wilko* Court contended that Congress specifically designed this "special right" to reduce the disparity in bargaining power between buyers and sellers inherent in the open securities market. The Court concluded that "[w]hile the Securities Act does not require [a claimant] to sue, a waiver in advance of a controversy stands upon a different footing. [I]t is clear that the [1933 Act] was drafted with an eye to the disadvantages under which buyers labor. Issuers of and dealers in securities have better opportunities to investigate and appraise the prospective earnings and business plans affecting securities than buyers. It is therefore reasonable for Congress to put buyers of securities covered by that Act on a different basis from other purchasers."[17]

The *Wilko* result was adopted by Professor Loss in the American Law Institute's FEDERAL SECURITIES CODE[18] to protect small investors against predispute waiver of the right to court determination of securities law claims. This decision was also justified by finding that despite the Congressional policy decision in enacting the Federal Arbitration Act that it could trade off judicial protection for the decreased court congestion, time, expense, and *increased* expertise that might result from industry arbitration, arbitration was not permitted. In any event, it is clear that under *Wilko* only predispute agreements were invalid; an agreement to arbitrate after a dispute had arisen would be enforceable.

2) *WILKO'S* PROGENY

For thirty-six years *Wilko* stood for the proposition that 1933 Act claims were not arbitrable. The principle has been eroded in a series of cases, culminating in the overturning of *Wilko* in *Rodriguez* in 1989.

In 1972 the Second Circuit found that the sale of securities in a private placement not involving an exchange transaction was clearly within the meaning of commerce under the Federal Arbitration Act.[19] The same result would probably result in almost any sale of securities, due to the use of the securities markets, NASDAQ trading, telephones, or the mails. Therefore, federal arbitration will render state arbitration statutes inapplicable to securities disputes. In 1974 the Supreme Court in *Scherk v. Alberto-Culver Co.*[20] decided that international securities arbitration was permissible. The Court determined that facilitating international trade was preferable to an expansive application of the securities laws by holding that *Wilko* prohibited Exchange Act claims arbitration. Because the Exchange Act claim under § 10(b) was subject to an implied private right of action, whereas § 12(2) of the 1933 Act had created an express statutory right of action, the Court felt justified in permitting international arbitration. But the basis of the *Scherk* decision was the international business aspects, which the Court found different from those controlling in *Wilko*. The forum selection in arbitration was controlling, "absent a strong showing that it should be set aside," which rejected the previous doctrine that international forum selection would not be respected by U.S. courts unless the forum was more convenient than the state in which suit was brought.[21] *Scherk* also said in dictum that a "colorable argument" was made that *Wilko* was not controlling in cases under the implied action provisions of the Exchange Act because of the jurisdictional and remedial differences between the 1933 and Exchange Acts.

The next Supreme Court case interpreting *Wilko* came in 1985. In *Dean Witter Reynolds, Inc. v. Byrd*,[22] a claim was made under the Exchange Act and various state law provisions for trading in a customer's account. Dean Witter, the broker, did not ask for a stay on the securities claim believing them non-arbitrable, but did request an order severing pendent state claims and requiring arbitration for them. The Court refused to determine whether *Wilko* was applicable to Exchange Act claims. It merely waited two years for *McMahon*. But it found that bifurcated proceedings, which would result if the arbitration agreement was enforced as to state claims, was what Congress had intended in the Federal Arbitration Act, even if the result was "piecemeal" litigation.

Therefore, *Byrd* held that it is proper to compel arbitration of pendent arbitrable claims, even where the result would be possibly inefficient bifurcated proceedings in different forums, finding this was the result of the preeminent concern of Congress in passing the Federal Arbitration Act.

Byrd caused confusion in the lower courts as to the continued application of *Wilko* to 1934 Act violations. Several courts interpreted *Byrd* to hold mandatory arbitration clauses unenforceable. In an interesting case involving claims under RICO, the Third Circuit found it could distinguish those claims that were based on § 10(b) of the Exchange Act and did not permit arbitration. But claims under RICO for mail fraud and wire fraud were, nevertheless, arbitrable.[23] The result of this bifurcated procedure meant:

> 1. When faced with the necessity to arbitrate state claims *and* litigate federal . . . claims . . ., it may be advisable to discontinue the arbitration and proceed only on the federal claims, to avoid . . . larger legal fees.
> 2. Where the arbitration proceeding is conducted first and the customer is fully compensated . . . § 28 of the [Exchange Act] would presumably preclude further recovery in subsequent federal litigation.
> 3. Where the customer has proven liability to an arbitration panel but [only recovers part of the damages sought], the broker-dealer may be encouraged to settle . . . in lieu of subjecting the facts to a jury.
> 4. Where the customer loses in arbitration, he or she may not want to pursue the more expensive and time consuming process of federal litigation.[24]

The result of this procedure was bifurcation at its most absurd. Neither the goals of protection of the investor of the securities laws nor the efficiencies and speed accomplished in arbitration were achieved as the result of *Byrd*.

In 1985 the Supreme Court also decided *Mitsubishi Motors Corp. v. Soler Chrysler-Plymouth*,[25] holding an agreement to arbitrate antitrust claims in an international commercial compact enforceable. Prior decisions had indicated that antitrust enforcement was not arbitrable, on much the same rationale as in the securities arbitration area: the public interest lay in antitrust enforcement in the courts, rather than by arbitration. The Second Circuit had previously found antitrust cases to be very complex and the judicial process was perhaps better suited to deal with this type complex litigation. The court in *American Safety Equipment* had also queried that since the antitrust laws were to be enforced against business and because arbitrators were typically business persons, perhaps industry arbitration was not in the public interest.[26]

In *Mitsubishi*, an agreement on the sale of inventory to Soler, a large Puerto Rican car dealer, called for arbitration in Japan. Mitsubishi sought arbitration by court order in a breach of contract action against Soler, and Soler counterclaimed against Mitsubishi and Chrysler International alleging conspiracy to restrain trade under the antitrust laws. The Supreme Court, as in *Scherk*, again focused on the international aspects of the transaction, but raised questions on the standards applied in *American Safety*, although not reversing it. The Court in *Mitsubishi* found an "emphatic federal policy in favor of arbitral dispute resolution." In fact, the opinion reads as an endorsement of arbitration, clearly further undermining *Wilko*:

> [A]daptability and access . . . are hallmarks of arbitration. The anticipated subject matter of the dispute may be taken into account when the arbitrators are appointed, and arbitral rules typically provide for the participation of experts . . . [T]he factor of potential complexity also does not persuade us that an arbitral tribunal could not properly handle an antitrust matter.[27]

These cases set the stage for the *McMahon* decision, which probably came as a surprise to few lawyers following these decisions. The Court had consistently concluded over 14 years that arbitration of other claims created by other federal statutes was an adequate, if not preferred less costly and more efficient means of resolution of these claims.

3) *McMAHON*

By 1987 confusion reigned in the federal courts regarding the standard to be applied in determining if predispute arbitration agreements in cases raising securities law claims were enforceable and a stay of litigation was required to permit resolution in a non-judicial forum. The Supreme Court's *Wilko* and *Byrd* decisions were seemingly consistent, but the Court had clearly sent forth the message that arbitration under the Exchange Act may not be governed by *Wilko's* prohibition. It had merely refused to say so expressly.

A majority of courts had adhered to *Wilko* as far as 1933 Act claims were concerned; and most concurred in the same result for Exchange Act claims as well. For example, in *Wolfe v. E. F. Hutton & Co.*,[28] the Eleventh Circuit expressly extended *Wilko* to Exchange Act § 10(b) claims implied as a private right of action under a series of cases dealing with Rule 10b-5. It based this decision on four grounds: (1) the refusal of the Supreme Court to limit *Wilko* to 1933 Act claims; (2) that both Acts provide a "special right" to investors; (3) the exclusive federal jurisdiction under § 27 of the Exchange Act was a more important safeguard for the investor than the concurrent jurisdiction of both federal and state courts in the enforcement of the 1933 Act under 1933 Act § 14; and (4) the express right of investors to sue under the 1933 Act was implied to exist in Exchange Act proceedings by a long line of precedent that Congress had not overturned, even in the 1975 amendments to the Exchange Act.

A similar rationale had been applied to RICO actions. Courts inferred that Congress intended to entrust the enforcement of RICO to the courts and not to arbitrators.[29] Surprisingly, courts mechanically accepted this rationale.[30]

The issue of the distinction between customer remedies for violation of the securities laws being express or implied was decided in *McMahon*. *McMahon* also resolved another issue by permitting arbitrators to award punitive damages.[31] In *McMahon*, the Court found that RICO mandated treble damages and fee recovery under Federal Arbitration Act authority. Still, state courts may resist these extraordinary remedies. Legislation may be required to overcome this resistance.

A) The *McMahon* Facts

The facts in *McMahon* were fairly simple. In 1984 the McMahons brought suit in federal court for losses of approximately $500,000 against Shearson/American Express, Inc., a brokerage firm with whom they had several accounts, and the Shearson registered representative who handled their accounts.[32] The complaint alleged the representative made false statements and omitted material facts in giving them advice and had churned their accounts, all in violation of (1) state law fraud and breach of fiduciary duty; (2) § 10(b) of the Exchange Act and Rule 10b-5; and (3) RICO, which would allow treble damages and recovery of attorney's fees and costs.

The McMahons had signed contracts with Shearson upon opening their account that contained predispute arbitration clauses.[33] Shearson moved to compel arbitration. The District Court ordered arbitration of the state and § 10(b) claims under the authority of *Byrd*, but not the RICO claim. Both parties appealed. The Second Circuit held the District Court erred in ordering arbitration of the § 10(b) claims,[34] but affirmed on the RICO and state claims disposition. The Court found RICO involved a fundamental federal public policy that would not be permitted to be resolved in an arbitral forum. Shearson appealed to the Supreme Court and certiorari was granted in order to "resolve the conflict among the Courts of Appeals regarding the arbitrability of § 10(b) and RICO claims."

B) *McMahon's* Holding

In a 5-4 split, made more obtuse by the concurring opinions, the Court reversed the Second Circuit and remanded to arbitration. The Court thus found that implied actions under the Exchange Act and securities claims under RICO were arbitrable. But the narrow and splintered majority, reversing the longstanding *Wilko* rationale, left many questions. Five Justices voted that implied actions under the Exchange Act were arbitrable under the rationale of *Byrd*, *Scherk*, and *Mitsubishi*, and all Justices agreed that RICO securities claims were also arbitrable under the "public policy" exception of *American Safety*. Justice Stevens wrote a short concurrence and dissent on the "longstanding interpretation" of *Wilko* for § 10(b) issues finding that the

Congressional intention in 1975 was not to overturn *Wilko*, but an implied acceptance of non-arbitrability for both 1933 and Exchange Act violations. This position was rejected by the bare majority of the Court. But Justice Steven's cogent argument that minimizes judicial activism and would have left the alteration of *Wilko* for both claims to Congress was proper. It would be preferable to have Congress expressly overturn a prevailing judicial interpretation of longstanding application by the courts that had given the statutes a clear meaning.[35] Justice Blackmun also dissented on the § 10(b) issue and was joined by Justices Brennan and Marshall.

Justice O'Connor, writing for the majority, began by noting the Federal Arbitration Act's creation of a strong federal policy favoring arbitration. She found that even when claims are grounded in federal statutes, the burden is on the party seeking to avoid arbitration to establish Congressional intent to provide an exception to the Federal Arbitration Act's presumption of arbitrability. The burden was not met in *McMahon* for either implied rights of action under the Exchange Act or RICO, despite the plaintiffs' contention that the non-waiver provisions of § 29(a) of the Exchange Act[36] were similar to the provisions in § 14 of the 1933 Act, which the *Wilko* Court had found persuasive. Moreover, Justice O'Connor clearly adopted a revisionist approach and wrote that *Wilko* was not a simple reading of the 1933 Act's non-waiver provision, but could be understood only "in the context of the Court's ensuing discussion explaining why arbitration was inadequate." Noting the decisions subsequent to *Wilko* had rejected the "general suspicion of the desirability of arbitration and the competence of arbitral tribunals," and the 1975 Exchange Act amendments giving the SEC power to supervise the industry arbitration rules,[37] she concluded that "An arbitration agreement does not effect a waiver of the protections of the [Exchange] Act." Arbitration was thus found "an adequate substitute" for a judicial forum, particularly so since it was procedural and not a "substantive right" under the *Scherk* understanding that the right to select a judicial forum exists only where arbitration is inadequate to protect the substantive rights at issue. Remarkably, the Court did *not* either define what constituted a substantive right or overturn *Wilko*.

Thus finding that the "suitability of arbitration as a means of enforcing Exchange Act rights is evident" and that "the mistrust of arbitration that formed the basis for the *Wilko* opinion in 1953 is difficult to square with the assessment of arbitration that has prevailed since that time," the Court rejected *Wilko* as it applied to implied actions under the Exchange Act. In *Mitsubishi*, the Court had examined arbitration and concluded that (1) such forums are capable of handling factual and legal complexities; (2) streamlined procedures do not restrict substantive rights; and (3) judicial review, though limited, suffices to ensure compliance with the statute. But, the Court did not distinguish between the *international* commercial aspects of *Mitsubishi* and the fact that the McMahons were consumers far less sophisticated than the large dealer and manufacturer in *Mitsubishi*. Neither did the Court address the issue that because there was no written opinion in arbitrations, less sophisticated investors would be less well protected from unfair practices in market transactions. In addition, the court also felt (1) *Scherk* was precedent, although in an international agreement, for § 10(b) claims being arbitratable; (2) the courts would enforce arbitration between members of an SRO of § 10(b) claims; and (3) *Wilko* does not apply to post-dispute agreements to arbitrate. The Court also noted that arbitration now adequately protects investors, apparently focusing on the SEC oversight provided after the 1975 Exchange Act amendments.

A similar analysis was applied to find RICO's Congressional intent also fell under the Federal Arbitration Act's strong public policy. The Justices all agreed that RICO claims were subject to arbitration. Arbitration could serve the interest of Congress in its "remedial and deterrent function," except in the criminal sense. But in "run-of-the-mill civil RICO claims brought against legitimate [business] enterprises," the Justices suggested mandatory arbitration was appropriate.

The dissenting Justices agreed with the majority's analysis of the Federal Arbitration Act's preference position, but disagreed on the Exchange Act claims arbitrability. Justice Blackmun first argued that Congressional action in amending the Exchange Act in 1975 to provide for SEC supervision of arbitration procedures of the SROs was not as clear a repudiation of the judicial interpretation of the substantive or procedural rights of investors as the majority had decided.[38]

Justice Blackmun argued *Wilko* had not been decided on the Court's belief that inadequacy of arbitration was insufficient for enforcement of 1933 Act claims. He centered on the almost identical non-waiver provisions of the two securities laws. Concluding that due to the investor protection purposes of the statute and that the laws are part of a comprehensive and integrated federal regulatory scheme for governing securities transactions, arbitration of either 1933 or Exchange Act claims, including those which the courts have recognized to exist by implication from the statutory purpose, still fails to protect the investor adequately. Justice Blackmun still had concern similar to that expressed in 1953 in *Wilko* in three areas: (1) there was still very limited judicial review of arbitration awards; (2) arbitrators need not rely on judicial precedent or make a record; and (3) the industry-sponsored forum selections gave no real alternative to the investor and was probably not effectively supervised by an already overworked SEC that does not have the power to initiate SRO rule changes.

Blackmun also found the SEC's change in position regarding arbitration "curious." Citing the rationale justifying the adoption of Rule 15c2-2,

Blackmun was unable to dismiss, as did the majority, the belief that *Wilko* did not bar the enforcement of predispute arbitration agreements dealing with violations of the "special rights" created by the securities laws.

C) Analysis of *McMahon*

The question prior to *Rodriguez* was whether the Court would adopt the interpretation of federal securities statutes under the "ignore Congressional inaction" approach of Justice O'Connor; the "inferred approval by Congressional inaction" approach of Justice Stevens; or the "enactment rule" of Justice Blackmun; both of the dissents would require express Congressional action to overturn a long-established judicial precedent. This inconsistency is nothing new with the Rehnquist Court, but as a result the lower courts needed additional guidance.

The Court, in a 1989 6-2 decision, decided that this stay under state law was permissible under the Federal Arbitration Act.[39] Chief Justice Rehnquist, writing for the majority, found that the state procedural statute did not undermine the goals of the Federal Arbitration Act, but rejected the state court's contention that there had been a waiver of the right to arbitrate under the Federal Arbitration Act. The federal policy in favor of arbitration was still paramount, but no federal right was found to have been created when this state law provision was used.

4) *RODRIGUEZ DE QUIJAS*

After *McMahon*, the confusion as far as arbitrability of Exchange Act and RICO claims seemed resolved. But what remained of *Wilko*? While *McMahon* did not overrule *Wilko*, it is obvious that the view of the Supreme Court toward arbitration has undergone striking change since 1953. As a result, there was a split in the federal courts regarding the non-arbitrability of § 12(2) claims, the very issue in *Wilko*.[40] A number of investors added § 12(2) allegations to their complaints against broker-dealers hoping to avoid *McMahon's* required arbitration despite Justice Blackmun's suggestion in *McMahon* that *Wilko* was placed in the graveyard of ideas. The Supreme Court's decision in *Rodriguez de Quijas v. Shearson/American Express, Inc.*[41] answered these questions.

A) The *de Quijas* Facts

This case involved a group of Texas investors who lost $400,000 in an account they opened at a local Shearson office. They brought action to recover the losses based on violation of the antifraud provisions of § 12(2) and other provisions of the 1933 and Exchange Acts which all parties agreed to be subject to arbitration under *McMahon*. The District Court ordered all claims, except those under § 12(2), to arbitration. The Fifth Circuit in *de Quijas* found that *McMahon* had effectively undercut every aspect of *Wilko*, finding that "[a]uthority no longer exists to deny arbitration of the § 12(2) claims. . . . Arbitration must be directed as to both the Securities Act claims and Exchange Act claims."[42] Judge Williams read *Wilko* as "barring waiver of a judicial forum only if arbitration is inadequate to protect the substantive rights at issue."[43] And *McMahon* made it clear that the Supreme Court, as a result of advances arbitration since *Wilko*, no longer felt arbitration inadequate to protect substantive rights of investors. Due to the similarities between § 14 of the 1933 Act and § 29(a) of the Exchange Act, both of which void any stipulation "to waive compliance with any" provision of the statutes, the Court felt Congress did not intend to draw such a "fine distinction" to prohibit arbitration in one and not the other.[44]

The Supreme Court again came out in favor of arbitration. With the retirement of Justice Powell, replaced by Justice Kennedy a supporter of arbitration as a Circuit Court Judge, there had been little doubt that the final nail was about to be driven into *Wilko's* coffin.

B) The *de Quijas* Holding

This opinion by Justice Kennedy, again a 5-4 decision, expressly overruled *Wilko* and held that arbitration of securities law violations of § 12(2) of the 1933 Act was permissible from *McMahon's* holding, in that there resulted inconsistency and violation of the principle that the securities acts should be construed harmoniously or as a part of an integrated system of regulation, since they "constituted interrelated components of the federal regulatory scheme governing transactions in securities."[45] Thus the Court has further embraced arbitration: federal and state courts are mandated to enforce predispute arbitration agreements for all claims under the federal securities laws.

The Court found that the current judicial view favors arbitration and rejected *Wilko's* outmoded "judicial hostility to arbitration," and its concern regarding procedural issues. It absolutely rejected once again the idea that the securities acts, because they were enacted after the Federal Arbitration Act, indicated Congressional intent to not subject claims to arbitration. Finding *Wilko* concerned primarily with the procedural protection of litigation, the Court concluded, again in light of the SEC's recently expanded authority "to oversee and regulate those arbitration procedures," the *Wilko* rationale no longer existed. But, perhaps even more significantly, the Court found that "the right to select the judicial forum and the wider choice of courts [so important to *Wilko's* justification] are not . . . essential features of the [1933 Act]."[46]

After reviewing the decisions over the last 14 years that stressed the validity of arbitration, Justice Kennedy concluded *Wilko* was obviously not correct because "the language prohibiting waiver of 'compliance with any provision of this title' could easily have been read to relate to substantive provisions of [the 1933] Act without including the remedy provisions."[47] Despite its affirmance of the Fifth Circuit's decision, the Court's opinion nevertheless chastised the Fifth Circuit for its impertinence in usurping the Court's "prerogative of overruling its own decisions" and forgetting its duty to follow the direct precedent.

While concluding that there was no reason to treat claims under the 1933 Act differently from those brought under the Exchange Act, the Court bound itself by the strong language of the Federal Arbitration Act's mandate that "arbitration agreements 'shall be valid, irrevocable, and enforceable.'" The Court, however, still left open the possibility of challenge to arbitration on the grounds of fraud or duress, or by a showing of "overwhelming economic power that would provide grounds for the revocation of any contract,"[48] although in *Rodriguez* there was no showing in the record of such defenses to arbitration.

Finally, the opinion overruled *Wilko* retroactively by finding such retroactivity would not "produce 'substantial inequitable results' . . . [because] our assessment that resort to the arbitration process does not inherently undermine any of the substantive rights afforded to petitioners under the Securities Act."[49]

The dissenters too found the Fifth Circuit had engaged in "indefensible . . . judicial activism,"[50] but found that although the Court is not subject to the same restraint as lower courts in upsetting its prior decisions, to do so in the face of "3 ½ decades" of Congressional acceptance of *Wilko* is to usurp the lawmaking responsibility of Congress. Finding "valid policy and textual arguments on both sides regarding the interrelation of federal securities and arbitration Acts,"[51] the dissenters did not agree that this area of the law, which had been settled for so long, should be upset by judicial action in the face of Congressional acceptance.

C) *de Quijas* Analysis

Both Securities Act of 1933 § 12(2) and Securities and Exchange Act of 1934 § 10(b) claims and the waiver provisions of those statutes in § 14 and § 29(a) are so similar that it is hard to conclude any other result would occur, especially looking at the caselaw developments up to *McMahon*. *McMahon* makes it clear that the Court no longer considers arbitration as inadequate to protect substantive rights, and the advances in arbitration procedures, particularly SEC oversight, apply equally to protection of the substantive rights under both the 1933 and Exchange Acts.

One commentator, however, agreed with the *Rodriguez de Quijas* dissenters that *McMahon* was a result of judicial activism reversing a longstanding judicial statutory interpretation that Congress seemed purposely to have left intact.[52] Finding, as did Justice Steven in *McMahon*, that there was no "gap" in the law to be filled by judicial construction due to the meaning *Wilko* had acquired from 25 years of judicial "gloss," this commentator felt that "the judiciary should not undertake the ongoing role of making policy determinations in a changing world." Further, "Congress should have exclusive power to overturn [such] a judicial statutory interpretation."

Consequently, the *Rodriguez de Quijas* holding is important for a number of reasons. First, predispute arbitration agreements will be enforced by the Federal courts to compel arbitration of both 1933 and Exchange Acts claims unless there is a showing of the invalidity of the contract under a very narrow group of theories. Second, the Court emphatically rejected any denigration of the arbitration process as unfair or inadequate, specifically noting that any judicial "suspicion of arbitration . . . has fallen far out of step with [the Court's] current strong endorsement of the federal statutes favoring this method of resolving disputes."[53] Third, the Court suggested that due to the preeminence of the Federal Arbitration Act, *Rodriguez de Quijas* should be applied retroactively even to those cases brought in federal courts under the prior holding in *Wilko*. The result has been court mandated arbitration in a number of pre-*Rodriguez de Quijas* cases.[54]

Both *McMahon* and *Rodriguez de Quijas* make the same basic assumption: that arbitration as a procedure can offer as much protection to the claimant as litigation in the federal courts. There is criticism of this assumption, and to date there is little concrete evidence to support the position that in reality this is true. The Supreme Court has clearly taken the position that securities arbitration is fair to investors.

5) WHAT IS NEXT?

McMahon and *Rodriguez de Quijas* have been retroactively applied under both the *Rodriguez de Quijas*' mandate and under application of the usual rule that federal cases are decided in accordance with the law as it exists at the time of decision and not as it exists at the time of filing.[55] The "strong federal policy in favor of arbitration--and the absence of any federal policy favoring securities litigation--suggests that the rule [in *McMahon*] should be applied retroactively."[56] Furthermore, *McMahon* and *Rodriguez de Quijas* "alter only the forum for resolving [the] dispute and not [the plaintiff's] substantive rights."[57]

In a case[58] decided just before *Rodriguez de Quijas*, however, the Supreme Court may have opened the door to further litigation. A construction contract predispute arbitration clause was read in conjunction with the choice of law provision and was found to be governed by a state law that did not permit arbitration of the issues in controversy. The Supreme Court agreed with the stay of arbitration and denied the argument that the Federal Arbitration Act preempted state law because the agreement provided that state law would govern.

In another case,[59] a court found that under state securities statutes, a non-arbitrable right of action was created for trading by brokers. Other claims proceeded to arbitration, but this issue was to be litigated without stay because the outcomes under the different state statutes would not be dispositive of each other.

Two states have attempted to modify *McMahon* and *de Quijas* through statute or regulation. In the first, Massachusetts' Securities Commissioner adopted a rule prohibiting any broker registered in the Commonwealth from precluding the right to court resolution of disputes with customers. This was found in violation of the Federal Arbitration Act in *Securities Industry Association v. Connolly*[60] in 1989. Despite *Connolly*, in 1990 Florida adopted a provision in their law concerning registration and licensing of registered representatives and broker-dealers that would require the brokerage agreement to permit customers to elect arbitration in a forum before the AAA "or other independent non-industry arbitration forum" as well as an industry-sponsored forum.[61] This law was found to conflict with sections 2 and 5 of the Federal Arbitration Act in *Securities Industry Ass'n v. Lewis*,[62] and struck down as an impermissible state incursion into a federally preempted area.

In a typical maneuver, the plaintiff in *Ferreri v. First Options of Chicago, Inc.*,[63] filed a securities cause of action after an arbitrator had awarded damages. The court held that arbitration provided a fair, complete, and adequate substitute for a judicial trial because (1) the arbitrators had expertise in the securities industry, a specialized field; (2) the plaintiff's economic loss was resolved from the evidence[64] in a complete proceeding; (3) plaintiff was represented by his own lawyer at the arbitration and changed lawyers to pursue litigation after the arbitration was complete; and (4) the rules and procedures used in arbitration were substantially the same as at trials. The court also noted that the damages recoverable for the arbitrated claim were the same as for the violations of securities laws. This should be the result in most arbitrable cases.

To date, the Supreme Court has not confronted the non-arbitrability of securities issues in connection with other laws as have the federal circuit courts. For example, in *Bird v. Shearson Lehman/American Express, Inc.*,[65] it was determined that arbitration could be compelled against participants in an employee retirement plan. Beneficiaries of an ERISA[66] plan could be compelled to arbitrate any issue or "controversy arising out of or relating to" the trust by the trustee's agreement with the broker.

In a number of cases concerning the language in customer agreements dating from SEC Rule 15c2-2 times, courts have found that the express language of the arbitration clause does not permit arbitration even under *McMahon* and *Rodriguez*.[67] As noted above, older customer agreements still state that the customer is required to arbitrate any dispute with the firm but specify that claims for violations of the federal securities laws could instead be litigated. Despite the preference for arbitration, some courts have found variants of the Rule 15c2-2 language to permit arbitration under the theory that it creates substantive rights to litigate rather than arbitration;[68] for example, when the clause said "to the extent [such claims] . . . may be litigated"[69] or where it referred to no waiver of a right to seek a federal forum "where such waiver would be void under the Federal Securities Laws."[70] But other courts have found the Rule 15c2-2 language was only an interpretation by the SEC of the law. As such it was only a notice provision and the language of the agreement would not prohibit arbitration of securities law claims since the parties did not make the law at the time a substantive part of the contract.[71] This enforces the Supreme Court authority endorsing arbitration as a method of dispute resolution.

In the two developments in connection with state laws or regulations directly interpreting or enforcing securities arbitration agreements, *Securities Industry Association v. Connolly* and *Securities Industry Association v. Lewis*, state regulations applicable only to predispute securities arbitration clauses were struck down. State rules applicable to all contracts, not just arbitration clauses, would, however, seem valid under *Perry v. Thomas* and *Volt Information Sciences Inc. v. Bd. of Trustees*, especially where the contract has a choice of governing law provision, which is normally the case in broker-customer agreements. In another case where the Delaware Securities Commissioner sought to abrogate arbitration in a customer's action in which the Commissioner was allowed by statute to represent the customer, the action deprived the firm of its rights under the Federal Arbitration Act. The court found that the enforcement authority granted the Commissioner to offer rescission to investors for violation of state law cannot be used to overcome disputants' rights to arbitration.[72] It is not clear if this rationale will be applied to situations where a state takes action on behalf of an entire class of customers or where relief other than for one particular customer is involved. It may also apply to remedies sought by the SEC or an SRO. There is always the possibility that the nature of the trading intended by the parties will remove the contract from application of the Federal Arbitration Act. If the agreement relates solely to securities within a state, and the duties are created and obligations performed within the state, state and not federal law regarding predispute arbitration agreements will apply.[73]

6) CONCLUSION

The courts have been moving away from the almost automatic application of the federal preference for arbitration, principally through examination of the language of the contract. While language conforming to SEC Rule 15c2-2 may still apply in a way to find arbitration not available for federal securities claims, some courts have found that after *Rodriguez*, Rule 15c2-2 language should be construed to permit arbitration.[74] Under *Volt*, there may be a tendency to examine arbitration clauses by state contract principles for state claims.[75] This may lessen somewhat the preference for arbitration, but the Federal Arbitration Act will surely govern when federal claims are presented.

NOTES

1 465 U.S. 1 (1984). *Southland* involved the arbitration of a dispute under the California Franchise Investment Law, in which the U.S. Supreme Court reversed the California Supreme Court's finding that arbitration was not available under that state's statute.

2 *See also* Moses H. Cone Memorial Hosp. v. Mercury Constr. Corp., 460 U.S. 1 (1983).

3 482 U.S. 483 (1987).

4 Shell, *The Role of Public Law in Private Dispute Resolution: Reflections on Shearson/American Express, Inc. v. McMahon*, 26 AM. BUS. L. J. 397, 401 (1988).

5 Malcolm & Segall, *The Arbitrability of Claims Arising Under § 10(b) of the Securities and Exchange Act: Should Wilko Be Extended?*, 50 ALA. L. REV. 725, 726 (1986).

6 *See* The Judicial Improvements and Access to Justice Act of 1988, Pub. L. 100-702, which provides for expansion of the pilot court-annexed arbitration from the ten District Courts in which it has been used to another ten Districts and gives Congressional blessing to use of compulsory arbitration in cases up to $100,000.

7 Pub L. No. 94-29, 89 Stat. 97 (1975). In fact, in 1975 Congress amended the Exchange Act to permit arbitration by the SROs but under supervision of the SEC. It was clearly an action read by the Court in *McMahon* to approve of arbitration. This was despite legislative history that stated there was a "clear understanding of the conferees that this amendment did not change existing law, as articulated in *Wilko v. Swan*." H.R. REP. No. 229, 94th Cong., 1st Sess. 91, 111 (1975), reprinted in 1975 U.S.C. CONG. & ADMIN. NEWS 179, 321. Of course, Justice Blackmun disagreed with this

conclusion in his *McMahon* dissent, in which Justice Stevens seemed to concur.

The SEC *amicus* brief in *McMahon* stated:

> In light of the Commission's oversight authority under § 19 of the Exchange Act, the customer-broker arbitration agreement in this case does not effect a waiver of the protections of the Act and should therefore be enforced. The same conclusion would apply to agreements to arbitrate any federal securities-law claims where the arbitration procedures are subject to the Commission's § 19 agreement to arbitrate pursuant to SRO arbitration procedures would be enforceable, even with respect to claims arising under § 12(2) of the 1933 Act, the section under which the claim in *Wilko* arose, as long as SRO procedures are specified.

8 Congressional Report at 91.

9 *Id.* at 111.

10 *See* the discussion of Rule 15c2-2 in chapter 6.

11 Federal Arbitration Act § 3. The *Wilko* court also noted that the customer agreement further stated that the brokerage firm was relieved of all liability for all "representation or advice by you or your employees or agents regarding the purchase or sale by me of any property." *Wilko*, 346 U.S. at 434. This language, read in conjunction with the 1933 Act's emphasis on full and fair disclosure for the protection of investors, seems most damning. The decision, therefore, to find the congressional intent to put buyers of securities on the same basis as other purchasers, especially when there is inequality in bargaining position, seemed only fitting.

12 *Wilko* stated the rationale in this way: "As the protective provisions of the Securities Act require the exercise of judicial direction to fairly assure their effectiveness, it seems to us that Congress must have intended § 14 . . . to apply to waiver of judicial trial and review." *Id.* at 437.

13 15 U.S.C. § 77n (1982).

14 *Wilko*, 346 U.S. at 438.

15 Justice Jackson, concurring in the *Wilko* result, nevertheless believed that there could be a judicial remedy for the arbitrator's error in interpretation of the relevant statute. The majority had determined that without a written record, such a review would not be possible. *Wilko*, 346 U.S. at 439 (Jackson, J., concurring); *See* Justice Reed's majority opinion, *id.* at 436.

But an even more convincing statement of the right of judicial review is contained in Justice Frankfurter's dissent. Finding nothing in the record or in the facts subject to judicial notice to indicate that the industry arbitral system as practiced in New York City and supervised by the Southern District was improper, Frankfurter concluded that the plaintiffs could be given all the rights to which they are entitled under the securities laws in arbitration. He further stated at 346 U.S. 440: "Arbitrators may not disregard the law . . . they are

. . . bound to decide in accordance with the provisions of § 12(2) . . . their failure to observe this law would constitute grounds for vacating [an] award [under § 10 of the Federal Arbitration Act]."

16 Section 10 of the Federal Arbitration Act limits the district court's power in vacating an arbitration award. The 1933 Act did not provide exclusive federal court jurisdiction; claims could be brought in state courts as well. *See* the discussion of finality of awards in chapter 5.

17 *Wilko*, 346 U.S. at 438.

18 2 FED. SEC. CODE § 1725 (1980). This provision exempts the "sophisticated investor" along with the other *Wilko* exceptions. The Federal Securities Code envisions a court determining if the investor truly has the financial and legal knowledge and bargaining position to be considered "sophisticated." 2 FED. SEC. CODE § 1725(b)-(3)(c) (1980).

19 Coenen v. R.W. Pressprich & Co., 453 F.2d 1209 (2d Cir.), *cert. denied*, 406 U.S. 949 (1972).

20 417 U.S. 506 (1974).

21 *Scherk v. Alberto-Culver Co.*, 417 U.S. 506, 518 (1974), *citing Zapata*.

22 470 U.S. 213 (1985).

23 Jacobson v. Merrill Lynch, Pierce, Fenner & Smith, Inc., 797 F.2d 1197 (3d Cir. 1987).

24 *See* Robbins, *A Practitioner's Guide to Securities Dispute Resolution*, in RESOLVING SECURITIES DISPUTES 44-45 (D. Robbins ed., 1986) (emphasis original).

25 473 U.S. 614 (1985).

26 *See* Am. Safety Equip. Corp. v. J. P. Maguire & Co., 391 F.2d 821 (2d Cir. 1968).

27 Mitsubishi Motors Corp. v. Soler Chrysler-Plymouth, Inc., 473 U.S. 614, 628, 633-34.

28 800 F.2d 1032 (11th Cir. 1986).

29 *See, e.g.*, S.A. Mineracao Da Trindade-Samitri v. Utah Int'l, Inc., 576 F. Supp. 566 (S.D.N.Y. 1984) and *Jacobson, supra* note 22.

30 But the Eleventh Circuit observed that "whether a RICO claim is a 'non arbitrable federal claim' is an open question in this circuit." Greenblatt v. Drexel Burnham Lambert, Inc., 763 F.2d 1352 (11th Cir. 1985).

31 *See* Katsoris, *Punitive Damages in Securities Arbitration: The Tower of Babel Revisited*, 28 FORDHAM URB. L. J. 573 (1991). Punitive damages are discussed in chapter 10.

32 Approximately $200,000 of the $500,000 decline was due to commissions. The McMahons were successful funeral home operators who had pension plans and other savings of over $1 million when the account

representative, a fellow parishioner in their church, persuaded them to invest on the promise that she could boost their income 25%. Based on their holdings, the McMahons would be considered "sophisticated" investors under SEC 1933 Act Rule 215, which looks for $1 million net worth and income of over $200,000 in the two years prior to a purchase in private placements. This would be ridiculous, however, since the McMahon's net worth was probably not in connection with securities trading, but their business.

33 The relevant clause in *McMahon* is reproduced in chapter 6.

34 The Second Circuit found the "broad policy concerns expressed in *Wilko* about protecting investors applicable to the McMahons' claims. The court declared that churning claims contain broad public interest because churning claims deter future fraudulent conduct. It concluded that 'the similarity of the non-waiver provisions [of the 1933 and Exchange Acts] . . . as well as the strong public policy concern inherent in the securities laws and the legislative history that preceded their enactment, support the compelling need for a judicial forum."

35 *Id.* at 2357 (Stevens, J., concurring and dissenting).

36 Section 29(a) provides: "any condition, stipulation, or provision binding any person to waive compliance with any provision of this chapter or of any rule or regulation thereunder, shall be void." 15 U.S.C. § 78cc(a) (1982).

37 Justice O'Connor found that the language of the House Report on the 1975 amendments did not remotely address the subject of arbitration and may have gone to the decision in *Scherk*. Or if it did, it probably went to support other explanations other than the non-arbitrability of Exchange Act claims as the McMahons proposed. Malcolm & Segall, *supra* note 5 at 744 state:

> Pursuant to § 19 of the Exchange Act, 15 U.S.C. § 78s (1982), the SEC has long been able to exercise broad regulatory authority over securities exchanges and other self-regulatory organizations (SROs). However, in 1975, Congress amended § 19 to expand that authority to cover all SRO rules. Securities Acts Amendments of 1975, Pub. L. No. 94-29, § 19, 89 Stat. 97, 146. The Commission now believes, in light of the amendment, that it has "the power to ensure that arbitration procedures prescribed by the SROs are adequate to enforce the rights of customers against brokerage firms that are members of SROs." Brief for the Securities & Exchange Commission as Amicus Curiae at 13, Shearson/American Express, Inc. v. McMahon, No. 86-44 (U.S. filed Nov. 1986).

Several commentators have found Justice O'Connor's analysis implausible.

38 Justice O'Connor found that the express reference to the non-affect in the Congressional Conference Report of *Wilko* did not extend it beyond the

1933 Act because (1) it would do so by enacting a law such a provision if it wanted *Wilko* applicable to Exchange Act claims, and (2) the Conference Report may have wished to make clear either the 1975 amendments to the Exchange Act did not affect the 1933 Act or really the Congress was approving *Scherk*.

Section 28(b) of the Securities Exchange Act of 1934, 15 U.S.C. § 78bb(b) (1982), was amended in 1975, as follows:

> (b) Nothing in the chapter shall be construed to modify existing law with regard to the binding effect (1) on any member of or participant in any self-regulatory organization of any action taken by the authorities of such organization to settle disputes between its members or participants, (2) on any municipal securities dealer or municipal securities broker of any action taken pursuant to a procedure established by the Municipal Securities Rulemaking Board to settle disputes between municipal securities dealers and municipal securities brokers, or (3) of any action described in paragraph (1) or (2) on any person who has agreed to be bound thereby.

The Conference Report had stated:

> The Senate bill amended § 28 of the Securities Exchange Act of 1934 with respect to arbitration proceedings between self-regulatory organizations and their participants, members, or persons dealing with members or participants. The House amendment contained no comparable provision. The House receded to the Senate. It was the clear understanding of the conferees that this amendment did not change existing law, as articulated in *Wilko* . . ., concerning the effect of arbitration proceeding provisions in agreements entered into by persons dealing with members and participants of self-regulatory organizations.

H.R. CONF. REP. NO. 229, 94th Cong., 1st Sess. 111, *reprinted in* 1975 U.S.C. CONG. & ADMIN. NEWS 179, 321, 342.

39 Volt Information Sciences, Inc. v. Board of Trustees of Leland Stanford Jr. Univ., 109 U.S. 1248 (1989). Justice O'Connor did not participate and Justices Brennan and Marshall dissented on the ground that a state court decision should not "effectively nullify a vital piece of federal legislation."

40 *See, e.g.*, Osterneck v. Merrill Lynch, Pierce, Fenner & Smith Inc., 841 F.2d 508, 512-13 (3d Cir. 1988), which states that: "[a]s long as *Wilko* stands, agreements to arbitrate claims under the 1933 Securities Act will remain unenforceable, but that is the only rule *Wilko* now stands for . . . § 507 of the Pennsylvania Securities Act, when applied to preclude arbitration that falls within the Federal Arbitration Act, stands as an obstacle to the full purposes and objectives of Congress and is therefore preempted."

"After examining the factors considered by the Court in *Wilko*, the only distinction between the two claims which has any merit is that implied rights of actions are different from specifically granted statutory causes of action." Lusardi, *Enforcement of Arbitration Agreements In Securities Fraud Disputes*, 41 RUTGERS L. REV. 541, 570 (1989).

41 Rodriguez de Quijas v. Shearson/American Express, Inc., 109 S. Ct. 1917 (1989).

42 845 F.2d 1296, at 1299 (5th Cir. 1988).

43 *Id.* at 1298.

44 845 F.2d at 1299. "Similarities between the Securities Act and the Exchange Act outweigh any differences between them."

45 845 F.2d 1299.

46 109 S. Ct. at 1921.

47 *Id.* at 1919.

48 109 S.Ct. at 1920 (citing *Mitsubishi* at 628).

49 109 S. Ct. at 1920.

50 109 S.Ct. at 1923 (Stevens, J., dissenting, joined by Brennan, Marshall, and Blackmun, JJ.).

51 *Id.*

52 *See The Supreme Court 1986 Term: Leading Cases Federal Statutes and Regulations--Arbitration: Arbitrability of Securities Law and RICO Claims*, 101 HARV. L. REV. 280, 281 (1987) (reviewing *McMahon*). Finding that the court in recent years has interpreted Congressional silence inconsistently this note concludes: "[T]he court [should] avoid decisions like *McMahon*, in which a narrow majority's views on a discrete policy issue result in the reversal of a longstanding judicial statutory interpretation that Congress has left intact." *Id.* at 290. *See also* Shell, *supra* note 4, at 410-13, 432.

53 *de Quijas*, 109 S. Ct. at 1920.

54 The retroactive application of *Rodriguez de Quijas* was immediately enforced. Elliott v. Albright, 209 Cal. App. 3d 1028, 257 Cal. Rptr. 762 (1989)(found *Wilko* no longer applicable for a § 7a violation on *McMahon's* authority); Campbell v. Dominick & Dominick, Inc., 872 F.2d 358 (11th Cir. 1989)(no manifest injustice will result from retroactive application of the new § 15(b) to the Federal Arbitration Act); Coffey v. Dean Witter Reynolds, Inc., 891 F.2d 261 (10th Cir. 1989); Rubashkin v. Phillips, Appel and Waldren, Inc., 722 F. Supp. 1135 (S.D.N.Y. 1989); Hamilton v. Dean Witter Reynolds, Inc., FED. SEC. L. REP (CCH) ¶94,823 (W.D. Pa. 1989).

55 *See de Quijas*, 109 S. Ct. at 1922 (citing St. Francis College v. Al-Khazraji, 481 U.S. 604, *reh'g denied*, 483 U.S. 1011 [1987]; United States v. Schooner Peggy, 5 U.S. [1 Cranch] 103, 109 (1801); Chevron Oil v. Huson, 404 U.S. 97, 106-107 [1971][court will limit decision to prospective application in appropriate cases; otherwise retroactive application is the rule]). In Villa Garcia, the court explained its view of retroactivity: "'The new law is

applied prospectively--that is, to decisions handed down after the new law is announced--but it has retroactive effects, because for a time parties come before the courts with controversies that unfolded while the old law was the standard for their behavior.'"

See also Bradley v. Richmond School Bd., 416 U.S. 696, 715 (1973)("[E]ven where the intervening law does not explicitly recite that it is to be applied to pending cases, it is to be given recognition and effect."); King v. Drexel Burnham Lambert, Inc., 825 F.2d 68 (5th Cir. 1987); Mayaja, Inc. v. Bodkin, 824 F.2d 439 (5th Cir. 1987), *remanded*, 107 S. Ct. 2332 (1987)(*McMahon's* position on RICO was also retroactively applied); Ketchum v. Prudential-Bache Sec., Inc., 710 F. Supp. 300 (D.C. Kan. 1989); Kavouras v. Visual Prod. Sys., 680 F. Supp. 205, 207 (W.D. Pa. 1988)("*Wilko* is now untenable. The non-waiver provisions of the two Acts are substantially the same."); Aronson v. Dean Witter Reynolds, Inc., 675 F. Supp. 1324 (S.D. Fla. 1987)(1933 Act claims submitted to arbitration); Goldberg v. Drexel Burnham Lambert, Inc., 1987 LEXIS 11782 (N.D. Ill. 1987) (the court distinguished between margin account activities and cash account, where margin agreement provided for arbitration and cash did not, finding parties' intention at the time agreements were entered into could not have supposed the *McMahon* result regarding arbitration of Exchange Act claims).

56 Noble v. Drexel Burnham Lambert, Inc., 823 F.2d 849, 850 (5th Cir. 1987).

57 *Id.* at 851; *See de Quijas*, 109 S. Ct. at 1922.

58 *Volt*, 109 U.S. Ct. at 1248.

59 McCowan v. Sears, Roebuck and Co., 722 F. Supp. 1069 (S.D.N.Y. 1989).

60 703 F. Supp. 146 (D. Mass. 1988), *aff'd*, 883 F.2d 1114 (1st Cir. 1989), *cert. denied*, 110 S. Ct. 2559 (1990).

61 Fla. Stat. § 517.122 (1990).

62 751 F. Supp. 205 (S.D. Fla. 1990).

63 661 F. Supp. 1186 (E.D. Pa. 1987).

64 A written transcript was referred to by the client in determining the arbitrators had detailed evidence provided by the plaintiff.

65 926 F.2d 116 (2d Cir. 1991).

66 Employee Retirement Income Security Act, 29 U.S.C.A. §§ 1001-1461 (West 1989). Securities arbitration claims can be raised under this statute. *See* chapter 11 for discussion of this issue.

67 Ballay v. Legg Mason Wood Walker, 878 F.2d 729 (3d Cir. 1989); Gooding v. Shearson Lehman Bros., Inc., 878 F.2d 281 (9th Cir. 1989); Kayne v. Paine Webber Inc., 703 F. Supp. 1334 (N.D. Ill. 1989).

68 *See* chapter 6 for discussion of SEC Rule 15c2-2 arbitration clauses.

69 Clark v. Merrill Lynch, Pierce, Fenner & Smith, Inc., 924 F.2d 550 (4th Cir. 1991), *cert. denied*, 112 S. Ct. 74 (1991); Esposito v. Hyer, Bikson & Hinsen, Inc., 709 F. Supp. 1020 (Kan. 1988).

70 Scher v. Bear Stearns & Co., 723 F. Supp. 211 (S.D.N.Y. 1989).

71 Bird v. Shearson-Lehman/American Express, Inc., 926 F.2d 116 (2d Cir. 1991); Scher v. Bear Stearns & Co., 723 F. Supp. 2ll (S.D.N.Y. 1989); McCowan v. Dean Witter Reynolds, Inc., 682 F. Supp. 741 (S.D.N.Y. 1987); Nemes v. Merrill Lynch, Pierce, Fenner & Smith, Inc., 741 F. Supp. 657 (E.D. Mich. 1990); Clark v. Merrill Lynch Pierce Fenner & Smith, Inc., 924 F.2d 550 (4th Cir.), *cert. denied*, 112 S. Ct. 74, (1991); Majeski v. Balcor Entertainment, 740 F. Supp. 563 (E.D. Wis. 1990); Blue Gray Corporations v. Merrill Lynch, Pierce, Fenner & Smith, Inc., 921 F.2d 267 (11th Cir. 1991).

72 Olde Discount Corp. v. Tupman, 1 F.3d 202 (3d Cir. 1993).

73 Ex Parte Jones, 628 So.2d 316 (Ala. Sup. Ct. 1993).

74 Majeski v. Balcor Entertainment Co., 740 F. Supp. 563 (E.D. Wis. 1990).

75 *See* Securities Industry Ass'n v. Lewis, 751 F. Supp. 205 (S.D. Fla. 1990).

Chapter 9

FORUMS FOR SECURITIES ARBITRATION

Due to the nature of the securities industry and historical development, a number of different arbitration forums have developed.

1) SRO FORUMS--WHEN CAN THEY TAKE A CASE?

Today, the different exchanges and securities broker-dealer organizations are registered with the SEC under Sections 15A and 15B of the Securities and Exchange Act of 1934.[1] The goal of the 1934 Act is market regulation, and the Act permits the industry to develop self-regulation through organizations it establishes. These organization's rules, including those dealing with arbitration of disputes, are subject to SEC approval.

The self-regulatory organizations (SROs) include: The American Stock Exchange; The Boston Stock Exchange; The Chicago Board Options Exchange, Inc.; Cincinnati Stock Exchange; Midwest Stock Exchange; Municipal Securities Rulemaking Board; National Association of Securities Dealers, Inc.; The New York Stock Exchange, Inc.; New York Mercantile Exchange; National Futures Association; Pacific Stock Exchange; and Philadelphia Stock Exchange.

The SROs are the operators of the securities exchanges. Under their rules, their boards of directors are composed principally of industry members of the exchanges, but the Securities and Exchange Act requires "one or more" directors to be representatives of investors.[2] The SROs must provide for self-enforcement of the securities laws, SEC rules, and exchange rules.[3] In the event a person engaged in the securities business is not a member of an SRO (which is highly unlikely), that person must register and be regulated directly by the SEC as "SECO" person (SEC only regulation).

The Commodities Futures Trading Commission and its only registered organization, the National Futures Association, conduct arbitrations in connection with trading and settlements in commodity futures contracts.

Forums for arbitration of disputes have been established by the SROs, including the New York Stock, American Stock, and Chicago Board Options Exchanges, the Municipal Securities Rulemaking Board (M.S.R.B.), and the National Association of Securities Dealers (N.A.S.D.). The bulk of the arbitration is done by the N.A.S.D. and N.Y.S.E. Due to the possibility of selection of more than one forum under the provisions of most arbitration clauses prevalent in the securities industry, a number of cases have discussed the issue of forum selection. Most arbitration clauses provide that all relevant issues shall be consolidated in the same SRO forum under authority of the Federal Arbitration Act, as applied by state law. Proposals have been made by the SIA to designate one SRO-sponsored agency to administer all customer-brokerage firm disputes. This would cure the delay problem when one SRO-sponsored agency might have a backlog while another has no current cases.

Those dealing in commodities futures have for arbitration alternatives not available to stock or option traders. See section 5 of this chapter.

A) Limits on Forum Jurisdiction

Normally one considers jurisdiction in terms of compelling attendance and ability to enforce a judgment. That is not the case in arbitration where the parties have "consented" to submit the claim and be bound by the decision. Some of the SROs limit the types of claims that their arbitration facilities will accept. For example, the C.B.O.E. rules limit arbitration to only C.B.O.E. matters,[4] whereas the N.A.S.D. will take stock options and commodity claims under its broad general language. In 1991, SRO rules were amended to allow the SRO, with customer's consent, to refer a claim to the SRO where the transaction occurred.[5]

Sometimes a case will be brought in more than one forum; in this case, the arbitration clause normally provides that all relevant issues shall be consolidated in the same SRO forum. Under the authority of the Federal Arbitration Act, even claims arising in the trading of different securities, for example, stocks and commodities and options, can be combined in arbitration because conflicting awards would defeat the statute's policy of encouraging arbitration uniformity.[6] See the discussion in chapter 2.

Often the forum will be asked to arbitrate issues which might be subject to a statute of limitations or other jurisdictional questions might be raised by one of the parties. These jurisdictional questions are discussed in chapter 12.

B) Arbitration of Customer Disputes

Disputes between non-members, such as a public customer, of the SRO or exchange and members are heard by panels established by the arbitration rules of the SROs. In order to determine the forum in which a customer dispute can be heard, one must examine the contract: the arbitration clause may specify a single arbitral forum. However, most provide alternatives because the SEC prohibits customer agreements that limit a customer to one arbitration forum.[7] But, an agreement specifying arbitration solely before the N.Y.S.E. was found not to violate the Exchange Act's antiwaiver provision because the "substantial similarities" between N.Y.S.E. and N.A.S.D. arbitration procedures did not waive any substantial protection. The court felt that "the customer's ability to demand arbitration before the arbitral forum of his choice dictates that he is equally free to agree to limit his recourse to a particular forum." Again, it is essentially an issue of freedom of contract.[8]

C) Arbitration of Securities Industry Disputes

The SROs normally agree that members and persons associated with members, that is, those engaged in industry activities, including registered representatives or account representatives who deal with investors in trading, clearing brokers, and other industry parties, abide by the constitution and rules of the body. The constitutions of the exchanges require members to arbitrate all disputes of whatever nature with other members as well as customers.[9] This means that a customer may force the broker to arbitrate before one of the SRO forums.[10] Courts, even prior to *McMahon*, interpreted this to permit arbitration because § 28(b) of the Exchange Act permits the exchanges to mandate arbitration of Exchange Act claims[11] and this falls under the "sophisticated investor" exception to *Wilko*.[12]

D) Rejection of Claim by Forum

One feature of the SRO forums is that they may decide to reject a claim for arbitration even when jurisdiction is present. The AMEX constitution § 2(a) provides: "The Board of Governors may decide in any case to permit the use of the arbitration facilities of this Exchange;" C.B.O.E. Rule 18.3 permits the Exchange to decline the use of its arbitration facilities where "such dispute, claim or controversy is not a proper subject matter for arbitration": as determined by the director of arbitration, subject to appeal of this decision to the Board of Directors; N.Y.S.E. Constitution, Article XI, § 3 and Rule 604 provide that the Board may decline to permit the use of arbitration facilities and can delegate that power; and the S.I.C.A. Uniform Code of Arbitration permits the SRO to decline jurisdiction, "having due regard for the purposes of the [SRO] and the intent of this Code" and to dismiss proceedings "and refer the parties to the remedies provided by law." The forum may also find the controversy "ineligible."

E) Dismissal of Proceedings

All the SRO forums provide for the dismissal of claims by the arbitrators on their own initiative or at the request of one of the parties. If the parties jointly request dismissal, the rules provide that the arbitrators "shall" dismiss. In this instance, the parties are left to their remedies at law.[13]

F) Forum Eligibility Requirements: A Private Statute of Limitations

Rules of the various SROs create an eligibility requirement for matters submitted to arbitration. These eligibility requirements are normally stated in a language similar to a statute of limitations.[14] The question of whether a request for arbitration is timely under the terms of the contract is an issue of a private statute of limitations and a jurisdictional issue for the arbitrators rather than a court.[15] For example, N.Y.S.E. Rule 603 states that,

> No dispute, claim or controversy shall be eligible for submission to arbitration under this Code where six (6) years shall have elapsed from the occurrence or event giving rise to the act or the dispute, claim or controversy. This section shall not extend applicable statutes of limitations, nor shall it apply to any case which is directed to arbitration by a court of competent jurisdiction.[16]

The time limitation dispute is further complicated since there are three groups that can, potentially, make decisions concerning whether the six years time limitation has elapsed. These three groups are: (1) the judiciary; (2) the particular arbitration panel appointed to the hearing; and (3) the director of arbitration. There currently exists no consensus within the courts as to who has this decision-making power.

In *Castellano v. Prudential-Bache Securities, Inc. & The New York Stock Exchange, Inc.*,[17] the claimant brought an action in federal court claiming that the Director of Arbitration of the N.Y.S.E. incorrectly interpreted Rule 603 in ruling that the six (6) year limitation had elapsed, which barred the claim from arbitration. The court stated that "[u]nder the N.Y.S.E.'s construction of [its] rules, the Director of Arbitration must first determine that a claim is eligible for submission to arbitration before it may be submitted to an arbitration panel for an award."[18] The court further noted that, "[t]he law regarding judicial deference to securities exchange interpretations of its own Congressionally-approved rules is clear: absent a wrongful application of its rules or regulations, a Court should permit national securities exchanges to construe and apply their own rules."[19]

Because broad discretion is granted exchange interpretations of their own rules, the Court's inquiry is limited to whether the N.Y.S.E. was "obviously wrong" in: i) construing the requisite "occurrence or event" of Rule 603 that triggers the limitations period to be the purchase date of the relevant security; and ii) allocating responsibility to the Director of Arbitration to determine a claim's eligibility for submission to arbitration. In *Castellano*, the court looked to the plain language of Rule 603 and held that "[t]he N.Y.S.E.'s interpretation that Rule 603 . . . allocates responsibility to the Director of Arbitration to determine as a threshold matter whether a claim is eligible for submission to arbitration is reasonable."[20] The court went on

> [w]hatever (sic) may be the court's view as to whether the determination of limitations questions is merely ministerial, Rule 603 allows for the N.Y.S.E.'s interpretation. Because the court concludes . . . that the N.Y.S.E. did not act "wrongfully" in interpreting its rules, enforcing the terms of plaintiff's . . . contract leaves him without remedy.[21]

The court in *Roney & Co. v. Goren*, accepted the reasons set forth in *Paine Webber v. Hartmann*[22] as to why such a claim is not arbitrable:

> First, the plain language of Rule 603 states that after six years from the events giving rise to the dispute have elapsed, the dispute "shall [not] be eligible for submission to arbitration . . ." Second, the only other appellate court to interpret, in a similar context, language identical to Rule 603, namely that found in §15 of the Code of Arbitration Procedure of the National Association of Securities Dealers (N.A.S.D.), reached the same conclusion. In *Farnam*,[23] the Seventh Circuit also reasoned that the word "eligible" must be given its plain and literal meaning and interpreted it as absolutely barring stale disputes from reaching arbitration.[24]

After considering the cases that consider this eligibility provision of the SROs, it is clear that there exists more than one line of thought on the issue. While the majority of decisions have held that it is within the province of the judiciary to decide such issues, it is still not settled. *Castellano*, although the only case addressing Rule 603 that holds that Rule 603 determinations are within the province of the Director of Arbitration of the N.Y.S.E. to decide, gives persuasive support for allowing such decisions.

Although *Hartmann*, *Castellano*, and *Roney* are the only cases that dealt directly with Rule 603, other courts have considered parallel issues of time limitations. The *Hartmann* court distinguished Rule 603 from those arbitration clauses that set forth procedures for the arbitration proceeding. The court determined that Rule 603 was not procedural in nature, and thus concluded the time limitation issue was properly left to the courts.[25]

This procedural/substantive law dichotomy articulated in *Hartmann* can be contrasted to another Third Circuit case, *Nursing Home & Hospital Union v. Sky Vue Terrace, Inc.*,[26] which arose in the context of a dispute involving a collective bargaining agreement. In considering the issue raised that the time limit for filing for arbitration had elapsed, the court stated that "the law is clear that matters of procedural arbitrability, such as time limitations, are left for the arbitrator once the court determines as a matter of substantive law that the parties have agreed in the contract to submit the subject matter of the dispute to arbitration."[27]

In considering Rule 702 of the C.B.O.E.'s Rules of Arbitration, the Second Circuit in *Conticommodity Services Inc. v. Phillip & Lion*,[28] held that the arbitration panel had the jurisdiction to decide the issue of timeliness. Rule 702 is a one (1) year time limitation, similar to the six (6) year limitation of Rule 603. The major difference between the two rules is in the procedures that Rule 702 provides in order to initiate an arbitration proceeding. It is this difference that the *Hartmann* court drew upon in holding the Rule is not procedural in nature; therefore, it is for the courts to decide whether the six (6) year time limitation has elapsed. The court held that the existence of a valid arbitration agreement was undisputed; therefore, under § 4 of the Federal Arbitration Act,[29] the court would be required "to send the dispute to arbitration, regardless of any procedural defenses, such as untimeliness."[30] The court further noted that "[a]rbitration is intended to provided the parties to a dispute with a speedy and relatively inexpensive trial before professionals."[31]

Both *Sky Vue* and *Conticommodity Services* can be distinguished from the cases that directly consider Rule 603, but both cases offer support for allowing arbitrators to decide time limitation issues. An important factor noted in *Conticommodity Services* is that determinations of the merits of the cases are determined by professionals.[32] Under the N.Y.S.E.'s Arbitration Rules, at least one member of the arbitration panel is a member of the securities industry; therefore, such a person is able to consider complex securities cases.[33] Such expertise may potentially be required to determine when the time limitation has elapsed. Since the "occurrence or event giving rise to . . . the controversy" under Rule 603 may not be easily determined, such input from a securities industry professional may prove to be quite useful.

A letter written by William J. Fitzpatrick of the Securities Industry Association stated that:

> The purpose of (Rule 603) was to deny access to arbitration for any claim based on a transaction which was over six years old. There is a basic pragmatic equitable reason not to accept jurisdiction in arbitrations involving transactions which are over six years old. This was understood by all the members of S.I.C.A., at that time.[34]

His letter further stated:

> Section 4 [of the Uniform Code of Arbitration] is not a statute of limitation. It is an eligibility rule and SRO's have no authority to accept an arbitration based upon events which took place more than six years before the request to arbitrate. *Arbitrators have no authority in these cases.* (emphasis added). Any submission to arbitrators of a matter which is over six years old can obviously result in a motion to vacate since the arbitrators are plainly without authority to hear it.[35]

Regarding the eligibility rules of the SROs, the absence of uniformity can be utilized as a tactical tool. Whether the six year time limitation of eligibility under the SRO rules has in fact elapsed is often open to interpretation. Considering the time bar created by these rules, different solutions may be reached depending upon which forum is chosen to lodge a dispute regarding the time limitation. It is clear, however, that the right to arbitration can be conditioned by the forum. If the forum refuses to take the matter, then the claimant is left to redress wherever she can find it: namely, in the court system. This was what the arbitration agreement attempted to avoid.

A question may arise regarding tolling of the limitations period, usually during the time a party was under a disability such as incapacity due to physical condition or mental defect, or drugs, or alcohol. In a decision regarding N.A.S.D. Code § 15, the court found it not to be a statute of limitations and thus could not be tolled for the period of disability.[36] Further, the court noted the only way to defeat the eligibility bar would have been for the party to have submitted to court for an order compelling arbitration, but the claimants did not do so and voluntarily submitted to N.A.S.D. arbitration, with the result that the claim was ineligible.[37] Charges of fraudulent concealment or misrepresentation will not toll the eligibility period.[38]

Recent court decisions have continued to consider the eligibility rules. In *Merrill Lynch & Co., Inc. v. Shook*,[39] the court found authority to interpret the eligibility provision citing federal precedent in *Paine Webber v. Hartmann*,[40] *Prudential Bache v. Archard*,[41] and *Merrill Lynch v. DeChaine*,[42] because the courts consistently hold that N.Y.S.E. Rule 603 and its equivalents in the other SROs go to the very power of the arbitration itself and must be satisfied before the claim can be arbitrable. *Prudential Securities, Inc. v. Kronman*,[43] found that Prudential attempts to stay the arbitration on time-bar grounds were ineffective and ordered all claims to arbitration under both federal and state law. New York CPLR 7502 and 7503, despite providing for a court to stay arbitration of untimely claims, states that if there are some claims which pass muster, the whole matter is submitted to arbitration (citing *Paver & Wildfoerster v. Catholic H.S. Ass'n of N.Y.*,[44] in which the Court of Appeals held that the courts should not, in the name of a time-bar issue under CPLR, bind the case to the technical rules of law that arbitration is designed to avoid; only if under no circumstances could the facts survive a time bar should the arbitration be barred).

The whipsaw nature of the statute of limitations is also represented in *Shearson Lehman Brothers, Inc. v. Rinzler*,[45] case where the court denied a stay of arbitration because the broker had earlier requested arbitration stating: "The reason for the lack of cases seeking stays by applicants who previously moved to compel arbitration is, perhaps, that no one has yet had the gall to employ this whipsaw."[46]

But in *Nomura Securities Int'l v. Carvolth*,[47] the court held that the claims were clearly arbitrable under the industry standard U-4 signed by the broker, whereby he agreed to arbitration of "any dispute, claim or controversy that may arise between me and my firm." The court found no jurisdiction over the matter and any statute of limitations must be determined by the arbitrators.

In *Paine Webber, Inc. v. Hall*,[48] the brokerage firm attempted to have the court rule on the statute of limitations period, but the court found that federal precedents "have consistently held that under the Federal Arbitration Act, the determination of all time-bar defenses--including the statute of limitations--is to be made by the arbitrators, not the courts."

The S.I.C.A. has recommended a rule change regarding eligibility. The new rule will place sole authority for promptly determining eligibility in the director of arbitration, but preserve the right of the party to proceed in court if eligibility is denied. While no guides will appear in the new rule, some guidelines were proposed, such as that wrongful conduct was felt to be necessary within the six-year period, but fraudulent concealment and continuing representations (continuous fraud) are examples of allegations that will meet the rule's requirements.[49]

In a case requesting vacatur of an award due to the arbitrator's failure to explain in its finding that claims were not time barred on the basis that it was "in manifest disregard of the law," *Trustees of Lawrence Academy v. Merrill Lynch Pierce Fenner & Smith, Inc.*,[50] found that the arbitrators are not required to make formal findings of fact or give reasons for the award. An argument at the hearing between counsel and one of the arbitrators on the eligibility issue is not sufficient to establish manifest disregard under § 10 and vacatur was denied.

A recommendation has been made that the letter of the director of arbitration or dismissal by arbitrators indicate that a determination of ineligibility is based on scope of arbitration under SRO rules and does not affect the parties right to proceed on the same claims in court.[51] This is not the normal language and should be suggested to the director or arbitrators when deciding an eligibility defense. The practical effect of the new S.I.C.A. proposal may be identical. This comports with the rules on dismissal of a case and leaves the parties to "the remedies provided by law."[52]

2) DEVELOPMENT OF SRO PROCEDURE

Before the 1975 Securities and Exchange Act amendments giving the SEC oversight authority over the arbitration activities of the SROs, the different arbitration forums applied differing rules of procedure. In 1976, as a result of SEC action pursuant to this Congressional mandate for the examination of the feasibility of developing a "uniform system of dispute grievance procedures for the adjudication of small claims,"[53] and a staff recommendation for adoption of new procedures and creation of an independent entity to provide arbitration facilities in the securities industry, the SROs proposed an industry task force to examine arbitration.

Another justification for the creation of the industry task force was that the volume of transactions created the possibility of generating so many disputes that the industry had to develop a private forum to resolve them in order to avoid tying up vast sums of working capital in protracted litigation. Initially, the task force was to consider development of a uniform arbitration code to establish a more efficient mechanism for resolving investor disputes, especially those involving small sums of money.[54]

A) S.I.C.A. and the Uniform Code of Arbitration

The 1976 task force evolved into the Securities Industry Conference on Arbitration (S.I.C.A.), established in April 1977. The S.I.C.A. developed simplified arbitration procedures for resolution of small claims,[55] which were the SEC's announced concern. But in 1978 the S.I.C.A. went on to develop, in many cases from the already existing procedures, the Uniform Code of Arbitration ("Uniform Code"), which was adopted after SEC approval by all the SROs in 1979 and 1980.[56] The S.I.C.A. has also prepared information concerning small claim filings and a booklet on procedures. As noted in the above discussion of SRO eligibility requirements for bringing claims, the S.I.C.A. continues to propose new arbitration rules.[57]

B) Small Claims

The small claim rules and procedures are discussed in chapter 11. By 1988 over 10,000 claims had been submitted to SRO under the small claims procedures or the Uniform Code.

C) Large and Complex Claims

Typically, complex actions such as class actions with numerous parties and complicated issues have not been heard in SRO arbitrations. But the SEC has encouraged development of new rules regarding large and complex arbitrations, as a result of which these types of claims are now being met with greater receptivity by the SROs. See the chapter 11 discussion.

The N.A.S.D. has recently announced that it is considering adoption of special arbitration procedures for complex securities claims totaling more than $1 million. These procedures will involve more conferences among the parties; discovery rules covering records and data which must be shared between the parties; and will be heard by special panels of well-qualified arbitrators.

3) AMERICAN ARBITRATION ASSOCIATION

The American Arbitration Association (AAA) is a non-profit national organization with 35 offices and more than 600 employees. By 1992 it had arbitrated one million claims, mainly in construction and labor matters. It does not handle many securities claims. In 1990 it administered over 60,000 claims including 381 securities cases involving claims of $84 million (16 percent of which were brought by brokers); in 1991, 586 securities claims for $329 million (20 percent brought by brokers); and in 1992, 485 claims of $166 million. In the first eight months of 1993, cases increased 35%. The increase is due in part to the N.Y.S.E., N.A.S.D. and "AAA window" filings, but is more likely due to more publicity regarding the AAA as a result of the new rules as well as the program for large and complex cases. Due to its procedures, which differ in several respects from the Uniform Code (see chapter 11), and which were revised in May 1993 by a Task Force consisting of members of the securities industry, customer's attorneys, and other neutral parties, many prefer AAA arbitration.[58]

The AAA, unlike the SROs, is not industry subsidized. As a result, arbitration fees are higher too. As of November 1, 1993, AAA fees in connection with commercial arbitrations increased. The increase was not reflected in securities arbitrations, as the advisory committees concerned with the Securities Arbitration Rules had not met to consider increases, but it is likely that the securities fees will continue to be comparable to those in commercial arbitration. For example, a $300 fee went to $500 and the other fees were similarly increased. One interested in filing an AAA claim should consult the local AAA office for the most recent fee schedule.

A) AAA Offices

The major offices are listed on the last page of Appendix F, AAA SECURITIES ARBITRATION RULES. In 1991 most AAA securities arbitrations occurred in Miami, New York, Charlotte, Orlando and San Francisco.

B) American Arbitration Association Securities Arbitration Rules

The AAA Securities Arbitration Rules were initially adopted in 1989 as a result of consultation with the securities industry, and amended by a 1991 Task Force that recommended changes adopted in 1993. They provide for expedited hearings, if the amount in controversy is less than $25,000, and encourage mediation where the mediator does not have the power to make a binding decision or award, but assists settlement negotiations between the parties under the AAA Commercial Mediation Rules. Otherwise, the rules are similar in procedure and panel composition to the other securities arbitration forums discussed above.

One of the major advantages of AAA arbitration is that the AAA does not impose arbitrators on the parties. A list of potential arbitrators is furnished, from whom the parties may strike those whom they do not want to sit. Typically, the AAA list is not skewed in favor of the industry with which the arbitration is concerned. If the parties desire, however, they may choose an arbitrator with industry expertise and experience. AAA arbitrators are not employees of the AAA, and they usually serve *pro bono* for the first day of a hearing. Thereafter they are paid by the parties, on a *per diem* basis, through assessment by the AAA.[59]

A 1983 report studying 1,500 contract and tort cases (including 147 AAA cases) in five federal judicial districts,[60] which were roughly divided equally between federal and state courts, made some startling discoveries:

- Only about 5 percent of court cases are fully litigated. Over 50 percent of AAA arbitrations are fully adjudicated.
- Caseload and administrative factors affect the speed of adjudication in both the courts and AAA arbitrations, but "[o]verall, the AAA is not slower than the courts, and it is usually faster."
- AAA arbitration is least expensive for small cases, but most expensive for cases in which over $25,000 is at controversy. The federal courts are least expensive for cases in the $5,000 to $10,000 range. State courts are least expensive in cases in which between $10,000 and $25,000 is at stake.

These results will probably extend to AAA securities arbitrations as well. As a result the authors conclude: "One does not save money by going to the AAA. However, given that the AAA is not substantially more expensive than the courts, it is likely that the cost of full adjudication in the AAA is less than the cost of full adjudication in the courts."

C) AAA Large, Complex Cases Program

In 1992 the AAA adopted supplemental procedures to respond to the challenges of large and complex cases for claims of at least $1 million--exclusive of interest, costs, and fees. The special rules under this program: (1) select arbitrators with the special experience, expertise, and availability for these cases; (2) encourage mediation; (3) provide for administration by trained, senior AAA staff; and (4) are governed as determined by the rules, parties agreement, or other AAA rules to the extent not inconsistent with the Supplementary Procedures. Normally, the parties will contract for this program, although court-ordered arbitration may also make it applicable to the dispute. In the first eight months of 1993, there were 21 securities claims of more than $1 million filed with the AAA.

D) AAA Arbitration Through The AMEX Window

One of the interesting features of SRO arbitrations is the provision in the American Stock Exchange Constitution[61] that states, "(c) if any of the parties to a controversy is a customer, the customer may elect to arbitrate before the American Arbitration Association in the City of New York, unless the customer has expressly agreed, in writing, to submit only to the arbitration procedure of the Exchange."

Plaintiff's attorneys have argued that because the AAA is an available arbitral forum through this provision of the AMEX Constitution, the parties did not enter into an arbitration agreement providing that their disputes would be resolved only by AMEX arbitration. Attorneys for brokerage firms, on the other hand, argue that the AMEX Constitution does not provide authority for plaintiffs to resolve their claims at the AAA, and it is an available forum only if designated in the parties' arbitration agreement.

The practice under the arbitration clause of the customer agreement is to permit a very limited time for the customer to elect the forum--for example, 5 to 10 days after service of a demand for arbitration.[62] If the election is not made within that relatively short time, the brokerage firm can file a notice of election, usually of an SRO forum.[63] Consequently, the AMEX Window election of AAA forum may be more of form than substance in practice. Two commentators noted:

> It seems inconceivable that the AMEX, an SRO, could divest itself of jurisdiction over its members in favor of the AAA, a non-SRO, which does not utilize the Uniform Code of Arbitration employed by all SRO arbitral forums and is not overseen by the SEC. This is especially so when the parties' arbitration agreement designates solely SRO arbitral forums and does not mention the AAA. The Director of Arbitration of

> the AMEX . . . in deposition testimony . . . has stated that the AMEX interprets Article VIII, § 2(c) of its Constitution as *not* providing authority for a public customer to commence an arbitration at the AAA. Notwithstanding the AMEX's interpretation, the AAA has stated that it will accept cases brought through the AMEX Window unless it is presented with a court order stating it has no jurisdiction.[64]

Where a customer signed customer agreements for option and margin trading that provided for arbitration of all disputes "in accordance with the rules" of any of three exchanges, the customer was permitted to select the AAA under the AMEX window.[65] The Court felt that the contract provision should be construed against the party which drafted it--in this case the brokerage firm. Since the AMEX was one of the exchanges listed in the customer agreement and it provided for AAA selection, the Court found that this did not call for arbitration "only" before one of the exchanges versus under the "rules of" any exchange listed. The New York Court of Appeals decision differs from several federal courts. In a Second Circuit opinion a week after *Cowan & Co. v. Anderson*, the court held that a provision requiring arbitration before an "arbitration facility provided by" AMEX was remanded to determine if arbitration before the AAA was precluded.[66]

E) New York Rejects The AMEX Window

The SEC and SRO requirements after May 1989 prohibit a brokerage firm from limiting or contradicting SRO rules in a customer agreement, which seems to permit the AMEX-AAA election by the customer. But Southern District of New York cases[67] have found that the AMEX Constitution provision was not a "rule" that would create another arbitration forum in addition to the ones specified in the customer agreement and" closed" the AMEX window, therefore an AAA election was not permitted as it would vary the terms of the customer contract.[68] Of course, since most brokerage customer agreements specify New York law as governing, the effects of these decisions is to limit the access to the AAA forum via the "AMEX window."

The AMEX Window was also closed for customers under a recent Eleventh Circuit opinion if they agreed to arbitrate disputes with a brokerage firm "before" and/or "in accordance with the rules of the N.Y.S.E., AMEX or N.A.S.D.[69] These customers could not compel the firm to arbitrate before the AAA under the AMEX constitutional provisions. The Court noted, however, that a more specific customer agreement can supersede the AMEX Window by providing that the proceedings can be brought other than under "rules" of the AMEX.

F) Present Status of the AMEX Window

Depending on the wording of the arbitration clause, the AAA window may still be open if it refers to the AMEX procedures or forums, but apparently not if the reference is to AMEX "rules," as is the usual case.

To some extent, the AAA Window controversy was lessened by an agreement in 1991 between several large brokerage firms and the AAA whereby on a case-by-case basis the firms agreed to voluntarily submit to AAA arbitration for a one year trial period, even though the AAA was not included as a possible forum in the predispute arbitration agreements. Consent of the customer *and* the firm is required, however.[70]

G) Location

Another question presented by the AAA Window is the location of the arbitration. The parties by contract can limit the arbitration to a particular location. The AMEX Constitution provision provides that a customer may "elect to arbitrate any dispute before the American Arbitration Association in the City of New York."[71] Claimants have often sought to arbitrate at one of the AAA locations outside the City. Some courts have held that arbitration must be in New York City,[72] while the AAA and other cases have taken the position that the reference is only to the fact that the AAA is headquartered in New York City.[73] To require only New York City hearings in AAA cases will be a considerable disadvantage to nationwide forums now being provided by the SRO's and will be an additional financial burden for customers and their attorneys. The AAA has taken the position that the reference to New York City only refers to the main office of the AAA. Otherwise, the AAA normally hears cases all over the country. The AMEX has filed a proposed constitutional amendment with the SEC to provide that the AAA reference is without reference to location.

4) SRO ARBITRATION FORUMS

A) Names And Addresses

The American Stock Exchange
86 Trinity Place
New York, NY 10006
Tel: (212) 306-1000

The Boston Stock Exchange
One Boston Place
Boston, MA 02108
Tel: (617) 723-9500

The Chicago Board Options Exchg. Inc.
LaSalle at Van Buren
Chicago, IL 60605
Tel: (312) 786-5600

Cincinnati Stock Exchange
205 Dixie Terminal Building
Cincinnati, OH 56202
Tel: (513) 621-1410

Midwest Stock Exchange
440 So. LaSalle Street
Chicago, IL 60605
Tel: (312) 663-2222

Municipal Securities Rulemaking
1640 King Street
Suite 300
Alexandria, VA 22314
Tel: (202) 223-9503

National Association of Securities
Dealers, Inc.
33 Whitehall Street
New York, NY 10006
Tel: (212) 858-4400

New York Mercantile Exchange
4 World Trade Center
New York, NY 10048
Tel: (212) 938-2222

The New York Stock Exchange, Inc.
11 Wall Street
New York, NY 10006
Tel: (212) 656-3000

Pacific Stock Exchange
301 Pine Street
San Francisco, CA 94104
Tel: (415) 393-4000

Philadelphia Stock Exchange
1900 Market Street
Philadelphia, PA 19103
Tel: (215) 496-5000

The four major industry-sponsored forums for securities arbitration are the New York Stock Exchange, American Stock Exchange, Chicago Board of Options Exchange, and the National Association of Securities Dealers. Each has its own rules and regulations concerning the operation of arbitration facilities, and a staff to assist in the arbitration of a disputes, all of which are discussed in relation to the procedures of bringing a claim and the hearing process in succeeding chapters. The other SRO arbitration facilities are not widely used and will not be discussed in this book. One may obtain information directly from the SRO on their arbitration procedures. One of the major differences in these panels is the composition of the arbitration panels, which is discussed in chapter 11.

B) National Association of Securities Dealers

The Board of Governors, elected by the membership of the N.A.S.D., appoints the National Arbitration Committee and Chairperson.[74] The National Committee is composed of public and securities persons, some of whom are not members. It sets the policy for arbitration staff. The Director of Arbitration is appointed by the Board of Governors, is responsible for the National Committee, and is charged with performance of all administrative duties in connection with arbitration. The Director composes panels from which persons the arbitrators are selected.[75]

i) Small Claims Procedures. The N.A.S.D. has adopted the $10,000 small claims cut-off, similar to the other SROs. For claims under that amount, arbitration is before one arbitrator,[76] but if more than that amount, the claim is heard by three to five arbitrators unless the parties agree to one.[77]

ii) Non-Member Disputes. Customer claims are resolved in arbitration under the Uniform Code of Arbitration.

iii) Member Disputes. Part II of the N.A.S.D. Code of Arbitration Procedure provides for industry and clearing controversies.[78] Members, associated persons, pledgees, participants, and other persons acting under the rules of a clearing organization that has elected to use the N.A.S.D. arbitration facilities, with claims of less than $10,000 are normally resolved by a panel of industry arbitrators, not less than one, that only reviews the submissions and does not take oral testimony or argument. For claims over $10,000 but not exceeding $30,000, one arbitrator is usual. Claims over $30,000 have three arbitrators. All panels consist of industry arbitrators only for member disputes.

C) New York Stock Exchange

The constitution of the N.Y.S.E. provides that the Board of Governors, elected by the members, can promulgate rules for arbitration and that the Chairman of the Board appoint a Director of Arbitration.[79] The Director of Arbitration is appointed by the Chairman of the Board. He is assisted by arbitration counsel and staff employees to administer the N.Y.S.E. arbitration program.

The Board has adopted rules, including the Uniform S.I.C.A. rules. The power to change the constitution rests in the members of the N.Y.S.E., but the Board can make, repeal, and change the rules. Rule 633 provides that the Chairman of the Board of Governors appoints the Board of Arbitration, subject to Board approval. The members of the Board of Arbitration can not be members of the Board of the N.Y.S.E., but can be present and former members, allied members, and officers of member companies.

i) Small Claims Procedures. The N.Y.S.E. small claims procedures are used for claims less than $10,000. These procedures are discussed in chapter 11.

ii) Non-member Disputes. A claim of less than $10,000 is heard under the small claims procedures discussed in chapter 11. Claims over

$10,000 are handled by three to five arbitrators, a majority of which are chosen from the non-securities, public panel unless the non-member has requested all securities industry panel arbitrators.

iii) Member Disputes. Members, allied members, member firms, and member corporations with claims of $10,000 or less are heard by one member of the Board of Arbitration unless non-members are also parties to the dispute; if over $10,000 in controversy, the hearing is before three to five arbitrators.

D) American Stock Exchange

The Board of Governors of the Exchange, elected by the members, have adopted the arbitration rules. The AMEX Chairman appoints two panels of arbitrators: Group 1 consists of members and associated persons (the securities industry panel), and Group 2 are non-members not in the securities business (the private panel).[80] The Chairman may designate an officer or employee of the Exchange as Director of Arbitration, and an Assistant Director and these persons are charged by Rule 600 with the duty of performing all ministerial duties in connection with matters submitted for arbitration.

i) Small Claims Procedures. Rule 623 provides for hearing of member and non-member disputes under $10,000 by a single arbitrator selected from Group 1.

ii) Non-member Disputes. Rule 602 provides for not less than three arbitrators for non-member claims of more than $10,000, the majority of which shall be from Group 2 unless the public customer has requested a majority of arbitrators from Group 1.

iii) Member Disputes. Rule 602(b) provides that arbitrations between members, member organizations, partners thereof or officers, where the amount in controversy is more than $10,000, shall be heard by not less than three arbitrators, all of whom are selected from Group 1.

E) Chicago Board Options Exchange

The Board of Directors, elected by the membership, governs the arbitration process not through the constitution of the C.B.O.E., but through the General Rules of the Exchange.[81] The chair of the Executive Committee appoints an Arbitration Committee and its chairperson, subject to Board approval.[82] There is no rule regarding the appointment of a director of arbitration.

i) Small Claims Procedures. The C.B.O.E. has no small claims procedures.

ii) Non-member Disputes. C.B.O.E. Rule 18.1 provides that any matter arising "out of the Exchange business of such member or a person associated with such member shall, at the request of the non-member and the approval of the Exchange's Director of Arbitration, be submitted for arbitration."

iii) Member Disputes. Members and associated person's disputes are resolved by panels consisting of not less than three members of the Arbitration committee in accord with the Uniform Code (Rules 18.5 to 18.33) as well as Rule 18.34 (payment for floor brokerage services).

F) Other SROs

The typical predispute arbitration agreement permits the use of the named forums, so in most cases a party has the option where to proceed. The type of trading may permit the choice of other forums. 1992 revisions to the Uniform Code, however, permit the transfer of the case to the forum where the transaction occurred, but requires the customer's consent.[83] The reader should review the rules of these exchanges and organizations, several of which are include in the Appendixes.

5) COMMODITIES ARBITRATION

Under Commodity Futures Trading Commission (CFTC) rules, arbitration of a customer claim arising as a result of commodity futures contracts trading or settlement of such contracts rules can be brought: (1) on the exchange where the transaction occurred or would have occurred; (2) before a registered futures association, that is, the National Futures Association (N.F.A.), which is the only registered commodities trading organization; or (3) at least one other organization that will ensure the customer an opportunity to select the hearing venues and composition of panel. However, § 14 of the Commodity Exchange Act[84] permits a customer to bypass arbitration and file a reparations claim directly with the Commission.

The CFTC Rules Relating to Reparation Proceedings[85] and N.F.A. arbitration procedures are examined in the chapter 12 discussion on bringing a claim.

Names and Addresses for Commodity Arbitration:

Commodity Futures Trading Commission
2033 K Street
Washington, D.C. 20581
Tel: (202) 254-6387

National Futures Association, Inc.
200 W. Madison Street
Chicago, IL 60606-3447
Tel: (312) 781-1300

6) OTHER ARBITRATION FORUMS

In addition to the SRO and AAA tribunals, parties may submit their disputes to arbitration in a number of other places. These include the New York and other chambers of commerce arbitration departments, better business bureaus, trade associations, and other groups.[86] It is beyond the scope of this book to discuss all arbitration forums possible: besides, in the securities industry, the customer agreement or requirement for brokerage firm consent in the absence of an agreement will result in SRO or AAA forum selection in almost all cases. There is no reason to permit the selection of an arbitration forum to sink to "forum shopping."[87] For this reason, the uniformity of procedural rules in the SROs, as evidenced by the Uniform Code, and the similar AAA Rules, is desirable.

7) PRIVATE ALTERNATIVE DISPUTE RESOLUTION

It is beyond the scope of this article to discuss the burgeoning industry now developing in alternative dispute resolution. Technically, there is no requirement under the Federal Arbitration Act or Uniform Law that arbitrations need to be conducted by any particular organization. Non-profits, such as the AAA, coexist with industry-sponsored forums, such as the SROs in the securities industry. But any organization can arbitrate disputes. They are now more than 50 profit and not-for-profit corporations specializing in private dispute resolutions, with names like United States Arbitration & Mediation, Judicial Arbitration & Mediation, and Judicate, Inc. Most have been formed in response to the crowded court dockets and high costs of litigation. Some use retired judges exclusively. Considering the present state of judicial salaries and the fact that such firms charge fees of $120 to $250 an hour, and more, for presiding over these private trials, one questions if this development is good for the judicial system. Several commentators have suggested that premature retirements of experienced and able judges are in response to these economic considerations, with the resulting decline in the quality of the judiciary.

8) CONCLUSION: PICK THE FORUM CAREFULLY

Due to the number of arbitration forms available to resolve disputes; the active encouragement of both state and federal laws for persons to use alternatives to litigation; and the nature of the securities disputes, for example, often complicated financial transactions with layers of law and business practice, the customer may be correct in choosing to arbitrate. In most cases, moreover, she will be required to arbitrate due to the predispute arbitration terms of the customer agreement. Once it is concluded that arbitration is either by choice or by necessity, the next question is obviously in which of these forums should the case be brought. For the industry member or employee, there is no choice to arbitrate or not; it is required by the terms of employment or SRO membership.

As discussed in chapter 11, picking the forum is one of the first strategy issues in preparing the case.

NOTES

1 15 U.S.C. § 78(o) *et seq.*

2 15 U.S.C. § 78(f)3.

3 15 U.S.C. § 78(f)(b)6.

4 C.B.O.E. Rule 18.1(b).

5 *See* S.I.C.A. Uniform Code § 1(c); N.Y.S.E. Rule 600(c).

6 State laws would also compel consolidation. *See* Bock v. Drexel Burnham Lambert, Inc., 143 Misc. 2d 542, 541 N.Y.S. 2d 172 (N.Y. 1989) (consolidation is permissible where evidence and testimony are common to several arbitration proceedings under the authority of the Federal Arbitration Act); Kanuth v. Prescott, Ball & Turben, Inc., FED. SEC. L. REP. (CCH) ¶ 94,430, (D. D.C. May 16, 1989) (employee initiated arbitrations before N.A.S.D. and N.Y.S.E. ordered consolidated before N.A.S.D. experience a real risk of conflicting awards that would "flout the strong federal policy encouraging arbitration.").

7 *See* the recommended form of arbitration clause in chapter 3.

8 Roney & Co. v. Goren, 875 F.2d 1218 (E.D. 1989).

9 *See* New York Stock Exchange, Inc., Const., Art. VIII, Secs. 1 and 5, N.Y.S.E. Rule 347 *New York Stock Exchange Const. & Rules*, N.Y.S.E. MANUAL (CCH).

10 In Scobee Combs Funeral Home, Inc. v. E.F. Hutton & Co., Inc., 711 F. Supp. 605 (D.C.S. Fla. 1989), the plaintiff relied on § 12(a) of the N.A.S.D. arbitration code which provided for arbitration on customer's demand or as provided in the written agreement; this section made the customer a third-party beneficiary of the firm's membership in the N.A.S.D..

11 15 U.S.C. § 78bb(b) (1982).

12 No similar provision was inserted for 1933 Act claims.

13 *See* chapter 3. One must always bear in mind the applicable statutes of limitations, as a problem could result if the dismissal caused the action to fall as time barred. *See* the chapter 12 discussion.

14 The statute of limitations defense to arbitration is discussed in chapter 12 under Motions to Dismiss.

15 Merrill Lynch, Pierce, Fenner & Smith v. Ainsworth, 630 So.2d 1145 (S.D. Fla. 1993). But see 1994 New York cases.

16 N.Y.S.E. Rule 603. This is the same as N.A.S.D. § 15 and S.I.C.A. Uniform Code § 4. There is no comparable AAA provision, but state law will provide a statute of limitations, usually there period applicable to contracts. *See* N.Y. CPLR 213 discussed in chapter 12.

17 FED. SEC. L. REP. (CCH) ¶95,321 (S.D.N.Y. 6/19/90).

18 *Id.* at 96,535. *See* Capos v. Mid-American Bank of Chicago, 581 F.2d 676. *In accord*, Roney and Company v. Sam Kassab; Akram Semaan, LEXIS 32429 (6th Cir. 1992).

19 Castellano, *supra* note 16, at ¶96,535.

20 *Id.* at ¶96,536.

21 *Id.*

22 Paine Webber v. Hartmann, 921 F.2d 507 (3d Cir. 1990).

23 Paine Webber v. Farnam, 870 F.2d 1286 (7th Cir. 1989).

24 Roney, *supra* note 17, at 12-13.

25 Hartmann, 921 F.2d at 513-514.

26 759 F.2d 1094 (3d Cir. 1985).

27 *Id.* at 1097.

28 613 F.2d 1222 (2d Cir. 1980). *Accord*, Wylie v. Investment Management and Research Inc., FED. SEC. L. REP. (CCH) ¶ 98,009 (Fl. Ct. App. 1994), which found that the time limitation for submission under forum rules is a procedural bar and thus for the arbitrators to decide under the Supreme Court's admonition that all doubts are to be resolved in favor of arbitration.

29 9 U.S.C. § 4.

30 Conticommodity Services, 613 F.2d at 1225.

31 *Id.* at 1224, citing Scherk v. Alberto-Culver Co., 417 U.S. 506, 510-511 (1974).

32. *Id.*

33. N.Y.S.E. Rule 607.

34. Letter to S.I.C.A., from William J. Fitzpatrick of the Securities Industry Association, dated September 18, 1991.

35 *Id. See also*, S.I.C.A. minutes, October 1, 1991, page 3, 7 (Discussion of S.I.C.A. Uniform Code § 4--Time Limitations Upon Submission).

36 See chapter 12 discussion of eligibility rules.

37 Edward D. Jones & Co., v. Sorrells, 957 F.2d 509 (7th Cir. 1992).

38 Merrill Lynch & Co., Inc. v. Shook, 5 SEC. ARB. COMM. 10, 1993 (N.Y. Cty. Sup. Ct. 1993); Prudential Bache v. Archard, 4 SEC ARB. COMM. 10 (1992); Merrill Lynch v. DeChaine, 5 SEC. ARB. COMM. 8 (1993).

39 18600/92 (N.Y. Cty. Sup. Ct. 1993), 5 SEC. ARB. COMM. 10 (Aug. 1993).

40 4 SEC. ARB. COMM. 3 (1992).

41 4 SEC. ARB. COMM. 10 (1992).

42 5 SEC. ARB. COMM. 8 (1992).

43 5 SEC. ARB. COMM. 11-12 (S.D.N.Y. 1993).

44 38 N.Y. 2d 669 (1976).

45 594 N.Y.S. 2d 593 (1993).

46 *Id.* at 596.

47 N.Y.L.J. 30:5 (March 2, 1993) (N.Y. Sup. Ct. 1993). *Accord,* Prudential Securities, Inc. v. American List Counsel, Inc. Profit Sharing Plan, 1993 WL 26735 (S.D.N.Y. 1993).

48 FED. SEC. L. REP. (CCH) ¶97,697 (Fla. Cir. Ct. 1993).

49 *See* 5 SEC. ARB. COMM. 9, 17 (1993).

50 FED. SEC. L. REP. ¶ 97,726 (D.C.N.H. 1993).

51 *See* 4 SEC. ARB. COMM. 4 (May 1992).

52 *See* Rejection of Claim by Forum, above.

53 *See* Sec. Exchg. Act Rel. No. 34-12,528 (June 9, 1976), discussed in chapter 8.

54 *See* Sec. Exchg. Act Rel. No 34-12,974 (Nov. 15, 1976).

55 Initially small claims were of $2,500 or less; this has been raised in increments over the years to where small claims are now $10,000 or less. *See* N.A.S.D. Code § 13.

56 *See* the Third, Fourth, and Fifth Reports of the Securities Industry Conference on Arbitration to the Securities and Exchange Commission (Jan. 31, 1980, Nov. 1984, and April 1986, respectively).

57 *See* chapter 17 discussion of new proposals being made for SRO arbitration rules.

58 The AAA Securities Arbitration Rules are contained in Appendix E. AAA panels of arbitrators are less industry-connected than SROs; AAA procedures were used as a model for the SRO rule reforms recently; the SEC has urged the SROs to improve arbitration by adopting the AAA procedures; and, perhaps most significantly, statistics indicate the customer prevails more in AAA than SRO arbitrations. (*See* chapter 10).

59 The national *per diem* is $400 for the first two days of hearings and thereafter as agreed.

60 *See* The Third, Fourth, and Fifth Reports of the Securities Industry Conference on Arbitration to the Securities and Exchange Commission (Jan. 31, 1980, Nov. 1984, and April 1986, respectively).

61 American Stock Exchange, Inc., Constitution Article VIII, ¶ 9,063, § 2(c). AM. STOCK EX. GUIDE (CCH) ¶ 9,063.

62 *See*, for example, the clause in the customer agreements and discussion in chapter 6.

63 There is also a short period to challenge arbitration--20 days after service of notice to arbitrate under N.Y. CPLR 7503(c).

64 Krebsbach & Friedman, *Prentice Hall Law & Business: Securities Arbitration*, in SECURITIES ARBITRATION UPDATE 24 (M. Fitterman & T. Krebsbach eds., 1989) (citations omitted). *But see* Cowen & Co. v. Anderson, N.Y.L.J. Apr. 4, 1989, at 22, col. 4 (N.Y. Sup. Ct. Mar. 28, 1989), *aff'd*, 546 N.Y.S. 2d 621 (N.Y. App. Div. 1989).

65 Cowen & Co. v. Anderson, 76 N.Y. 2d 318, 559 N.Y.S. 2d 225 (1990).

66 Formica v. Malone Associates, 907 F.2d 397 (1990).

67 Merrill Lynch, Pierce, Fenner & Smith v. Georgiadis, 903 F.2d 109 (2d Cir. 1990); Roney & Co. v. Goren, (1989).

68 Georgiadis found that the parties signing the agreement superseded the AMEX Constitution. Other cases agreed, finding the AMEX Constitution not a "rule" permitting creation "of a fourth electable forum." Painc Webber, Inc. v. Pitchford, 721 F. Supp. 542 (S.D.N.Y. 1989), *aff'd*, 903 F.2d 106 (2d Cir. 1990). *See* Haskel, *Opening the AMEX Window to Securities Customers Seeking an Independent Arbitral Forum*, 63 N.Y.S. B. J. 20 (1991).

69 Luckie v. Smith Barney, Harris Upham & Co., Inc., FED. SEC. L. REP. (CCH) ¶97,723 (11th Cir. 1993).

70 Through the first three quarters of the pilot program, 29 claims were submitted for AAA arbitration. The firms in 20 instances offered the customer the option of participating in the pilot program; only 12 customers accepted. In 22 requests by customers to proceed under the pilot program, the firms consented in 17 cases.

71 *See* Am. Stock Ex. Const. Art. VIII, §2(c); 2 AM. STOCK EX. GUIDE (CCH) ¶ 9063.

72 *See* Paine Webber v. Rutherford, 903 F.2d 106 (1990); Bear, Sterns & Co. v. Bennett, 938 F.2d 31 (2d Cir. 1991); Smith Barney, Harris Upham & Co., Inc., v. Garfield, FED. SEC. L. REP. (CCH) ¶97,225 (S.D.N.Y. 1992).

73 *See* SEC Rel. No. 34-27459 (Nov. 30, 1989). Boudreau v. L.F. Rothschild & Co., No. 89-250-CIV-18 (M.D. Fla. Feb. 23, 1990), cited by Nesseman, *The State of the Law*, SECURITIES ARBITRATION (D.E. Robbins ed., 1992), which held that the reference to the City of New York was not a venue selection provision for AAA arbitration location.

74 *See* N.A.S.D. Article VII, § 1(a)(3) of the By-Laws and § 2, Code of Arbitration Procedure ("N.A.S.D." Code).

75 *See* N.A.S.D. § 1-4.

76 N.A.S.D. § 13(a).

77 N.A.S.D. § 3(d).

78 *See* N.A.S.D. § 1-8.

79 N.Y.S.E. Constitution Article XI; N.Y.S.E. Rules 600-637; N.Y.S.E. Guide (CCH).

80 AMEX Rule 601.

81 C.B.O.E. Rule 18.1ff.

82 C.B.O.E. Rule 2.19(a) specifies that the Arbitration Committee is charged with administration of the Constitution of the Rules of Arbitration.

83 N.A.S.D. § 12(c); N.Y.S.E. Rule 600(c).

84 7 U.S.C. § 18.

85 41 F.R. 3993, revised 49 F.R. 6602.

86 *See* generally R. RODMAN, COMMERCIAL ARBITRATION 1-6 (1984).

87 *See* Lundquist, *The New Art of Forum Shopping*, 15 LITIGATION 21 (1988). Of course, given the preference for arbitration and freedom contract, such forms could be developed by an ologopolistic industry to take advantage of the consumer by setting up panels biased in favor of the industry. There are both industry and regulatory checks on brokerage firms in this regard.

Chapter 10

LITIGATION OR ARBITRATION? SECURITIES INDUSTRY ARBITRATION PANELS

This chapter reviews the question of whether to litigate, arbitrate, or mediate a dispute in light of the advantages and disadvantages of each method. Ultimately, this decision must take into account the claims made and evaluation of the strength of the case.

1) ARBITRATION OR LITIGATION?

The first step in evaluating a dispute is to determine if arbitration is a viable alternative to litigation. The reasons why an investor or brokerage firm might prefer arbitration are discussed in chapter 7.

If a predispute arbitration agreement exists, arbitration is probably the only process to resolve the dispute (unless defenses to the agreement exist--see chapter 6). If an arbitration clause is present and the contract defenses unavailable, there will be little choice if the other party wants to arbitrate: he or she will merely move for a stay in the event litigation is commenced.[1] If there is no predispute agreement, in order to arbitrate the parties must mutually agree to submit the dispute to arbitration.[2]

For industry related claims, members of an exchange have normally agreed to arbitrate disputes under either the rules of the exchange or the SRO of which they are members.[3] A party involved in the industry but a non-signatory to the account agreement may also be required to arbitrate any dispute arising from the actions in the account under agency principles.[4] For them, there is no option and arbitration will be the method to resolve any disputes.

A) Types of Claims

The types of claims that can be brought in customer and industry disputes are discussed in chapter 11. The same claims are available in litigation or arbitration; the question is the appropriate forum to hear the dispute.

B) Questions to Consider

If a party has the decision to arbitrate or litigate, certain basic questions are normally raised:

i) Recovery. As demonstrated by several studies, arbitration does not result in remarkably different recoveries compared to litigation, but does result in different costs.[5] Customers are not disadvantaged in arbitration in industry-sponsored SRO forums.[6] However, in a recent study of California's requirement of a mini-trial before an arbitrator prior to a case claiming under $50,000 in damages going to trial before a jury, in 45 of 148 cases where the arbitrator's decision was rejected and the parties went to trial, the jury's verdict came out better for the defense than the arbitrator's award in 73 percent of the cases.

One major difference was in who initiated the action in arbitration. The 1992 GAO study[7] found if the broker initiated the claim, chances of recovery were 3.3 times as large as when a customer initiated the claim. One ground for this result, however, is that most broker-initiated actions are for balances due in margin accounts, and the GAO suggested perhaps this was an easier claim to prove since it was based on documents.

ii) Success in Recoveries. The 1992 GAO Report surveyed some 6,600 arbitration cases closed between January 1989 and June 30, 1990, and some 100 cases filed in the Federal District Courts in D.C., Maryland, Northern Illinois, Southern New York, and Eastern Virginia. It found no significant differences between independent (AAA) and SRO forums (average of customer awards approximately 60 percent), while only 14 percent of the court cases resulted in a decision in favor of investors (39 percent).

iii) Settlement. The N.A.S.D has indicated that while generally people are able to settle business disputes out of court or arbitration as much as 85 percent of the time, in securities disputes it is only 50 to 55 percent. With the 1993 caseload of the N.A.S.D. expected to rise 18 percent to 5,200 cases and the large number of limited partnership claims from investments in the 1980s, mediation may be an answer. But factors against arbitration may include the reluctance of the brokerage industry to settle and lack of experience in securities arbitration by claimants and their lawyers.

The GAO Report found that the major result in both litigation and arbitration was settlement: in litigation, 48 percent of cases were settled and 38 percent dismissed, while in arbitration about 44 percent of claims were settled at the SROs and 33 percent at the AAA.

iv) Comparison of Arbitration and Litigation Procedures. The following table was contained in the 1992 GAO Report:

Comparison of Arbitration and Litigation Procedures

	Securities SROs	AAA	Court
1. Discovery (determining the elements of an opponent's case)	Extensive pretrial discovery permitted in courts is not available in SRO arbitration proceedings. Discovery in arbitration is more focused than in litigation. The Uniform Code encourages the parties to exchange documents and information before the first hearing session and establishes procedures to resolve contested requests for information. The Uniform Code also establishes timetables for the transfer of documents and provides for prehearing conferences	AAA prehearing rules provide that an administrative conference can be scheduled to expedite the arbitration hearings. In large or complex cases, a preliminary hearing may be held to specify the issues to be resolved, stipulate the uncontested facts, and consider any matters that will expedite the arbitration proceedings.	Federal and state rules of civil procedure provide extensive opportunities to discover the elements of an opponent's case. Discovery is controlled by the parties rather than the courts. Attorneys have a considerable range of discretion in serving interrogatories and taking depositions.
2. Right to appeal	An arbitration award is final and the parties are bound to it; however, an award can be modified or vacated by a court for limited reasons, including arbitrators' partiality or misconduct, prejudicial conduct of the hearing, corruption or fraud in procuring the award, and manifest disregard of the law.	Like SROs awards, AAA awards are also final and binding, subject to the same limited review by the courts.	Unlike arbitration, a court decision can be appealed, which may prolong the final resolution of the dispute.
3. Punitive damages	The federal appellate courts are split on whether punitive damages are available in arbitration. None of the SROs prohibit arbitrators from hearing claims for punitive damages or awarding them.	AAA rules neither permit nor prohibit punitive damage claims. The rules state "the arbitrator may grant any remedy or relief which the arbitrator deems just and equitable and within the scope of the agreement of the parties...	Punitive damage awards are not available in causes of action arising under express liability provisions of the Federal Securities Acts. Courts prohibit such awards in causes of action implied from the provision. However, exemplary awards are available in court when litigants join pendant state claims with federal claims where the underlying state law so provides.

	Securities SROs	AAA	Court
4. Attorney fees	Investors can request attorney fees. While the general legal rule is that each party bears its own legal expenses, arbitrators do award legal fees in some cases if a statutory or contractual basis exists.	Same as SROs. Also see comments for punitive damages.	The right to recover attorney fees from one's opponent in litigation does not exist in common law. It must be authorized by statute, a rule of court, or some agreement of the parties. In federal court, attorney fees may be awarded in various cases under federal statutes, including the 1933 and 1934 securities acts. No attorneys' fees are available in securities fraud litigation.
5. Preservation of a record	The Uniform Code requires that "a verbatim record by stenographic reporter or tape recording of all arbitration hearings shall be kept." A party requesting a transcript must pay for it, unless the arbitrators direct otherwise.	A verbatim record of the proceedings is not required; however, AAA rules indicate that parties wanting a record of the proceedings must make arrangements directly with a stenographer and notify the other parties of these arrangements in advance of the hearings.	Each district court must appoint one or more court reporters who are required to record verbatim all open proceedings in cases unless the parties, with the judge's approval, agree otherwise.
6. Rules of evidence	Federal Rules of Evidence do not apply in arbitration hearings. Arbitrators can determine the materiality and relevance of any evidence presented and can accept whatever information they deem necessary to understand and determine the dispute.	Same as SROs.	Federal Rules of Evidence govern federal court proceedings. The rules govern the definition of relevant evidence; the treatment of irrelevant evidence as inadmissible; the exclusion of relevant evidence on the grounds of prejudice, confusion, or waste of time; privileges; and exceptions to the hearsay rule.
7. Availability and rationale of arbitration and court awards	SRO arbitration awards are available to the public. The awards disclose the names of the parties (NYSE and Amex will exclude the names of customer parties if requested), a short summary of the dispute and issues involved, damages requested and awarded, and the names of the arbitrators. (NASD excludes arbitrators' names on public information about awards.) The arbitrators generally do not give reasons for their decisions.	AAA rules are less specific than SRO rules regarding the content of awards. Like SRO awards, AAA awards will generally not be accompanied by an opinion. AAA has no specific requirement with respect to publicizing awards; however, it does give a confidentiality pledge to the parties involved, which makes the awards unavailable to the public.	Court decisions are available to the public and contain findings of fact and conclusions of law and give substantive reasons for the decision. However, the large number of filings in litigation does not allow every court decision to have a written opinion.
8. Production of documents and appearance of persons.	SRO arbitrators can direct the appearance of industry personnel or the production of documents in control of industry personnel without a subpoena.	AAA arbitrators may establish, at a preliminary hearing, the extent of and schedule for the production of documents.	A court may order discovery of documents or subpoena appearance of persons or production of documents.

The General Accounting Office reported to Congress in 1994 that the panels of arbitrators in securities industry forums lacked subject matter expertise in the area of discrimination. It recommended establishment of arbitrators with such experience and knowledge and that the SEC scrutinize such cases. In addition, the GAO recommended enhanced disclosure of industry and criminal convictions of arbitrators and regular cycles of review of broker-customer cases (which the SEC has agreed to do).

v) Investor Disadvantage? Commentators have observed:

> Generally, investors are at a disadvantage with large brokerage firms that often are members of the self-regulating organizations (SROs) that typically conduct the arbitration proceedings. Brokerage firms also are intimately familiar with the arbitration process, whereas investors [and perhaps their lawyers as well] rarely understand this process prior to arbitrating an actual dispute. As such, the investing public perceives forced arbitration of their disputes with brokers as inherently unfair, which undermines the integrity of the financial markets and serves to impede the flow of capital upon which our economic system depends.[8]

vi) Conclusion. If a party can decide whether to litigate or arbitrate a claim, there may be perceived advantages of one to another. But, in reality, it appears that arbitration is less costly and a decision is reached more quickly. There is, however, a price paid for these advantages: a loss of some procedural advantages of litigation, not insignificant among which is the right of appeal.

2) ARBITRATION OR MEDIATION?

The mediation process has been briefly discussed in chapter 1. Basically, the mediator is a neutral party, with some expertise in the securities industry, who will assist the parties in coming to a settlement of the dispute. In the event that a settlement can not be reached by the parties with the help of the mediator, they can resort to either litigation or arbitration as the facts will permit.

The major advantage of mediation is time: the mediator will typically meet quickly with the parties. There are few formalities, with the resulting savings in both time and expense of discovery, hearings, and the like. Mediation has a high success, often as many as 80 percent of the matters submitted are resolved. It should be seriously considered as a inexpensive alternative for litigation *or* arbitration. And even if mediation is not successful, it probably has refined the issues that should make discovery, and the arbitration or litigation process less expensive and faster. It is for this reason that mediation is gaining adherents in the business community generally, as well as in securities disputes.

A) The Mediation Process

The mediation session is informal; geared mainly to the exchange of information in a non-threatening atmosphere. The mediator will normally: (1) hear an exchange of positions, as usually presession submissions are not made and there is no formal statement of claim; (2) following the joint session, the mediator will work with each party individually to discuss their positions confidentially, often having the confidential authority to suggest terms from the other side; and then (3) caucus with both sides to accomplish a settlement, often with the mediator suggesting reasonable positions which the parties might not otherwise accept. The mediation is accomplished by an administrative framework similar to arbitration except that the administrator does little more than facilitate meetings and review case progress regularly.

B) Pilot Mediation Program at AMEX

The American Stock Exchange initiated a pilot mediation program for investor-brokerage firm disputes. It is designed to provide the parties a structured method to analyze the risks of litigation or arbitration, with a goal of settlement. The AMEX does not administer mediations, but refers the parties to ENDISPUTE, Inc., a firm with offices in New York, Chicago, Boston, and Washington, D.C., which maintains a roster of mediators with knowledge of the securities industry. The mediator has no authority to make a binding decision or require the parties to accept a proposed settlement.

The mediation has no effect on ultimate arbitration or litigation. The information exchanged is confidential and settlements proposed may not be admitted in later litigation or, parties' arbitrations, as such disclosure would undoubtedly prejudice the parties positions.

If a party is interested in more information about mediation or serving as a mediator, the AMEX will put them in contact with ENDISPUTE.

C) AAA Mediation

Under § 10 of the Securities Arbitration Rules, the AAA will refer a dispute to a mediator to assist them in reaching a settlement. The mediator is encouraged to have meetings with the parties separately. From these caucuses the mediator is able to determine in a non-confrontational environment the issues of the dispute. With that knowledge, he assists negotiations between the parties, helping them settle their disputes. There is a high success rate--75 to 80 percent.[9]

D) N.A.S.D.-AAA Mediation

A joint N.A.S.D.-AAA pilot project was begun in 1989 and offers mediation as an alternative to parties who submit securities arbitration claims to the N.A.S.D. in New York, Chicago, and San Francisco. In 1990 the AAA and United States Arbitration and Mediation Service undertook specialized mediation training for attorneys having securities expertise. Judicate, Inc., was added to the program in May 1991.

3) SECURITIES INDUSTRY ARBITRATION PANELS

The arbitration panels will be determined by the customer's agreement terms or the submission agreement. SRO panels provide for one arbitrator for either non-monetary or claims up to $10,000,[10] and three or more ("no less than three") for claims in excess of $10,000.[11]

Two questions are continuously raised regarding SRO arbitrations: (1) is the proceeding biased in favor of the industry-member of the SRO; and (2) are there too many arbitrators with industry affiliations? In response to the first question, the SRO provides the facility and personnel to process the arbitration. The SRO personnel do select the arbitrators, but have little input into the process, and will not advise on issues of substantive law nor participate in the deliberations of the panel. In fact, the personnel of the SRO will often assist the *pro se* claimant in the presentation of his or her materials to the panel, through advice about the procedures and process (outside the hearing, of course). With either SRO or AAA arbitrations, there is a problem in discovery compared to litigation, which is discussed in chapter 13.

In 1987 the SEC wrote the S.I.C.A. that it recommended a number of changes in arbitrator selection in order to "improve" SRO arbitrations. Discussed below are the SRO responses to the SEC recommendations regarding arbitrator selection from public and industry panels; disclosures; training; evaluation of competence, preparedness and fairness; and challenges for cause.

A) Classification of Arbitrators

Under the Uniform Code, arbitrators are chosen from two lists--public arbitrators and industry arbitrators.[12] The N.Y.S.E. has adopted guidelines giving a precise definition distinguishing between public and industry arbitrators.[13] These guidelines comply with the amendments to N.Y.S.E. Rule 607 defining industry arbitrators as compared with public arbitrators. The major change in that Rule is that a person associated with a member or other investment house is an industry person if the individual: (1) has been associated in the last five (the N.A.S.D. and Uniform Code § 8 use three) years; (2) is a retired person who spent "a substantial part of his or her business career" in the industry; (3) is an attorney, accountant, or other professional who devoted 20 percent or more of professional work to clients in the securities industry in the last two years; (4) or has a spouse or other member of the household who is a person associated with the industry.[14] It is clear, however, that the practice of the SROs is different in classifying arbitrators.

Under SRO rules, affiliated persons include any person associated with a member, broker/dealer, municipal securities dealer, or investment advisor for the last five years or a retired person who spent a substantial part of his or her career in these businesses. Also included are attorneys, accountants, and other professionals who in the last two years devoted more than 20 percent of their work effort to clients in the securities industry, or persons whose spouse is in the industry.[15]

The AAA classifies arbitrators on the same basis as the SROs. The AAA has a national panel of arbitrators from which all arbitrators are appointed.[16] An "affiliated" arbitrator is defined as "one with a direct or indirect involvement or relationship with the securities brokerage industry for a minimum of three years if [still] employed . . . or five years if no longer so employed."[17] Lawyers and accountants are also included. Under AAA Rule 15, the parties may have provided for the appointment of certain arbitrators by party selection, in which case challenges (see below) are not permitted for these arbitrators. This recognizes the contractual nature of the arbitration before the AAA versus the more coercive SRO procedures. The AAA will, if the party-selected arbitrator cannot agree on the other(s), appoint a neutral arbitrator from the national panel who shall act as chairman.[18] AAA Rule 17 provides that where the parties are nationals of different countries, if requested neutral arbitrators from other nations will be appointed.

B) Disclosure

The disclosure regarding arbitrators was one of the major concerns of the SEC after *McMahon*. The disclosures to non-industry parties of the nature of the contacts of the proposed panels is important to improve the impression that the SRO forums are impartial. Federal Arbitration Act §10 requires arbitrators to disclose any interests that might create an impression of possible bias. The question of bias is one of perception. Therefore, the arbitrator is encouraged to withdraw even if disclosures do not rise to the level that would disqualify the arbitrator from serving in a particular case.[19]

The N.Y.S.E. and N.A.S.D. established procedures in 1988 whereby disclosures regarding employment histories of the arbitrators, and other pertinent information, is sent to the parties before the arbitration begins.[20] The following information is disclosed by the SROs about the arbitrators:[21]

- Name
- Employment history for the last 10 years
- Conflicts of interests, including accounts at particular firms, retention by particular securities client, etc.
- Publicly available awards in which party was arbitrator or represented a party is also available
- All other information that the arbitrator has disclosed pursuant to the rules, which is a continuous requirement (the arbitrator has a commitment to keep this information current even during an arbitration)

AAA Rule 20 also requires disclosure of circumstances that are "likely to affect impartiality, including financial or personal interest in the result of the arbitration or a past relationship with a party or their representatives." The AAA will also furnish additional biographical information on request.[22]

The S.I.C.A. ARBITRATOR'S MANUAL has completed a guide outlining the arbitrator's duty to avoid any appearance of bias through full disclosure throughout the proceeding, the arbitrator's ethical responsibilities, the procedure under the Uniform Code, and the role of the arbitration staff. The AAA also has adopted ethical rules of conduct for arbitrators in commercial and securities disputes.[23]

C) Selection of Arbitrators

The SROs select arbitrators (agency selection) while the AAA permits the parties to pick from its lists (party selection). Selection of the names is normally a function of the director of arbitration at the SROs or the AAA staff. Both normally select panel members on the basis of their skills, background, and experience, usually in regard to the type of case.[24] At the AAA, the parties can unilaterally select an arbitrator for the panel or other method of arbitrator appointment.[25] If the parties are unable to select arbitrators from the lists submitted by the AAA, they must notify the AAA within 20 days and a final list is circulated. One preemptory challenge is allowed on this final list and the AAA then appoints from the remaining persons.[26]

Although prior to 1987 no industry panelists were present on AAA selection lists, today in AAA arbitration each party will be given two lists, industry and non-industry arbitrators, from which to select the panel.[27] Two arbitrators are appointed from the non-industry list and one from the industry list based on the parties selection, which must be done within 20 days or the staff will make the appointment.[28] In some cases the parties may provide that two party-designated arbitrators select a neutral third panelist. If the appointment is not made within ten days from the appointment of the last party arbitrator, the staff will appoint the third arbitrator who will act as chair of the panel.[29] If the claim is less than $25,000, then the AAA expedited procedures apply and only one non-industry panelist will be selected.[30] This is the same as SRO small claims, where one arbitrator is appointed for claims less than $10,000.[31]

D) Challenges

If a party desires to have an arbitrator omitted from the panel at the SROs, this is done through a challenge. The challenge must be made prior to the hearing. An unlimited number of challenges are permitted for cause,[32] and each party is allowed one peremptory challenge.[33] With the new rules requiring disclosure of information about arbitrators and past awards (discussed below), the parties can evaluate the arbitrator and utilize the challenges allowed.

The SRO director of arbitration is required to notify the parties of the identity of the arbitrators at least eight days in advance of the hearing, and challenges must be made within five days of notification. Usually the naming of SRO arbitration panels occurs well in advance of the first hearing. Normally a challenge is initially informal, when the attorney for a party discusses the matter with the forum staff. The director will seek to avoid cause in the appointment in the first place and may change the arbitrator after notification of a problem. If the director will not change the arbitrator, under the SRO rules a challenge must be made within five days of notification unless the director extends this time.

The AAA selection procedures minimize the need for challenges since the parties are able to strike persons from the lists of potential arbitrators furnished by the AAA staff, and each party also ranks the remaining names in order of preference.[34] The arbitration staff appoints based on greatest preferences, or in the event that no agreement can be reached, then the staff can make an appointment from the National Panel without regard to the parties input. A challenge, by notifying the AAA of stricken names, must occur within 20 days after the lists of affiliated and public arbitrators are submitted to the parties. The right to challenge would come after disclosure by the arbitrator of information that would affect impartiality, but the AAA's decision to disqualify or not is final.[35]

E) Disqualification or Disability of Arbitrator

In the event an SRO arbitrator resigns, dies, withdraws, is disqualified, or otherwise is unable to serve as an arbitrator after the commencement of the first hearing (which can be the preliminary hearing), the remaining arbitrators can continue to decide the matter unless a party objects within 5 days after being notified of the vacancy by the director of arbitration.[36] The director of arbitration is required to name a new arbitrator to fill out the panel if an objection is timely made. The SRO rules regarding challenge apply to the newly appointed arbitrator as well.

At the AAA, the AAA can declare a vacancy if "for any reason an arbitrator is unable to perform" his duties.[37] Vacancies are filled under the other rules, but if the hearings have commenced, the remaining arbitrators can continue with the hearing and determine the case, unless the parties otherwise agree. Otherwise the new panel determines if any of the prior hearing shall be repeated.

The courts retain the right to appoint an arbitrator when the arbitration clause is silent on the matter, or when a vacancy occurs in the named arbitrators even in a private arbitration.[38]

F) Bias--A Perception Problem or Grounds to Challenge?

One of the major problems in the perception of the public regarding industry-sponsored arbitration is the impression of bias of the panel. The parties in arbitration are "not only entitled to present their claims to an impartial judge, but to one who by no act on his part has justified a doubt as to his impartiality."[39] While non-neutral arbitrators may be permitted under the Federal Arbitration Act through agreement or consent of the parties, arbitrator bias is one justification discussed in chapter 15 for setting aside an award.

An arbitrator must disclose any past or present relationship with the parties that might create an impression of possible bias. This extends to both business and personal dealings.[40] Justice White stated in his concurring opinion in a 1968 case that "[a]rbitrators are not automatically disqualified by a business relationship with the parties before them if both parties are informed of the relationship in advance, or if they are unaware of the facts but the relationship is trivial. I see no reason automatically to disqualify the best informed and most capable potential arbitrators."[41]

In fact, presumptively, biased arbitrators may nonetheless make the best arbitrators, if the arbitration requires industry expertise, and they are the unimpeached experts in the field. In *Mitsubishi Motors v. Soler Chrysler-Plymouth, Inc.*, the Supreme Court noted that "adaptability and access to expertise are hallmarks of arbitration. The anticipated subject matter of the dispute may be taken into account when the arbitrators are appointed, and arbitral rules typically provide for the participation of experts either employed by the parties or appointed by the tribunal."[42]

Situations that typically find the existence of bias include those where the arbitrator is a party to the proceeding, or is related by consanguinity, affinity, or business (including employee, agent, employer, debtor, creditor, attorney, or client). Impermissible arbitrator bias is best described as requiring actual bias in the process. Because each party has the right of procedural due process, the right to have a "realistic and fair opportunity to prevail in the dispute"[43] is guaranteed. This minimal level of integrity of the process requires that the arbitrator both disclose any conflict, or appearance of conflict of interest, as well as be capable of deciding the case on the basis of the evidence presented.[44] A more direct bias is obvious if the arbitrator had a personal or financial interest that will be affected by the outcome and is substantial enough to influence the arbitrator's decision.

Even if there is an appearance of bias, there is no guarantee that the bias will be sufficient to vacate an award or disqualify a forum. Cases of arbitrator bias justifying vacatur of an award are not uncommon, but usually are unsuccessful.[45] Failure of the arbitrator to advise parties that he was sued by one party's law firm in another action is potential bias.[46] Membership in the same organizations, personal acquaintance, work referrals without payment, and past business dealings alone are not enough to create the necessary bias. This is particularly true if the parties have the right under the rules of the forum to disqualify all who show the requisite potentiality for bias.

The controlling question on a motion to vacate an award, however, is whether the interest was disclosed to the parties. If the parties proceeding in arbitration either knew, or should have known, of the potential bias, there will be a waiver and the award is impregnable.

If the nature of the bias is industry-connected, however, the courts have a harder time vacating an award or staying arbitration. In some instances, they will find the arbitration clause unenforceable as being adhesive.[47] Of course, if the industry- or firm-sponsored arbitration process requires the use of presumptively biased arbitrators, it will be found unconscionable. Potential industry bias, however, is not sufficient to disqualify the forum itself.[48] In other cases there may be institutional pressure exerted on the arbitrator, either overtly or covertly, to render a decision in favor of one of the parties. When the institution has control of the arbitrator selection as well as forum for arbitration, bias can almost be presumed. This would certainly be the case, for example, if a broker had set up his own captive forum, using his own employees, or former employees, on variable or discretionary pension, or paid arbitrators, and then required customers to submit disputes to this panel. For example, a biased or impartial forum might be where one neutral and two non-neutral arbitrators must, under the forum rules, decide a claim by a unanimous vote. Since decisional (or veto) power is exercised by one biased arbitrator, the process would fail as not meeting the minimal levels of integrity.

As in the SRO arbitrations, where the forum selects the arbitrators, a perception that the institution-sponsored forum is biased can be considered almost presumptive. This is especially true if there is limited disclosure to the non-industry parties of the backgrounds and affiliations of the arbitrators for the purpose of challenging an arbitrator being impaneled. The use of such a presumptively biased forum would certainly permit a court's review of the process and outcome, or award under notions of procedural fairness, a judicial concept.

The composition of arbitration panels is principally white male. The General Accounting Office reported to Congress in 1994 that when minorities and women in the securities industry file discrimination claims, the arbitration is likely to be determined by 60 year old white males. The Report also indicated that the panels lack "subject matter expertise" on discrimination and that only 11 percent of the arbitrators are women; less than one percent Asian or Black.

4) ARBITRATOR TRAINING

As noted above, the use of experts, such as industry personnel, as arbitrators is one attribute of arbitration in difficult cases. In the securities area, with the complicated nature of the marketplace and the complex mix of different rules of both internal and external regulation and law, normally a degree of expertise is essential.

Until recently, most of the SROs have not had training programs for arbitrators, relying instead on a belief that the panels from which they select arbitrators have sufficient expertise, or that the parties will elect to disqualify a person whose disclosures indicate they are not sufficiently well qualified to sit. Nevertheless, change is taking place. As a result of the SEC's 1987 letter to the S.I.C.A., both the N.A.S.D. and N.Y.S.E. hold training sessions for arbitrators. The N.Y.S.E. has used video tapes prepared by the AAA for assistance to arbitrators generally. The N.A.S.D. has held educational forums at various locations. The American Law Institute-American Bar Association Committee on Continuing Professional Education (ALI-ABA) has developed, and offers to interested viewers, a videotape entitled *A Guide to the Discovery Rules for Securities Arbitration*. The S.I.C.A. has developed a manual[49] covering the ethical responsibilities of arbitrators, the conduct of the hearing, discovery, motions, and the special authority of arbitrators.

After 1992 the AAA and SROs require all securities arbitrators to complete a training course before they can serve and attendance at confirming training programs to remain on the "active" panels. The 1992 G.A.O. Report recommended mandatory training at both the SROs and AAA.[50] Training courses, as a result, have increased tremendously. Under a July 1992 agreement, the AAA, N.A.S.D., N.Y.S.E., and AMEX all agreed training at one forum's program will receive credit at all organizations. Every issue of the SECURITIES ARBITRATION COMMENTATOR lists courses available throughout the country.

5) EVALUATION OF ARBITRATORS

The SROs and AAA responded to SEC concern regarding arbitrator's competence by sending an evaluation form to the parties or their representatives after the case is closed (AAA) or prior to the award (SROs).[51] The SROs also request peer evaluation from the other arbitrators on the panel[52] and do staff evaluation.[53]

One troubling issue has been the SEC's request for "evaluation" of the members of SROs arbitration panels. First, there is uncertainty regarding the scope of the SEC's requested evaluation: does it go toward establishing a "track record" of wins and losses for the investor versus the broker; or is it toward determining the qualifications of the arbitrator, based on his participation in the process--the evaluations should not become a "popularity contest," with votes cast *after* the award by the victorious or losing party? At the present time there is an informal evaluation process, in the nature of selection of arbitrators from the panels by the SRO arbitration personnel. It appears that this process works well. Further, to identify arbitrators (like many labor arbitrators) as "pro-industry" or "pro-investor," will not be good. Arbitrators may try to protect their independence by looking at the decisions they are about to make and their "record." There is reason to evaluate on a case-by-case basis the bias of arbitrators, as well as the fairness of the private dispute resolution forum.

6) CONTINUING CONCERNS

One of the continual concerns of the SEC staff is that customers be made aware of other arbitral forums, especially the AAA. Minor concerns for the future include the ability of arbitrators to enforce interim decisions, especially in discovery, and review of the handbook acquainting arbitrators with the process, rules, and law. In a related SRO change approval, the SEC acted on the request of the C.B.O.E. to change rules concerning service of pleadings, selection of arbitrators, to disclosure of arbitrators' background, discovery, and publication of award summaries similar to the changes previously approved for the N.Y.S.E., AMEX, and N.A.S.D. Continuing its practice, the C.B.O.E. also required highlighting of the arbitration provisions and an explanation to customers of their rights vis-à-vis mandatory arbitration agreements. The 1993 revisions of AAA Securities Arbitration Rule 42(f) now allow public access to awards, but the names of the parties are redacted. Many securities arbitration lawyers circulate awards to each other or make them available to the media. SRO arbitration decisions are now routinely available.[54]

NOTES

1 This is done by a motion to compel arbitration made to the federal or state court. *See* N.Y. CPLR 7503(b).

2 This will be done on the Uniform Submission Agreement form, currently used by the AAA and all SRO forums. *See* the Uniform Submission Agreement reproduced in chapter 12.

3 Often a member of an exchange will not be an SRO member. In these cases, the arbitration agreement is only with the exchange, and the claimant can not bring the arbitration in any other forum.

4 *See* Lee v. Chica, FED. SEC. L. REP. (CCH) ¶ 97,315 (8th Cir. 1993), where the customer's account representative was bound to arbitrate under the firm's agreement, even though he had not signed the agreement between the customer and the firm. This was due to the employment relationship and the fact that he was responsible for the transactions in her account from which the claims arose.

5 *See* the discussion in chapter 7 of cost savings. The Deloitte Study indicated, in fact, that customers make larger claims in litigation, but recover a greater percentage of the claims made in arbitration.

6 An AAA study of 4,223 commercial arbitrations completed in 1992, however, found that "splitting-the-baby" is not prevalent. In only one of ten cases was an award roughly midway between the parties positions. In 25% of the cases the arbitrator awarded at least 80% of the plaintiff's claim; in one-third of the cases the claim was totally rejected. *See* WALL STREET J. B:2 (September 27, 1993). The SEC. ARB. COMM. survey of awards from May 1989 to August 1990 found that customers won in 58.1% of SRO awards versus 57.6% in AAA awards.

7 General Accounting Office Report to Congressional Requesters, GAO/GGD-92-74, GAO Publication B-24 7464 (May 11, 1992).

8 Gregory and Schneider, *Securities Arbitration: A Need for Continued Reform*, 17 NOVA L. REV. 1223, 1224 (1993).

9 *See* G. Friedman, *AAA Securities Arbitration: What You Need to Know*, SECURITIES ARBITRATION 417 (D. Robbins ed., 1991); but in the 1992 edition of SECURITIES ARBITRATION, Mr. Friedman notes success is 60% in securities cases..

10 N.Y.S.E. Rule 607; Uniform Code of Arbitration §8(a)(1). The N.A.S.D. § 9 provides one arbitrator for claims to $30,000 and three for all claims in excess; § 10 covers the small claims, those not exceeding $10,000.

11 Uniform Code of Arbitration § 8 provides for 3 panelists in all cases over $10,000. Today under N.A.S.D. § 19 and N.Y.S.E. Rule 60, there is one arbitrator for claims of $10,000 or less; and three for all others (except one in N.A.S.D. arbitrations up to $30,000 unless claimant requests three and

three to five if claimant requests in all other cases).

12 N.A.S.D. § 8(a)(1) and (2) provide that a public customer dispute shall be resolved by a panel "at least a majority of whom shall not be from the securities industry." On the other hand, disputes among member firms can be resolved by industry-only panels.

13 New York Stock Exchange Guidelines for Classification of Arbitrators.

14 N.Y.S.E. Rule 607(3).

15 N.Y.S.E. 609(a)(2) and (3).

16 AAA Rule 4.

17 AAA Rule 13.

18 AAA Rule 16.

19 *See* S.I.C.A. Arbitrator's Manual.

20 *See* N.Y.S.E. Rule 610 and Rule 608, which require disclosure of any potential conflict and employment history, respectively; AAA Rule 19 requires disclosure of any circumstance likely to affect impartiality.

21 *See* Uniform Code §§ 8 and 9; N.A.S.D. §§ 21 and 23; N.Y.S.E. Rules 607 and 608.

22 AAA Rule 14. This includes past awards.

23 *See* the AAA CODE OF CONDUCT. After appointment under AAA Rule 19, the arbitrator under Rule 20 is required to notify the AAA of potential conflict. As a practical matter, however, AAA staff will normally inquire both as to availability and potential conflicts at the time lists are prepared before forwarding to the parties under Rule 14. AAA Rule 13 defines the qualifications of the party-designated (Rule 15) as well as neutral or industry-affiliated arbitrator.

24 *See* N.A.S.D. §20; N.Y.S.E. Rule 607(b); AAA Rule 13.

25 AAA Rule 15.

26 AAA Rule 14. Under the previous practice, AAA staff could complete the panel without circulation of the second list.

27 AAA Rules 14, 19, and 52. *See also* G. Friedman, *Securities Regulation at the AAA*, SECURITIES ARBITRATION 366 (D. Robbins ed., 1992) which indicates that of 3,628 persons on the Securities Panel, 1,802 (49.7%) were affiliated persons, 1,627 (44.9%) non-affiliated, and 197 (5.4%) of the customer's bar.

28 AAA Rules 14 and 15.

29 AAA Rule 16.

30 AAA Rules 18 and 52.

31 Uniform Code §2(f) and (i) and N.A.S.D. § 10. N.Y.S.E. Rule 601 does not provide for decision on the papers only.

32 N.A.S.D. § 22; N.Y.S.E. Rule 609.

33 N.A.S.D. § 22; N.Y.S.E. Rule 609. If there are multiple parties to the arbitration, all claimants and respondents have only one peremptory challenge, unless the director of arbitration determines that the interests of justice requires more.

34 AAA Rule 14.

35 AAA Rule 20.

36 N.A.S.D. § 24; N.Y.S.E. Rule 611.

37 AAA Rule 21.

38 *See* Federal Arbitration Act §5, 9 U.S.C. § 5 (1988), and N.Y. CPLR 7504.

39 Matter of Friedman, 215 A.D. 130, 135, 213 N.Y.S. 369, 374 (1926).

40 Johnston v. Security Ins. Co., 6 Cal. App. 3d 839, 86 Cal. Rptr. 133 (2d Dist. 1970), held even though the state statute did not provide for vacatur due to bias, the award was vacated due to the arbitrator's undisclosed acquaintanceship with the plaintiffs' attorney-appraiser.

41 Commonwealth Coatings, Corp. v. Continental Casualty Co., 393 U.S. 145, 149-150, 89 S. Ct. 337, 21 L. Ed. 2d. 301 (1968) (White, J. concurring).

42 Mitsubishi Motors Corp. v. Soler Chrysler-Plymouth Inc., 473 U.S. 614, 633, 1105 S. Ct. 3346, 87 L. Ed. 2d 444 (1985). This attitude is a considerable change from *Wilko* in 1953. In addition, many arbitrators are lawyers specializing in securities litigation or practice, sophisticated business, financial, or accounting executives, financial and business consultants, college deans, and professors.

43 Graham v. Scissor-Tail, Inc., 28 Cal. 3d 807, 825, 623 P.2d 165, 176, 171 Cal. Rptr. 604, 615 (1981).

44 Hines v. Anchor Motor Freight, Inc. 424 U.S. 554, 96 S. Ct. 1048, 47 L. Ed. 2d. 231 (1976).

45 *See Survey of Post Award Proceedings*, 4 SEC. ARB. COMM. 12, 1 (1992).

46 Rollins v. Paine Webber, Inc., 5 SEC. ARB. COMM. 7, 16 (Cal. Ct. App. 1993).

47 Of course, if the industry or firm sponsored arbitration process requires the use of presumptively biased arbitrators, it will be found unconscionable.

48 Arrieta v. Paine, Webber, Jackson & Curtis, Inc., 59 Cal. App. 3d 322, 130, Cal. Rptr. 534 (1976), to the effect that the customer had an opportunity to disqualify biased arbitrators, and potential bias is not a ground for vacatur of award. *But see* discussion of Hope v. Superior Court, 122 Cal. App. 3d 147, 175 Cal. Rptr. 851 (1981), which relied on Graham v. Sissor-

Tail, Inc., *supra* note 35, in holding that the N.Y.S.E. arbitration procedure was unconscionable. One commentator concluded that there is "danger of over-intrusive lawmaking by courts armed with substantive unconscionability. . . . Moreover, courts are not competent to evaluate the fairness of the arbitration." Note, 70 CAL. L. REV. 1014, 1046 (1982).

49 *See* THE S.I.C.A. ARBITRATOR'S MANUAL.

50 *GAO Report*, *supra* note 7.

51 *See* MORRIS, MASUCCI, and CLEMENTE, *Securities Arbitration at Self-Regulatory Organizations*, SECURITIES ARBITRATION 289-290 (D.E. Robbins ed., 1992).

52 Each arbitrator is asked to evaluate the others in terms of understanding of (1) the issues in the case; (2) the legal principles involved; (3) demeanor; (4) about the chair's performance; and (5) asked for a rating (excellent, very good, adequate, inadequate). *See Peer Evaluation Questionnaire*, the 1992 edition of SECURITIES ARBITRATION at 287.

53 *See id.* at 291.

54 *See, for example*, THE SECURITIES ARBITRATION COMMENTATOR. Decisions are also reported in THE WALL STREET JOURNAL and other publications.

Chapter 11

TYPES OF CLAIMS IN SECURITIES CASES

When a securities client seeks a remedy for some perceived unfairness or wrongful conduct by his or her broker, the first step is to evaluate the case from the viewpoint of arbitration. Several questions need to be asked: What document forms the basis for the client/broker relationship? Has it been signed by the client?[1] Will it sustain a challenge as a valid contract? If it is one of the typical customer agreements containing an arbitration clause, arbitration will probably be required. What type of claim or claims can be made? Where can they be resolved? Even after *Rodriguez de Quijas*, although it may be possible to bring some claims in litigation, still others have to be resolved in arbitration.

1) EVALUATION OF CUSTOMER CLAIMS IN ARBITRATION DISPUTES

A) Step One: Prefiling Analysis

The first step in making a decision to arbitrate is to evaluate the claim. It is essential to obtain as much and as good information from the claimant as possible. This chapter examines the evaluation of the allegations to determine if the dispute justifies filing a claim.

i) Factual Determination. It is important to understand the case in detail before commencing the arbitration; the statement of claim will, of course, be more compelling if the facts are fully set out.

a) Client and Initial Documents. The first caveat in evaluating a claim is not to make the mistake of completely believing the story of every customer. Often the customers' memories will be selective. Customers may not give the full picture, feeling that to do so will make the case less appealing. Therefore, the first thing to do is carefully discuss the case with the customer. In this discussion, it is important to assess the customer's willingness and ability (physical and psychological) to undertake a case; understanding and sophistication regarding securities and the transactions complained of and prior trading history at this and other firms; communications (oral and written) with the brokerage firm; and the credibility of the customer as a witness, as well as matters which could be used to challenge credibility, such as prior litigation, criminal convictions, and license revocations.

At the same time, the customer should have furnished account documentation and any correspondence with the firm. After review of this information, a second interview might be in order in which the customer could be questioned in depth about the transactions at issue.

ii) Public Information. After this elicitation of information from the customer, the next step is to obtain information from public sources regarding the brokerage firm and employees. While this material may be considered part of the discovery process discussed in chapter 12, it does not logically fall into the materials that are requested of the other party.

Newspapers, particularly *The Wall Street Journal* and *The New York Times*, often discuss arbitration cases that are being brought by investors, as well as outline the awards given and review disciplinary sanctions imposed on brokerage firms and registered representatives. Other magazines and newsletters also review developments in arbitration from time to time. These sources give general information, but occasionally will discuss areas where abuses have arisen. If available, a search on one of the computer retrieval networks could prove helpful in developing theories and finding similar cases in progress or already decided.

Because of the state and federal regulation of the exchanges, disciplinary actions against firms and individual employees are reported. This public information is available from the N.A.S.D. and state securities commissions. In 1993 the SEC gave approval to establishment of a N.A.S.D. hotline for information regarding brokers and firms. Information that can be obtained includes (1) pending and final disciplinary actions; (2) criminal indictments and record; (3) civil judgments; and (4) arbitration awards. The telephone number is 800-289-9999.[2]

An excellent source of materials on arbitration is a monthly publication, the SECURITIES ARBITRATION COMMENTATOR (14 Highland Place, Maplewood, N.J. 07040; tel. 201-378-5880, fax 201-761-1504). Another source of information regarding sanctions is compiled by the Mortgage Asset Research Institute, Inc., available on LEXIS. These sources include disciplinary actions and sanctions collected from the N.A.S.D., SEC, stock exchanges, as well as reports by other federal and state agencies, HUD (Mortgage Review Board), and the media.[3]

B) Step Two: Analysis of Types of Claims in the Broker-Customer Relationship

What are the types of claims for actions by a broker that may arise in the broker-customer relationship?

The following is a non-exclusive list of the types of claims that can exist in the broker-customer relationship and may be subject to resolution through the arbitration process. Most claims are for fraud. Approximately 50 percent of all N.Y.S.E. complaints involve unauthorized trading. Churning and suitability are also common. RICO claims are becoming more prevalent.

i) Transactions Giving Rise to Customer Claims. In determining whether a claim that can lead to a recovery exists, two questions must be resolved. First, is there a transaction which itself gives a right to relief? Second, what is the specific grounds for relief? In the following discussion, the general duties of a customer's account executive or registered representative and the brokerage firm are discussed.

Most customer claims exhibit a number of potential grounds for claiming relief. Generally, there are certain duties that the representative and firm undertake. These duties vary to some degree by the nature of the business. For example, long-term bond investing may be more conservative than stock trading; stock trading more "safe" than options or futures speculation. Consequently, in reviewing the claim, the first attention should be given to the customer and the type of trading.

These claims may be phrased in terms of brokers professional "malpractice." Under New York CPLR 214(6), there is a three year statute of limitations on such claims. But by alleging "professionalism," the issue of fiduciary duty arises, which may toll the period or invoke the continuous transaction doctrine, both of which are discussed below.[4]

a) Shingle Theory. In addition to the other rules and regulations applicable to brokers, common law duties and fiduciary obligations also exist. One of the most basic is the "Shingle Theory," which requires the broker to exercise the standard of care in dealing with customers that other brokerage firms exercise in dealing with the public. In making recommendations for the purchase and sale of securities, for example, there is an implied representation that the broker has done the research and has an adequate basis for the recommendation. The Shingle Theory intertwines with the other duties of the broker to the customer, in reality due to the broker's holding himself out as having expertise. It is a factual question if the customer has relied on this representation of adequate professional performance and been damaged.

The Shingle Theory carries with it certain responsibilities for those engaged in the industry. These responsibilities are set forth in not only the general principles of the trade, but in the securities industry rules and regulations regulating the conduct of those doing business with the public. These regulations arise from the Securities and Exchange Commission as well as SRO, exchange, and other sources. The broker, for example, is required to exercise the "fair and equitable principles" of the securities business, evaluate the capacity of the customer for risk based on "knowing the customer," execute trades in a professional manner, and the like. Failure to perform these basic duties will result in claims, probably for breach of contract or negligent performance of duty.

b) The "Know Your Customer" Rule. The N.A.S.D. and SROs require that, "every member organization [broker] is required . . . to . . . [u]se due diligence to learn the essential facts relative to every customer, every order, every cash or margin account accepted or carried by such organization and every person holding power of attorney over any account accepted or carried by such organization."[5]

c) Violation of Exchange Rules. Unfortunately, investors do not have a private right of action against an exchange for violating or failing to enforce exchange rules. Under § 6(b) of the 1934 Act, the SEC is required to ensure that the exchange has promulgated rules to prevent fraudulent practices, promote just and equitable principles of trading, perfect the mechanism of a free and open market, and demonstrate a capacity to comply with and enforce compliance by its members.

A recent case has determined that this is merely the prerequisite of a broker's registration, and investor's can not sue traders who allegedly violated exchange trading rules and against the exchange for failure to enforce compliance.[6] This is opposed to the older view, where the courts implied a right of action and Congress has then revised the statute without disturbing the previous implied private right of action remedy.[7]

d) Common Stock, Bond, Convertible Securities, Options, Commodities, and Other Trading. Most investors are familiar with trading in ownership interests in productive companies through common stocks and bonds, convertible securities, and similar securities, as opposed to purchasing an asset itself. Some, probably the more sophisticated, invest in options to be exercised in the future to purchase (a "call" option) or sell (a "put") securities. Fewer invest in other futures transactions such as the right to buy or sell commodities such as oil, gold, or orange juice. Today, most small investors do not themselves invest in individual securities, but instead buy mutual fund shares. The mutual funds in turn then invest in stocks, bonds, and other investment securities, usually dependent on the objective of the fund. For example, a growth fund will concentrate on investments that promise future growth, while an income fund will invest in high yield securities.

It is beyond the scope of this book to discuss investment strategies and appropriate vehicles for various investors. But in evaluating a claim, it is important to understand the nature of the trading in relation to the customer and her investment objectives. Obviously, something has gone wrong in the customer's opinion regarding her investment plan; otherwise, there would be no reason to seek recovery.

Most losses in securities transactions do not give rise to a right to recover from anyone. They are just poorly made or timed investments. The securities markets are, by their very nature, volatile and securities prices fluctuate widely depending on the market and economic conditions as well as the particular company or investment. The following discussion will examine those areas where a broker's influence on the customer to invest in particular investment vehicles may result in recovery in the event such advice turns out to have been wrong and the customer loses money.

e) Short sales. If an investor believes that the price of a security will decline, she can sell the security in the marketplace, borrowing it from the broker. Ultimately, the "short sale" will have to be "covered" by the purchase of the security to replace the one sold from the seller's account, and the seller will be responsible for any dividends or distributions paid on the shorted security during the period it is borrowed. Because it is risky to sell something not owned with the hope of buying back later at a lower price, the broker must explain the risks carefully to the customer. The SEC has regulated short sales since 1938.

f) Margin Accounts. Margin sales occur when the customer trades in securities on credit. In order to trade on credit, or margin, the investor normally has signed a margin account agreement. This may be unlike a cash account where no agreement may be required by the firm. The term "margin" normally refers to the initial amount the customer must invest in order to purchase the securities. The balance of the purchase price is on loan from the brokerage firm. The amount of margin is set by The Federal Reserve System as part of the Fed's control over extension of credit, and has been typically 50-55 percent of the purchase price.[8]

Obviously, because the brokerage firm is providing loans to customers, it ties up firm capital. Under margin rules,[9] the customer must provide collateral to secure the loan. If the value of the securities used as collateral goes down, additional collateral may be demanded (in a "margin call"). Before a broker will permit trading on margin, the firm will usually require a margin account agreement.[10]

After the initial purchase of the securities, where the Fed's margin must be met by the brokerage firm, the firm can continue to provide loans to the customer. This can also occur when there is no initial margin on a purchase of a security, but the customer desires to borrow against the securities in his or her account. The amount of margin required in these transactions (called "maintenance margin") is set by the brokerage firm under SRO or exchange rules, not the Fed. Typically, it is the same as the Fed's margin, that is, 50 percent of the loan is required as continuing collateral. If the price of the securities constituting the collateral fall, the amount of the margin loan remains the same as the initial loan amount, and the firm will require additional collateral to meet internal or maintenance margin requirements. When this occurs, the industry practice is to give notice either oral or written, which requires the customer to deposit additional funds or securities. This notice is known as a "margin call." If a call is not met, the securities may be liquidated and debt repaid. Often brokerage firms will feel overextended if too many customers have margined a particular stock, however, and will reduce the amount of loans outstanding on that stock by calling for repayment of margin loans by those customers despite the fact that the internal margin collateral is met. The questions in arbitration cases normally relate to the call and how the later liquidation sale was made by the firm.[11]

g) Boiler room sales. Unscrupulous brokers will often make cold calls to individuals who are not customers for the purpose of recommending purchase of securities in a high pressure sales campaign. While the SEC has taken the position that this does not *per se* constitute a fraudulent activity, because the customer's interests are not related to the recommended security, the "know your customer" and "Shingle Theory" may form the basis of a claim. Further, the sales personnel probably have not been registered to sell securities and have not performed due diligence in obtaining information about the securities recommended. Offenses are primarily brought by the N.A.S.D. and state securities commissioners rather than private claimants.

h) Unregistered Brokers and Securities. In some cases, a customer who understood and was able to bear the risks will still be able to recover the amount of her investment, plus interest and attorney's fees. This is due to statutory provisions, which must be observed in an arbitration.[12]

For example, where the brokerage firm or the customer account representative is not registered in the state where the customer is located, the failure to meet the registration requirements of the state's Blue Sky Law (see below discussion) will permit rescission of the transactions effected while not registered. Where the securities are not registered for sale, and are not subject to an exemption from registration, under both the 1933 Act[13] and the Blue Sky Laws of some states,[14] the customer will be permitted to rescind the purchase, recover interest and attorney's fees.

Both of these grounds for recovery are statutory. A few jurisdictions will permit the broker to raise equitable defenses against rescission, usually estoppel and ratification.

New York law will govern many cases, however, due to the governing law provision in most brokerage firm customer agreements. New York does not permit a private right of action for failure to register under its Blue Sky Law,[15] which may well preclude action on these grounds before arbitrators.

i) Clearing Firms. A clearing firm is the one that settles trades for the accounts on exchanges where the customer's firm, which initiates the trading and has the customers, is not a member, and often mails confirmations and monthly statements to customers for smaller firms that may not be able to meet recordkeeping or other regulatory requirements. The customer's firm is known as the "introducing firm" and pays a fee to the clearing firm.

Because the relationship of most clearing firms with the customer is tenuous, claims will result in recovery only if the customer can establish some duty owed by the clearing firm. Often this is by showing the clearing firm is a control person or it acted in aiding and abetting[16] the violations of the introducing firm or its employee.

j) Class Actions in Arbitration.[17] The class action permits many persons with common claims to sue or be sued through a single representative. Federal Rule of Civil Procedure 23(a) requires that the class action litigation can be maintained if: (1) joinder of the number of parties, each with their own legal representatives is impractical; (2) the class has common questions of fact or law; (3) the representative presented has common claims and defenses typical of other class parties; and (4) the representative will protect the class members. The joinder of claims into class actions increases the efficiency of the litigation or arbitration, principally through eliminating duplication. It may also permit actions by those injured but in amounts too small to justify expenditures for individual action.

Class actions can be arbitrated despite the procedural problems of certifying the class, selecting counsel, providing notice, and safeguarding the class against improper settlement.

Arbitration as a class action is improper unless the arbitration agreement provided for consolidation. The relation between class actions and consolidations is that in a class action many persons with similar claims are represented by one "lead" attorney while in a consolidated action, the similar factual issues allows a joinder of claims with each party still represented individually. Under Federal Rule of Civil Procedure 42(a), consolidation of arbitration proceedings has been held to further the federal preference for arbitration. This rule does undermine policies supporting class actions,[18] because the result--a hybrid proceeding--is inefficient.

Originally the S.I.C.A. recommended that class arbitration actions should be referred to the courts for resolution of the certification issue, followed by arbitration. This would have resulted in a hybrid action: the courts resolving certification, notice to class members, and supervising the process including settlement for the protection of the absent class members; and the arbitrators determining the facts of the dispute in accord with the arbitration agreement,[19] but in 1992 the S.I.C.A. adopted a rule that does not permit arbitration of class actions.[20] This will not apply in AAA arbitrations, since the AAA has no such rule, and the SRO rules apply only to agreements after October 29, 1993. This will also preclude a party from demanding arbitration of a class action brought in court, even if there is a valid arbitration clause designating an SRO forum. Under the S.I.C.A. Uniform Code of Arbitration § 1(d)(ii), a party to a class action can be heard by the AAA as a non-self-regulatory organization, if ordered by a court, if the parties agree, or if the claimant demonstrates he has not elected to participate in or has withdrawn from the class action. The issue of whether a party is within the class is determined by arbitrators. No industry party can seek arbitration against any customer who has initiated a class action or is a member of a class.[21]

C) Step Three: Typical Claims in Securities Cases

The following discussion briefly examines the different claims that may arise in securities cases. Each cause of action set forth may exist in conjunction with other claims. The list should be considered as additive; one claim does not necessarily exclude another. And even those that might be considered to do so can be plead in the alternative: if one permits recovery, the claimant can elect to proceed on that basis; if it is precluded due to failure to prove the elements of that claim, then the claimant can proceed on the other claims. The claimant should carefully examine the law in light of the facts of each case in determining to use these claims.

In most cases only actual damages are recoverable. The claimant has the burden of proof of damages and normally must pay his or her own attorney's fees and other costs of the arbitration.

The arbitration provisions provide what kind of claims are arbitrable, usually in the broadest terms. For example, the S.I.C.A. arbitration clause in brokerage firm-customer cases will cover "all controversies and disputes arising out of" the relationship and covers therefore all possible matters relating to the nature of their contract and all activities related thereto. The question of exclusions of certain areas from arbitration, such as the clause excluding violations of federal securities law claims in older customer agreements, is one of the first questions that must be addressed in evaluating a case.[22]

i) Fraud. In many cases the customer will believe that he or she has been defrauded by the misrepresentations and/or conduct of the broker. Fraud is a concept from the ancient tort common law, giving damage recovery to the injured person only if the elements of fraud are present. In different jurisdictions the necessary elements to prove fraud may differ, so it is important to examine the law as the claim is drafted to be sure to include all of the requirements; otherwise, the claim can be held defective with the requirement of revision and perhaps the inability to thereafter bring the claim due to the statute of limitations[23] or some other defect in pleading.

a) Common law fraud. In many cases the customer will believe that he or she has been defrauded by the misrepresentations and/or conduct of the broker. When a party intentionally and deliberately misrepresents a material, important fact for the purpose of inducing the other person to make an agreement or do an act, fraud occurs. At common law there were three major elements to fraud claims: (1) the party making the misrepresentation must know it was false or have made it in reckless disregard or indifference to the truth; (2) he must have intended to deceive the other party; (3) and the other party must have actually relied on the misrepresentation and sustained damage as a result of relying on the misrepresentation.

Several factors apply to establishing fraud. First, the misrepresentation can be oral, written, or arise from conduct. Second, intent to deceive is often hard to establish. Third, silence is not usually fraud; there must be a duty to disclose. This duty is not normally present but may exist in a fiduciary relationship where one relies on the utmost disclosure, for example, with trustee and beneficiary or attorney and client. This fiduciary relationship also exists between the broker and customer.[24] Fourth, if a party knows the other party is under a misapprehension and fails to set him right, the failure to correct may be fraud. Fifth, the reliance on the misrepresentation must be justified, and no recovery will be allowed if the true facts could have been readily discovered without difficulty. Exaggerated statements of opinion, advertising claims, and statements regarding value are not misrepresentations, particularly if part of sales talk or "puffing" the attributes of a product.

In different jurisdictions the necessary elements to prove fraud may differ, so it is important to examine the law as the claim is drafted to be sure to include all of the requirements; otherwise, the claim can be held defective with the requirement of revision and perhaps the inability to bring the claim due to the statute of limitations.[25] The elements of fraud required to be set forth in the claim and proved under New York law are referred to as the "five fingers of fraud" and include:

1) Representations;
2) Falsity;
3) Scienter (an intent to make the misrepresentation, or recklessness disregard in making it without knowledge);
4) Deception of the party to whom made; and
5) Injury due to justified reliance on the misrepresentation.[26]

b) Federal Securities Fraud. Fraud is a major feature of the federal securities laws. These statutes usually make it easier than common law to prove fraud.

1) 1934 Act Fraud: Rule 10b-5. The Securities and Exchange Act of 1934[27] contains one of a number of provisions permitting private actions for violations of federal securities laws. While some provisions of the Securities Act of 1933 and the Securities and Exchange Act of 1934 permit private actions directly, in other sections an implied private right of action has been found to exist by the courts. This is the case with § 10(b) under the 1934 Act.[28] Under this provision, the Securities and Exchange Commission has adopted Rule 10b-5 in order to prohibit fraudulent actions, devices, schemes, misstatements and omissions.[29] The relevant provisions are:

- *Section 10(b): Regulation of the use of manipulative and deceptive devices:*
  It shall be unlawful for any person, directly or indirectly, by the use of [1] any means or instrumentality of interstate commerce or [2] of the mails, or [3] of any facility of any national securities exchange--
  (a) To effect a short sale, or to use or employ any stop-loss order in connection with the purchase or sale, of any security registered on a national securities exchange, in contravention of such rules and regulation as the Commission may prescribe as necessary or appropriate in the public interest or for the protection of investors.
  (b) To use or employ, in connection with the purchase or sale of any security registered on a national securities exchange or any security not so registered, any manipulative or deceptive device or contrivance in contravention of such rules and regulations as the Commission may prescribe as necessary or appropriate in the public interest or for the protection of investors.

- *Rule 10b-5: Employment of manipulative and deceptive devices:*
  It shall be unlawful for any person, directly or indirectly, by the use of [1] any means or instrumentality of interstate commerce, or [2] of the mails, or [3] of any facility of any national securities exchange,
  (a) to employ any device, scheme, or artifice to defraud,
  (b) to make any untrue statement of a material fact or to omit to state a material fact necessary in order to make the statements made, in the light of the circumstances under which they were made, not misleading, or
  (c) to engage in any act, practice, or course of business which operates or would operate as a fraud or deceit upon any person, in connection with the purchase or sale of any security.

Therefore, the Rule 10b-5 action is one concerning a violation of federal securities laws. The first issue in arbitration is whether this claim, since based on federal law, is outside the predispute agreement to arbitrate. If so, there is a right in the claimant to take this issue to court instead. See the discussion of 1934 Act Rule 15c2-2 language in chapter 6 and the motion to dismiss in chapter 12.

Whether in arbitration or court, the claimant for a Rule 10b-5 recovery must establish:

1. jurisdictional means--usually easy to do by proving use of an instrumentality of interstate commerce, such as the telephone, the mails, or the facilities of a national securities exchange, such as trading over one of the exchanges.
2. standing to sue--the claimant must be either a purchaser or seller of securities.
3. misrepresentation or omission--the fraud must be established. Note that an omission (silence) is included, which is a departure from common law fraud principles.
4. scienter--the respondent must have acted with intent; negligent action is not enough unless the representation or omission is made in reckless disregard of the truth.[30]
5. materiality--the misstatement or omission must have influenced the investor-claimant's decision to purchase or sell the security. This is a question that will depend in large part on the facts.
6. justified reliance--the question of the reasonable reliance by the claimant on the misrepresentation or omission is also largely a question of fact. The proof of reliance is especially difficult in an omission case and may be dispensed with. The courts have developed, however, a theory of "fraud on the market" whereby if there is a showing that the marketplace for securities has placed some value on the questioned information, such as an effect on the price of the stock when the true information is disclosed, the reliance requirement will be satisfied. Reliance is closely connected to the causation factor.
7. causation--this is the "in connection with" requirement. The claimant must establish that the injury has resulted from the misrepresentation or omission.

This list of factors to consider in a Rule 10b-5 action is sketchy at best, and any analysis of a claim must entail careful preparation and research. For example, in addition to the questions presented by the requirements listed above, the statute of limitations may be one or three years for the claim.[31] There are many treatises and articles regarding 10b-5 actions and they should be consulted if needed.

2) 1933 Act Fraud. In addition to common law and Rule 10b-5 fraud claims, it is also possible to claim fraud under § 11 and 12 of the

Securities Act of 1933[32] for misstatements and omissions in a registration statement. Under § 5 of the 1933 Act, registration statements, basically a disclosure document called a "prospectus," are required to be filed *prior* to the sale of securities and the prospectus delivered to the purchaser. This statute allows a direct action by the party who purchases the securities.

Section 11 provides:

> In case any part of the registration statement, when such part became effective, contained an untrue statement of a material fact or omitted to state a material fact required to be stated therein are necessary to make the statements therein not misleading, any person acquiring such security (unless it is proved that at the time of such acquisition he knew of such untruth or omission) may, either at law or in equity, in any court of competent jurisdiction, sue--
>
> 1. every person who signed the registration statement;
> 2. every person who was a director of (or person performing similar functions), or partner in, the issuer at the time of the filing of the part of the registration statement with respect to which his liability is asserted;
> 3. every person who, with his consent, is named in the registration statement as being or about to become a director, persons performing similar functions, or partner;
> 4. every accountant, engineer, or appraiser, or any person whose profession gives authority to a statement made by him, who has with his consent been named as having prepared or certified any part of the registration statement, or as having prepared or certified any report or valuation which is used in connection with the registration statement, with respect to the statement in such registration statement, report, or valuation, which purports to have been prepared or certified by him;
> 5. every underwriter with respect to such security.
>
> If such person acquired the security after the issuer has made generally available to its security holders an earning statement covering a period of at least twelve months beginning after the effective date of the registration statement, then the right of recovery under this subsection shall be conditioned on proof that such person acquired the securities relying on such untrue statement in the registration statement or relying upon the registration statement and not knowing of such omission, but such reliance may be established without proof of the reading of the registration statement by such persons.

Section 12 of the 1933 Act provides:

> Any person who--
>
> 1. offers or sells a security in violation of § 5, or
> 2. offers or sells a security (whether or not exempted by the provisions of § 3, other than paragraph (2) of subsection (a)

> thereof), by the use of any means or instruments of transportation or communication in interstate commerce or of the mails, by means of a prospectus or oral communication, which includes an untrue statement of a material fact or omits to state a material fact necessary in order to make the statements, in the light of the circumstances under which they were made, not misleading (the purchaser not knowing of such untruth or omission), and who shall not sustain the burden of proof that he did not know, and in the exercise of reasonable care could not have known, of such untruth or omission, shall be liable to the person purchasing such security from him who may sue either at law or in equity in any court of competent jurisdiction, to recover the consideration paid for such security with interest thereon, less the amount of any income received thereon, upon the tender of such security, or for damages if he no longer owns the security.

3) Other Securities Statutes. The Investment Company Act of 1940[33] imposes registration and disclosure requirements that encompass broad anti-fraud prohibitions through rules on mutual funds and investment companies, including mutual funds and their distributors, which may include stockbrokers. An implied private right of action has been found for most violations of the Act, so claims can be made in a securities arbitration.

The Investment Advisor's Act of 1940[34] requires registration of investment advisors, periodic reporting including disclosure of fees and the identity and background of associated persons, and prohibits misrepresentations and fraud in connection with giving investment advice.[35] Although technically exempt from the Act because they are not being compensated separately for advice apart from the normal commissions, brokers must be careful in making investment recommendations to customers. If the broker is, however, paid contingent on the profit made or paid for advice, there is potential for Investment Advisers Act remedy.

ii) RICO. The Racketeer Influenced and Corrupt Organizations Act[36] includes securities fraud in its organized crime and racketeering activities. *McMahon* held that RICO claims were arbitrable. Several states have also enacted similar legislation, known as "little RICO" statutes. There is no requirement that the participants actually engage in organized crime; it is enough if their actions fall within those prohibited. RICO is violated whenever two persons associated with an "enterprise" engage in a "pattern of racketeering activity," which is defined as two predicate acts occurring within 10 years of each other.[37] The enterprise can be informal, but is more easily proved when there is a group with a common purpose, continuity of personnel, and organization. RICO claims are not easy to plead or prove.

Since § 1962(c) of RICO requires two separate entities--(1) a RICO enterprise employing (2) a person--it is necessary to establish that the person acted in violation of the Act; the enterprise is often a passive instrument or victim of the racketeering activity. Consequently, a brokerage firm may be found to be the instrumentality even if it is not the person committing RICO violations.[38] On the other hand, if the brokerage firm has participated in the RICO actions, it too will be actively committing the violation. Consequently, the claimant bringing a RICO action must have a good understanding of the predicate RICO acts, the facts of the case, and knowledge of the RICO statute of limitations (four years).[39]

Unlike a simple damage recovery in Rule 10b-5 cases, if RICO has been violated, the actual damages shown are trebled and attorney's fees and costs are recoverable even in arbitration proceedings.[40] It is for these reasons of recovery that RICO violations are attractive for arbitration or litigation. But RICO is not a common securities arbitration claim, and the claimant will have to educate the panel. There is also reluctance to find treble damage awards, just as arbitrators hesitate to award punitive damages.[41] But one of the major advantages is recovery of attorney's fees. This factor may improve settlement positions as well.

iii) ERISA Claims. As discussed in chapter 8, a retirement plan governed by the Employee Retirement Income Security Act (ERISA)[42] can be forced to arbitration.[43]

ERISA imposes significant liabilities on persons who render financial advice to a retirement plan for compensation. These persons are labeled "fiduciaries." The Department of Labor has determined that a broker can be considered a fiduciary if (1) compensation is received for advice regarding value of the plan's assets, recommending purchases or sales of securities, *and* (2) the advice given is for this plan's particular needs and will serve as the primary basis for the plan's investment decisions.[44] The investments recommended must be diversified and "prudent." In determining if the mix of recommendations for a plan are prudent, the suitability determination of the recommendation must take into account safety, possibility of gain, and plan purposes. This is similar to the question of suitability for the individual investor. But a broker will not be considered an ERISA fiduciary if his or her duties are only executing trades in plan securities.

The statute of limitations under ERISA is the earlier of (1) six years after occurrence or the last date the fiduciary could have corrected the violation, or (2) three years after actual knowledge of the violation.[45]

iv) Blue Sky Law. As noted in the RICO discussion above, state laws may also include a racketeering prohibition. But most state remedial provisions are contained in the "Blue Sky" or state securities laws. A common statute is the Uniform State Securities Act[46] that governs distribution of securities within the state; tender offers; provides for registration and regulation of broker-dealers and investment advisors; and may provide antifraud penalties similar to Rule 10b-5.[47] See, for example, Uniform Securities Act § 101, which provides:

> Any person who:
> 1. Offers or sells a security in violation of subsection (2) of § 17 or 101 or 62-151, or of any rule or order under § 5 which requires the affirmative approval of sales literature before it is used or of any condition imposed under § 165 or 169; or
> 2. Offers or sells a security by means of any untrue statement of a material fact or any omission to state a material fact necessary in order to make the statements made, in the light of the circumstances under which they are made, not misleading, the buyer not knowing of the untruth or omission, and who does not sustain the burden of proof that he did not know, and in the exercise of reasonable care could not have known, of the untruth or omission;
>
> is liable to the person buying the security from him, who may sue either at law or in equity to recover the consideration paid for the security, together with interest at six per cent per year from the date of payment, costs, and reasonable attorneys fees, less the amount of any income received on the security, upon the tender of the security, or for the damages if he no longer owns the security. Damages are the amount that would be recoverable upon a tender less the value of the security when the buyer disposed of it and interest at six per cent per year from the date of disposition.

There may be other state legislation or regulation that will provide grounds for a claim in securities arbitration. The claimant should carefully examine local securities laws to see if any are applicable to the facts of the claim. Unfortunately, New York does not have such a provision.[48] Local laws may also permit claims based on a particular type of investment. For example, real estate syndication laws may impact on publicly traded real estate limited partnerships.

v) Breach of Contract. A common securities arbitration claim is for breach of contract. Where one party promises, either impliedly or expressly through oral communication or in writing, to perform a certain thing and refuses or fails to do so, the other party has an action for the failure or breach of the promisor's obligation. Recovery is usually compensatory; the monetary amount the claimant proves is necessary to put him in as good a position as if the promise had been performed in full. Normally all damages flowing from the breach that are reasonably foreseeable are also recoverable as incidental or consequential to the breach. But if the damage is unusual or unexpected, it is not foreseeable and recovery will be denied. Also the non-breaching party has a duty to take any action necessary to make sure that the damages are mitigated, that is, kept to the minimum, even though he has done nothing wrong. Breach of contract may also permit specific performance, an order requiring the breaching party to perform as promised, but this is an unusual remedy and requires, among other things, that money damages would not adequately compensate the claimant. Specific performance would not be available in securities cases because money damages will normally make the claimant whole.[49]

If there are particular promises made to the claimant, a breach of contract claim may exist. Particularly, this will be the case in employment contracts for intra-industry arbitrations. A customer may also claim representations of the broker rise to the level of a promise, which if not performed can give rise to a claim.

Some promises may be implied due to the nature of the business, as discussed above under the Shingle Theory. Here, if the brokerage firm fails to execute orders, mail confirmations and statements, and the like, a claim for breach of this contractual duty may exist.

Where a promise is made by a brokerage firm employee to a customer and it induces the customer to take some action, a claim under promissory estoppel may exist. Literally, the promisor is stopped from denying responsibility for the actions taken by the promisee/customer in reliance on the promises made. Here the customer must prove that (1) the promise was made; (2) the customer justifiably relied on the promise in taking some action or not taking an action; and (3) damage to the customer has resulted as a direct consequence of taking this action in reliance on the promise. The recovery will be an amount that will put the customer back in the position he would have been in if the action had not been taken. Usually promissory estoppel recovery will be less than for breach of contract, but the advantage is that the claimant will not have to prove existence of a traditional contract.

Claims may also be made on the basis of ERISA requirements that brokers must exercise a standard of care of a prudent fiduciary in rendering investment advice. This statute thus creates a higher duty than normal for brokerage firm behavior. These claims were found arbitrable in *Byrd v. Shearson Lehman/American Express, Inc.*[50]

vi) Unsuitability. The concept of "suitability" derives from the obligation of a broker to "know your customer" and "know the product."

The suitability guidelines of the N.A.S.D. provide:

> In recommending to a customer the purchase, sale or exchange of any security, a member shall have reasonable grounds for believing that the recommendation is suitable for such customer upon the basis of the facts, if any, disclosed by such customer as to his other security holdings and as to his financial situation and needs.[51]

The obligation of brokers to know their customer and to make suitable recommendations requires that recommended purchases and sales should be appropriate to the specific customer's situation and needs. The broker must "make a customer-specific determination of suitability and . . . tailor his recommendations to the customer's financial profile and investment objectives."[52] An unsuitable investment recommendation may be actionable.[53]

Brokers are not obligated to do business with anyone who walks through the door and have a duty to not do business with those judged to be unsuitable as investors or poor credit risks. In fact, a broker must review the trading, even at the customer's demand, and refuse to accept trades if they are not appropriate for this customer and her investment objectives. Much of the brokerage business is done on the basis of an oral agreement--a telephone call ordering or selling thousands of dollars of securities. It is clearly a fiduciary relationship-- one requiring the trusted party (broker) to act in the best interests of the customer. This "know your customer" rule, in turn, requires the broker not to sell securities to a customer that are unsuitable for his or her investment objectives and risk-taking ability.[54]

Because of the application of the Shingle Theory, a broker who gives information and makes recommendations concerning securities or trading or engages in discretionary trading or otherwise is in control of the account, clearly has a fiduciary relationship with the customer. With a discount broker, on the other hand, who gives no advice but merely executes orders, this liability should not attach.

Brokers have argued that suitability provisions create only an ethical and not a legal obligation, but that argument has not won acceptance. In fact, internal brokerage firm control procedures concerning knowledge of the customer and trades may also be used to prove a violation of this duty.

In suitability cases, for example, the duty of the salesman are heightened in the context of transactions involving speculative, low-priced stocks whose values depend on events such as acquisitions rather than company earnings. In such cases, the recommendation must come after the broker has obtained knowledge about the customer's other securities, financial situation, and other "know your customer" information under N.A.S.D. Rules of Fair Practice.[55] Because of the professional status of the salesman, he is required to possess this knowledge, and if the customer placed reliance in his recommendations and they were false, the broker can be sanctioned.[56]

The SEC has proposed a rule which would require an investment advisor to make only suitable recommendations to clients.[57] Under the proposed rule, before providing investment advice, advisers would be required to make a reasonable inquiry into the client's financial situation, investment experience, and investment objectives. This information must be updated periodically, depending upon what is appropriate under the circumstances. Compliance with the proposed rule would not override the obligations of an investment adviser that also is a broker-dealer to meet the suitability requirements imposed on broker-dealers by the federal securities laws and the rules of various self-regulatory organizations.

vii) Churning. As part of the brokerage firm's fiduciary obligation to its customers under the suitability doctrine, not only must the broker consider the risk that the customer can take in making recommendations, but the broker must not trade the account excessively. Because the account registered representative is compensated at most firms according to the commission income his or her sales generate, there is a built-in conflict of interest: the more the trading, the more the broker's commissions. Since much securities trading results from advice given to customers--like insurance, securities are more often sold than a customer asking for them--and this method of compensation,[58] there is inducement to have frequent trades. As a result of this conflict, brokerage firms have strict internal compliance policies regarding the frequency of trading in a customer's account.

When the account has excessive trading, the customer may be able to claim that the account has been "churned." In analyzing if churning has occurred, the account's investment objective and the nature of the customer are important. But three elements are necessary:

1. The broker must have exercised *control* over the account, which is a factual question often depending on the naiveté and lack of securities experience causing a reliance on the expertise of the broker's advice;
2. The *trading is excessive* in light of the customer's financial resources, knowledge of the risks of such trading, and investment objectives of the account; and
3. The broker acted with *fraudulent intent*, or reckless disregard for the customer's interest.

This requires that the broker, and not the customer, initiated the trading activity. Obviously a discretionary account will result in finding a broker in control. But the customer who authorizes each trade in advance may still have a churning claim if the overall amount of trading is excessive and results from trust and confidence in the broker's recommendations.

Churning is normally tied to a pattern of fraudulent activity. Therefore, the elements of a state common law fraud claim must be established and punitive damages can be recovered. Churning itself can also be Rule 10b-5 fraud. The SEC has adopted Rule 15c-7 that prohibits excessive trading by a broker for any discretionary account, finding it a "manipulative, deceptive or other fraudulent device or contrivance."[59]

Excessive trading is found by examining the frequency of trades in the account. This is usually exemplified by the "turnover" in the account:

$$\frac{\text{Amount of Purchases in period}}{\text{Amount Invested}^{60}} = \text{turnover for period}$$

However, the nature of the trading must also be examined because the market for some securities, such as commodities, options, and high-risk stocks, are held for a much shorter period than long-term investments. In some accounts, the turnover will, due to the nature of the investment objective, be higher than in others. Market patterns of trading will also factor into the determination of excessive trading.

Churning normally results in large commissions from this frequent trading. Accordingly, the size of commissions itself can be grounds for a churning claim. For example, a broker may liquidate a position that a customer has had for a long time for the purpose of obtaining commissions. This is often done regardless of the tax consequences. Again it is an unsuitable trade. Because it is a trading pattern that is at issue, a customer is entitled to recover for the excessive commissions resulting from churning even if a profit was made in the account.[61] This is due to the abuse of the customer's confidence in the fiduciary relationship with the broker. Often a clearing firm will be held liable under the theory of "control person" or *respondeat superior*, as discussed below.

The defense most often raised in churning cases is that the trading was initiated by the customer, or he acquiesced in it. Often the firm will write the customer advising against excessive trading when there is a pattern of large trading commissions from an account. These letters are called "comfort" or "activity" letters and result from the firm's supervisory responsibilities. The defense, of course, is that the customer was alerted to the risks of excessive trading by the letter and, if the activity continued, ratified this pattern of trading.

There is a fair amount of literature on the question of churning and excessive trading measurement.[62] One of the easiest defenses against churning is to show that the customer has engaged in this pattern of excessive trading in the past at other firms or contemporaneously. It is for this reason that the broker will request information about the customer's activity in other brokerage accounts in discovery (see chapter 13).

Churning can be found when there are no losses from the trading. In *Davis v. Merrill Lynch, Pierce, Fenner & Smith, Inc.*,[63] the federal court, relying on South Dakota law, found that churning alone was recoverable, even though the 87 year old widow-plaintiff had *no actual losses*. the broker had earned $43,000 in commissions in a 31 month period with average account equity of $144,000. In addition, the Court found the investor entitled to recovery of what the account would have been worth if it had been properly handled. Punitive damages of $2 million were also rewarded, despite compensatory damages of only $100,000, due to the recklessness of the employer in hiring and failing to supervise the employee who engaged in deceitful and fraudulent acts in the regular course of business. The broker argued that there was ratification and waiver of the trading because the plaintiff had received confirmations, monthly statements and even "activity" letters, some of which had been reviewed by her son, and she did not make timely objection. But the court found she lacked capacity for waiver and that individually received documents (even if reviewed by others) do not tell the investor if churning has occurred on an overall basis, since continuous activity is of the essence in churning. The broker was required to establish not only that the account documentation was sent out, but that it was received *and understood* by the investor/customer.

viii) Unauthorized Trading. Where trades are made by the broker without authority, the customer has a claim for unauthorized trading. This is basically an agency question: has the broker acted without authority? Authority can be granted orally, as is the case with most telephone conversations between the broker and client that today account for a vast majority of the trading. As a result of the customer receiving confirmations of trades[64] and monthly statements, a firm will often defend against allegations of unauthorized trading by arguing ratification of the activity by the customer. This is particularly true of a trading pattern established for a long period of time.[65] New York law presumes that a confirmation sent is received.

This assumes that the customer has not granted the broker discretionary authority or limited "time and price" authority to purchase a security. It may be considered a conversion to sell stock without authority. In reality, the question of authority is one of fact. There is no SEC rule covering unauthorized trading, unlike Commodity Exchange Act § 4b,[66] but it can constitute a Rule 10b-5 violation.

ix) Failure to Execute. When the broker fails to execute a customer's order to either purchase or sell a security, the customer will have a claim for failure to execute due to negligence. This might occur when the broker fails to enter the order or the firm fails to act timely on the order and misses the market or fails to notify the customer that the trade did not occur. This often arises when a customer has requested the broker to enter a "stop loss" order and if the order is not entered fails to sell the securities which fall in value. Again, like unauthorized trading, it is difficult to establish these orders if oral. Often a customer will not realize that a written confirmation should be received when orders are given the firm. Most simply, failure to execute is a breach of the brokerage firm's contract with the customer.

x) Mistaken Orders. Mistaken orders are those that have been erroneously made by the broker. This might be due to misunderstanding of the order the customer gave or clerical error in entering the order. Customers will have difficulty here too in establishing exactly what their instructions on the trade were. Ratification occurs when the confirmations and monthly statements are sent the customer and there is a failure to object within 10 days.

xi) Margin Account Litigation and Margin Calls. As noted in the discussion of opening account agreements, most brokers will require arbitration of disputes in margin accounts.[67] If the required margin is not maintained, the customer's margin agreement will normally give the broker the right to liquidate collateral at any time the margin falls below a certain amount. This means sale of the collateral, normally the securities in the account. As noted above, a margin call will normally be sent by the brokerage firm to the customer requiring additional collateral be deposited and warning that otherwise liquidation of some or all the securities in the account will occur.

In times when the market falls quickly, such as occurred in October 1987, firms may be forced to liquidate securities without notice to maintain security on loans. This is normally permitted by the customer's margin account agreement.[68] This is the risk of trading on margin: the leverage of using borrowed money to purchase securities produces a reward if the price of the security goes up, but, conversely, if the price declines, the customer may be wiped out and wind up owing the brokerage firm the balance of the loan.

Margin complaints can also be in terms of a broker recommending trading on margin. If this leverage trading is too dangerous for the customer, it can be grounds for a suitability and perhaps a Rule 10b-5 claim. There is a good chance of success in a claim (1) where the broker did not explain to the customer or customer did not understand the risk that the stock collateral could be liquidated to meet margin calls; (2) if the brokerage firm liquidated the collateral either without sending a margin call or giving the customer prior notice and the ability to cover; (3) where the broker liquidated a portion of the collateral without permitting the customer to select which securities were sold.

There is no private right of action for Regulation T violations since Section 7 of the 1934 Act imposes the margin requirements on "creditors," and the rules are imposed to protect the brokerage firm in the extension of credit to the customer. However, the SRO and brokerage firm margin maintenance requirements and rules regarding over leveraging adopted to conform to the SEC regulations may allow claims based on these rules enacted for the protection of the investor.

xii) Misrepresentations or Omissions. Where the registered representative mischaracterized the nature of a security or fails to inform the customer of material facts about the investment, the customer can maintain common law or statutory action under federal or state law for fraud. Sometimes the customer can also raise failure to provide information under the suitability doctrine or exchange rules.

xiii) Know the Product Rule: Broker Ignorance in Areas "Too Dangerous and Too Complicated."[69] Due to the fast changing nature of the securities markets, products offered to investors vary greatly. In essence, the broker owes a duty to the customer to recommend a security only after studying it sufficiently to become informed as to its nature, price, and financial prognosis.[70] While the broker represents that she has expertise, the types of financial products available have proliferated in the recent past to such an extent that almost no one can claim to have a complete grasp of all aspects. Accordingly, the customer will have a claim if the broker has given inaccurate advice regarding a particular investment or trading strategy. A former SEC Chairman, Professor David Ruder, has suggested that some financial products are "simply too dangerous or too complicated" for the individual investor. As new products are developed by the marketplace to meet different investment objectives and risks, it is necessary under the Shingle Theory and suitability for the broker recommending such securities to understand the risks and fully explain them to the customer.

xiv) Forgery. In some cases the broker will have forged the customer's signature to account opening agreements, margin agreements, and the like, arguing that he was authorized to do so in order to open the account quickly since the customer wanted to trade. In other cases, the broker may have the customer sign the agreements in blank and then the broker fills in the blanks with inaccurate information that will permit the broker to exercise discretionary, option, and other high-risk trading that might not otherwise be allowed if information regarding the customer and her account objectives had been correctly recorded. See the discussion in chapter 3 regarding forgery in the execution of account opening agreements. This will also be the claim when the customer signs documents in blank and the broker fills them out incorrectly, often misrepresenting the customer's financial position and investment sophistication to permit unsuitable trading.

xv) Failure to Supervise Employees by the Brokerage Firm. If the account representative has engaged in practices that are actionable, often the firm also has liability because of their failure to supervise. Failure to supervise might also make the firm directly liable as a control person[71] or for a RICO violation.[72]

A brokerage firm is required as a result of this statute by SRO and exchange rules to maintain and enforce a reasonable system of oversight of employees because they deal with customers' funds and securities. This is similar to control person liability, but is directly due to a failure by the firm and not derivative from actions of the controlled employee. A typical example is found in a churning case, where the account activity is excessive considering the nature of the investor and his objectives. As noted above, the firm will normally have created some "paper trail" if the office manager or other compliance personnel have detected a potential problem, such as an activity letter (often a filed acknowledgment from) to the customer indicating the activity levels are authorized.

a) Failure to Supervise as a SEC Violation. The SEC has taken the position that the brokerage firm's duty to supervise is a critical component of the regulatory scheme envisioned by the federal securities laws. In 1964 Congress authorized the SEC to impose sanctions against broker-dealers where the firm had "failed reasonably to supervise, with a view to preventing violations [of the federal securities laws], another person who commits such violation, if such person is subject to his supervision"[73] While there is question as to what the term "subject to his supervision" means, it appears clear that failure to reasonably supervise another person will result in the imposition of sanctions.

However, no sanction under § 15 will result as long as the supervisor "reasonably discharged the duties and obligations incumbent upon him by reason of his firm's procedures" and had no reasonable basis for believing that those procedures were not being followed.[74] Therefore, a question arises if the brokerage firm personnel is truly a supervisor. Often office managers and "line personnel" are supervisory; office personnel, such as compliance officers normally are not.[75] The "statutory supervisor" test is two pronged: (1) was the person in fact a supervisor of the wrongdoer, and (2) did he act reasonably in discharging that supervisory duty.

In failure to supervise cases, the SEC has taken the position that compliance and legal officers of brokerage firms may become liable if they have the degree of responsibility, ability, or authority to affect the conduct of the employee who is the wrongdoer. The reasonable efforts look to more than merely identifying wrongdoing, such as taking steps to see that the violation does not recur. As long as the employee is charged with the duty to supervise, including the power to "hire or fire, reward or punish," as well as when the person is looked to by management to recommend and devise a course of action responding to the misconduct and prevent violations.[76]

While the existence of SEC violations in an arbitration case are not strictly part of a claim, if a failure to supervise is at issue, there is a duty to report the firm's conduct.

b) Firm Compliance Manuals. Firm compliance and supervisory manuals given to the branch offices and home office supervisory personnel, such as those providing procedures to be followed by compliance personnel and the branch managers in reviewing account openings and customer trading activity, will be helpful in pinpointing where the supervisory duty of the firm exists. The claimant should request copies of any compliance manuals, supervisory manuals, letters and memoranda or other documents in discovery (see chapter 13) to see if the internal controls should have alerted the firm to the trouble in the account, and if they failed to take appropriate action. One source for information regarding the activities of brokerage firm's employees, who are often the focus of these claims, is the N.A.S.D. information office. This office will provide public disclosure of information on disciplinary and other actions concerning member firms and associated persons. See also the other sources discussed in the section on Public Information, above.

xvi) Trading Actions. Because a broker is in a position to get information in advance of the customers and makes recommendations, he can trade in securities for his own account. Later on, customers can be brought in. The broker can also trade for himself (or others affiliated with him) prior to executing the customer's order. The broker can also buy for the purpose of selling to the customer at a mark-up or profit. These activities are called "scalping," "front running," and simple price manipulation. There are a number of claims that can result from this activity, but all have a common problem: proving the broker traded in violation of fiduciary duty. This proof may be obtained from SEC or other investigations. Otherwise, it is difficult to find.

xvii) Insider Trading. The broker may trade on "inside information." It is illegal under Rule 10b-5 and The Insider Trading Sanctions Act of 1984 (ISTA)[77] to purchase or sell a security "while in the possession of material non-public information." The ISTA provides for, among other things, treble damages to be assessed against a violator and a bounty of as much as 10 percent of the recovery to private individuals who provide information that results in a disgorgment or recovery by the government. But this type of trading is likely to produce no claim for damage by an investor since it is essentially fraud on the marketplace generally. If the customer, however, can establish the broker had a duty to advise him of the information, a claim may exist. One problem here is that often the customer will have been a "tipper" or "tippee" of the inside information and will be unable to make a claim on the basis of his own actions.

xviii) Limited Partnership and Derivatives. One of the areas of conflict, after the recent well-publicized settlements in the area of unsuitability of limited partnership investments,[78] may be the growing market in derivative securities. Derivatives are financial products whose value is derived from an underlying asset, rate or index. They usually apply to options on individual stocks or stock indexes, financial futures, contracts, and currency or commodity futures and hedges. Other financial practices, such as short sales, reverse repurchase agreements, firm or standby purchase agreements and interest rate swaps, also are sometimes referred to as deviations.

Derivatives are securities where the characteristics of the underlying securities are separately marketed, for example, treasury bonds and long-term mortgages are divided into a zero coupon obligation to pay the principal at maturity and the flow of interest to maturity. Each element is sold and traded separately, often in "pools" of similar investments. Derivatives result from a variety of novel structures, including international currency "swaps" and equity options and indexes, such as the Standard & Poors index futures, or indexes of "baskets" of securities in particular industries, such as utilities, Japanese stocks, or bonds. No one knows how these instruments will react in stressful markets since they have not been tested by time. One troubling concern is the risk to the market makers and participants in these developing securities. This new product market is exploding and the potential risk is unknown in many derivatives. Regulation of net capital for dealers and end-users of these products and margin levels may result.[79]

Another possible source of future concern in limited partnership sales issues is the possibility of imposition against wrongdoing brokage firms of punitive damages in multiple cases. Such a result has been held to not in itself be unreasonable so as to violate substantive due process even though the same conduct gives rise to the recovery.[80] Such awards arguably could bankrupt major investment firms.

D) Intra-Industry Claims

One of the first uses of arbitration in the securities industry was to resolve disputes among the firms themselves.[81] As a means of quickly, efficiently, and economically resolving disputes, the industry experience lead to arbitration with employees as well as customers. Today, a large number of arbitrations within the industry concern employment matters. The N.Y.S.E. reports 440 cases filed in 1991 and decided 124 cases in 1992 between registered representatives and brokerage firms. This was about 40 percent of the N.Y.S.E. caseload, versus the normal 25-30 percent.[82] The N.A.S.D. received 638 cases in 1992 and decided 110.

The SRO arbitration forums typically impose different fees and slightly different procedures for member arbitrations than with public-customer arbitrations.[83] The AAA makes no such distinction.

i) Contract Claims. Between the industry firms, arbitration is still the way to resolve disputes arising out of business activities.[84] These disputes are commonly a result of disagreements regarding settlements of trades, delivery of securities and funds, transfer of accounts, and the like. But parties outside the industry can also avail themselves of arbitration; witness a landlord action against a brokerage firm that was compelled to arbitration even though the landlord was not an exchange member. The arbitration as a result of the firm being a member of an exchange that required members to arbitrate disputes connected to the business.

ii) Employment Claims. Brokerage firms will typically require registered representatives to execute an employment agreement containing a predispute arbitration clause. The uniform registration application, known as the U-4 form, which is used to have the representative registered under the broker's aegis with the state securities regulators and N.A.S.D., or brokerage firm employment or training agreements, all contain an arbitration clause. In addition, the broker will be deemed to have impliedly agreed to arbitration under the rules of the SRO requiring arbitration among affiliates of the SRO members.[85] Even a terminated representative can be required by earlier agreements to arbitrate customer and firm claims. The requirement to arbitrate does not cease with resignation.[86]

a) Arbitration Issues. Typical sexual harassment and discrimination claims brought by employees have resulted in various positions on arbitration. In *Gilmer v. Interstate/Johnson Lane Corp.*,[87] the Supreme Court concluded that arbitration was appropriate even in the case of statutory claims for age discrimination under the Age Discrimination in Employment Act. In a remand of a Title VII sexual harassment claim, compulsory arbitration was enforced in *Dean Witter Reynolds, Inc. v. Alford*.[88] *Gilmer* and *Alford* were covered by the industry arbitration employment agreements. Both decisions relied on the thesis that Congress could have expressly precluded arbitration for violations of these statutes, but did not do so. On the other hand, if the claim is for violation of some statutory provision outside the scope of the contract's arbitration clause, it will not be included under a simple reading of the contract.[89] In two 1993 cases, New York accepted the *Gilmer* precedent for arbitration of age discrimination claims, overturning a 1979 case that found a predispute arbitration clause contained in a U-4 form was unenforceable in a dispute claiming race and sex discrimination in employment.[90]

Section 1 of the Federal Arbitration Act also enumerates certain employment claims that are excluded from arbitration. In *Reid v. Goldman, Sachs & Co.*,[91] a sex discrimination claim was submitted to arbitration because the arbitration clause was with the exchange and not "an employer," which would have triggered the Federal Arbitration Act's prohibition of an employment contract requiring arbitration. But in another case sex discrimination was not found to be within the Form U-4 as it did not arise out of "industry and clearing disputes arising out of . . . business transactions."[92]

b) Discrimination. Typical employment related discrimination claims arise from violations of a member of federal laws:

- The Civil Rights Act of 1964,[93] Title VII, prohibits discrimination on the basis of race, color, religion, sex, or national origin. The Civil Rights Act of 1991[94] expands Title VII and the ADA provisions and provides new remedies. The major claim is sexual harassment.[95]
- The Age Discrimination in Employment Act of 1967[96] prohibits age discrimination, if the employer has more than 20 employees, in hiring, firing, compensation, conditions, privileges, and terms of employment of those over 40.
- The Americans with Disabilities Act of 1990 (ADA)[97] applies to employers with more than 25 employees[98] and prohibits discrimination due to disabilities in hiring, promotions, demotion, transfer, layoff, termination, recruitment, advertising and job application procedures, rates of compensation or fringe benefits, job assignments, leaves of absence, social, recreational and other activities, and any other term of employment.
- The Federal Equal Pay Act of 1963, § 6 of the Fair Labor Standards Act,[99] prohibits discrimination in pay on the basis of sex for equal work performed under similar working conditions where the job requires equal skill, effort, and responsibility.

State and local laws may also impact on pay and discrimination on the basis of race, color, national origin, ancestry, pregnancy, medical condition, marital status or sexual orientation, religion, age, and other factors.

c) Claims in Connection with Termination. The N.A.S.D. has filed rule changes with the SEC regarding Code §§ 1 and 8, which will provide that employment or termination of employment of associated persons will be arbitrable, and clarify that employment discrimination claims and public policy issues will have a panel of a majority of public members. Disputes over compensation, employment contracts, etc., will still be by panels of industry arbitrators.

Typically, termination-connected allegations are asserted by former brokerage firm employees and include the following:

- Wrongful discharge. Although the presumption is that an employee is dischargable anytime, this "At Will" doctrine has become modified in recent law. Often an employment handbook or contract will form the basis to find that there must be "cause" for discharge; that the employment was for a term; or that certain procedures must be followed (a due process concept) to discharge an employee. If there is a contract, whether oral, written, or implied, this can also constitute the grounds for a wrongful termination claim. A statute of frauds defense may be available if the employment contract is not in writing and lasts for more than a year.

- Public policy may also permit a finding that the discharge has been wrongful. Examples of this are discharge for jury duty, political and union activities and affiliations, and whistle blower protection for an employee who reports violations by the employer and is subject to retaliatory discharge.
- Appropriation of customers. Often a broker will leave one firm and take with her customers of the former brokerage firm. In these cases the former employer may seek an injunction against both the former employee and new firm, prohibiting them from using the names and contacts developed that are arguably an asset of the first employer. Sometimes an employer will also argue that there may have been appropriation of trade secrets or processes, such as computer programs and customer lists which are proprietary.

d) Other Employment-Related Claims. Most employment-related claims in securities arbitration relate to money: breach of contract and compensation. In many cases, a defamation claim will also be raised due to the firm's answers on the N.A.S.D. and state regulators Uniform Notice of Termination (U-5), that acts as notice that a reported representative is no longer working for the firm that previously filed the U-4 registration form.[100] It may also inform regulators of any reason why an investigation of the employee's conduct might be appropriate.

In a recent case,[101] a brokerage firm was ordered to pay $1.5 million to a former branch manager who was fired for refusing to condone the office's practice of forging customer's signatures. The firm had filed a U-5 with the N.A.S.D. answering "yes" to the question regarding the employee's being under investigation for fraud, wrongful taking of property, or violating investment related statutes regulations, rules, or industry standards of conduct. The employee argued that such an answer was permanently damaging his reputation in the securities industry, because the U-5 is part of the broker's permanent record. In addition to $750,000 in compensatory damages and ordering the broker to correct the false statement with the N.A.S.D., $750,000 in punitive damages was also awarded.

Normally, however, claims are related to commissions that have not been paid or refund of a "signing bonus," where a representative with a profitable client following will agree to work for a number of years in exchange for a bonus paid upon joining a new brokerage firm and then leaves prior to the time passing.

E) Step Four: Who To Sue?

One of the first questions is which parties can be sued.

i) Direct Liability. Obviously, two parties are named as

respondents in most customer claims: the brokerage firm as the principal or active wrongdoer, and the account representative as an active wrongdoer and agent of the firm. Through the facts of a case, it may develop that other parties are also involved: typically other registered representatives in the brokerage firm; sometimes a firm which acts as a clearing broker; and there may be other individuals who might also have some connection with the claim who should be named as respondents.

One of the major reasons to seek to join others in an arbitration is practical--a better chance to get recovery of damages exists when there are multiple responsible parties, particularly if they are jointly and severally liable, which means that the entire damage award may be collected from any one of the respondents. In the event that one respondent pays the claimant, he is normally entitled to contribution from the other respondents subject to the award but it is collectable at his risk.

Of course, all the respondents must be made subject to the arbitration. This is usually not a problem in industry arbitration or where industry personnel and SRO firms are involved: they are bound to arbitrate disputes;[102] but if private parties are also named, there must be a submission agreement for them to be bound by the arbitration. This may result, however, in limiting the forums where arbitration can be conducted to only those SROs where all industry parties are associated. See the discussion in chapter 6 regarding which disputes are arbitrable. The result may be a bifurcation of the action--one in arbitration pursuant to an arbitration agreement with some of the parties and another in court because parties not subject to the arbitration agreement refuse to agree to arbitrate.

ii) Controlling Person Liability. Under the federal securities laws "[e]very person who, directly or indirectly, controls any person liable under any provision of this chapter or any rule or regulation thereunder shall also be liable jointly and severally with an to the same extent as such controlled person."[103] Thus, an employer may be found to control, or have the right to control, the employee and be responsible, jointly and severally, as a "control person" for the wrongs of the employee. This is often used in securities claims to include the brokerage firm where the action is really for only the registered representative's actions. A similar concept would be common law *respondeat superior* or conspiracy.

iii) Aiding and Abetting Liability. While the person who is the primary violator is obviously a proper respondent in an arbitration claim, any person who may have assisted the primary violator in the conduct complained of may be jointly and severally liable as a secondary party for the injury sustained. These cases usually require "substantial assistance" and knowledge of the violation by the aider and abettor.

A recent U.S. Supreme Court case severly limited the rights to raise aiding and abetting claims in violation of the federal securities laws.[104]

iv) Agency Liability. A party involved in the industry but a non--signatory to the account agreement may also be required to arbitrate any dispute arising from the actions in the account under agency principles.[105]

F) Step Five: Damages or What to Claim?

In addition to the question of which claim or claims to pursue, upon reviewing the facts, the relief that can be claimed will also be discerned. Under the arbitration forum rules, a claim must specifically state the relief sought, which, if possible, will include an amount for money damages.[106] While the arbitrators can give non--monetary relief including specific performance, injunctive relief, declaratory relief, and can order an accounting to assist in such determination, most recovery sought is money.

Monetary recoveries can include:

i) Losses Sustained. If the contract between the broker and customer has been breached by conduct of the broker, a logical place to begin to assess damages recoverable is to tally up the losses and gains realized from the trading. In most cases the customer's income tax records regarding short- and long-term capital gains (Federal Income Tax Schedule D) will give this information easily.

After examination of the total losses in the account, a more detailed financial analysis is probably necessary. Here it may be argued that tax consequences also resulted from the trading patterns that are subject to the claim. For instance, included in a claim for churning or unsuitable trading, may be federal and state taxes required to be paid by the customer due to the broker's liquidating a portfolio of appreciated securities for the purpose of generating commissions or funds with which to engage in additional transactions.

ii) Breach of Promise. If the broker has promised a particular performance, say a return of 15 percent per annum, a breach of contract (promise) claim may be available. This claim will be calculated as if the promised performance had been reached, thus fulfilling the investor's expectations in dealing with the broker-promisor. It is typical contract law. Here the problem is due to the oral nature of the securities business; if there is a promise in writing the evidentiary problem may be overcome.

iii) Commissions. The amount of commissions generated on the trading activity is also easily determined: either from the commissions noted on the slips confirming trades or in discovery from the brokerage firm's commission statements to the broker on the account activity. Of course, commission recovery is part of the churning claim and, as noted above, exists regardless of profit in the trading.

iv) Interest. Most claims will request interest on the amount of damage sustained from the date of the injury, especially if there has been a monetary loss due to the actions complained of by the claimant, based on common law notions of fairness and to fully compensate for the breach of duty. In addition to interest on the award, margin violations will permit recovery of margin interest paid. Margin interest may also be a part of unauthorized trading activities, fraud, unsuitability, and other claims. RICO, the 1933 Act, and other statutes expressly permit recovery of interest.

v) Legal Fees and Costs of Arbitration. Normally, attorney's fees are not recoverable in litigation or arbitration for the reasons discussed in chapter 15. If the contract does provide for recovery of legal fees by the prevailing party, however, they can be part of the recovery. Some statutes expressly permit recovery of attorney's fees, such as RICO. Costs of the arbitration are normally apportioned between the parties as the arbitrators deem appropriate.[107]

A rule proposed recently by the N.A.S.D. suggests a modified English approach to recovery of attorney's fees in arbitration. Under this proposed rule, an investor who turns down a settlement offer by a brokerage firm in an arbitration case of more than $250,000, could be forced to pay the firm's attorney's fees and costs, including expert witness fees, if the subsequent award rendered by the arbitrators is less than the settlement offer; but if the award is more than the settlement offer, the customer will be entitled to his attorney's fees and costs in addition to the damages awarded. The proposed rule is opposed by plaintiff's attorneys and investor organizations as an attempt by members of the N.A.S.D. to discourage their clients even more in the mandatory arbitration process.

vi) Punitive and Statutory Multiple Damages. In addition to the actual damages sustained by the claimant, often she will seek punitive damages as well. Literally, punitive damages are assessed to punish the wrongdoer, to deter him and those in his position from acting in a similar wrongful manner with others. Normally, malice must be proved. In theory, punitive damages have no bearing on the amount of actual damages that are intended to compensate a party for actual damage resulting from the complained of actions. They can exceed actual damages many times. Statutes, such as RICO's treble damage award, impose a type of punitive recovery, known as multiple damages, to discourage violation as well as encourage private parties to bring action against violators.

Assessment of these damages is within the arbitrator's powers if permitted under the agreement and state law. In New York, however, punitive damages are not recoverable in most arbitrations under the *Garrity* case.[108] (See the detailed discussion of punitive damage award issues in chapter 15). Several states have recently enacted statutes providing that punitive damage recoveries should accrue to the public. In a recent case under a Florida statute that required 60 percent of a punitive damage award to be paid to the state, the certified question (if the statute applied to arbitration awards) was sent to the Florida Supreme Court to answer.[109] If so, the award would have to be divided between the claimant and state under state law grounds.

vii) Conclusion on Damages. In preparing your case, it is essential to have the relevant facts so that the statement of claim damages can be precise and supported by the proof.

G) Step Six: Do You Need A Lawyer?

i) When is it Time to Get a Lawyer? It may be possible for the investor to work out the problem within the brokerage firm's grievance procedures. Typically a customer will complain to the broker and receive little or no relief. He or she will then complain to the office manager, perhaps with the same result. Finally, the customer should write to the compliance department of the firm. If, after the firm's internal investigation, no relief is offered or the offered relief is unacceptable, the customer will then need to consider whether or not to get a lawyer. But this also may depend on what relief is desired. There are circumstances where an attorney is not warranted. Moreover, an attorney is not required and a claimant can be represented in arbitration by a friend, financial advisor, accountant, or other representative.[110]

If the claim is less than $25,000, few attorneys will take the case, unless attorney's fees and costs can be part of the recovery, as in a RICO action, for example. The predispute arbitration clauses are silent on the recovery of attorney's fees and costs by the customer. It is not likely that the contract between customer and broker will be drafted to provide for recovery of attorney's fees and costs in event of a breach by the firm, since the firm drafts these agreements. Therefore, particularly in small claims, the investor will represent himself. This is referred to as *pro se*--one representing or "for" himself.

The Uniform Code of Arbitration §§ 13 and 27, adopted by the Securities Industry Association Committee on Arbitration in 1979, approved by the SEC in the same year, and adopted by all SROs in 1979 and 1980, specifies a small claims procedure for claims of less than $10,000 which is especially designed for the *pro se* claimant. This dollar limit was changed several times, the last time in 1989. The director of arbitration, under § 27 of the Uniform Code, is permitted to select only one arbitrator for claims between $10,000 and $30,000, unless the parties disagree. AAA Rules 51-55 cover "Expedited Procedures" for claims under $25,000 or under Rule 9 by agreement of the parties. The small claims procedures are discussed in detail in chapters 9 and

12.

In fact, panels are felt to be more generous to the *pro se* claimant where the amount in controversy is small, unless the claimant representing himself is a lawyer (apparently a lawyer-investor is presumed to have more knowledge than a layman).

Common failings of *pro se* claimants include generalized and unsupported statements of the claim; failure to read and understand the answer; failure to prepare properly for the hearing; intimidation, both by the forum and process, as well as the presence of the broker's counsel; lack of litigation skills, such as knowledge of the procedures to subpoena witnesses and documents, cross examination, and inability to use expert witnesses. Generally, *pro se* claimants tend to present a case on emotion, not facts and law. Even in small cases it may be advisable to retain an attorney to draft the complaint or submission. Once a claim goes to arbitration, the procedure is standardized by the Uniform Code as adopted by the SROs or AAA Securities Arbitration Rules.

The 1992 GAO Report[111] found that investors who used attorneys prevailed in the same number of cases whether at the SRO forums or AAA. Moreover, the size of the award when represented was 1.6 times more likely to be in excess of 60 percent of their claim, but for claims under $20,000, those represented were 3.7 times more likely to get 60 percent.

ii) Can You Get By Without a Lawyer? One of the advantages of arbitration is the ability to not use a lawyer. Normally, this is the choice of the *pro se* party, who then goes on to represent herself against the lawyers from the brokerage firm. As the number of securities arbitration cases has roughly doubled from the 1987 *McMahon* decision, however, a number of firms have offered their services, as non--lawyers, to help a party conduct an arbitration. At the present time, there is no prohibition against non--lawyers assisting a party in arbitration.[112] As a result, these firms have engaged in advertising, touting their expertise in the securities business as much as the inability of investors to get lawyers in cases involving losses of less than $100,000 or to find lawyers who are expert enough in securities industry matters to not have to hire an expert to educate them regarding the products and processes used. In many cases, lawyers have been unwilling to take a securities arbitration case on a contingent fee.

In late 1993 the S.I.C.A. proposed an amendment to the Uniform Code of Arbitration which would preclude non--lawyer groups from representing parties in SRO arbitrations. While noting that arbitration is one method where you do not have to have an attorney, there are problems including malpractice and unauthorized practice of law claims. Consumer groups including the American Association of Retired Persons (AARP) and the American Association of Private Investors oppose this rule as precluding those claimants who do not have large enough claims to justify hiring a lawyer to represent them.

2) CONCLUSION

Whether in arbitration or litigation in the courts, the most important element is to be sure that the ground for the claims made exist. Consequently, the facts must be carefully reviewed to determine exactly which claims can be supported by the proof. While some evidence may be unavailable at the time of filing the statement of claim, the evidence that does exist should clearly support the allegations made or point to the existence of other evidence that can be obtained through discovery. Outrageous claims will only make the case look more suspect to either a jury or arbitrators, although the statement of claim can be amended.[113] More importantly perhaps, a carefully prepared claim with exhibits supporting allegations of fact will be conducive to settlement before arbitration or trial.

NOTES

1 For example, a husband's agreement to arbitrate disputes in any brokerage account in which he had an interest did not bind his wife in her separate account since she did not sign the agreement. This was so even though he had been authorized by her to act in a joint account. Any problems arising between the wife and the brokerage firm regarding either the joint account or her separate account would not be affected by the husband's agreement. Dillard v. Cooper, FED. SEC. L. REP. (CCH) ¶ 94,521 (W.D. Okla. 1989).

2 The telephone number of the N.A.S.D. Office of Administrative Services is 301-590-6708.

3 On LEXIS as "Sanctn" file.

4 J. Markham, *Fiduciary Duties Under the Commodities Exchange Act*, 68 NOTRE DAME L. REV. 199 (1992). *See also* the chapter 12 discussion of eligibility requirements.

5 N.A.S.D. Rules of Fair Practice, Article III, § 2; N.Y.S.E. Rule 405.

6 Spicer v. Chicago Board of Options Exchange Inc., 977 F.2d 255 (7th Cir. 1992), where the Court reserved the question if violation of other rules of the exchange might permit an implied private right of action under the four tests of Cort v. Ash, 422 US 66 (1975), for such private right. *Spicer* looked principally at the second factor and found that "[i]n discerning Congress' intent, we look to the language and structure of the statute, the circumstances of its enactment, the legislative history, the contemporary legal context in which Congress acted, and the other Cort factors." The allegation was that the

exchange rules were violated by exorbitant prices charged for index options, and market maker's failed to appear and trade on Black Monday (in October 1987) in breach of C.B.O.E. Rules 4.1 and 8.7(a).

7 *See* Merrill Lynch Pierce Fenner & Smith Inc. v. Curran, 456 U.S. 353 (1982), dealing with the private right of action implied under the Commodity Exchange Act.

8 Reg. T, 12 C.F.R. §§ 220.1 *et seq.* Since Reg. T applies to brokerage firms and not customers, no private right of action exists for its violation by the firm.

9 Section 7 of the 1934 Act regulates the extension of credit for securities transactions. The Federal Reserve System Board of Governors is delegated the authority to set rules governing the amount of margin that may be permitted and on which securities the customer may leverage his investment. Regulation T applies to broker-dealer's extension of credit; Regulation U to bank loans secured by securities; and Regulation G to other lenders. But these rules apply to the initial extension of credit, and it is up to the lender (brokerage firm) as to the maintenance of margin when the price of the collateral goes down. The exchanges and N.A.S.D. have imposed margin maintenance requirements for accounts. *See* N.Y.S.E. Rule 431(b); AMEX Rule 462(b); N.A.S.D. Rules of Fair Practice, Art. III, § 30.

10 This is the typical customer agreement and contains a predispute arbitration clause.

11 *See* the discussion of margin account claims below.

12 If not observed, this is grounds for appeal of the award. *See* the discussions in chapters 5 and 15.

13 1933 Act § 11, 15 U.S.C. § 77m.

14 *See*, for example, Uniform Securities Act § 201.

15 *See* the discussion of Blue Sky Laws.

16 *See* the discussion later in this chapter of control persons and aiding and abetting.

17 *See* S. Kupperman & G. Freemen, *Selected Topics in Securities Arbitration*, 65 TULANE L. REV. 1546, 1577-1593 (1991); Comment, *Classwide Arbitration and 10b-5 Claims in the Wake of Shearson/American Express, Inc. v. McMahon*, 74 CORNELL L. REV. 380 (1990); Note, *Classwide Arbitration: Efficient Adjudication or Procedural Quagmire?* 67 VA. L. REV. 787 (1989).

18 Champ v. Siegel Trading Co., 132 F.R.D. 1; FED. SEC. L. REP. (CCH) ¶95, 605 (N.D. Ill. 1990).

19 This was the approach in Keating v. Superior Court, 31 Cal. 3d 584, 645 P.2d 1192 (1982), *rev'd sub nom.*, Southland Corp. v. Keating, 465 U.S. 1 (1984). Southland is discussed in chapter 6.

20 *See* N.A.S.D. § 12(d); N.Y.S.E. Rule 600(d). This rule is reflected in the customer agreements. See page 82.

21 Uniform Code § 1(d)(iii); N.A.S.D. § 12. This further provides that arbitration can be had once the certification is denied; the class decertified; the customer excluded from the class; or the customer elects not to participate or withdraws.

22 If the Court is convinced that arbitration does not apply to this matter, a stay of arbitration is granted. *See* the discussion in chapter 6.

23 *See* the discussion in chapter 6.

24 *See* the discussion below in "Unsuitability" regarding the fiduciary nature of the broker- customer relationship.

25 *See* the discussion in chapter 6.

26 135 Misc. 2d 1021, 517 N.Y.S. 2d 675 (Sup. Ct. N.Y. Cty. 1987).

27 15 U.S.C. § 78.

28 15 U.S.C. § 78j(b).

29 17 C.F.R. § 240.10b-5.

30 Reckless conduct has been defined in Sundstrand Corp. v. Sun Chemical Corp., 553 F.2d 1033 (7th Cir. 1977), *cert. denied*, 434 U.S. 875 (1977); as:

> . . . [A] highly unreasonable omission, involving not merely simple, or even inexcusable negligence, but an extreme departure from the standards of ordinary care, and which presents a danger of misleading buyers or sellers that is either known to the defendant or is so obvious that the actor must have been aware of it.

31 *See* Lampf Pleva Lipkind Prupis & Petigrow v. Gilbertson, 111 S. Ct. 2773 (1991), *reh'g denied*, 112 S. Ct. 27 (1991). This case held that Rule 10b-5 actions must be commenced within one year from discovery or three years from the date the violation occurred.

32 15 U.S.C. § 77k.

33 15 U.S.C. § 80a-1 *et seq.*

34 15 U.S.C. § 80b-1 *et seq.*

35 § 206(1), 15 U.S.C. § 80b-6, prohibits "any device, scheme or artifice to defraud and client or prospective client," or "operates as a fraud or deceit," self-dealing with a client, and "fraudulent, deceptive, or manipulative" acts or practices in a manner similar to 1934 Act § 10(b) and Rule 10b-5.

36 18 U.S.C. §§ 1961-1968.

37 *See* 18 U.S.C. § 1961 for the elements in a RICO claim.

38 Leonard v. Shearson Lehman/American Express, Inc., 687 F. Supp. 177 (E.D. Pa. 1988).

39 *See* Agency Holding Corp. v. Malley-Duff Associates, Inc., 483 U.S. 143, 107 Sp. Ct. 2759 (1987), which held civil RICO claims were more closely related to the Clayton Act national enforcement provisions than

different state periods for fraud or other federal periods.

40 § 1964(c).

41 *See* the discussion of claims below and punitive damage awards in chapter 15.

42 29 U.S.C. §§ 1001-1461.

43 *See* Byrd v. Shearson Lehman/American Express, Inc., 926 F.2d 116 (2d Cir. 1991), discussed in chapter 8; *Enforceability of Contract Provision to Submit to Arbitratio Disputes involving Claims under Employee Retirement Income Security Act*, 116 A.L.R. Fed. 525 (1993).

44 Labor Regs. § 2510.3-21(c)(1).

45 29 U.S.C. § 1113.

46 7 Uniform Laws Annotated 695 (1958). An excellent examination of the Blue Sky Laws is L. LOSS and E. COWETT, *Blue Sky Law* (1958).

47 *See* Loss and Cowett discussion.

48 *See* N.Y. Executive Law § 63 which does not permit a private person to bring an action, but does give the Attorney General power to bring action against fraudulent buyers and sellers. Section 10(b) and Rule 10b-5 were also silent on a private right of action, but the courts interpreted them to imply such a right, unlike the New York statute.

49 Of course, attorney's fees are still not recoverable in breach of contract cases. Consequently, many claimants will feel that damages do not really "fully" compensate them for the losses incurred. But this is simply a fact of recovery in our legal system. Other nations permit recovery of such expenses, but in the United States they are not part of a damage award absent express statutory authority, such as in RICO (discussed above) and in cases where the parties contract expressly permits such recovery.

50 926 F.2d 116 (2d Cir. 1991)

51 N.A.S.D. Const., Art. III (Rules of Fair Practice), § 2.

52 F.J. Kaufman and Company of Virginia, SEC Rel. No. 27535 (December 13, 1989), 45 SEC DOCKET 120, 125-26.

53 Unsuitability can also be a violation of Rule 10b-5 and ERISA.

54 *See* N.Y.S.E. Rule 405, N.Y.S.E. Manual (CCH) ¶405.

55 N.A.S.D. Policy relating to Art. III, § 2 of the N.A.S.D. Rules of Fair Practice.

56 *See* In Re Hellie, SEC Rel. No. 29468 (July 23, 1991), FED. SEC. L. REP. (CCH) ¶ 84,834; Philips & Co., 37 SEC 66 (1956); Eugene Erdos, 47 SEC 985 (1983), *aff'd*, 742 F.2d 507 (9th Cir. 1984).

57 SEC proposed Rule 206(4)-(5) under the Investment Advisors Act of 1940 (March 16, 1994).

58 *See* Note, *Churning by Securities Dealers*, 80 HARV. L. REV. 869 (1967); Winslow & Anderson, *A Model for Determining the Excessive*

Trading Element in Churning Claims, 68 N.C. L. REV. 327 (1990); Poser, *Option Account Fraud: Securities Churning in a New Account*, 39 BUS. LAW. 2 (1984).

59 17 C.F.R. §240.15c1-7.

60 This may include not only the amount initially invested, but also additional investment, dividends, interest, capital gains and losses, etc.

61 Davis v. Merrill Lynch, Pierce, Fenner & Smith, Inc., 736 F.2d 1206 (8th Cir. 1990); Nesbit v. McNeil, 896 F.2d 318 (5th Cir. 1990).

62 *See* Winslow and Anderson, *A Model for Determining the Excessive Trading Element in Churning Cases*, 68 N.C. L. REV. 327 (1990); Brodsky, *Measuring Damages in Churning and Suitability Cases*, 6 SEC. REG. L.J. 157 (1978); Note, *Churning by Securities Dealers*, 80 HARV. L. REV. 869 (1967).

63 906 F.2d 1206 (8th Cir. 1990).

64 Uniform Commercial Code § 8-319 provides: "(c) within a reasonable time a writing in confirmation of the sale or purchase [of securities] . . . has been received by the party against whom enforcement is sought and he has failed to send written objection to its contents within 10 days after receipt."

65 *See* Merrill Lynch, Pierce, Fenner & Smith, Inc. v. Cheng, 901 F.2d p. 1124 (D.C. Ct. App. 1990), which held that there was no ratification because a broker's duty to the customer included the duty to inform him that there was a right to reject unauthorized trades, and failure to do so was a breach of that duty.

66 7 U.S.C. § 4b.

67 *See* chapter 6.

68 *See* the former Supreme Court Justice Lewis Powell's opinion in Prudential-Bache Securities, Inc. v. Stricklin, 890 F.2d 704 (4th Cir. 1989), which found that the client agreement permitted the broker to liquidate without prior notice.

69 *See* Ricks, *SEC Chief Calls Some Financial Products "Too Dangerous" for Individual Investors*, WALL ST. J., Jan. 7, 1988, at 46, col. 5. There may be products too risky to be suitable for any investor.

70 *See* Csordas v. Smith Barney, Harris Upham & Co., Inc., FED. SEC. L. REP. (CCH) ¶ 97,230 (Fla. Cir. Ct. 199).

71 1Section 20(a) of the 1934 Act. *See* discussion of Who to Suebelow.

72 *See* "control persons" and RICO under securities law violations discussion above.

73 *See* Section 15(b)(4)(E) and (b)(6) of the 1934 Act.

74 Section 15(b)(6) of the 1934 Act.

75 *See* Huff, FED. SEC. L. REP. (CCH) ¶ 84,719 (SEC 1991).

76 *See* Comments of SEC Commissioner Mary L. Shapiro to the Sixth Annual N.A.S.D. Educational Seminar reported in FED. SEC. L. REP. (CCH)

No. 1579 (Oct. 25, 1993); Goldman, Sachs & Co., Exchg. Act Rel. No. 33,576 (Feb. 3, 1994).

77 15 U.S.C. § 78u.

78 *See* various articles in late October 1993 concerning the $387 million settlement between the SEC and Prudential Bache Securities for recommending unsuitable real estate limited partnership investments in the 1980s to investors who lacked the ability to understand that they were not the "safe income" promised by the brokerage salesmen who were paid high commissions and other incentives for sales.

79 *See* FED. SEC. L. REP. (CCH) No. 1579 (Oct. 25, 1993).

80 TXO Production Corp. v. Alliance Resources Corp., 113 S.Ct. 2711, 61 LW 4766 (3d Cir. 1993).

81 *See* the history of securities arbitration discussion in chapter 7.

82 *See* E. Morris, D. Masucci & R. Clemente, *Securities Arbitration at Self-Regulatory Organizations*, in SECURITIES ARBITRATION 165 (D.E. Robbins ed., 1992); Masucci and Clemente, *Securities Arbitration at Self-Regulatory Organizations*, in SECURITIES ARBITRATION at 141 (D.E. Robbins ed., 1993).

83 *See* the discussion of industry arbitration procedures in chapter 14.

84 The SROs typically require arbitration of disputes among those affiliated with the SRO. For example, N.Y.S.E. Constitution, Article XI, Sec. 1, requires arbitration as follows:

> Any controversy between parties who are members, allied members or member organizations and any controversy between a member, allied member or member organization and any other person arising out of the business of such member...or the dissolution of a member organization, shall at the instance of any such party, be submitted for arbitration in accordance with the provisions of this Constitution and such rules as the Board may from time to time adopt.

Raiding of a firm's sales force by another is another example of the inter-broker claim. *See Merrill Lynch, Pierce, Fenner & Smith, Inc. v. Salvano*, 999 F.2d 211, No. 92-3854 (7th Cir. 1993), where simultaneous proceedings in three forums were all conducted in under a month! The district court was not precluded by arbitration from issuing an injunction against soliciting former clients, despite arbitrators refusal to give Merrill Lynch injunctive relief. But the Circuit Court of Appeals found that once the arbitrators had acted, the courts should withdraw.

85 *See* N.Y.S.E. Rule 347, which states, "any controversy between a registered representative and any member or member organization arising out of the employment or termination of employment of such registered representative by and with such member or member organization shall be settled by arbitration, at the instance of any such party, in accordance with the arbitration procedure prescribed elsewhere in these rules." N.A.S.D. § 8 is

similar.

86 O'Neal v. N.A.S.D., 667 F.2d 804 (9th Cir. 1983); Fleck v. E.F. Hutton Group, Inc., 891 F.2d 1047 (2d Cir. 1989) (where statement on U-5 regarding termination of employee "arose out of" the employment under N.Y.S.E. Rule 347).

87 111 S. Ct. 1647 (1991).

88 111 S. Ct. 2050 (1991).

89 *See* Alexander v. Gardner-Denver, 415 U.S. 36 (1974), where a union collective bargaining agreement was held to operate only to arbitrate contract claims.

90 Fletcher v. Kidder, Peabody & Co., 81 N.Y. 2d 623, 601 N.Y.S. 2d 686, 619 N.E.2d 998 (1993); Reid v. Goldman, Sachs & Co., 601 N.Y.S. 2d 686 (1993).

91 Sup. Ct. N.Y. City. April 21, 1992, 1992 N.Y. Misc. LEXIS 318. In agreement are other cases including Spellman v. Securities, Annuities and Ins. Services, 8 Cal. App. 4th 452, 10 Cal. Rptr. 2d 427 (Cal. Ct. App., 2d Dist. 1992); Skewes v. Shearson Lehman Brothers, Inc., 250 Kan. 574 (1992); Saari v. Smith Barney, Harris Upham & Co., Inc., 968 F.2d 877 (9th Cir. 1992); Neubrander v. Dean Witter Reynolds, Inc., 610 N.E.2d 1089, 81 Ohio App. 3d 308 (Ohio Ct. App., 9th Dist. 1992); Mago v. Shearson Lehman Hutton, Inc., 956 F.2d 932 (9th Cir. 1992).

92 Higgins v. Los Angeles Superior Court, 1 Cal. Rptr. 2d 57 (1991).

93 42 U.S.C. §§ 2000e *et seq.*

94 42 U.S.C. § 6(b).

95 *See* 4 SEC. ARB. COMM. 1 (Jan. 1993).

96 29 U.S.C. §§ 621 *et seq.*

97 42 U.S.C. §§ 12101 *et seq.*

98 This 25 limit is reduced to 15 after July 26, 1994.

99 29 U.S.C. §§ 201-209.

100 Fahnestock & Co., Inc. v. Waltman, 935 F.2d 512 (2d Cir. 1991) (defamation awarded employee).

101 Glennon v. Dean Witter, Discover & Co., reported in WALL ST. J. C1:6 (Oct. 12, 1993).

102 *See* the chapter 6 discussion of arbitration of industry disputes.

103 Section 20(a) of the 1934 Act , 15 U.S.C. § 78t(a); *See also* § 5 of the 1933 Act, 15 U.S.C. § 77o.

104 Central Bank of Denver v. First Interstate Bank of Denver, 114 S. Ct. 1439 (1994) (review of law in a Rule 10b-5 case).

105 *See* Lee v. Chica, 983 F.2d 883 (8th Cir. 1993), where the customer's account representative was bound to arbitrate under the firm's agreement, even though he had not signed the agreement between the customer

and the firm. This was due to the employment relationship and the fact that he was responsible for the transactions in her account from which the claims arose.

106 *See* S.I.C.A. Rule 13(a); AAA Rule 6.

107 *See* the chapter 15 discussion of the rules relating to apportionment of costs of arbitration in the award.

108 Garrity v. Lyle Stuart, Inc., 40 N.Y. 2d 354, 386 N.Y.S. 2d 831, 353 N.E.2d 793 (1976).

109 Miele v. Prudential Bache Securities, Inc. 5 SEC. ARB. COMM. 7, 15 (11th Cir. 1993).

110 *See* N.A.S.D. § 27; N.Y.S.E. Rule 614; AAA Rule 23.

111 GAO REPORT TO CONGRESSIONAL REQUESTERS, GAO/GGD-92-74 (May 1992).

112 *See* AAA Rule 23 ("Any party may be represented by counsel or *other authorized representative*" [emphasis supplied]), N.A.S.D. § 27; N.Y.S.E. Rule 614.

113 *See* AAA Rule 8.

Chapter 12

PROCEDURES TO ARBITRATE A CLAIM IN SECURITIES ARBITRATION

1) BRINGING THE CLAIM

A proceeding is commenced in arbitration by the Statement of Claim[1] or notice, known as a Demand.[2] A Uniform Submission Agreement[3] may also be used, which will bind the executing parties to any award, including a decision on counterclaims. The filing fees in securities arbitration are set by the SRO[4] or AAA.[5]

A) Uniform Submission Agreement

This standard form is used to submit the claim after voluntary assent of each party to the arbitration. The standard form also refers to the rules of the arbitration organization, whether SRO, AAA, or another group, the governing procedures and agreement to be bound by the award.

The Uniform Submission Agreement covers the requirements of the SROs regarding the content of a claim: a statement of the relevant facts and the remedies sought. Under all SRO rules, all pleadings except the statement of claim must be served on the opposing parties and director of arbitration of the forum selected with sufficient copies for the arbitrators. The person initiating the claim must file with the director of arbitration of the forum an executed Submission Agreement and Statement of Claim in sufficient copies, together with the required fee. The arbitration staff will then mail one copy of the Submission Agreement and the Statement of Claim to the respondent

The AAA will take a submission under either a notice to arbitrate pursuant to a contract provision or if the parties have executed a submission to arbitrate. In either case, the fees must be paid at filing.

Uniform Submission Agreement

____

(Name of Sponsoring Organization With Which Claim is to be Filed)

In the Matter of the Arbitration Between

Name(s) of Claimant(s) (Please print or type)		Name(s) of Respondent(s)
____________________		____________________
____________________	and	____________________
____________________		____________________

1. The undersigned parties hereby submit the present matter in controversy, as set forth in the attached Statement of Claim, Answers, and all related Counterclaims, and/or Third-Party Claims which may be asserted, to arbitration in accordance with the Constitution, By-Laws, Rules, Regulations, and/or Code of Arbitration Procedure of the sponsoring organization.
2. The undersigned parties hereby state that they have read the procedures and rules of the sponsoring organization relating to arbitration.
3. The undersigned parties agree that in the event a hearing is necessary, such hearing shall be held at a time and place as may be designated by the Director of Arbitration or the arbitrator(s). The undersigned parties further agree and understand that the arbitration will be conducted in accordance with the Constitution, By-Laws, Rules, Regulations, and/or Code of Arbitration Procedure of the sponsoring organization.
4. The undersigned parties further agree to abide by and perform any award(s) rendered pursuant to this Submission Agreement and further agree that a judgment and any interest due thereon, may be entered upon such award(s) and, for these purposes, the undersigned parties hereby voluntarily consent to submit to the jurisdiction of any court of competent jurisdiction which may properly enter such judgment.
5. IN WITNESS WHEREOF, the parties hereto have signed and acknowledged the foregoing Submission Agreement.

Claimant(s) Signature(s)	Respondent(s) Signature(s)
____________________	____________________
____________________	____________________
____________________	____________________

FOR CLAIMANTS WHO ARE INDIVIDUALS*
State of ____________, County of ____________, ss.:____________________

On the ____________day, of ______________, ____________, before me personally appeared ________ to me known and known to me to be the person(s) who executed the foregoing instrument and (_he_) acknowledged to me that (_he_) executed the same.

____

Notary Public

**A corporate claimant is required to execute an acknowledgment in the form approved by the state in which it has its principal office. If assistance is required. please contact the Director of Arbitration.*

B) Notice of Intention to Arbitrate

Under the Federal Arbitration Act and Uniform Arbitration Act,[6] a party intending to submit a claim to arbitration serves a notice of intent to arbitrate in the same manner as service of a summons under the state law. The notice must specify the agreement provision providing for arbitration to resolve a dispute, the name and address of the party serving the notice, and state that the party will submit the claim to arbitration within 20 days after service of the notice. If the party served does not object within the 20 days, he is precluded from objecting that a valid agreement to arbitrate was not made *and* that any statute of limitations is applicable to the claim in a legal action.

If a party is served with a notice of intention to arbitrate, she must promptly move to stay arbitration within the 20 day period.[7] Failure to seek stay within 20 days forfeits right to contest arbitration[8] and the right to object to a valid arbitration request is precluded from judicial review.

C) Securities Arbitration Notice; Forum Selection

In securities arbitration, the notice of intention to arbitrate can also specify the forum pursuant to the predispute arbitration clause used in most brokerage customer agreements that specify that the customer may select the forum, but the customer is only given 20 days to do so. After notice of intent is served by either the broker or customer, the broker will demand customer selection of a forum. In the event that the customer does not respond properly within the period, the broker can select the forum. If the customer has a preferred forum, the failure to respond can preclude its use. (See the customer agreement discussed in chapter 6 and selection of forum discussed in chapter 9).

D) Stay of Litigation

If the arbitration is not consented to by the parties, but provided for in agreement, the party seeking arbitration can go to court and demand arbitration pursuant to the arbitration statutes.[9] In such a case, the court shall order arbitration and stay further proceedings pending the outcome of the arbitration. If there are issues in a legal action that are not subject to arbitration, the court will retain jurisdiction over those matters and refer the arbitrable issues to arbitration.[10] Appeal of this stay is considered in chapter 16.

E) Location

The locale for arbitration depends on the forum.[11] The different forums are discussed in chapter 9. AAA arbitration will permit the parties to agree on the place, but in SRO arbitrations, the director of arbitration will decide the first hearing place, and the arbitrators will decide for subsequent hearings.[12] The SROs conduct hearings regularly in many locations throughout the United States and Puerto Rico.[13] The AAA has 34 regional offices.

2) SERVICE OF PLEADINGS

Service on the director of arbitration or any other party to be served pleadings can be effected by first-class postage prepaid, other overnight mail service, or by hand delivery. Claims can be filed in any office of the forum. If a member firm of an SRO and person associated with the firm, such as a account representative or investment advisor, are both named in the statement of claim, the firm may be required to serve the associated person. If the firm does not want to undertake future service on the associated person, it must advise all parties and the director of arbitration of that fact and provide a current address for the associated person.

3) STATEMENT OF CLAIM

There are two requirements for the Statement of Claim under SRO or AAA Rules:

> The claimant shall file with the Director of Arbitration an executed Submission Agreement, a Statement of Claim together with documents in support of the claim and the required deposit. Sufficient additional copies of the Submission Agreement and the Statement of Claim and supporting documents shall be provided to the Director of Arbitration for each party and each arbitrator. The Statement of Claim shall specify the relevant facts and the remedies sought. The Director of Arbitration shall endeavor to serve promptly by mail or otherwise on the Respondent(s) one (1) copy of the Submission Agreement and one (1) copy of the Statement of Claim.[14]

Drafting the Statement of Claim allows the claimant to state his or her strongest case. Following are three Statement of Claim examples.

A) The Ineffective Statement of Claim[15]

> On or about February 1, 1993, claimant, my client, opened an account No. 22 22222 with respondent firm, his broker, through its agent, servant or employee, Y, a registered representative.
>
> On and after February 1, 1993 and up to an including December 31, 1995, Yablons was careless, reckless and negligent in his handling of the account herein before referred to, breaching both his contractual and fiduciary obligations to claimant, as a result of which my client suffered substantial damages.

My client claims damages in the amount of $50,000.

B) The Effective Statement of Claim[16]

In July, 1993, Shirley Jones (Claimant) opened Account No. 22222 (the Account) with XYZ Securities (Broker) with a deposit of $50,000 cash. At the time she was a student with no investment experience or business sophistication. She met with Y (Account Executive) to whom she had been recommended by a friend. She told him she wanted to invest her money in low-risk securities and that she needed a return of approximately $400-$500/month to meet her school and living expenses.

At that meeting, the Account Executive represented to her that he could achieve a 20 percent annual return in stocks and a 15 percent annual return on bonds. He told her he would manage her portfolio very conservatively investing primarily in bonds. He also told her because of the income and capital appreciation the account would generate, she could withdraw $500/month without reducing her capital. Claimant signed papers relating to the opening of a margin account at that time, but the Account Executive represented that these were mere formalities and she need not read them.

The Account Executive completely controlled the Account during its entire existence and never consulted with Claimant. Instead of being invested in bonds, her Account was primarily invested in common stocks. Instead of being conservatively managed, the Account was heavily margined and traded with an annualized turnover ratio of approximately 5.1 in 1993 and 6.5 in 1994. Commissions totaled $4,250 in 1993, $5,800 in 1994 and $2,100 in 1995. These figures constituted respectively 13 percent, 18 percent, and 10 percent of the average net equity in the account in those years. Interest on the margin account resulted in charges totaling $2,500 in 1993, $4,000 in 1994, and $2,000 in 1995. When you add the interest charges to the commission charges for each year, the account would have to have had to earn 19 percent, 35 percent, and 30 percent respectively simply to pay for those charges. Instead of achieving a 20 percent or even 15 percent annual return, the account generated an income of $600 in 1993, $1,500 in 1994, and $800 in 1995. At 15 percent the income for 1993, 1994, and 1995 on the $50,000 invested should have been $7,500 per year or $22,500 versus the actual $2,900. The account had steadily declined in net equity from her original $50,000 in July, 1993 to $15,000 at the end of 1994. At the end of 1995, the account was essentially closed out by the withdrawal of $14,000. This resulted in a loss of $36,000 principal and income promised of in excess of $19,600.

Investments in the account were not in accordance with representations made by the Account Representative and the trading and securities were clearly unsuitable to Claimant's objectives. Trading was excessive in light of those objectives, and the account was managed in a manner more conducive to generating commission and interest income for Respondents than to serving Claimant's interests.

Claimant seeks recovery of her losses of $36,000 principal and $19,600 interest, or $55,600 plus interest and costs of this action. A copy of her monthly account statements from July, 1993, through December, 1995, is attached hereto as Exhibit A.

C) The More Detailed Statement of Claim

Some attorneys prefer to use a Statement of Claim more detailed than the above specifically referring to the different violations of law, but arbitrators will prefer a statement much more brief than the formal complaint used in legal actions. The following is an example of a very detailed statement of claim.

IN THE MATTER OF AN ARBITRATION
BEFORE [FORUM NAME]

....

[Name]		X	
	Claimant	X	
		X	
		X	STATEMENT
	- against -	X	OF
		X	CLAIM
		X	
[Name]		X	
	Respondents.	X	
		X	

....X

_________, by his attorney, _________, as and for his Amended Statement of Claim, hereby submits this claim for arbitration to the [Forum] in [location], pursuant to the arbitration clause in his Customer Agreement with Respondent Company, Inc., and its successors, and alleges:

1. _________ (hereinafter "*Claimant*") is a resident of New York, New York and had a margin account which traded, among other things, in Chicago Board of Options Exchange options.

2. Respondent [Brokerage Company, Inc.], (hereinafter "*Respondent*") and acting through its employees, including those named as respondents herein (hereinafter referred to collectively as "*Company*") at all times is and was a registered broker/dealer in securities and commodities and a member of the New York Stock Exchange Inc., the American Stock Exchange, Inc., the National Association of Securities Dealers, and the Chicago Board of Options Exchange, among others, with a main office at New York, New York and a branch office in Los Angeles, California and is a "control person" under Sec. 20 of the Securities and Exchange Act of 1934 (15 U.S.C. 78) of the other Respondents.

3. Respondent _________ (hereinafter "*Employee A*") was an employee of and registered representative at Company's Los Angeles, California office from October 1, 1955 through July 25, 1996 and a registered representative of XYZ Securities, Inc., prior to October 1995.

4. Respondent _________ (hereinafter "*Employee B*") was the assistant to Employee A and an employee of Company assigned to Employee A at Company's Los Angeles, California office from October 1, 1995 through July 25, 1996.

5. Respondent _________ (hereinafter "*Employee C*") was the supervisor of Employee A, and an employee of Company at its Los Angeles, California office.

6. Respondent _________ (hereinafter "*Employee D*") was a registered representative and employee of Company at its Los Angeles, California office.

7. Respondent _________ (hereinafter "*Employee E*"), from August 29, 1986 through the present, was a registered representative and Managing Director of Company in its Los Angeles office. At various times during Employee A's representation as account executive for Claimant, Employee E handled matters for the Claimant's account.

8. Respondents' in their dealings with Claimant and his account at Company's Los Angeles office continually concealed a series of fraudulent activities, including: (1) churning, (2) trading and recommending securities which were unsuitable for Claimant's risk preferences and ability to bear losses, (3) market manipulation, (4) self-dealing, (5) unauthorized trading in a margin account and advice to the Claimant to ignore margin calls, (6) misrepresentations regarding securities including those concerning the risks attendant in the purchase and sale of naked options, (7) operating Claimant's account as a discretionary account without the customer's consent or prior written approval to do so, (8) multiple breaches of fiduciary duty on each option trade by withholding material information concerning Employee A's past history of fraudulent trading and by failing to disclose to the Claimant that Employee A and Company would make unauthorized trades in his non-discretionary account in complete disregard of Claimant's financial situation, his needs and his express wishes and (9) by failing to properly maintain accurate, true and complete books and records of Claimant's account in violation of Sec. 17 of the Securities and Exchange Act of 1934, (15 U.S.C. 77q).

9. As a result of the Respondents' activities, Claimant's account declined in value from approximately $94,882.00 transferred from XYZ Securities to his Company account on October 25, 1995, to a value of $33,859.00 on July 25, 1996, or a loss of approximately $61,000.00 in only ten months.

10. Respondents directly and indirectly, by use of means of interstate commerce, of the mails and wires and of a facility of a national securities exchange, employed a scheme, device and artifice to defraud, made untrue statements of material fact and omitted to state material facts necessary in light of the circumstances under which they were made, not misleading, and engaged in acts, practices, and a course of business which operated as a fraud and deceit upon the Claimant and others in connection with the purchase and sale of securities in violation of the Securities and Exchange Act of 1934, section 10(b) (15 U.S.C. 78(j)) and Rule 10b-5 (17 C.F.R. sec. 240.10b-5).

11. Respondents are liable jointly and severally to Claimant.

12. By reason of contract entered into between and by Claimant and the Respondents, Respondents agreed to manage, invest, supervise and advise concerning safe and secure income-producing investments for Claimant in a diversified portfolio of prudent investments for a man of Claimant's financial sophistication and experience. The account was non-discretionary.

13. At the time Claimant opened his account with Company at the time he transferred his account from XYZ Securities, he advised Employee A that his account objectives were growth and safety of principal. Trading in options, such as Standard and Poors Index Futures by Company and Employee A was not a suitable investment for Claimant's risk position.

14. Respondents breached their fiduciary obligations to the Claimant by failing to adequately supervise Employee A and other registered representatives at its Los Angeles officer permitting excessive trading in Claimant's non-discretionary margin account without authorization and by its failure to discover Employee A's false statements concerning Claimant's ability to bear the burden of a risk of his investment.

15. Respondent Employee A has been involved in many other cases similar to the actions alleged by Claimant herein and has been found liable to customers other than Claimant before and after the time Claimant held the Company Account about which this Claim is made. Respondent Company knew, or should have known in the exercise of due care and diligent supervision, of Employee A's past actions at other brokerage firms, but did nothing to stop Employee A from engaging in such course of conduct with customers, including Claimant and other members of the general public. Such conduct of Respondents Employee A and Company was taken despite their fiduciary duty owed to the public in general and to the Claimant. Such conduct involves a high degree of moral culpability in gross disregard of such duties and Respondents' actions were motivated by greed and self dealing with the Claimant and other customers for their sole profit.

16. Respondents breached their continuing obligations to investigate each account and each investment for its suitability for the Claimant's purposes and thereby damaged the Claimant as set forth herein. Such callous disregard of their fiduciary duties to Claimant and the public justifies imposition of punitive damages of at least $500,000 against Respondents.

17. By reason of a relation of trust, confidence and dominance encouraged by Respondents, the Claimant was justified in assuming that Respondent Employee A and his employer, Respondent Company would not act in a manner inconsistent with the Claimant's welfare and would deal with the Claimant fairly and in good faith.

18. Respondents deliberately and fraudulently failed to disclose and actively concealed from the Claimant Employee A's past and then present history of fraudulent, unauthorized, excessive and unsuitable trading in customer accounts at XX, Company, and other brokerage firms. As a result, Claimant opened a margin account at Company and is entitled to restitution damages, incidental and consequential damages, including commissions and fees.

19. Employee A and other Respondent employees of Company' Los Angeles office made material misrepresentations to Claimant concerning (1) the type and nature of the risk associated with the purchase and sale of naked options, including Standard and Poors Index options; (2) the type and nature of the risk of the other investments recommended for Claimant's account; (3) the sale of positions on a margin call after Employee A advised the Claimant that the notification of a margin call was a mistake and that his margin positions would not be liquidated; (4) that Employee A and Respondents would only recommend safe and secure investments; and (5) that Respondents would only act in his best interests; and (6) that Employee A and Company would guarantee a high rate of return of income from their recommended investments without unreasonable risk to Claimant's principal.

20. Respondents failed to manage, invest, supervise and advise Claimant concerning safe, secure, and diversified prudent investments for a man of Claimant's investment ability, objectives, sophistication, and age, and actively concealed its failures by providing Claimant with "special account statements," generated to deceive Claimant and misrepresent his margin account.

21. Respondents' conduct damaged the Claimant in a sum in excess of $133,928.00, calculated as follows:

i) actual losses of $61,000.00, plus commissions and margin interest; and

ii) Interest and profits calculated as:

	Investment	10% Return*	Total
1986	$ 72,000	$ 7,200	$ 79,200.00
1987	$ 79,000	$ 7,920	$ 87,120.00
1988	$ 87,120	$ 8,712	$ 95,832.00
1989	$ 95,832	$ 9,583	$105,415.00
1990	$105,415	$10,541	$115,956.00
1991	$115,956	$11,595	$127,551.00
1992 (6 MOS)	$127,551	$ 6,377	$133,928.00
		$61,928	

*Rate of return promised Claimant by Employee A.

22. Employee A, with other participants in an enterprise, engaged in the purchase and sale of securities, affecting interstate commerce and foreign commerce, conducted, and participated directly and indirectly through a pattern of racketeering activity such enterprise affairs.

23. Employee A directly and indirectly, has received income through a pattern of racketeering activity using and investing, directly and indirectly the whole and parts of such income and proceeds of such income in the acquisition of an interest in, the establishment and operation of an enterprise which engages in and the activities of which affect, interstate and foreign commerce. Employee A, through a pattern of racketeering activity, acquired and maintains, directly and indirectly, an interest in and control of an enterprise which is engaged in and whose activities affect interstate and foreign commerce.

24. That the predicate acts committed by Employee A include, but are not limited to, two or more violations of the United States mail fraud statute (18 U.S.C. 1341), wire fraud statute (18 U.S.C. 1343) and securities fraud (15 U.S.C. 78i, 78j, 77q, 77w, 80b-6, 80b-7, 80b-8).

25. Respondent Company has knowingly controlled Employee A, violated, conspired to violate, and aided and abetted the violations by Employee A and others of the United States mail fraud statute (18 U.S.C. 1341), wire fraud statute (18 U.S.C. 1343) and securities fraud (15 U.S.C. 78i, 78j, 77q, 77w, 80b-6, 80b-7, 80b-8).

26. Employee A, and Company having damaged the Claimant in the sum of at least $133,928.00, which under Title IX, Racketeering Influenced and Corrupt Organizations Law, 18 U.S.C. 1964, is to be tripled to at least $401,784.00, together with costs, disbursements and attorney fees by the aforesaid United States statute (18, U.S.C. 1964(c)).

27. Plaintiff has not brought this action until this time due to representations by Company that these matters were being resolved, as they amounted to record keeping errors and trading desk errors.

WHEREFORE: Claimant requests an award of $133,928, tripled to $401,784, costs disbursements and attorneys fees and punitive damages in the amount of $500,000.00 and such other and further relief as the Arbitrators shall find right and just.

Dated: Respectfully,
New York, New York

____
Claimant's Attorney

4) FEES

As noted in the Task Force Survey, arbitration is normally regarded as being cheaper than litigation. This is not always true. In fact, the filing fees in arbitration are probably much higher than filing fees in state or federal courts. For example, New York State courts filing fees are typically $100, with additional fees for requests for judicial action. Federal courts require a filing fee of $120 for initiating an action. The fees charged for securities arbitration vary depending on the SRO forum and are subject to SEC supervision. In comparing the forums, there is a considerable difference between SRO and AAA fees. This is principally due to the subsidization of the SRO process by the members of the exchange or broker-dealers.

Arbitration forum fees are typically paid prior to the commencement of the hearing, but in appropriate cases the administrator can waive the fee payment to a later time.[17] In hardship cases the fees may be completely waived, but the arbitration directors will require good evidence to justify waiver of fees. If a case is settled or withdrawn, a refund of a portion of the fee is made.

The fees charged by the SRO forum rules and the AAA are set forth in the rules contained in the Appendixes. N.Y.S.E. and AMEX arbitration fees in public cases range between $15, for a claim or counter-claim in the amount of $1,000 or less, to a fee of $1,500 for disputes over $5,000,000.[18] Additional charges are made for hearing sessions. This can quickly add up to much more than litigation fees. In the absence of a dollar amount in dispute, a $200-250 filing fee and $600 hearing deposit is assessed.[19] The arbitrators may include in the award an assessment of forum fees to the parties as they determine.[20] In order to discourage adjournments, there is a small adjournment fee, payable by the party causing the adjournment of any scheduled hearing.

Under the 1992 AAA Securities Arbitration Rules, fees are no longer based on the amount of the claim or counterclaim, but to make parties pay for the services they use. Under the old schedule, the fees charged were percentages of the amount of the claim as is still the case in SRO arbitrations. The AAA found that the costs incurred by the Association often had little to do with the amount in controversy. Cases involving claims in the thousands of dollars were taking far longer to resolve than multimillion-dollar disputes. The 1992 AAA fee schedule sets non-refunding filing fees based on the amount of the claim in dispute and includes fixed fees for services such as hearings and postponements. For example, hearings before a single arbitrator will cost each party $100, and processing fees of $150 per party will be assessed for cases that remain on file for more than 180 days. The lowest filing fee charged under the new schedule will be $300 for claims under $25,000. For claims of $25,000 to $100,000, the fee will be $1,000. Under the old system, the fee would have been $1,750. The fee on a claim of $5 million or more will be $4,000. Under the old system, the fee would have been $15,000, plus one-tenth of 1 percent of the excess over $5 million. In November, 1993, the AAA commercial arbitration fees were raised, and it is anticipated that securities fees will also be increased proportionally.

5) THE PRESENT SITUATION

There is no reason to suppose that non-SRO facilities and procedures are any less cost-effective than litigation. The GAO 1992 Report found securities arbitration not substantially cheaper, but definitely faster, than litigation. For this reason, there may be a rationale to provide arbitration forums that are *not* affiliated with the industry, in order to provide the appearance of fairness and an unbiased system for dispute resolution. Despite the author's impression, based on his participation as an arbitrator, that the personnel of the SRO are scrupulously fair, the impression of bias still remains in the mind of the customer, who is forced by the forum selection clauses of the predispute arbitration agreement to choose between two equally undesirable SRO-sponsored forums. This can be resolved by permitting choice of AAA or other forums. The best solution for the industry may be to establish a single forum for arbitration, unaffiliated with any exchange or broker-dealer organization. But the S.I.C.A. rejected this suggestion in 1991.

The SEC and commentators have raised several questions regarding the affiliation of arbitrators. Presently, the courts will presume that the arbitrators are fair and unbiased. Based on this arbitration experience, the presumption is correct. Industry and retired industry personnel, in fact, seem most outraged at industry conduct that is not in accord with the fair and equitable standards by which brokers are to treat customers. While taking an oath to be impartial is no guarantee of impartiality, it is, nevertheless, another indication of a fair deliberation.

6) COMMODITIES ARBITRATION

As noted in chapter 9, two arbitration forums serve exclusively commodity futures trading: the Commodity Futures Trading Commission (CFTC), which is the agency charged with enforcement of the Commodity Exchange Act (CEA),[21] and the SRO for the commodities trading part of the securities industry, The National Futures Association (N.F.A.). Addresses of both are given in chapter 9. The procedure for claims in these forums are slightly different than for SRO arbitration.

A) CFTC Rules Relating to Reparation Proceedings[22]

Section 14(a) of the Commodity Exchange Act provides, "any person complaining of any violation of any provision of this Act may, at any time within two years after the cause of action accrues, apply to the [CFTC] for an order awarding damages approximately caused by such violation."

The CFTC has adopted regulations concerning reparation proceedings. The Complaint must (1) set forth the violation specifically by reference to the rule, regulation, or order alleged to have been violated; and (2) a "description of all relevant facts concerning each and every act or omission" claimed to be a violation. Counterclaims can also be adjudicated if they arise out of the same course of events as the claim.

The proceeding is adjudicated before the Commission due to its "obvious expertise in applying the Act and its own regulations."[23]

While originally thought only to apply to claims for commodity violations by those registered under the CEA, there has been an extension of jurisdiction. Today, commodities reparations proceedings permit the CFTC to entertain claims and counterclaims under state law as long as they are incidental to and completely dependent on the federal commodities violation.

In a reparations proceeding, the complaint must set forth "all relevant facts concerning each and every act or omission which it is claimed constitutes a violation of the Act."[24] The U.S. Supreme Court held in *Commodities Futures Trading Commission v. Schor* that the CEA empowers the Commission to decide state law and common law counterclaims arising from the same events as the main CEA claim, on the theory that many of the same factual issues should be resolved without allocating jurisdiction among many tribunals. This was felt to be the effective way to provide a limited federal regulatory scheme on the commodities industry by a body that had "obvious expertise" and thus other matters which are clearly incidental to, and completely dependent on, the reparations claim.

In *Bahr v. Murlas Commodities, Inc.*,[25] the scope of reparations proceedings were extended even further. There initial investments in commodity transactions were followed by tax shelter investments to which the CEA did not apply at all. The CFTC found that because of the solicitation, inducement, and action in reliance on the commodities futures advisor in the tax shelter, the two were sufficiently related to permit reparations in both under the CEA.

B) National Futures Association

The N.F.A. is not technically a "securities" arbitration SRO since it only arbitrates disputes in commodity trading. It is not a participant in the S.I.C.A. and is not a self-regulatory organization under the 1934 Act. But it is registered as the only self-regulatory organization under the CEA. Its panels are composed entirely of commodities industry arbitrators, unless a customer requests otherwise, in which case there will be two non-industry and one industry arbitrator.

In 1988 the N.F.A. opened 401 new cases, a number exceeded only by the N.Y.S.E. and N.A.S.D. The N.F.A. is subject to oversight by the CFTC, similar to the SRO and SEC relationship.

There appeared little industry bias in a study of N.F.A. claims from 1983 to 1988 reported in the SECURITIES ARBITRATION COMMENTATOR.[26] While more than 95 percent of the claims were non-industry, industry-member only panels awarded 38.74 percent of claims in 258 cases heard, while public member majority panels only 14.03 percent in 128 cases. Thus, the conclusion reached is that N.F.A. industry panels awards favor the customer. This evidence of no bias has been used to bolster the argument that other SRO industry panels are presumptively not biased. Of course, this is a limited sample and in a non-securities product that may lead to the need for greater expertise in arbitrators who are evaluating a claim.

The procedures for raising a claim with the N.F.A. are essentially identical to those involving a securities claim at an SRO arbitration forum. Counterclaims can also be raised.

7) RESPONDING TO A CLAIM

Under the state and federal arbitration laws, there is no requirement that the statement of claim be responded to by an answer from the respondent.

Under SRO and AAA arbitrations, however, general denials or failure to submit an answer within the rules may bar presentment of any facts or defenses at the hearing.[27]

> An arbitrator looks upon a non-responsive [answer or no response] in a number of ways: (a) ...important enough to warrant time to an answer; (b) accepted the claim as presented; (c) leaves the arbitrators free to conclude their own findings; (d) is usually accepted as an admission of guilt; and, (e) wastes valuable time of all parties involved.[28]

A) SRO Answer Rules[29]

The respondent must serve each party and the director of arbitration with a copy of the executed Submission Agreement and Respondent's Answer within 20 days from receipt of the claim, unless that time is extended by the director of arbitration.

A general denial, as noted above, or failure to be specific in an Answer may, in the discretion of the arbitrators and upon objection by a party, result in a bar from presenting what might be relevant facts or defenses at the time of the hearing. While it is probably rare for the arbitrators to preclude, abuse of the process will justify such a bar being applied.

The answer shall specify all available defenses and relevant facts that will be relied upon at the hearing as well as any related counterclaim the respondent may have against the claimant. In addition, where the respondent has claims arising out of the same facts raised by the claimant, the Answer may contain (1) any cross-claim the respondent may have against any other respondent named in the claim, and (2) any third-party claim against another party that is based on any existing dispute, claim, or controversy subject to arbitration. Fees in the same amount as for a customer dispute are required when the respondent files counterclaims, cross-claims, or a third-party files claims in the proceeding. Third-party respondents have the same 20 day period to respond to service of a claim made against them by the respondent.

Any claimant must respond to a counterclaim within 10 days of receipt of any Answer containing a counterclaim, with copies sent as well to the director of arbitration and arbitrators.

B) AAA Answer Rules

Once a claim is filed, the staff will give notice to the respondent who "may" file an answering statement within 20 days with the AAA and send a copy to the claimant under AAA Securities Arbitration Rule 6. If no answer is filed, it will be treated as a general denial, but the claimant can serve a written request for an answering statement, which, if not answered within ten days, may bar the party from presenting any matter, argument, or defense, at the arbitrators discretion (usually determined prior to the hearing) There is no default judgment, however.[30]

If a counterclaim is asserted it must set forth (1) the nature of the claim; (2) amount involved, if any; and (3) remedy sought; and be filed with the AAA together with the appropriate fee.[31] The same is true if a respondent wishes to interject a claim against a third party.[32]

The AAA Rule 8 provides for changes in claim or counterclaim to be filed with the AAA, with copies to the other parties who then have 10 days to answer, up to the time that an arbitrator has been appointed. After appointment of the arbitrator, no new or different claims may be submitted without the arbitrator's consent.

8) OTHER PRE-ANSWER MATTERS

Either in conjunction with filing the Answer to a Statement of Claim or before filing the Answer, certain procedural "defenses" are available to the respondent in a securities arbitration, similar to litigation defensive strategies. These include:

A) Wrong Forum: Order to Show Cause

The first defensive maneuver is related to the forum: if the claimant has chosen the wrong forum, the proper response is to seek judicial intervention to require the claimant to show why the claim should not be resolved at the contract specified forum. This often occurs when a customer seeks to arbitrate before the AAA and the agreement specifies only an SRO forum, such as N.A.S.D., N.Y.S.E., or AMEX. The Order to Show Cause will have to meet the requirements of the state or federal court in which it is brought. The courts will review on the basis of the applicable arbitration statute.

In New York, the following form is for an order to show cause under CPLR § 7503.

The Supreme Court of the State of New York,
County of ____

--X

IN THE MATTER OF THE ARBITRATION	)	
BETWEEN	)	
[Name],	)	[Forum] Arbitration
	)	No.
Claimants,	)	
	)	ORDER TO SHOW
	)	CAUSE
-against-	)	Index No.
	)	
	)	
[Broker]	)	
and [Registered Representative],	)	
	)	
Respondents.	)	

--X

Upon the affidavit of _____, the exhibits thereto, and respondent's memorandum of law annexed hereto and made a part hereof, it is ORDERED, that claimant _____ show cause at Term ____, Part _____ of this Court, at [location], New York, on the _____ day of _____, 19___, at _____ o'clock in the _____ noon of that day, or as soon thereafter as counsel can be heard, why an order should not be made and entered pursuant to CPLR Section 7503 and Section 2201 staying this action on the ground that all of the claims alleged in the statement of claim are subject to arbitration; and it is further

ORDERED, that the time within which respondent must serve an answer to claimant's statement of claim is hereby extended until the hearing of the motion brought on by this Order to Show Cause; and it is further

ORDERED, that personal service of a copy of this Order and the papers upon which it is granted upon the claimant's attorney by _____ o'clock _____ on the _____ day of _____, 19___, shall be good and sufficient service; and it is further

ORDERED, that any answering papers shall be served personally by _____ o'clock _____ on the _____ day of _____, 19___.

The above-entitled action is brought to [explain nature of action].

ENTER,

____
J.S.C.

B) Motion to Dismiss; Statute of Limitations

A respondent may bring a motion to dismiss a claim brought in arbitration which is barred by an applicable statute of limitations.[33] Under New York CPLR § 7502(b), a party in arbitration can file a motion in court to dismiss the arbitration altogether if "the claim sought to be arbitrated would have been barred by limitation of time had it been asserted in a court of this state, a party may assert the limitation as a bar to the arbitration on an application to the court as provided in § 7503 or subdivision (b) of 7511." Failure to apply for such an order, moreover, will not defeat the ability of a party to bring the statute of limitations defense before the arbitration panel, but if a party appears and participates in the arbitration without raising this defense, the arbitrators decision will be upheld. Consequently, it is important to raise a statute of limitations defense immediately.

The question of the applicable statute of limitations is determinative. Normally, securities violations are subject to specific statutory limitations, for example, the action must be commenced within one year from discovery or three years from sale of securities under the 1933 Act or for Rule 10b-5 violations. Otherwise, typically a six year contract statute is applicable.

Once the party has prevailed on a motion to stay an action and compel arbitration, it is improper to permit them to then argue that a statute of limitations exists to bar the arbitration. However, the arbitration forum is the only forum in which the limitations defense can be raised. A recent New York case found no cases in support of such a position, noting that "perhaps, . . . no one has yet had the gall to employ this whipsaw."[34] The better approach would have been to not ask for a stay to compel arbitration, but defend the litigation on the grounds of the limitations period having run. The SRO rules provide that "the time limitations which would otherwise run or accrue for the institution of legal proceedings *shall be tolled*" for the period (1) the forum has jurisdiction over the matter, or (2) if submitted to the court while the court retains jurisdiction.[35]

Closely related to statutes of limitations are the SRO forum "eligibility" rules, discussed directly below.

C) Arbitration at Forum Discretion; Eligibility Rule

As discussed in chapter 9, the forum rules normally provide that the director of arbitration has discretion *not* to accept certain disputes if they are found not proper for forum determination. Where the parties are directed to proceed with an arbitration proceeding, despite the contention of one party that it had previously submitted the same claim to arbitration, with resulting relitigation of extensive procedural and substantive issues before the court, there is no reason why the forum should find the dispute a proper subject matter for arbitration under its rules.[36]

One of the ways that the SRO eligibility period (discussed in chapter 9) is utilized is to petition New York courts to stay arbitration even if the conduct occurs outside New York under the governing law provision of most brokerage firm contracts. Under New York CPLR § 7503, however, a court will be precluded from deciding time limitation and eligibility issues, but only if the specific requirements of § 7503 are met, particularly, service of the demand to stay within 20 days of service; and service in the same manner as a summons or by return receipt, registered, or certified mail. The arbitration forum may not serve within that period due to delays inherent in their systems.

Chapter 9 suggests that if a claim is determined ineligible for arbitration, the parties should be left with any available legal remedy.

9) JOINDER AND CONSOLIDATION OF CLAIMS

The director of arbitration in an SRO forum is authorized to determine whether a counterclaim, cross-claim or third-party claim is directly related to the matter raised in the Statement of Claim. If so, other parties can be joined in the dispute only if they have agreed to arbitrate. Other arbitration actions can be consolidated for hearing and award purposes. The final decision on joinder and consolidation, however, rests with the arbitration panel. See N.A.S.D. § 25(d) and N.Y.S.E. Rule 612(d); AAA Rule 6 is similar.

NOTES

1 N.Y.S.E. Rule 612; N.A.S.D. § 25(a).

2 AAA Rules 5 and 7.

3 N.Y.S.E. Rule 612; N.A.S.D. § 12.

4 N.A.S.D. § 43 (Customer Disputes) and § 44 (Industry and Clearing Controversies); N.Y.S.E. Rules 629 and 630.

5 *See* fee schedule following AAA Rule 55.

6 *See* Uniform Act § 103; N.Y. CPLR 7503(c). The New York provision permits service by mail.

7 N.Y. CPLR 7503(c); Federal Arbitration Act § 3, 9 U.S.C. § 3 (1988).

8 City of Long Beach v. Catalyst Waste-to-Energy Corp. of Long Beach, 543 N.Y.S. 2d 1013 (Sup. Ct. N.Y. Cty. 1988).

9 Fed. Arbitration Act § 4; *See also* N.Y. CPLR 7503 Application to Compel or Stay Arbitration.

10 *See* the chapter 3 discussion of this bifurcation under the *Prima Paint* doctrine.

11 N.Y.S.E. Rule 485; N.A.S.D. Code of Arbitration Procedure 26; AAA Rule 12.

12 N.A.S.D. § 26; N.Y.S.E. Rule 613; AAA Rules 12, 22.

13 In 1988, the N.A.S.D. conducted hearings in 52 cities and the N.Y.S.E. in 33 cities. In 1990, the N.Y.S.E. held 65% of all its hearings outside New York City (in 38 cities). The N.A.S.D. conducted 80% of its 1991 hearings outside New York City (in 46 locations).

14 N.A.S.D. §§ 13(b) and 25(a) (small claim simplified procedures); N.Y.S.E. Rules 612(a) and 601(b) (small claims). AAA Rule 5 requires the Notice of Claim to set forth the nature of dispute, amount involved, remedy sought, hearing locale, and copies of the arbitration provision of the contract (Rule 5) or Submission Agreement (Rule 7).

15 From D. Masucci and R. Clemente, *Securities Arbitration at Self-Regulatory Organizations*, in SECURITIES ARBITRATION 245, 246 (D. Robbins ed., 1993).

16 *Id.*

17 N.A.S.D. § 43; N.Y.S.E. Rule 629; AAA Rule 48 .

18 N.Y.S.E. Rule 629; N.A.S.D. § 44.

19 N.Y.S.E. Rule 629(e), but the director of arbitration or arbitrators can require a "greater or lesser" amount, not exceeding $1,500 (the highest fee).

20 *See* N.Y.S.E. Rule 629(g) which refers to the assessment of fees and costs under Rules 617, 619, and 623. There are different fees for member controversies (see N.Y.S.E. Rule 631; N.A.S.D. § 44(g)).

21 7 U.S.C. § 18 *et seq.*

22 41 C.F.R. § 3993, as amended 49 C.F.R. § 6602.

23 Commodity Futures Trading Commission v. Schor, 478 U.S. 833, 106 S. Ct. 3245, 92 L. Ed. 2d 675, COMM. FUT. L. REP. (CCH) ¶ 23,116 (CFTC 1986).

24 CFTC Regulation §12.13(b)(iv)(A).

25 2 COMM. FUT. L. REP. (CCH) ¶ 24,481 (CFTC 1989).

26 No. 8 (Nov. 1988).

27 N.A.S.D. § 25(b); N.Y.S.E. Rule 612(c); AAA Rule 6 (only after claimant demands answer and there is failure is bar effective).

28 Comments of Michael P. Golden, Senior Home Office Compliance Director of Merrill Lynch at "SIA Forum: Byrd's Eye View of Arbitration" (Sept. 19, 1985), reprinted in SECURITIES ARBITRATION 121 (D. Robbins ed., 1989). N.A.S.D. § 8(a)(1) and (2) provides that a public customer dispute shall be resolved by a panel "at least a majority of whom shall not be from the securities industry." On the other hand, disputes among member firms are resolved by industry-only panels.

29 *See* N.A.S.D. §§ 13 and 25(c); N.Y.S.E. Rule 601 (Simplified Arbitration) and 612(c).

30 *See* AAA Rule 6.

31 *Id.*

32 AAA Rule 6 provides that a third party joinder is an issue for the arbitrators to decide.

33 N.Y. CPLR 213, which sets a six year time ban for contract actions.

34 Matter of Shearson Lehman, N.Y.L.J. (March 2, 1993), page 30, col. 5 & 6.

35 N.A.S.D. § 18; N.Y.S.E. Rule 606. There is no AAA rule.

36 *See* Kevin Connors & Co. L.P. v. Salomon Brothers, Inc., FED. SEC. L. REP. (CCH) ¶ 97,213 (1992).

Chapter 13

DISCOVERY AND OTHER PREHEARING MATTERS

Compared to litigation, discovery in arbitration is limited. Federal and state rules of civil procedure provide extensive opportunities to discover the elements of an opponent's case that hopefully leads to better presentment of the issues and eliminates surprise. It may also encourage settlement in lieu of trial as the parties become more aware of the facts regarding the dispute.

While the information required to develop the statement of claim should be rather detailed as noted in chapter 11, the discovery process under SRO and AAA rules, called "exchange of information," can be used to get additional documentation and identify additional witnesses that can be used in the arbitration hearing, or in preparation for the hearing. Clearly, however, discovery (called Requests for Information in arbitration, and not interrogatories or requests for admission as in litigation) is not extensive. But this is a great advance from only a few years ago when document production in securities arbitration was almost non-existent since it was voluntary, and it produces a less expensive procedure for bringing the controversy to an end. Under today's rules the customer, employee, and firm will be required to produce relevant documents in their possession in advance of the hearing. The result must be an improved hearing procedure as both sides to the dispute can better plan the presentation of the case.

There are no detailed discovery procedures in arbitration. Discovery is not necessary for a party to respond to a motion to compel arbitration since it is irrelevant to the issue of arbitrability.[1] Interrogatories are not permitted and depositions of key personnel are not generally available under present SRO rules. Arbitration by ambush thus continues to be a problem. The SEC has been especially critical of the few discovery tools available in SRO arbitration forums. The situation is little changed despite a 1987 letter of Richard G. Ketchum, SEC Director of Market Regulation, that observed:

> Under existing rules, documents that a party requests pursuant to subpoena do not have to be produced until minutes before a hearing is to begin. We do not believe that is sufficient time for a party to prepare for a hearing. . . .There is . . . no established enforcement mechanism to ensure that parties cooperate in document production.

The N.A.S.D. had an informal policy prior to 1989 allowing an unsatisfied party in an arbitration to seek information or documents by writing to the N.A.S.D. requesting aid in obtaining the document or information. The opposing party would thereafter respond by production or submit its refusal, with the arbitration panel deciding the refused requests prior to the scheduled hearing on the merits.

In 1989 the SEC approved SRO arbitration rule changes.[2] As a result, N.Y.S.E. Rule 619, AMEX Rule 607(a), and the N.A.S.D. Code of Arbitration Procedure § 32(a) now formally declare, "parties shall cooperate to the fullest extent practicable in the voluntary exchange of documents and information to expedite arbitration." A N.A.S.D. Board of Governors Resolution originally adopted in 1973 states, "It may be deemed conduct inconsistent with just and equitable principles of trade and a violation of Article III, § 1 of the Rules of Fair Practice for a member or person associated with a member to fail to . . . produce any document in his possession or control, as directed pursuant to N.A.S.D. Code of Arbitration Procedure." AAA Rule 11 provides that the arbitrator "may" provide for (and resolve any dispute regarding) exchange of documents and limits of witnesses.

The basic way to receive information in an arbitration, then, is to use the voluntary exchange. The following sections discuss the less voluntary subpoena process, as well as the more usual document request and prehearing conference to comply with the need to obtain information by both the customer, employee, and/or brokerage firm.

1) BEFORE FILING CLAIM

As discussed in chapter 11, the person bringing the claim should carefully review documents that are available, and list those that she does not have. This will serve as a basic checklist for requested documents.

In addition, chapter 11 also discusses the sources of information available upon request. SEC, state securities commissions, and other public filings and certain SRO documents can be obtained prior to filing a claim. After the claim is filed, the SRO discovery rules should permit requests for information to exchange documents from each side's files.

2) INFORMATION AND DOCUMENT PRODUCTION IN SECURITIES ARBITRATION

Within the confines of an arbitration, the SRO forums permit each party to request information and documents in the possession, custody, and control of the other party.[3]

All the SRO discovery rules[4] provide that 20 days must pass after service of the Statement of Claim before a Claimant or Respondent may serve information requests. Essentially this allows the respondent to serve the information requests together with its answer (due to 20 days after service of the claim). The information request is normally made by written letter to the other party. A letter specifying the specific documents and information sought will suffice as a document request; no particular form is required. See the Sample Document Request set forth below.

An objection to the document request, a response, or the documents must be served within 30 days of service. If a party objects to the information request served upon it, it must first seek to resolve the objection with the requesting party. If after attempting a resolution of the dispute, the parties cannot resolve the objection, the objecting party must thereafter serve all parties and the director of arbitration with a specific written objection, setting forth all attempts to resolve the objection with the requesting party. Thereafter and within ten days of the receipt of an objection, the requesting party may make a written response to the objection. The reply must be served on all parties and the director of arbitration. The director of arbitration will then normally try to mediate the dispute; if that fails, a single arbitrator will be asked to rule on the issue presented in a prehearing conference. See the discussion later in this chapter.

Ten calendar days prior to the first hearing, all parties must serve on all other parties' copies of all documents that they intend to present in evidence, as well as a list of all witnesses to be called. This does not cover documents or witnesses used for cross-examination or rebuttal.[5]

If a party is dissatisfied with the results of the prehearing or mediation discovery, it is possible to go to court seeking "aid" for the arbitration. For example, New York Civil Practice and Law Rule 3102(c) provides, "before an action is commenced, disclosure to aid in bringing an action, to preserve information or to aid in arbitration may be obtained, but only by court order. The court may appoint a referee to take testimony." But the courts are reluctant to "aid" arbitration, feeling the arbitrators are in the best position to judge the relevance of discovery requests as opposed to a mere disagreement as to the relevance of documents and witnesses. The arbitrators are given the powers to accomplish discovery, and the courts will be reluctant to grant requests to aid arbitration discovery where the arbitrators have refused such requests previously.[6] Special circumstances will probably be required before the court will step in.[7]

Further, because of the arbitrators' decision-making discretion, a losing party will not normally be able to vacate an award due to the arbitrators' conduct,[8] including failure to permit certain discovery. For example, in a case arguing for vacatur of an securities arbitration award on the grounds that discovery was denied, the Sixth Circuit found that

> [e]ven if the arbitrators failed to hold a prehearing discovery conference within the meaning of N.Y.S.E. Rule 619(d), this would not enhance our power to vacate the arbitration award. The purpose of a discovery conference is merely to 'seek to achieve agreement among the parties' . . . which does not rise to the level of misconduct sufficient to warrant vacating an arbitration award pursuant to [Federal Arbitration Act §10(a)(3)-arbitrator misconduct in refusing to hear evidence pertinent and material to the controversy; or other misbehavior by which the rights of any party have been prejudiced].[9]

Further, the case held that failure to produce a document during discovery does not necessarily amount to fraud, relying on the three-part test of *Bonar*[10] that an award can be vacated on grounds of corruption, fraud, or undue means only by a showing that (1) the plaintiff must establish the grounds by clear and convincing evidence; (2) the fraud must not have been discoverable upon the exercise of due diligence prior to or during the arbitration; and (3) the petitioner must demonstrate that the fraud materially related to an issue in the arbitration.

In another case where the discovery requested included a "speculative" request for daily "order tickets" which would have been a burden based on the "vast number of these documents generated daily," the arbitrators were upheld in refusing to order production. The investors had full and fair opportunity to litigate the issue during arbitration and confirmation proceedings concerning a clearing broker's inducement to enter customer agreements with an unregistered introducing broker and unauthorized liquidation of accounts. As a result the doctrine of *res judicata* barred securities law fraud claims raising the registration and liquidation issues.

Types of information that an Information Request may ask for include:

A) Customer Discovery From Brokerage Firm

Almost without exception, customers do not have copies of their opening account forms. In addition, trading confirmations and monthly statements often are missing from the customer's records. Although customers are expected to retain these documents, they are available from the brokerage firm (or clearing firm). These documents are essential in order to conduct a financial analysis and often to substantiate a claim. The documents are on microfiche at the brokerage or clearing house if the hard copy is not available.

i) Microfiche Copies. A specific and all too common problem encountered by the customer in connection with the production of essential documents is production of illegible copies as the "best available from the firm's microfiche." A customer encountering this should request the director of arbitration's permission to make copies from the microfiche. Very often the result will be that the firm will produce more legible copies, rather than permitting the customer access to the firm's files.

ii) The Problem of Specificity. Underscored in every arbitration is the undertaking that "the parties shall cooperate to the fullest extent practicable in the voluntary exchange of documents and information to expedite arbitration."[11] As a practical matter, however, each brokerage firm names its various documents differently, and that as a result customers and even attorneys can rarely specifically name the document as the firm names the documents. Brokerage firms often respond to information requests by demanding that the requesting party name the forms and documents requested by the specific name. The failure to specifically name the document may result in an objection to producing the requested document as "no such document exists." Another common justification for refusal to furnish requested documents is that compliance with the request will require expensive and/or time consuming searches of volumes of records "in storage." The requesting party should keep in mind that brokerage firms maintain records on microfiche; a request should be made to inspect these documents. Also it is wise to request a copy of all indexes to operation and compliance manuals used by the firm compliance department, regional and office managers that would shed light on both the existence of and a specific name that the brokerage firm uses to name its documents.

iii) Cost of Production. The SRO rules provide that the person requesting the "appearance of a person or the production of documents" shall bear all reasonable costs.[12] The AAA does not have a comparable provision, but Rule 42 provides that the award can assess expenses.

iv) Sample Document Request. The following is a form of document request that might be used in a typical customer suitability or churning case. The request must be tailored with regard to the specific documents that are in the specific customer's possession and the specific nature of the claim. It is necessary to define the terms that you are using in the rest of this request. This should describe the parties, dates, documents, and the like.

SAMPLE DOCUMENT REQUEST

XYZ Securities, Inc.
2 Wall Street
New York City, New York 10005

Attention: [Lawyer in charge of case]

Re: Case Name
[Forum] Arbitration No. ...

Dear Mr. ...:

Claimants, [by their attorneys, ...,] hereby request that respondents [Names] produce the following information and documents now in their possession, custody or control. For your convenience, the following terms are used to include and define:

"Claimants" include [name].

"Respondents" includes XYZ Securities, Inc. (Broker) and/or AA (Registered Representative), as well as each of their directors, officers, partners, parents, affiliates, subsidiaries, employees, agents or representatives, including their attorneys, or any employee, agent, investigator or representative of their attorneys.

"Document" includes electronic, recorded, taped, printed and written matter and non-identical copies, with illegible signatures identified and those contained in the definition in Rule 34 of the Federal Rules of Civil Procedure and Rule 1001(1) of the Federal Rules of Evidence. Where different designations or names are used, all documents within the functional definition generally used are included within this term regardless of the name or term used by you. If any of the documents referred to herein were once in the possession, custody or control but are no longer, identify such documents by stating the type of document, the date, the author, addressee, and the reason such document is no longer in your possession, custody or control. In the event that any document requires a computer key, code or other item to decode it, this request will extend to your production of any such key or code. If any document is asserted to be privileged, identify such document and the basis for the claim of privilege with sufficient specificity to allow Claimant an opportunity to object to the claim of privilege.

"Securities" includes all stocks, bonds, and other securities of whatever nature traded for claimant's accounts including, but not limited to, the following: [list all securities subject to this arbitration claim]

Claimants reserve the right to request additional information and documents.

Unless otherwise specified, the following requests relate to the time period from [Date].., to the date of full compliance with these requests, and shall constitute a continuing request if and when you receive additional relevant information in addition or inconsistent with any documents furnished.

REQUESTS

1. Copies of all account opening forms pertaining to the accounts of Claimants, or any IRA or trust, including customer agreements, new account forms, executed and non-executed documents and internal documents of Broker including all opening account qualification documents, including customer objectives, customer qualification for direct investments, financial condition, and manager opening, review or approval papers; margin records ;

2. All disclosure statements, sales literature, recommendations, advisory letters, research reports and other investment information given or transmitted by respondents to the Claimants;

3. All advertisements, marketing and promotional information with respect to any seminars conducted by respondents relative to [securities subject to the arbitration claim] and other financial products, together with the names of all publications, media and/or other methods of distribution of such notices;

4. All correspondence between Claimants and any of the respondents, including all activity letters;

5. All electronic stored data, print-outs, records, memoranda and other documentation reflecting telephone calls made and received between Claimants and any of the respondents, their agents and employees.

6. Records of any meetings, conferences, sales presentations, etc., between Claimants and any of the Respondents, including their dates, meeting sites, matters discussed, persons present and length of meetings;

7. All exception reports and/or activity concentration print-outs whether or not prior to [date] concerning respondent Registered Representative's trading and/or investment activities;

8. Year-end statements for all accounts of Claimants, containing information as to capital gains, capital losses, dividends, interest, distributions together with any internal year-end statements of respondents containing different or additional information including, but not limited to, commissions, mark-ups and/or production credits;

9. Copies of all product holding pages, order tickets; confirmation slips; account statements; blotters; diaries; brokerage orders; notices; ledgers; position book; dividend and interest sheets; securities received and failed to deliver sheets; account card; and posting books of or concerning Claimants;

10. Copies of all canceled checks issued by or on behalf of the Respondents to the Claimants;

11. All respondents' profit and loss analyses or other financial summaries performed by or on behalf of Respondents with respect to any and all accounts of the Claimants;

12. The name and address, including present employment, of any and all branch managers of Respondent for the period [date], to date;

13. Copies of all customer complaints of any date whether or not prior to [date] pertaining to Registered Representative and/or his branch manager as well as any other

agent or employee, registered representative or manager of respondents who earned compensation in any form directly or indirectly as a result of the trading activity that took place in the accounts of the Claimants;

14. All records showing the number of accounts constituting respondent Registered Representative's book of business at Broker for each of the years 19.. through and including the time Registered Representative left the employ of Broker, together with an identification of the number of accounts for which each of the Securities were purchased.

15. All W-2 statements, commission runs, and broker's monthly statements and all other compensation documents relating to the earnings and compensation of respondent Registered Representative and any other agent or employee, registered representative or manager of respondents who earned money or compensation directly as a result of the trading activity that took place in the accounts of Claimants;

16. Copies of all personnel files; questionnaires or employment applications; U-4; U-5; for Broker, [branch manager] and [supervisor] termination letters and notices, letters of resignation, recommendation, probation or reprimand; any SRO correspondence about such persons;

17. All documents showing any criminal conviction or regulatory body disciplinary action, including Form RE-3, pertaining to any respondent and any legal action, arbitration, and other customer complaint brought by any present or former customer against Registered Representative and any agent, employee, registered representative or manager of respondent Broker who earned monies directly as a result of the trading activity that took place in the accounts of Claimants;

18. Copies of monthly statements provided by Respondents to Claimants for each of Claimants' accounts [for any period missing];

19. Copies of respondents' questionnaires designed to obtain financial information such as assets, net worth, etc., regarding each claimant.

20. Suitability standards considered by respondents with respect to each security purchased for the respective accounts of the Claimants.

21. Respondents written guidelines and/or criteria setting forth the content, frequency and/or method of review of all customers' accounts;

22. Respondents written procedures for investigation designed to familiarize, direct any guide [Broker] compliance personnel when presented with claims of possible misconduct by registered representatives and/or account executives;

23. Respondents written procedures and guidelines designed to insure that deficiencies in supervision of registered representatives are corrected;

24. Respondents written instructions provided to supervisory and other personnel pertaining to their compliance responsibility, including a description of such compliance responsibilities;

25. Copies of all Respondents registered representative and supervisory manager training, operation and compliance manuals, memoranda, compliance information papers, inter-office notes, tapes, letters and updates and any other documents concerning (i) opening and qualification of accounts and customers; (ii) know your customer; (iii) supervision; iv) recommendation of purchases;(v) recommendation of sales; (vi) sales of direct investments; (vii) discretionary accounts; (viii) suitability of investment;(ix) registered representative-customer fiduciary duties; (x) necessary approvals; (xi) qualifications for direct investments; (xii) management account review

(xiii) exercise of discretion, (xiv) opening of discretionary accounts,(xv) necessary approvals for discretionary accounts,(xvi) solicitation of accounts (xvii) trade authorization, (xviii) margin accounts, (xix) activity letters (xx) low priced securities, (xxi) speculative securities (xxii) completion of and meaning of terms on new account statements; (xxiii) an complete index of all compliance, operation and advisory publications.

26. Records showing whether any of the securities purchased for any and all of the accounts of the Claimants were part of an initial public offering, and if so, an identification of which securities were part of an initial public offering;

27. Copies of prospectuses for all securities purchased for the accounts of Claimants;

28. Copies of all records, including internal documents of respondents, showing the compensation of Registered Representative and Broker for customer transactions in the securities underwritten by Broker;

29. The most recent valuations of any and all of the Securities purchased at any time for the accounts of Claimants (itemized in Request No. 14 above) together with the identification of the source and date of such valuation;

30. All notes and records of Respondents, their agents and employees, including notes describing telephone conversations or meetings, pertaining to the accounts of Claimants;

31. All commission runs, production runs, execution slips, records showing mark-ups and mark-downs, and other internal reports showing investment costs incurred by the Claimants and commissions received by respondents with respect to any and all of the Claimants' accounts; all transfer documents and correspondence between you and any other brokerage house concerning Claimants; copies of other statements of claim, complaints, discovery, interrogatories, affidavits, documents produced in connection with any claim or lawsuit brought concerning a product sold to Claimants or any trust created by or for Claimants; copies of other statements of claim, complaints, discovery, interrogatories, affidavits, documents produced in connection with any claim or lawsuit brought against Broker, [supervisor], or [branch manager]; copies of other statements of claim, complaints, discovery, interrogatories, affidavits, documents produced in connection with any claim or lawsuit brought against Broker, [branch manager], [supervisor], or firms other than Respondents by Broker or visa versa; all management account reviews of Broker's client accounts and (ii) all management account reviews of claimant's accounts.

32. Copies of (i) all prospectuses and correspondence concerning financial products sold to Claimants, (ii) copies of all letters and correspondence between you and the management of such product; (iii) copies of all investigations done by you in connection with the recommendation of financial products to your customers ("due diligence");(iv) copies of all correspondence between you and/or concerning Claimants investment in such products; (v) copies of all qualifications made concerning Claimants investment in such products.

33. A list of each of Respondents witnesses, including expert witnesses, that either respondent will call at the hearing to be held herein, together with their employment applications and resumes and written statement of their testimony;

34. Copies of all documents that Respondents will or intend to introduce at the hearing to be held herein;

In accordance with § 2 of the N.A.S.D. Code of Arbitration Procedure or other forum rule], the information and documents requested herein shall be satisfied or objected to within thirty (30) calendar days from the date of service.

Very truly yours,

copy to: [Name of Forum--Arbitration Counsel]

B) Brokerage Firm Document Requests

While the above documents are advisable for the customer, a brokerage firm will also want to request information concerning the customer as it prepares its case in arbitration. This may be used to establish the customer is not as naive as it might otherwise seem--especially if the loss on a transaction which is claimed to be unauthorized is treated as a trade, for example, taken on the tax return. Specifically, the firm might request documents from the customer regarding:

1. Other brokerage accounts, mutual fund, retirement, IRA and bank accounts; monthly statements, opening account forms for individual and joint accounts or those where claimants had trading authority;
2. Customer copies of confirmations and monthly statements;
3. Account statements at other brokerage firms;
4. Tax returns, K-1s;
5. Financial data, including financial statements;
6. Other investments data;
7. Diaries, notes, trading records and correspondence to and from brokerage firm and third parties, including confirmations, monthly statements, etc.;
8. Educational and employment background; resume;
9. Loan applications;
10. Telephone records, tapes, etc., of conversations relating to investments;
11. Account or investment analysis prepared by or for claimants regarding damages;
12 Subscriptions to financial, investment, and business services, newspapers, and periodicals;
13. Correspondence with the SEC, N.A.S.D., exchanges, and other regulators.

C) List of Witnesses

As part of the preparation for hearing, the parties will exchange identification on witnesses to be called.[13] In the event of a problem in getting this information, it can be ordered by either staff or an arbitrator in a prehearing conference. Lists are commonly prepared on forum forms.

D) Information Regarding Expert Witnesses

One area that both parties should carefully consider is the request for documentary information regarding the position that might be taken by an expert witness. (See item 33 of the Sample Document Request). Of course, the information about the expert's education, employment, pay, writings, prior testimony, and the like can assist in evaluating his or her testimony and giving an insight regarding cross-examination.

3) SUBPOENAS

Subpoenas are permitted in arbitration under the rules of all the SROs to compel production of documents and the presence at hearings of witnesses. The claimant's attorney, respondent's attorney, and the arbitrators may issue subpoenas, pursuant to state or federal law. The party issuing the subpoena must serve copies upon all parties, director of arbitration, and the arbitrators. Unless a prehearing conference is scheduled, documents or persons subpoenaed do not have to be produced before the first substantive hearing. It is therefore imperative to schedule a pretrial conference and make the subpoena returnable at a time before this first substantive hearing, to avoid undue surprise. Alternatively, one might call for an adjournment of the first hearing after production of the discovery materials.

A) Arbitration Rules

Arbitrators can subpoena witnesses[14] and documents[15] under the Uniform Code,[16] the Federal Arbitration Act,[17] and most state arbitration statutes,[18] but enforcement is left to the judiciary in the event the subpoena is not observed after service.[19] Presently there is no way to determine compliance until the prehearing conference or hearing when the persons or documents must be produced. The party requesting the subpoena must pay the reasonable costs of production or attendance.

While under the SRO rules, the arbitrators can compel appearance and production of documents in the possession of any party employed by or associated with any member organization of that SRO; the parties should remember that legal subpoena power also exists. But this is limited to subpoenas that would be permitted under applicable laws. It is also not limited to SRO members and associates. No SRO rule precludes a party from serving a subpoena upon another party.

The N.A.S.D. Code of Arbitration Procedure § 33(a) provides:

> *Subpoenas*. The arbitrators and any counsel of record to the proceeding shall have the power of the subpoena process as provided by law. All parties shall be given a copy of a subpoena upon its issuance. Parties

> shall produce witnesses and present proofs to the fullest extent possible without resort to the subpoena process.

N.A.S.D. § 33, N.Y.S.E. Rule 619(f), and AMEX Rule 610 parallel this language, exactly. The AAA provides for issuance of subpoenas by the arbitrators as provided under state law, as it has no coercive power (as do the SROs) over members. Because there is no corresponding penalty for the failure of a public customer to comply with SRO discovery requests, however, there is a risk of being assessed costs for a postponement of the hearing resulting from failure to produce documents in a timely fashion or failure to appear.[20]

While the issuance of subpoenas and voluntary exchange of information was permitted under prior practice, the new SRO rules[21] permit discovery as well as providing a forum for determining issues of disclosure--the prehearing conference.

B) Federal Law

Under § 7 of the Federal Arbitration Act, a single arbitrator, or a majority of the arbitrators, issue the subpoena. Section 7 provides in relevant part,

> the arbitrators . . . or a majority of them, may summon in writing any person to attend before them or any of them as a witness and in a proper case to bring with him or them any book, record or document, or paper which may be deemed material as evidence in the case. The fees for such attendance shall be the same as fees of witnesses before masters of the United States courts. Such summons shall issue in the name of the arbitrator or arbitrators, or a majority of them, and shall be directed to the said person and shall be served in the same manner as subpoenas to appear and testify in court.

In general practice, the *Subpoena Duces Tecum* requires the presence of the person to testify and/or production of documents and papers.

Federal Rules of Civil Procedure 45(e) permits the Clerk of the District Court to sign a subpoena for service within the district or within a one hundred mile radius of the district. Service of the subpoena may be made by a non-party over the age of 18, and if a witnesses' attendance is required, the witness fee for one day's attendance and mileage fees must be tendered.[22]

C) State Law

In addition to the subpoena process available under federal practice, a party may also avail themselves of the subpoena process of the state in which the hearing is to be held. States differ on the law of subpoenas. New York State is typical of most state practice under the Uniform Act.

In New York the arbitrator or any attorney of record may issue a subpoena in the arbitration proceeding outside of court or court intervention.[23] Subpoenas are served with the tender of witness fees and mileage. However, if substitute methods of personal service are used and require that the affidavit of service be filed, the subpoena and affidavit of service need not be filed with the court clerk.[24]

Enforcement of subpoenas may be judicially enforced pursuant to the law of the issuing jurisdiction. In New York, enforcement is made pursuant to the civil practice rules,[25] but can only be enforced within the state, while in Federal practice subpoenas are enforced in the "same manner provided by law for securing the attendance of witnesses or their punishment for neglect or refusal to attend in the courts of the United States,"[26] so a nationwide service is permitted.

D) Form of Subpoena

The following is a form of subpoena that might be used in New York to compel production of documents, in this case from a non-party to the arbitration.

---X
IN THE MATTER OF THE ARBITRATION)
BETWEEN)
[Name],) [Forum] Arbitration No.
Claimants,)
)
-against-) SUBPOENA DUCES TECUM
)
[Broker])
and [Registered Representative],)
)
Respondents.)
---X

THE PEOPLE OF THE STATE OF NEW YORK

To: Office of General Counsel
National Association of Securities Dealers, Inc.
1735 K Street, N.W.
Washington, D.C. 20006
Attention:

GREETINGS:

WE COMMAND YOU, That all business and excuses being laid aside, you produce the following documents at the offices of ... on or before [date--usually 30 days after date of subpoena] the following:

All records maintained by the National Association of Security Dealers, Inc., including CRD records, pertaining to [Name], on information and belief, a broker with [Broker] for at least the period 198.. through and including 199.. and at present with XYZ Securities, Inc.

Failure to comply with this subpoena and to produce the aforesaid documents will subject you to penalties, including but not limited to the proceeding provided for in CPLR 2308 of the State of New York and cause liability for damages sustained by reason of your failure to comply.

DATED: Huntington, New York
March 20, 199 .

[Name, Address, and Telephone]

[Add Affidavit of Service]

4) POWER TO DIRECT APPEARANCES

Typically a subpoena will require or compel a witness to appear before the arbitration tribunal and/or produce books, records, and other documents. All parties are given a copy of the subpoena on its issuance. But the SRO rules normally try to have the parties produce witnesses and documents without resorting to the more formal subpoena process.[27] The party seeking the subpoena against parties who are not parties to the arbitration must bear the reasonable costs of such appearance or production, which may be recoverable in the costs.

Without any resort to the subpoena process, SRO arbitrators may direct a member firm to produce documents or information. This right is unavailable in AAA arbitration. N.A.S.D. Code of Arbitration § 33(b), N.Y.S.E. Rule 619(g), and AMEX Rule 611, all provide:

> *Power to Direct Appearances and Production of Documents.* The arbitrators shall be empowered *without resort to the subpoena process* to direct the appearance of any person employed or associated with any member of the Association and/or the production of any records in the possession or control of such persons or members. Unless the arbitrators direct otherwise, the party requesting the appearance of a person or the production of documents under this Section shall bear all reasonable costs of such appearances and/or production. [Emphasis supplied].

Non-compliance with a directive of an arbitrator by a firm or broker may lead to the possibility of referral of the matter for disciplinary action by the SRO as conduct "inconsistent with just and equitable principles of the trade" and, thus, a violation of the rules of fair practice.[28] Rarely, if ever, has this occurred. Member firms will generally obey the directive of the arbitrators to produce documents, brokerage firm employees, or information subject to this rule.

5) THE PREHEARING CONFERENCE

When all information requests, objections, and reply have been served and filed with the SRO arbitration forum, the director of arbitration may either (1) hold a prehearing conference and select a person (not necessarily an arbitrator) to preside, or (2) select a public arbitrator to preside at the prehearing conference and decide the issues on the papers. Also upon a written request of a party, a prehearing conference will be scheduled to resolve any outstanding issue before a single public arbitrator appointed by the forum director of arbitration. This can be done by written submission, hearing, or telephone conference call.

An interim, unwritten, mediation step is usually imposed by the case administrator who will first attempt to resolve the issues without involving an arbitrator. AAA Rule 10 provides for administrative conferences, preliminary hearings and mediation conferences, all run by members of the AAA staff.

A) The SRO Preliminary Hearing

The aim of the prehearing conference is to obtain the parties cooperation in the exchange of information; the parties consent to produce requested documents and the identification of witness. However, the prehearing conference is not limited to discovery issues. In addition and at the discretion of the person presiding, the prehearing conference may deal with exchange of hearing documents, stipulations of fact, identification of disputed issues, briefing of contested issues, scheduling of hearings, and other matters that might expedite the arbitration.

B) SRO Mediation

If the case administrator acts as the person conducting the prehearing conference, he or she may attempt to mediate any dispute and suggest resolution. The case administrator holds no power to order a party to do anything. A major problem in expediting arbitration is injected when the arbitration counsel insists on mediating a discovery dispute. If the parties are truly fixed in terms of their positions on production, the question will have to be decided by an arbitrator in any event. Under most circumstances a brokerage firm, customer, or employee will make an evaluation of the ability of the case administrator's influence on the arbitrator's decisions. If the brokerage firm or claimant conclude that the case administrator is weak or will be unable to persuade the panel or sole arbitrator of the case administrator's suggestions for the resolution of discovery disputes, the brokerage firm or attorney will not produce the information or the documents requested. As a result, the time spent before a weak case administrator will be wasted, and it may be more economical to demand the prehearing conference.

A major practical problem with case administrator mediation is that after an initial hearing, subsequent prehearing conferences are difficult to obtain. Sometimes three months may pass between mediation and a subsequent prehearing conference. If a large period of time elapses between prehearing conferences, a party may lose momentum and coherence of his or her case. Respondents rarely complain about this difficulty, with the result that parties often may not receive documents until ten days before the final hearing and only then the documents that the party intends to use at the hearing.

C) Need for Written Order

A favorite delay tactic is to wait and not respond after the arbitrator's decision on discovery matters decided. Commonly, the response will be the firm was "waiting for the written order" or "there was no written order." It is therefore essential that at any prehearing conference the parties obtain a specific time frame to produce and a commitment as to whether a written order will follow. If a customer's counsel does not deal with these problems, she may find that documents and information are not provided until the day of the hearing, if at all. Or the customer's counsel may find that additional time will be wasted by rearguing at additional prehearing conferences these same issues in trying to obtain the information and documents already ordered to be produced.

D) Second Preliminary Hearing

If after the initial mediation or prehearing conference, the party who agrees or is directed to produce information or documents does not produce the requested material--or if the issues raised at the prehearing conference are not resolved--the director of arbitration may appoint a single arbitrator to resolve the remaining differences. Some SRO case administrators are reluctant to take this additional step. As a result, the party requesting information and documents may need to become very forceful and demand a single arbitrator resolve these difficulties.

If a single arbitrator is appointed to resolve the remaining difficulties, a second prehearing conference may also be held to resolve the remaining differences. Generally, the arbitrator's decisions are immediate. Decisions regarding discovery may be in writing, but more often are oral.

E) The AAA Preliminary Hearing

Under AAA Securities Arbitration Rule 10, at the request of any party or at the discretion of the AAA administrator, an administrative conference is scheduled in appropriate cases to expedite the arbitration. There is no administrative fee. This is particularly true in large and complex cases where the AAA staff will address with the parties or their representatives regarding: (1) appointment and technical qualifications of arbitrators; (2) compensation of arbitrators; (3) schedule of future hearing dates and estimated time for completion of arbitration; (4) fix the hearing locations under Rule 12; and (5) other matters that will expedite the proceedings.

AAA Rule 11 provides for a preliminary hearing before an arbitrator to establish (1) the extent and schedule for production of relevant documents and other information; and (2) identification of witnesses to be called and the nature of their testimony. The arbitrator can order these matters.

In addition to those matters specifically covered by AAA Rule 10, the preliminary hearing will also consider the following in order to expedite the arbitration: (1) stipulation of uncontested facts; (2) specification and clarification of claims and counterclaims; and (3) other evidentiary and procedural matters.

F) AAA Mediation

AAA Rule 10 provides that the AA can arrange a mediation under the AAA Commercial Mediation Rules, unless the parties agree otherwise. There is no additional administrative fee. The mediator may not be an arbitrator assigned to the case and cannot impose a settlement on the parties. Mediation is totally confidential; offers of settlement can not be used in subsequent litigation or arbitration. The AAA reports mediation has a 50 to 60 percent success rate.[29]

The AAA and N.A.S.D. are engaged in a joint mediation pilot project offering AAA mediation to parties in an N.A.S.D. arbitration.[30] The project uses an AAA staff mediator who has securities industry experience. See the discussion in chapter 9.

6) DEPOSITIONS

While the arbitrators are empowered to order production of witnesses from the SRO members and can compel attendance by subpoena, there are few cases where arbitrators have ordered depositions of witnesses prior to the hearing. This is permitted but has been seldom used to date. The rationale is that depositions add a layer of expensive, time consuming discovery and may cause delay in hearing the claim. It may be appropriate to require a deposition if the witness is unavailable at the hearing due to geographical or perhaps health reasons, the necessity to preserve a witness' testimony and other factors bearing on the efficiency and fairness of the proceeding. Depositions should be permitted only in the careful exercise of the arbitrator's judgment.[31]

Depositions in arbitration proceedings may be permitted under state law. Otherwise the panel will be asked to rule to permit them. There may be a question if arbitrators have that power absent forum rule permitting depositions. The SROs do not have such a rule. Some arbitrators have taken the position that AAA Rule 50, which permits the arbitrator to "interpret and apply these rules as they relate to the arbitrator's powers and duties," includes the power to order depositions in appropriate cases.

7) CONCLUSION

Discovery in arbitration is in flux. The SEC is aware of the failure of discovery in arbitration and the S.I.C.A. and SROs are currently working on new discovery rules and procedures to maintain the speedy resolution available in arbitration while avoiding unfair surprise at the arbitration hearing. All are seeking to avoid unnecessary difficulty obtaining necessary documents and information. This information will provide two functions: first, to avoid surprise and permit orderly presentation of a case in arbitration and, second, to encourage settlement once the facts are make known.

One of the most significant SRO rule changes permits arbitrators to enforce their orders.[32] This can result in an adverse inference against a party that does not comply with an order; assessment of costs and fees (including attorney's fees) caused by non-compliance; strike all or part of a pleading; or initiate a disciplinary referral. Consequently, if a party refuses to cooperate in discovery or fails to appear, ask for sanctions!

NOTES

1 ARW Exploration Corp. v. Aguirre, 1990 WL 270291 (W.D. Ok. 1990), appeal 947 F.2d 450 (10th Cir. 1991).

2 Exchange Act Release No. 34-26805, FED. SEC. L. REP. (CCH) ¶ 84,414 (1989).

3 In 1991, the N.Y.S.E. distributed a memorandum to arbitration staff and securities arbitration lawyers that listed the documents that should be produced in prehearing conferences and arbitration discovery. Included in documents from the broker were: key documents about brokers compliance and legal problems (particularly the N.A.S.D. RE-3 forms that disclose any settlement award or judgment involving more than $15,000, which may affect the broker's credibility); brokers employment and termination notices (U-1 and U-4 Forms); monthly statements and order confirmations, if necessary; relevant parts of the firm's compliance manual; research reports, client agreements, and opening account documentation (which relate to the customer's investment objectives, financial condition and needs); correspondence with regulators; marketing manuals; order tickets; profit-and-loss analysis; information regarding the broker's commissions; and other similar customer complaints. *See*, *Big Board Urges Broader Disclosure in Investor Disputes*, WALL ST. J. C:1 (April 12, 1991).

4 *See* S.I.C.A. Code of Arbitration ("Uniform Code") § 20; N.A.S.D. § 32(b); N.Y.S.E. Rule 619; and AMEX Rule 607(b), which provide:

> (1) Any party may serve a written request for information or documents ("information request") upon another party twenty (20) business days or

more after service of the Statement of Claim by the Director of Arbitration or upon filing of the answer, whichever is earlier. The requesting party shall serve the information request on all parties and file a copy with the Director of Arbitration. The parties shall endeavor to resolve disputes regarding an information request prior to serving any objection to the request. Such efforts shall be set forth in the objection.

(2) Unless a greater time is allowed by the requesting party, information requests shall be satisfied or objected to within thirty (30) calendar days from the date of service. Any objection to an information request shall be served by the objecting party on all parties and filed with the Director of Arbitration.

(3) Any response to objections to an information request shall be served on all parties and filed with the Director of Arbitration within ten (10) calendar days of receipt of the objection.

5 *See* Uniform Code § 20; N.A.S.D. § 32; N.Y.S.E. Rule 608(b).

6 *See* Cotter v. Shearson Lehman Hutton, Inc., 126 F.R.D. 19 (S.D.N.Y. 1989), where the arbitration panel refused to allow plaintiff's motion for discovery in aid of arbitration, except upon showing of relevance to the claims being arbitrated. The plaintiff had sought documents and testimony from defendants and others. In other cases, the chief executive officer of a brokerage firm was subpoenaed to testify on compliance issues, as this was ultimately his responsibility.

7 *See* Merrill Lynch, Pierce, Fenner & Smith, Inc. v. Hower, 726 F.2d 1286 (8th Cir. 1984); Cotter v. Shearson Lehman Hutton, Inc., 126 F.R.D. 19, FED. SEC. L. REP. (CCH) ¶94468 (S.D.N.Y. 1989).

8 *See* 9 U.S.C. §§ 10,11 (1982); N.Y. CPLR 7511.

9 Pontiac Trail Medical Clinic, P.C. v. Paine Webber, Inc., 1 F.2d, 1241, (6th Cir. 1993).

10 Bonar v. Dean Witter Reynolds, Inc., 835 F.2d 1378, 1383 (11th Cir. 1988), set up this test in response to a claim of fraud. Pontiac Trail extended the test to Section 10(a)(1) "undue means," citing A.G. Edwards & Sons, Inc. v. McCollough, 967 F.2d 1401, 1403 (9th Cir. 1992), which held "undue means" "clearly connotes behavior that is immoral if not illegal . . . [M]ere sloppy or overzealous lawyering does not constitute 'undue means.'"

11 N.Y.S.E. Const. Art. XI, N.Y.S.E. Rule 619(a); AMEX Const. Art. VIII, AMEX Rule 607(a); N.A.S.D. By-Laws, Art. XV, N.A.S.D. § 32(a).

12 N.A.S.D. § 33(b); N.Y.S.E. Rule 619(g).

13 N.A.S.D. § 32(d)(1); N.Y.S.E. Rule 619(d); AAA Rule 11.

14 *Subpoena ad testificandum*.

15 *Subpoena duces tecum*.

16 Uniform Code § 20(a); N.A.S.D. § 32; N.Y.S.E. Rule 619--all limited to SRO members and associates. But these rules are limited to subpoenas that would be permitted under applicable laws. *See* N.Y. CPLR

7505.

17 9 U.S.C.§ 7 (1982 & Supp. 1988).

18 N.Y. CPLR 7505.

19 *See*, Page, *Subpoena Practice in Arbitration*, WIDE WORLD OF ARBITRATION 32 (AAA ed.,1978).

In Tinway v. Merrill Lynch & Co., 658 F. Supp. 576 (S.D.N.Y. 1987), the court was "unable to infer a ground for the arbitrators' decision from the facts of [the] case" and vacated the award on the basis of the "evident partiality" of the arbitrators.

20 One commentator notes:

> [t]he failure of a broker-dealer party to an arbitration to produce documents, under certain circumstances, may be deemed inconsistent with SRO rules requiring that their members conform with just and equitable principles of trade. There is no corresponding penalty for the failure of a public customer to comply with discovery requests. However, there is a risk for either party of being assessed costs for a postponement of the hearing resulting from one party's failure to produce documents in a timely fashion.

Djinis, *Securities Industry Arbitrations: The System, Practice and Procedure*, in SECURITIES ARBITRATION UPDATE 50, 68 (M. Fitterman & T. Krebsbach eds.,1989).

21 N.A.S.D. § 32; N.Y.S.E. Rule 619.

22 29 U.S.C. § 821.

23 N.Y. CPLR 7505, 2302.

24 N.Y. CPLR 2303.

25 N.Y. CPLR 2308.

26 9 U.S.C. § 7.

27 *See* Uniform Code § 20(f); N.A.S.D. § 33(a); N.Y.S.E. Rule 619(f).

28 N.A.S.D. Board of Governors Resolution (May 7, 1991).

29 *See* Friedman, *AAA Securities Arbitration: What You Need to Know*, SECURITIES ARBITRATION (Robbins ed., 1992).

30 *See* the discussion in chapter 9.

31 *See* S.I.C.A. ARBITRATOR'S MANUAL 9.

32 N.A.S.D. § 35; N.Y.S.E. Rule 621 (1992 Amendments).

Chapter 14

THE HEARING

An arbitration hearing is very different from a trial. This chapter will review the preliminary hearing or prehearing conference briefly in light of discovery (which was more fully examined in chapter 13) and other matters involving the hearing including the setting of the hearing; rules for commencing a hearing; attendance of parties and who may attend the hearing; creation of a record of the proceeding; adjournments; presentation of the case; evidence rules; briefs; and reopening the hearing. There is normally a period of several months before the hearing. The arbitration forum personnel will arrange for service of the claim, answer, and other matters during this time.

1) WHEN NO HEARING IS REQUIRED

No hearing is required in two situations:

A) Small Claims

If the matter is submitted under the Simplified Procedures rules of the SROs or Expedited Hearing rules of the AAA, no hearing is required. The small claims amounts and jurisdiction are discussed in chapter 9.

In small claims cases, the arbitrator will consider the case based on written submissions of the parties.[1] As long as both the customer and firm have consented to this procedure, it will be binding.[2]

B) Waiver of Hearing

If the parties have waived their right to a hearing, the arbitrators can decide the case on submissions. However, the SRO rules provide that the arbitrators can still require a hearing or submission of additional evidence.[3] The principal reason why the arbitrators would want a hearing would be to assess the credibility of the parties or witnesses through a hearing. Sometimes the equities of a case are also better presented by a witness in a hearing, as, for example, when sophistication of the claimant or lack of knowledge of the broker is at issue.

2) LARGE CASE PROCEDURES[4]

> Recognizing that large, complex arbitrations often present unique procedural problems, the AAA, working with attorneys, arbitrators and industry advisory groups, has developed special Supplementary Procedures for Large Complex Disputes as part of its Large, Complex Case Dispute Resolution Program. (See also the discussion in chapter 9) The overall purpose of these procedures is to provide for the efficient, economical, and speedy resolution of larger disputes (i.e., cases involving claims in excess of $1,000,000). Cases are administered by senior AAA staff. The procedures provide for an early administrative conference with the AAA and a preliminary hearing with the arbitrators. Documentary exchanges and other essential exchanges of information are facilitated. The procedures also provide that a statement of reasons may accompany the award, if requested by the parties. The procedures are meant to supplement applicable rules that the parties have agreed to use. They include the possibility of the use of mediation to resolve some or all issues at an early stage.
>
> The procedures are party driven. They will apply only where the parties agree to their use (unless a court or another entity directs their application), and the parties are free to modify any provision of the procedures. Indeed, the entire process may be tailored to suit the particular requirements of the parties to any single dispute.

3) PREPARING FOR THE HEARING

A) Discovery

As noted in chapter 13, there is no discovery as would be allowed under the Federal Rules of Civil Procedure[5] or state law for litigation, but the SRO rules, as a result of SEC criticism, were amended in 1989 and now provide for "voluntary exchange" of documents which will serve to expedite the arbitration.

B) Notice of Panel Composition

The composition of panels and information regarding the industry connections of the potential panelists were of major concern to the SEC and resulted in many of the 1989 SRO rule changes. "Arbitrator profiles," which give past award information and a biography of the potential arbitrators selected by the SRO for a given case, are being sent to parties. Selection of arbitrators, discussed in chapter 10, is, as a result, a little less hit-and-miss than under prior practice.

C) Contact with Arbitrators

After the appointment of the panel and when the names are known to the parties, it is improper for the parties to contact the arbitrators *ex parte*. All communication should be in the prehearing conferences, which may be held by telephone, or at the hearing when both parties are present. Otherwise, the appearance of impropriety will exist, and there may be an opening to challenge an award. When the arbitrator is appointed, the parties may not contact him or her. If the parties contact the arbitrator, he or she should inform the forum director of arbitration or staff.

THE AAA CODE OF ETHICS FOR ARBITRATORS IN COMMERCIAL DISPUTES provides that, unless the agreement of the parties or rules otherwise provides,

> [A]rbitrators should not discuss a case with any party in the absence of each other party, except in any of the following circumstances:
>
> (1) . . . concerning setting the time and place of hearings or making other arrangements for the conduct of the proceedings.
>
> (2) If a party fails to be present at a hearing after having been given due notice, the arbitrator may discuss the case with any party who is present.
>
> (3) If all parties request or consent that such discussion take place.

All written communications should be copied to all parties. If an arbitrator receives a writing or fax that has not been sent to the other parties, he or she should send it to them.

4) THE PREHEARING CONFERENCE

The SRO Rules provide for a prehearing conference at the request of a party, an arbitrator, or the SRO director of arbitration.[6] This is now normal practice, and no fee is assessed for this staff service. The AAA rules provide for a prehearing conference at a party's request or at the discretion of the AAA.[7]

At the prehearing conference, "housekeeping" matters are resolved. The director may appoint a single member of the panel to determine these matters, usually the chair of the panel. This person can issue subpoenas, direct appearances from industry personnel and production of documents, and set deadlines. The arbitrator can also refer matters to the full panel.[8] The conference may be by telephone conference call.

The prehearing conference will consider such matters as:

1. Exchange of information requested--the discovery discussed in chapter 13.
2. Exchange of documents--also covered in chapter 13.
3. Identification and exchange of hearing documents, including the statement of claim, answer, and exhibits.
4. Stipulations and admissions of facts agreed to by the parties, which will expedite the hearing by not requiring proof of these facts in the hearing.[9]
5. Identification and briefing on contested issues of fact and law.
6. Identification of witnesses that will be used at hearing by both sides, including expert witnesses.
7. Logistical matters such as the location of the hearings[10] and dates that are mutually convenient for the arbitrators and the parties.
8. Determination of prehearing motions. As noted in chapter 11, motion practice is limited in arbitration but various motions can be made in response to the statement of claim. The S.I.C.A. ARBITRATOR'S MANUAL notes that at least seven motions can be included in the Answer (see discussion in chapter 11). Included would be motions relating to the procedure and substance of the claim, for example, motions to dismiss, for a more definite statement of claim or to bar defenses or facts when respondent has made a general denial, regarding the applicable statute of limitations or forum eligibility rule, to strike a defense, for joinder of parties or consolidation or severance, discovery motions, motions for change of venue, and the like. Often these are argued at the preliminary conference, sometimes after briefs are presented to the arbitrators, but often the decision is not known until the award is rendered.
9. Other matters that will expedite the arbitration proceeding.

5) THE HEARING

The SRO rules require that the parties be given eight days notice of the initial hearing by certified or registered mail or personal service, unless the parties waive notice.[11] After the first hearing, the type of notice is determined by the arbitrators. Attendance is waiver of notice.

A) Hearing Procedure

Neither the Federal Arbitration Act nor state statutes patterned after the Uniform Act provide for procedure in arbitration. The following describes a normal arbitration proceeding, but this can be varied by the arbitrators as long as there is a full and fair opportunity to all parties for the presentation of any material and relevant evidence.[12] This will require testimony under oath and full right of cross-examination by the parties. The presentation of the case is the same in public (customer) and industry (employment, breach of contract, etc.) arbitrations.

Before the hearing, the person responsible for presenting the case for the claimant (usually his attorney) should become familiar with the rules of the SRO or AAA. The forum staff also provide information regarding the procedures used at a hearing. Necessary reading should also include the S.I.C.A. ARBITRATOR'S MANUAL for SRO arbitrations and A GUIDE FOR COMMERCIAL ARBITRATORS for AAA proceedings. These materials are reproduced in the Appendixes.

i) Physical Setting. The main factor to remember in arbitration is the informality of the proceeding. Typically in a conference room at the SRO or AAA offices, or in a hotel if in another location than where the forum has offices, arbitrators and parties are seated at a small table. There are no robes or bench for the arbitrators, and normally no lectern nor podium from which the parties or their attorneys can stand to present their case. It is much less intimidating than the power and majesty of the law presented in the typical courtroom setting.

ii) Role of the Chair. The chairman of the panel of arbitration normally begins the proceeding, and also ends it. While he or she is merely one among equals, it falls on the chair to direct the proceedings so that the hearing progresses, while at the same time making sure that the parties have had a full and fair hearing. An important role is given to the chair at two stages: one, at the beginning when the chair will begin the arbitration by the opening statement; the second, when the chair closes the arbitration (see discussion of both these statements below). Both are usually read from a script prepared by the forum and inform as well as obtain the consent of the parties to the procedures and applicable rules.

Since the hearing is adversarial, often the chair will have to caution the parties or their attorneys when tensions run too high and the tone of the hearing becomes acrimonious. Because of the close proximity of the parties and the arbitrators, it is advisable not to let emotions run high. Argumentative, abusive, disrespectful, loud, and condescending behavior will not be appreciated by the arbitrators.

iii) Role of Arbitration Staff. Normally the director of arbitration assigns a staff person to the hearing. While not required, often the staff will sit in on the hearing, to answer procedural questions. They will not participate in the deliberation on an award and may be asked by the arbitrators to leave the room for all or part of the hearing.

iv) Burden of Proof. The claimant has the burden to prove the claim. Usually, an attorney will understand this, whereas the *pro se* party may not. It is important to focus on what issues are present: elements of the claim must be proved, and damages must be understandable. The evidence presented should meet these goals; otherwise the case presentation will be rambling, incoherent, and may be ineffective in the arbitrator's minds.

v) Rules of Evidence. Rules of evidence are not applied in arbitration due to the premise that "the arbitrators' sophistication permits them to delineate the probative from the prejudicial . . . [and] determine the materiality and relevance of any evidence presented."[13] The award must be based, however, only on the evidence presented and not as a result of the arbitrator's special knowledge. This informality, coupled with a less adversarial nature, are two real advantages of arbitration over litigation.

While rules of evidence do not apply, the arbitrators do not have to admit everything presented. The S.I.C.A. ARBITRATOR'S MANUAL indicates that the evidence must be relevant. If there has been a violation of discovery requirements, for example, the arbitrators can bar the document or witness.

"The parties are entitled to be heard, to present evidence and to cross-examine witnesses."[14] The order of proceedings are opening statements, the claimant's presentation of the case which is subject to cross-examination and questions from arbitrators,[15] respondent's presentation and cross, and panel inquiry as to the completeness of the presentation.

Often the parties will not present a witness and request either an affidavit or perhaps a deposition instead.[16] It is up to the arbitrators to determine whether to admit such evidence. One issue is whether the other party has had the opportunity to question this witness; if not the panel should consider this in giving weight to the testimony so introduced. The key consideration in the hearing is fairness to each party.

The AAA Securities Arbitration Rules, for example, provide: "The parties may offer such evidence as is relevant and material to the dispute and shall produce such evidence as the arbitrator may deem necessary to an understanding and determination of the dispute."[17] Under SRO rules, an arbitrator "shall determine the materiality and relevance of any evidence proffered and shall not be bound by the rules governing the admissibility of evidence"[18] in litigation.

vi) Interpretation of Rules. The SRO and AAA rules specifically provide that the arbitrators are empowered to interpret and determine the rules of the proceeding and that their decisions are final and binding.[19] This finality has been upheld by the courts.[20] This fact is crucial for the attorney who may be used to the more formal proceedings in litigation and the right of appeal.

vii) Sequestration of Witnesses. Since arbitration is a private proceeding, only the parties (and lawyers) are present. Witnesses can be excluded by the arbitrators order upon request by a party. Expert witnesses are typically permitted to attend and assist in the case presentation.[21]

viii) Absence of a Party. The arbitration can proceed without a party, providing there is jurisdiction. After being given notice of the hearing (or continuation in the case of an adjournment),[22] if a party fails to appear or obtain a postponement, under SRO and AAA rules the arbitrators can, in their discretion, proceed with the arbitration.

Under SRO rules, any award rendered is binding if the party entered an appearance in the matter.[23] The AAA Rules, however, provide that no default of a party can justify an award, and that the party present must submit evidence required to make an award.[24]

ix) Adjournments. Adjournments can be requested by the parties or arbitrators own initiative.[25] Adjournments are permitted in the discretion of the arbitrators. Frivolous, last minute requests for adjournment are discouraged by the imposition of adjournment fees in SRO and AAA arbitrations. Courts have vacated awards, however, where the arbitrators refused to grant a legitimate adjournment request.[26]

x) Death or Incompetence of a Party. Where a party dies or a committee of the property or person is appointed after making an agreement to arbitrate, the person's executor, administrator, or committee is given notice of intent to arbitrate.[27]

xi) Interim Relief. Interim relief is permitted if deemed necessary to protect the property that is the subject matter of the arbitration pending the final outcome of the proceedings.[28]

xii) Record. Under the SRO rules, a verbatim record by court reporter or tape of all arbitration hearings is made.[29] The AAA does not require a record, but if one of the parties wanted, he could provide for it. The party requesting transcription of the record must pay for it unless the arbitrators direct that the record be transcribed at joint cost. This usually will occur only in multiple sessions with complex facts or legal issues.[30]

xiii) Arbitrator's Death or Vacancy. As discussed in chapter 10, absent agreement of the parties, the sickness, incapacity, death, or other unavailability causing a vacancy of an arbitrator may be filled under AAA Rule 21. In other forums, the vacancy may remain empty or be filled, or if a party objects the arbitration may have to begin again with a new panel.

xiv) Interpreters. AAA Rule 25 permits the use of interpreters at the expense of the party using such service.

B) Order of Proceeding

The proceeding normally follows forum guidelines. The SRO forums have more or less adopted the AAA order of proceedings, with some additions. The presentation of the case thus follows the following "script:"

i) Introduction of the Arbitrators. The first step in the arbitration hearing is for the staff person to introduce the parties and their representatives, if any, to the arbitrators.

ii) Arbitrator Oath.[31] While the arbitration law, federal and state, does not require oaths, most forums will require one. The AAA does not require an oath, if the law does not, but requests one in advance of the initial hearing. A typical oath is:

> Do each of you, as the arbitrators selected to hear and decide the matter in controversy, solemnly swear or affirm that you are not an employer of, employed by, or related by blood or marriage to any of the parties or witnesses whose names have been disclosed to you; that you have no direct or indirect interest in this matter; you know of no existing or past financial, business, professional, family or social relationship which would impair you from performing your duties; and that you will decide the controversy in a fair manner and render a just award?

iii) Oath of Parties. Witness are normally sworn.[32] Sometimes the arbitrators will cause the oath or affirmation to be administered to all witnesses at one time, usually the beginning of the arbitration, rather than just before the testimony of each party. This will ensure that any comments made in the course of the informal proceeding are under oath. The AAA allows, but does not require, witnesses to be sworn.[33]

iv) Record. The Chair will note if a transcribed or other record is being kept.[34] Normally the record of the proceedings kept by the arbitration forum will note those present. Some SRO forums transcribe or tape hearings.[35] AAA Rule 24 permits a party to make arrangements "directly" for transcription (and pay therefor). If it is an official record of the proceeding, the transcript must be available to other parties for inspection and probably copying.

v) Introduction of the Statement of Claim and Answer. These are introduced into evidence, with exhibits, normally as Arbitrator's Exhibit No. 1.

vi) Chair's Opening Statement. This statement includes that the arbitrators have taken the oath; confirming that no party has objection to any arbitrator; explains the hearing procedure and role of arbitration staff, if present; that the arbitrators have read the prehearing submissions, which include the Statement of Claim and Answer and other briefs or documents submitted prior to the initial hearing as a result of the prehearing conference; and that the decision will be final.

vii) Opening Statements of Parties. The parties will be asked if they desire to make a general statement of their case. This usually is an outline of the facts which they will try to prove, with the legal arguments also briefly covered. While the parties may decide not to make an opening statement and go directly into the case, this would be a lost opportunity to begin to inform and persuade the panel about the case.

From first hand experience, the panel can initially be favorably impressed or not by the opening statement. If it is disjointed and not concise, questions will be drawn as to the ability of the party making the statement which can have serious implications on his believability later on. Since the arbitrators are usually sophisticated and have read the submissions of the parties, windy and repetitious openings are not recommended. At the AAA, however, a detailed opening from the respondent may be appropriate when there was no answer or a general denial submitted in response to the statement of claim.

The opening statement should not state as fact anything which there may be a problem proving. Opposing counsel no doubt will draw attention to this failure of proof later on.

viii) Claimant's Case in Chief. The claimant is normally accorded the right to present his or her case first, followed by the respondent, with the claimant's right to then rebut. With counterclaims, the process sometimes permits the claimant to present the case and then the respondent to present the counterclaims case, and in other cases to present the counterclaim and defenses as the facts are developed, but the rules are silent on the procedure so it is determined in each case by the arbitrators as part of their inherent power to control the process.

Often due to multiple parties and difficulties with witness schedules, the arbitrators will bifurcate the presentation. Since a jury is not involved and the arbitrators sophisticated, this normally is not felt to be a problem. When one side objects, the arbitrator has the inherent power to order the proceedings to continue.

Occasionally the defense will be that no damages were sustained. In these cases, the issue of damage can be tried first, because if none are found there is no reason to examine whether liability exists.

a) Direct Testimony. The director of arbitration, as part of the preparation for the case, will normally request an estimate of the time to present the case and a confidential list of the witnesses planned to be used by each party. The arbitrators in the prehearing conference will also ask for witnesses, so there is usually little surprise in this regard.

The testimony can be either in response to questions, which is a good strategy on cross-examining a witness or dealing with an adverse party, or narrative, where the witness tells the "story." With narrative testimony there is a chance that information can come out which may properly be objected to (see below).

The most important question relates to the credibility of witnesses. If the arbitrators believe the witness, his or her testimony is accepted as the version of the facts which occurred rather than "just one side's story." This is very important where oral communications are involved--and this is the normal way customers purchase and sell securities.

b) Order of Witnesses. The strategy of presenting the case depends on the presentation of witnesses. It is advisable to follow a strong opening statement with strong initial witnesses, rather than weak or ineffective testimony.

Usually the testimony will be in a chronological order. Often a useful lead witness will be one who can testify broadly. Normally, the first witness is the claimant, who testifies as to the nature of the transactions in question to give an "overview" of the controversy. Sometimes, however, the first witness can be a person who can testify not to the details, but to the nature of the interrelationship of the basic facts in dispute. Although not usual, it may be appropriate to call first the opposing side as an adverse witness, especially if questions can be narrowly phrased in order to make an effect on the panel.

Due to scheduling, sometimes a witness is not available when it would be most appropriate to hear the testimony. If this occurs, the arbitrators will normally understand, but the party should call attention to this in closing, so as not to let the testimony fall flat.

c) Witness Preparation. One problem is when the witness is used to "over try" the case; when the facts have already been established and the testimony becomes repetitious. Questions should probably be prepared in advance for direct, to be sure that the witness covers the essential elements of the case. Questions should be simple, and the witness should be encouraged to answer as simply as possible with only those details which are necessary to assist the arbitrators in understanding the case. The witness should be prepared so that he or she does not become verbose, confused or addled.

One of the dynamics of a hearing is like a trial--witnesses, even if prepared, often give ineffective answers to questions. This may be due to factors such as nervousness, unfamiliarity with the setting and sometimes failure to listen to the question. This requires that the question be rephrased, but if another imprecise answer follows, the point becomes harder to make as repetitious questions will not be looked on favorably by the arbitrators who wish to move through the proceedings. Also, the credibility of the witness may suffer as the arbitrators may feel the attorney or person representing the party is leading the witness to a particular answer.

d) Expert Testimony. Many securities arbitration cases are complicated, particularly in the areas of violations of fiduciary duties that come from the nature of the relationship of broker and customer and in the calculation of damages. While the arbitrators are themselves normally experts and there is less need for parties to introduce an expert to educate the panel, they may not have the expertise necessary to understand the case at hand.

Therefore, it will be appropriate to use an expert rather than rely on the arbitrator's general expertise.

The expert will need to be both a master explainer and believable. He or she will also have to be able to withstand cross-examination.

It is important to get your expert witness early in the proceeding. The expert can give valuable insight into not only the evaluation of the claim, as well as indicating what information to seek in arbitration's limited discovery, workings of the case, and offer suggestions on discovery and even claims which the less experienced, non-industry person might miss. It may be wise to have the expert attend the hearing and give suggestions regarding the presentation of the case.

Typically, an expert will be asked to testify as to technical matters, such as turnover ratios in churning cases, trading practices in cases dealing with improper executions, and evaluation of the risks of the investment and the customer's financial acumen and ability to take risk in cases of suitability. The expert's task is simple: to educate the arbitrators regarding a particularly technical aspect of the case.[36]

Normally the expert will assist in the development of damage analysis. Often this is done by an academic. Industry experts are useful to set forth the supervisory duties that would have been normal industry standard applied to the facts at issue.[37]

Experts can not be consulted by arbitrators outside the hearing. This will be grounds for overturning an award. The arbitrators can, however, call witnesses themselves under the SRO rules without resort to subpoena under the power to direct appearance of any person employed by or associated with a member firm in order to assure a full and complete hearing.[38]

It is often difficult to obtain an expert witness in litigation, and the same is true in arbitrations. Industry members are bound to appear if subpoenaed under exchange and N.A.S.D. rules, but this will hardly produce a favorable climate for examination of an expert. Experts can be found in a number of ways. Probably the most productive is to ask others about who they used in similar cases. A list is available from the Public Investors Arbitration Bar Association, 610 Brazos Street, Austin, Texas 78701, and from the editor of THE SECURITIES ARBITRATION COMMENTATOR. After identification of expert witnesses, it is important to review their credentials and past testimony, as well as industry affiliations in the past for possible conflicts of interest, which may affect their credibility in this case.

e) Unavailable Witnesses. SRO member firms have an obligation to produce affiliated persons for the arbitration,[39] and the parties can subpoena witnesses as discussed in chapter 13. Sometimes, however, the party will simply not show up at the hearing and there will be little ability to force attendance by a witness who is not within the subpoena's jurisdiction. In these cases, there is little alternative but to continue with the hearing. The absence of the subpoenaed or required witness should be drawn to the arbitrators attention by the party seeking that testimony, particularly if the brokerage firm has not produced the person, who may be an employee, where attendance is required by Exchange or SRO rules.

Sometimes depositions or telephone conference calls can be arranged to take testimony. This should be arranged in advance either with the director of arbitration, staff, or by order at a prehearing conference with the arbitrators. If an objection is made to eliciting testimony in this manner, this is a fact which the party will want the arbitrators to know as they evaluate the case without the testimony.

As noted above, affidavits may be prepared for absent witnesses and are usually admitted as evidence, despite objection since there is no ability to cross-examine. They are accepted by the arbitrators, who note the objection, "for what they are worth."[40]

f) Documents and Exhibits. Some of the documents regarding a claim may be submitted as exhibits to the Statement of Claim.[41] Otherwise, documents can be submitted in connection with testimony. In securities cases the confirmations, monthly statements, prospectus, and other documents can be voluminous, and general references by the witness usually are preferable to going over each transaction in detail.

It may be most helpful for the arbitrator's understanding of complicated cases, such as a churning case or one with difficult damage calculations, to ask the witness to testify using a chart or summary, which is introduced as evidence. After admission, the arbitrators can then read the document and absorb the detail that may be confusing if only presented orally. It is a mistake to present the evidence without helping the arbitrators understand the type of calculations by which they can determine the relief sought.

If documents are to be produced, copies for each arbitrator and the other parties should be prepared. Once admitted, the arbitrators will mark each document into evidence. If there are many documents, all may be received at one time by the arbitrators rather than each one separately, but this requires that the party seeking the admission must vouch for the relevancy and materiality of all and that any objection to introduction as evidence is overcome.

The arbitrators themselves can agree to require submission of documents and other evidence, even after the hearing if all parties agree.[42]

g) Lie Detector Tests. Since credibility is a major issue, often polygraph examination results will be introduced as evidence. It is, however, the arbitrator's function to assess the credibility of witnesses.[43] Like any instrument, the scientific instrument is only as good as the person operating it.

Therefore, it is important to review the credentials of the technician as well as the questions asked to elicit the measured responses.

ix) Objections. Arbitrators are the decisionmakers on the relevancy and admissibility of testimony and documents. In arbitration, objections to questions or admissibility of a document are generally not encouraged. The arbitrators often consider themselves sophisticated in the field and feel they are able to fairly evaluate evidence, sifting out that which is irrelevant and immaterial or procedurally improper.

After an objection, often the arbitrator will "note the objection," but permit the answer or evidence to the extent it is received with the arbitrator reserving judgment on its weight, normally by saying "for whatever it [the answer] is worth" or similar statements. The arbitrator will consider the answer or evidence in light of the objection as they deliberate the decision. This is a more informal procedure than litigation, where objections are more usual.

The real issue in making objections is if the answer or document would prejudice the fairness of the hearing. If so, a timely objection may be necessary to ensure both the fairness of the hearing and that there was no waiver of the defect.

Typical objections are:

- Poorly framed question--if the question is confusing, misleading, ambiguous, vague, overbroad, or just unintelligible
- Speculative question
- Compound question--one that asks two questions
- Opinion unless an expert, the witness should only testify to the facts
- Repetitious questions--those already "asked and answered"
- Irrelevant question or document--does the testimony or evidence advance the case?
- Immaterial question or document--does it relate to the case?

Objections that are probably not going to succeed in arbitration due to the relaxed nature of the proceedings and the arbitrator's freedom to accept and then disregard evidence are:

- Leading question--questions that lead to an answer
- Hearsay--facts that the witness did not personally receive or observe
- Insufficient foundation for question--no basis laid for the fact or conclusion asked
- Non-responsive answer--one to a question not asked

- Parole evidence rule--if there is a writing, the document will be evidence of what it said, and oral or written testimony should not be admitted that contradicts the writing
- Best evidence rule--the necessity to produce the original of a document is generally only an issue when there is an issue of the authenticity of the original or copy
- Privileged communication--doctor/patient or attorney/client are most common, but also husband/wife, clergy, business trade secrets, etc.

x) Cross-Examination. The state arbitration statutes normally provide that the parties are entitled to be heard, to present evidence material to the controversy and to cross-examine witnesses appearing at the hearing.[44]

The forum rules will also normally provide for cross-examination.[45] Cross-examination is usually limited to the matters covered in the scope of the direct testimony, but again arbitrators may permit expanded cross. Since depositions are rare in arbitration proceedings, it is difficult to prepare in advance for the cross-examination of witnesses.

In cross, there are several areas where the witness should be examined without giving him or her the ability to retestify. The first is prior inconsistent statements, which can bring question to the credibility of the witness. Here questions may also go to matters covered on direct, and then examination of any inconsistent statements of the witness in documents produced in discovery. This may be particularly beneficial with experts. To the extent possible, a good technique is to be calm and helpful, putting the witness at ease. Do not be hostile or argumentative. In this manner, if a question is seen as non-threatening, the witness may be less careful in answering than if he or she thought about the possible inconsistency with earlier testimony or writings.

Second, other witnesses can refute the statements made on direct and cross. Third, if the testimony is at variance with industry practice, the arbitrators themselves may question this; on cross this inconsistency can be highlighted. Finally, if the witness has exaggerated somewhat on direct, cross may elicit additional exaggeration that may also lead the arbitrators to question the witness' credibility or competence.

Often, witnesses on cross will attempt to answer the questions with more than a "yes" or "no," in order to tie any possible inconsistency to their earlier testimony or to reiterate it. While a party may request the witness to so answer questions, arbitrators will normally allow the witness to explain his or her answer, because a simple answer will often not assist them in understanding the case.

xi) Redirect Examination. After cross-examination, questions can be asked that relate to or explain further the testimony on direct and cross.

Sometimes the redirect will be limited only to those matters covered in cross, but, again, the informality of the arbitration proceeding permits leeway.

xii) Motion to Dismiss. As noted in the discussion of defenses against claims in chapters 11 and 12, if the claimant's case is not proved by the testimony and evidence, at the conclusion of the claimant's presentation the respondent should orally move to dismiss either the entire case or the claims not proved. There is no SRO nor AAA rule that addresses this motion practice. Clearly, however, the arbitrators, as they are in control of the procedures, can grant such relief under analogy to federal and state procedural rules.[46]

Often arbitrators will take this motion under advisement and continue by hearing the respondent's case. If this occurs, the motion should be restated again in respondent's summation so that the arbitrators will concentrate on the issue of claimant's lack of proof and/or meritless claim.

xiii) Respondent's Case. After the presentation of claimant's case in full, the respondent will introduce testimony and documents to defeat the claimant's case. In securities arbitration, the defense will normally indicate that the trading was by the customer's initiative; that the statements made were not misleading; that the trading was suitable; and that there was full disclosure to and acquiescence in the trading by the customer. One of the major defenses is lack of injury--no damages--even if a wrong is established.

The same pattern of presentation by respondent will follow, including expert testimony to refute the claimant's expert.

In industry arbitrations, the defenses will relate to the nature of the industry and the employee relationship, with appropriate documentation.

xiv) Claimant's Rebuttal. The claimant will offer additional evidence to rebut matters raised for the first time in the respondent's case. Normally new evidence regarding the claims will not be permitted, but, again, in the informal arbitration this may be permitted to assist the arbitrators in fully understanding the case.

xv) Closing Statements. When each side has presented its case, the chair asks if either has any further evidence to offer or witnesses to be heard.[47] Any objections to the presentation of evidence that were sustained should be objected to again at this stage to ensure that there was no waiver.

Each party will then be given the opportunity to present a closing statement. This will be in the nature of a summation of the evidence and claims or defenses presented during the hearing. It is especially important in multiple day hearings, where the summation will present the opportunity to tie together the evidence, attack witness credibility, and point out inconsistencies in law and facts. When the arbitration is held in a single day, a brief summation may be more appropriate. But the summation is the opportunity for a party to categorize the evidence in the most favorable interpretation and should not be carelessly waived.

Normally, the respondent sums up first, with the last word given to the claimant. The N.A.S.D., however, provides that the claimant sum up first, but gives an ability to rebut.

xvi) Closing of the Hearing. After the summations, the chair will again inquire if either party has anything further to present to the arbitrators. Then the chair will ask if each party believes that he or she has had an equal, fair, and full opportunity to present their case. After response, the chair will read the closing statement outlining the procedures to render and deliver the award and declare the hearing closed.[48]

If a party fails to object or respond, and the hearing proceeds, that will constitute a waiver of right to object unless preserved in writing.[49]

xvii) Post-Hearing. The arbitrators can permit the parties to submit briefs to assist in the deliberations in complicated cases. Briefs may be particularly helpful in multi-session cases, where marshaling the facts presented may be necessary, and in bifurcated proceedings to assist in determining the collateral estoppel effect of an award. In calculating damages, it is not unusual for the panel to request specific calculations from the parties, under the power to "require the parties to brief and explain."[50] Each claim should be itemized, so that the panel can select those elements of the total damage that are supported and reject the others, rather than include all together in a lump sum. It is also wise to separately calculate interest.

A hearing may be reopened prior to the rendering of an award, on the application of a party or by the arbitrators.[51]

6) DISCIPLINARY ACTIONS AND ARBITRATION

Often a claim against an SRO or exchange member will result in a filing of disciplinary action. Often these actions are against a customer's registered representative or associated person of the firm that is the SRO member. In these cases, a question arises regarding the admissibility in the arbitration of the results of the related disciplinary action.

The N.A.S.D. is a part of the Securities and Exchange Act of 1934's regulatory scheme for the brokerage industry and is one of the SROs that engages in self-regulation. As such, the SRO determines whether a party is engaged in the industry, a member or affiliated person of the SRO who has engaged in conduct that is in violation of the SRO rules and regulations or federal securities laws. Only in 1993 did the N.A.S.D. make publicly available its internal Sanction Guidelines.[52] If a person is charged with a violation, there is a disciplinary hearing where the SRO, as a self-regulating body of peers (businessmen-brokers), sits in judgment of the practices in question. The hearing is not an arbitration; in fact special rules of procedure apply.[53]

While an arbitration is brought by a party seeking relief, the N.A.S.D. disciplinary matter is brought by N.A.S.D. staff; the hearing is transcribed;[54] and the decision is made by the businessmen serving on the supervisory group. Sanctions can be informal if the hearing stage is not reached and a letter is placed in the member's record. These informal letters vary in severity depending on the seriousness of the violation: a de minimus letter; letter of caution; letter of future observance and compliance; and staff interview. After the hearing, the sanctions are in writing and can include censure; fines and costs; suspension; expulsion, revocation of registration, and bar from future association with the securities industry. The decision is appealable to the Board of Governors, and to the SEC and then the appropriate U.S. Court of Appeals as an appeal of an agency decision; ultimately it may go to the Supreme Court.

Copies of final disciplinary actions are made available upon request to the public and others. All complaints, hearings, and other information are confidential. Federal law requires copies of the disciplinary actions to be filed with the SEC and are publicly available. With any disciplinary action resulting in suspension, bar, or expulsion or a fine of $10,000 or more, the N.A.S.D. publicizes the decision.

In 1988 the Regulatory Review Task Force of the N.A.S.D. issued a Report that considered the requirement that an arbitration panel refer matters for possible N.A.S.D. regulatory action. It was particularly concerned with detection of deceptive sales and trading practices, but also the report of arbitration awards that might impact on the firm's ability to meet capital requirements. One problem is the confidentiality of certain disciplinary actions and arbitration proceedings.

Information regarding disciplinary actions can be obtained from state regulators and the N.A.S.D and may be useful in proving the type of conduct of a registered representative and firm supervision. (See the chapter 13 discussion on discovery.)

7) CONCLUSION

The hearing is where the claimant must present the evidence to support his claims. The procedures and rules are quasi-judicial in form and substance, but much more flexible than litigation. This is based on the expertise and experience the panel is presumed to possess, which allows presentment of proof which perhaps would not be admissible in a court. It is a factor to be considered if there is an option to arbitrate or litigate the dispute.

NOTES

1 *See* the discussion in chapter 11 of small claims. The rules are from S.I.C.A. Uniform Code § 2; N.Y.S.E. Rule 601; N.A.S.D. §§ 13 and 10 (Simplified Industry Arbitration); and AAA Rule 38 (waiver of oral hearing for claims not exceeding $5,000) and Rules 51-55 (Expedited Hearings for claims less than $25,000 under Rule 9).

2 *See* McLaughlin, Piven, Vogel, Inc. v. Gross, 699 F. Supp. 55 (E.D. Pa. 1988), which held that the broker had waived the right to challenge procedures because it submitted to the MSRB's small claims arbitration rules.

3 Uniform Code § 3; N.Y.S.E. Rule 602; N.A.S.D. § 14(b); AAA Rule 38.

4 The following section is quoted from the AAA SECURITIES ARBITRATION RULES. *See also* chapter 9 and 11 discussion of large, complex cases.

5 Fed R. Civ. P. 26.

6 Uniform Code § 20; N.A.S.D. § 32; N.Y.S.E. Rule 619(d).

7 AAA Rule 10.

8 Uniform Code § 20; N.A.S.D. § 32; N.Y.S.E. Rule 619. AAA Rule 10 provides similar procedures. There is no administrative fee for the "first" preliminary AAA hearing even if before an arbitrator, but the SRO fee for the prehearing conference is the same as scheduled for a hearing session with a single arbitrator. N.A.S.D. § 43(b); N.Y.S.E. Rule 629(b).

9 It may be wise to request the ability to brief complicated legal issues that will be presented in the arbitration. Both sides should be afforded the right to submit briefs.

10 AAA Rule 12 provides the parties may fix the place of hearing. If a party requests a particular location and the other party does not file an objection within 20 days after AAA notice, the locale will be as requested. Otherwise the AAA's decision is final and binding. *See also* AAA Rule 22 (date, time, and place of hearing).

11 *See* Uniform Code § 14; N.A.S.D. § 26; N.Y.S.E. Rule 613. Under AAA Rule 22, the notice of date, time, and place of each hearing must be 10 days in advance, but there is no requirement of type of notice delivery. AAA Rule 23 specifies that notice can be given to a representative of a party, once notified of representation.

12 *See* AAA Rule 32.

13 D. ROBBINS, SECURITITES ARBITRATION PROCEDURAL MANUAL 128 (1992). *See also* N.A.S.D. § 34; N.Y.S.E. Rule 620; AAA Rule 32.

14 N.Y. CPLR 7506(c).

15 One of the major advantages of arbitration is that the arbitrators can use their industry expertise to draw out facts that the parties and their counsel may have ignored or overlooked.

16 AAA Rule 33.

17 AAA Rule 32.

18 *Id. See also* N.A.S.D. § 34; N.Y.S.E. Rule 620.

19 N.A.S.D. § 35; N.Y.S.E. Rule 622; AAA Rule 50.

20 *See* the discussion of finality of arbitration decisions in chapters 5 and 16.

21 *See* AAA Rule 26 which permits experts to remain "generally," but gives the arbitrator discretion to permit attendance or not of "a party or essential person during the testimony of any other witness." *See also* N.A.S.D. § 28; N.Y.S.E. Rule 615.

22 The party must have been notified of the hearing itself, not just the arbitration proceedings. *See* AAA Rules 22, 31; N.A.S.D. § 29; N.Y.S.E. Rule 616.

23 Uniform Code § 17; N.A.S.D. § 29; N.Y.S.E. Rule 616; AAA Rule 30.

24 AAA Rule 31.

25 *See* AAA Rules 22, 27, 31; N.A.S.D. §§ 29, 30; N.Y.S.E. Rule 616, 617. N.A.S.D. § 30; N.Y.S.E. Rule 617.

26 In general, an arbitrator's refusal to postpone hearings must be reasonable and fair. If unreasonable, it can be grounds for vacating the award. *See* Polygon Co. v. Katten Machine Co. of Brooklyn, Inc., 433 N.Y.S. 2d 400 (Dist. Ct Suff. Cty. 1980). *See also* Leblon Consultants, Ltd. v. Jackson China, Inc. 92 A.D.2d 499, 457 N.Y.S. 2d 93 (1983); *contra*, Local Union No. 251 v. Narragansett Improvement Co., 503 F.2d 309 (1st Cir. 1979); Harwyn Luggage v. Henry Rosenfeld, Inc., 90 A.D.2d 747, 456 N.Y.S. 2d 3 (1982).

27 N.Y. CPLR 7512.

28 *See* AAA Rule 35; N.Y. CPLR 7502(c) permits a party to *seek* a temporary restraining order in court prior to commencement of the arbitration.

29 AAA Rule 24 does not require a record, but if one of the parties wanted it he could provide for it.

30 N.A.S.D. § 37; N.Y.S.E. Rule 623.

31 *See* N.Y. CPLR 7506(a); Uniform Code § 25; N.A.S.D. § 38; N.Y.S.E. Rule 624; AAA Rule 28.

32 AAA Rule 28 allows, but does not require, witnesses to be sworn unless "required by law or requested by any party." But N.A.S.D. § 38 and N.Y.S.E. Rule 624 do require an oath or affirmation.

33 AAA Rule 28.

34 *See* AAA Rule 24.

35 N.A.S.D. § 37, N.Y.S.E. Rule 623. A party or arbitrator can have stenographic transcription.

36 *See generally* Poser, *Securities Arbitration and the Expert*, SECURITITES ARBITRATION 683 to 689 (D. Robbins ed., 1988).

37 For examples of the questions one might ask an expert regarding supervisory responsibilities of the brokerage firm and branch office management *see* F. Ormsten and N. Arnoff, *Sources and Basis of Broker-Dealer Supervisory Responsibility Set Out in the Context of an Expert's Direct Examination and Cross-Examination*, in SECURITIES ARBITRATION 65 (D. Robbins ed., 1992).

38 This is true of SRO forums where the arbitrators can require the attendance of persons associated with members of the SRO. N.A.S.D. § 33(b) (power to direct appearances and production of documents); N.Y.S.E. Rule 619(g); AAA Rule 33.

39 N.A.S.D. § 33; N.Y.S.E. Rule 619(g).

40 *See* AAA Rule 33: "shall give it only such weight as the arbitrator deems it entitled to after consideration of any objection made to its admission."

41 *See* the discussion in chapter 12.

42 *See* N.A.S.D. § 40; N.Y.S.E. Rule 626; AAA Rule 33.

43 *See* discussion of admissibility of polygraph examinations in ROBBINS *supra* note 13, reproduced in SECURITIES ARBITRATION 569-574 (D.E. Robbins ed., 1992); Arther, *The Use of the Polygraph by Attorneys*, in SECURITIES ARBITRATION 389 (D. Robbins ed., 1993).

44 N.Y. CPLR 7506.

45 *See* AAA Rule 30.

46 For example, *see* Fed. R. Civ. P. 41(b) and N.Y. CPLR 4401.

47 AAA Rule 36.

48 *See Id*.

49 *See* AAA Rule 39.

50 *See* S.I.C.A. ARBITRATOR'S MANUAL.

51 AAA Rule 37; N.A.S.D. § 40. *See* the discussion in chapter 15.

52 N.A.S.D. Notice to Members 93-52.

53 *See* N.A.S.D. Code of Procedure governing the conduct of N.A.S.D. disciplinary proceedings.

54 Unlike N.A.S.D. arbitrations which are only recorded (*see* above discussion).

Chapter 15

THE AWARD

After the hearing or upon review of the evidence if there has been no hearing,[1] and review of the evidence and any post-hearing briefs, the arbitrators render their decision which takes the form of an award. The award is the determination on the merits of the case submitted to binding resolution through arbitration.

The parties may also reach a settlement and request the arbitrators to enter a "consent award." This will have the same impact as a rendered award for enforcement purposes. Only the AAA requires agreement to the consent award in writing signed by all settling parties,[2] but this would probably be reflected in any transcript if the settlement is reached at a hearing.

This chapter will examine the award: its form; how it is reached by the arbitrators; how it is given to the parties and the public; and finally confirmed by a court. Chapter 16 will examine how an arbitration award can be challenged.

1) FORM OF AWARD; STATE LAW REQUIREMENTS

The award need not be in any particular form under the Federal Arbitration Act. Under state law,[3] however, the award must be:

A) In Writing

The award must be in writing[4] and signed by the arbitrators concurring in the award. In some jurisdictions, the signatures on the award will have to be acknowledged before a notary. An arbitrator who does not agree with the result reached may sign the award document but indicate his dissent. The arbitrators signatures may be affixed to the award at different times and places.

B) Submitted Within the Time Specified by the Parties

If no time is specified in the arbitration agreement, the parties may agree to a time; if no agreement, state law normally provides that the award shall be rendered in such time as the court shall direct upon application by a party.[5] The Federal Arbitration Act is silent.

The arbitration forum rules may also supply a time, which is binding due to the agreement of the submitting parties to abide by these rules. Usually the timing is in terms of the last hearing or the submission of post-hearing briefs or other evidence to the arbitrators.[6] SRO rules[7] provide that the award either shall be made no later than 30 days after the date of close of hearing or the arbitrators shall "endeavor" to render the award within this period.[8] A party who does not notify the forum or arbitrators that the award was not made within the required time will waive this objection.[9]

C) Delivered to the Parties

Under forum rules the parties are to receive the award from the director of arbitration or forum by (a) registered or certified mail to the party or counsel; (b) by personal service; or (c) by delivery or service or filing in such a manner as has been authorized by law.[10] Often at the conclusion of the hearing, the chair will ask the parties to agree to this delivery of award. Their consent will be part of the record.

State law may have to be satisfied. For example, New York arbitration law provides that delivery of the award shall be in the manner provided under the agreement or, in the absence of a provision, then by certified or registered mail, return receipt requested.[11] A letter of transmittal of the award to parties is *prima facie* proof of delivery.[12]

2) DELIBERATION AND AWARD

The arbitrators are required to have read the pleadings before the hearing. They normally take extensive notes during the hearing. Because of their knowledge and expertise, arbitrators normally can understand the complexities and intricacies of a case. They will determine, as a finder of fact, the credibility of the witnesses and the weight to be given the evidence presented.

The arbitrators normally devote considerable attention to the case presented by the parties. While in long and complex cases they will request a copy of the record, it is more usual in securities arbitrations to have the deliberations immediately follow the hearing, especially if the hearing is one or a few days in duration. As far as the parties are concerned, the hearing is just the culmination of much preparation--preparation of the statement of claim and answer, exchange of documents, review of the witnesses testimony, and the like. A quickly made and not thought through determination is a disservice to them.

The deliberation will normally be a combination of a review of the facts established in the hearing and the submitted documents, including the statement of claim and answer, and the law. The arbitrators will normally apply their common sense to determine if the claimant was truly wronged and is entitled to relief. In some cases, however, the claimant may simply have failed to prove any grounds for recovery, often through failure to produce evidence necessary to sustain the claim or lack of any damages attributable to the respondent's conduct. As noted in the chapter 14 materials, the claimant must consider these issues in preparation for and presentation at the hearing.

A) Application of Law

The arbitrators are to determine the case by applying the rules or law to the facts as presented in the evidence--the documents of the parties, including statement of claim and answer, testimony of the witnesses, including the parties, and legal arguments. The arbitrators can reach a remedy that is based on equitable considerations. They are not strictly bound by legal rules.[13]

> The practice of commercial arbitration in the United States is indeed that the arbitrator has the freedom of determining the disputed questions according to his sense of justice of the case. Unless parties expressly or impliedly wish the arbitrator to determine the question by application of a specific law, the arbitrator appears free to resolve the dispute on the basis of his just and fair appreciation. This situation was rightly described when a court said that the parties "leave the issues to be determined in accordance with the sense of justice and equity that they may believe reposes in the breasts of self chosen judges". . . Nevertheless, arbitrators do not favor disregarding substantive law. It is interesting to note . . . [A 1961 study of the actions of arbitrators][14] reported 80 percent of the arbitrators questioned thought they should make their dispute determination within the framework of principles of substantive law; but 90 percent thought that they were not obligated to do so if they believed a more just decision could otherwise be made.[15]

B) Statement of Reasons in Award; No Opinion Required

Arbitrators have not been required to state the reasons for their award.[16] There is no opinion where the principles of law are applied by the arbitrators to the facts found by the trier of fact, also the arbitrators. As a result, it may be difficult to understand what facts and legal theories were used by the arbitrators to reach the award rendered. As noted in chapter 16, this general statement nature of the award makes judicial review difficult and limits the precedential value of the case in future arbitrations. An arbitrator who dissents from the award will normally not give reasons for his reaching that position either.

The new SRO standards for contents of awards (discussed below) and AAA Rule 42 requirements give some more information regarding the claims that were decided, but arbitrators are encouraged to make the awards as simple as possible, and no "opinion" or detailed justification of how the arbitrators resolved the issues is required. As a result, this sometimes leads parties to question the decision on the grounds that the arbitrators failed to follow the correct substantive law or omitted to consider some important fact in evidence. If the parties agree, the arbitrators can be required to give the reasons for their award. This is a most unusual situation, however, and will probably be discouraged by the forum director of arbitration or staff as not being in line with the normal practice. Where no opinion is given, however, it is difficult to establish either ground to sustain appeal of the award.

It is doubtful that SRO practice will change and a formal legal reasoned opinion will be rendered. This is due to the fact that three arbitrators are the norm in securities arbitrations, and all will have to agree in an decision written in all probability by one. Further, the payment to arbitrators will have to be adjusted from the present modest levels if legal research and writing opinions is added to the burden.

C) A Reasoned "Opinion"

In a recent case considering a more formal "opinion" by the arbitrators, *Advest, Inc. v. Asseoff*, there were a host of issues presented including disqualification of an arbitrator and two arbitrator's opinions totaling over 100 pages. In a motion of vacatur due to arbitrator bias, the court must find clear evidence of impropriety, which was not shown by the arbitrator's questioning of witnesses because "questioning of witnesses by an arbitrator to clarify important issues is a legitimate method of providing the speed and informality typical of the arbitration process."[17] Further, it is not improper for an arbitrator to state his views as long as they arise from the evidence and not from an impermissible source such as personal or financial interest.[18]

D) Industry Rules and Practice

The arbitrators will normally take into account the industry practices which they believe applicable to this case's circumstances. Usually this will result from a review of the applicable principle in testimony during the hearing, often through use of experts, but the arbitrator's own sense of industry practice will be determinative.

E) Lawyers as Arbitrators

Arbitrators are not required to be attorneys nor have any training in law. Their knowledge comes from normal practices in their experience, or as far as they are "instructed" in the hearing by the parties or the attorneys representing parties, through the testimony and documentary evidence. If there is one attorney on a panel, there may be some deference to her on interpretation of legal issues. Parties should brief and argue applicable legal issues to the entire panel, however, so that all arbitrators will have a good picture of the law they are being asked to interpret.

F) "Splitting the Baby"

Often participants in an arbitration will believe that the arbitrators have not applied the law. As is most disputes, there are often good arguments on both sides: otherwise, a settlement is more likely than going to trial or hearing. If arbitrators decide to use equitable principles, often a compromise result will occur--each side will be given something. A 1988 study found that approximately 40 percent of attorneys felt that arbitrators "split the baby" or rendered compromise awards, not justified by the law.[19] The term "splitting the baby" refers to the early Biblical decision by King Solomon when each side seeking a child's custody had merit and were unwilling to compromise.

But it is clear that the arbitrators can not in equity ignore the law. This will be grounds to overturn the award. See discussion in chapter 16 of manifest disregard of the law. The problem is due, of course, to the absence of reasons that lead to the award rendered.

3) THE AWARD

The award must be within the bounds of the agreement to arbitrate and the law.[20] Usually the award is based on unanimity, but the rules require only a majority.[21] Arbitrators normally award compensatory damages, which may include consequential damages and interest.[22] An award of a lump sum, for example, is presumed correct.[23]

A) SRO Form of Award

Before 1989 the award did not normally indicate anything other than the result reached by the arbitrators. The SRO rules now require the award to outline:

1. the names of the parties;
2. a summary of the issues in controversy;
3. the damages and/or other relief requested;

4. the damages and/or other relief granted;
5. a statement of other issues presented;
6. the number, dates, and locations of hearings; and
7. the names and signatures of the arbitrators.[24]

B) Form of Award Under AAA Rules

In 1993 the AAA amended Rule 42(b) to provide for more detailed awards, providing the parties with more information regarding the basis and underlying calculations for the award. The award now contains:

1. the names of the parties and representatives (such as attorneys), if any;
2. the names of arbitrators;
3. a summary of the issues including type(s) of any security or product in controversy;
4. the damages and/or other relief requested and awarded;
5. a statement disposing of statutory and any other issues resolved;
6. the date the case was filed;
7. the date of the award;
8. the number and dates of hearings;
9. the location of the hearings; and
10. the signatures of the arbitrators concurring in the award.

Additionally, the awards are to be made public.[25] Any party can request copies of all prior awards by arbitrators impaneled in their case.[26] As a result of these new requirements regarding public disclosure of the issues decided, there is a possibility of more "precedent value" to the award than in the past. The awards, upon disclosure, are routinely reported in the press, such as THE NEW YORK TIMES and WALL STREET JOURNAL, and compiled by the SECURITIES ARBITRATION COMMENTATOR.

4) JUDICIAL CONFIRMATION OF AWARD

The parties can apply for a judgment to be entered on the arbitration award, which will then have the same force and effect as a judicial judgment.[27] As noted in chapter 16, *res judicata* and collateral estoppel apply to arbitration awards.[28]

5) AWARD BY SETTLEMENT

If the parties agree to settle the dispute prior to the hearing or during the hearing process, they can request the arbitrators to set forth the terms of the agreed settlement in an award. This is known as a consent award.[29]

6) AWARD BY CONFESSION

Under state law an award by confession may be made for money due or to become due before an award is otherwise made. The award will be made by the arbitrator (or agency designated to name the arbitrator) within three months after receipt of a verified statements by all parties authorizing the award to be made and specifying the sum due and the facts under which the liability arose.[30]

Confession awards occur in securities arbitrations where the brokerage firm is suing for a margin balance due from a customer and the customer agrees as to the amount owed.

7) TYPES OF RELIEF AVAILABLE

The arbitrators may grant any remedy or relief that is deemed just, equitable, and within the scope of the agreement of the parties. This power is normally the same as those types of relief that could be available to a court with jurisdiction over the dispute. Money damages are the rule, but arbitrators can also award specific performance of a contract.[31]

A) Money Damages

With a claim for money damages, often a claim is presented for not only the actual damages sustained, but also for consequential damages. If the arbitration clause permits the arbitrators to determine damages generally, they will be permitted to assess damages in accordance with the interpretation of the contract. On the other hand, if the contract limits recovery in arbitration to actual damages, that will be the recovery. The same is true if liquidated damages are specified; the arbitrators will have to award that amount as long as it is found to be due and enforceable as related to actual damages that might result from breach and that the parties contemplate at the time of contract formation.

B) Punitive and Multiple Damages

Punitive damages claims are being sent to arbitration, and it is clear that statutory mandated treble or multiple damage provisions, such as RICO, are arbitrable in federal cases.[32] Normally, an arbitrator is presumed to have the power to award punitive damages, especially where so authorized by statute or the provisions of the parties' agreement.[33] Most federal court decisions have relied on *McMahon*, which permits the assessment of statutory multiple damages. The problem has been in state actions, particularity New York where *Garrity*[34] still rules and arbitrators are forbidden to assess punitive damages.[35] Of course, award of statutory multiple damage claims, including RICO as in *McMahon*, or under antitrust laws that provide for treble damage recoveries, are permitted in arbitration, even in New York. The SEC, in approving the new SRO rules, indicated that it construes the remedies to prevent a broker from attempting to limit a customer's right to seek, and an arbitrator's right to award, punitive damages.[36]

As noted in chapter 11, there is split of authority among the states as to whether arbitrators have authority to grant punitive damages.[37] The significance of an award of punitive damages as a part of an action is illustrated by the news of an unreported South Dakota jury verdict that found against a broker for $200,000 in compensatory damages and $2.27 million in punitive damages. While no such extreme arbitration findings are reported, punitive damages can be a measure of damage assessed by arbitrators. Punitive damages awarded in an Oklahoma arbitration were subject of a vacatur motion in federal court not under the question of the power of the arbitrators to make such an award, but rather interpretation of the contract.[38] The argument made was that although the Federal Arbitration Act permits punitive damage awards, the contract provided in a choice of law provision that New York law would apply. The contract also provided for governance of the arbitration under the N.A.S.D. Code, not New York law. The court found that the punitive damages may have been awarded within requirements of the New York substantive law, as the award was within a reasonable interpretation of the parties arbitration agreement. *Garrity* was thus determined to be procedural.

Under Colorado arbitration law, arbitrators are barred from awarding punitive damages, but in *Pyle v. Securities U.S.A., Inc.*,[39] the Federal District Court found that the arbitration agreement did not specify that state law would apply[40] and this action was brought under the Federal Arbitration Act. The court concluded that the issue of punitive damages was central to the case, not collateral in which case state law would govern. Therefore, federal law governed and permitted an award of punitive damages even though the arbitration agreement did not specifically mention such relief.[41] Further, the court found that the N.A.S.D. rules include an ability to award punitive damages.[42]

If the claimant has requested punitive damages, the arbitrators should clearly state in the award that no punitive damages were awarded in jurisdictions where they are not permitted, such as New York.[43] Otherwise a party can argue the award is ambiguous and, since punitive damage recoveries are in manifest disregard of the law, this creates a possible argument for vacating an award. Even in states where punitive recoveries are permitted, it may be advisable to set forth the amounts for actual and punitive damage claims separately.

C) Specific Performance

While not normal in securities disputes, arbitrators under their usual equitable powers can award specific performance to resolve a dispute. While neither the Federal Arbitration Act nor Uniform Act expressly state that specific performance remedial relief is available, it has been implied from the general power to "determine the controversy." Further, forum rules generally provide that the "arbitrator can grant any remedy or relief . . . deem[ed] just and equitable . . . including, but not limited to, specific performance of a contract."[44] The parties may have provided in the contract or submission agreement that the arbitrators can grant specific performance, but more often than not this will not be expressed and will have to be implied as a reading of the parties intention.

Therefore, both substantive law and forum rules support the arbitrator's power to grant specific performance and other equitable relief.[45]

D) Injunctive Relief

Under the same rationale as specific performance, arbitrators can fashion temporary relief that is just and equitable under the circumstances.[46] New York law, for example, specifically provides for the court in which jurisdiction the arbitration is pending or if not commenced yet, in a special proceeding, to

> entertain an application for an order of attachment or preliminary injunction in connection with the arbitrable controversy, but only upon the ground that the award to which the applicant may be entitled may be rendered ineffectual without such provisional relief.[47]

This would mean that the party seeking relief in aid of the arbitration should first file a Statement of Claim or Demand for Arbitration, and then ask the court for these actions in aid of arbitration.[48]

Under both SRO and AAA rules, a prehearing conference may be used to consider preliminary relief necessary to protect the arbitration rights of the parties. This is specifically covered in the language of the rules that permits the preliminary hearing to consider "any other matter that will expedite the arbitration proceedings."[49] AAA Rule 34 specifically provides that the arbitrator can "issue such orders for interim relief as may be deemed necessary to safeguard the property that is the subject matter of the arbitration."

E) Award of Administrative Expenses and Fees

Typically the parties agree in the contract or submission agreement to equally divide the administrative expenses of the arbitration forum, including filing fees and other expenses such as hearing, adjournment, postponement, and processing fees.

In the absence of such a provision, the forum rules will direct the arbitrators to determine the proper amount of these fees, which are payable by the parties. The normal procedure is for a claimant to request in the Statement of Claim that the respondent, as alleged wrongdoer, pay these expenses, while the respondent's answer will demand claimant pay them. The Uniform Code and other SRO rules provide that

> The arbitrators, in their award, shall determine the amount chargeable to the parties as forum fees and shall determine who shall pay such forum fees. Forum fees chargeable to the parties shall be assessed on a per hearing session basis and the aggregate for each hearing session may equal but not exceed the amount of the largest initial hearing deposit deposited by any party. . . . The arbitrators may determine in the award that a party shall reimburse to another party any non-refundable filing fee it has paid.
> . . . In addition to forum fees, the arbitrator(s) may determine in the award the amount of costs incurred pursuant to [adjournment fees], [prehearing fees, including document production, subpoenas, appearance of witnesses] and [cost of record of proceedings] and, unless applicable law directs otherwise, other costs and expenses of the parties and arbitrator(s) which are within the scope of the agreement of the parties. The arbitrator(s) shall determine by whom such costs shall be borne. . . .[50] The hearing deposit will be refunded . . .[51]
> Fees and assessments . . . shall be paid immediately on receipt of the award by the parties. Payment of such fees shall not be deemed ratification of the award by the parties.[52]

AAA Rule 47 was amended to clarify that while expenses are advanced equally by the parties, expenses of the arbitration can be allocated by the arbitrator in the award. AAA Rule 48 provides that the $400 arbitrator's compensation for the first and second day shall be equally advanced by the parties. Thereafter, the compensation is set by agreement, or, if no agreement, by the AAA.

F) Award of Attorney's Fees

Awards governed by state statutes similar to the Uniform Arbitration Act prohibit arbitrators from awarding counsel fees. This is in accord with the "American Rule" in litigation whereby each litigant pays his own attorney's fees, even if successful, versus the "English Rule" where the prevailing party can recover attorney's fees. This means that attorney's fees in both the arbitration and for court action in confirmation of the award are normally borne by the parties. One problem lawyers encounter as a result of this rule is that clients who prevail and establish a loss cannot understand how they have been "made whole" when they must pay their attorney from the loss recovery--and they are right.

If the agreement provides, however, costs of the arbitration including reasonable attorney's fees are to be part of the recovery, they can be made part of the award.[53]

A rule proposed by the N.A.S.D. suggests a modified English approach to recovery of attorney's fees in arbitration. An investor who turns down a settlement offer by a brokerage firm in an arbitration case of more than $250,000, could be forced to pay the firm's attorney's fees and costs, including expert witness fees, if the subsequent award rendered by the arbitrators is less than the settlement offer; but if the award is more than the settlement offer, the customer will be entitled to his attorney's fees and costs in addition to the damages awarded. The proposed rule is opposed by plaintiff's attorneys and investor organizations as an attempt by members of the N.A.S.D. to discourage their clients even more in the mandatory arbitration process. This proposed rule was withdrawn.

G) Sanctions

Arbitrators are not entitled to enforce sanctions, other than to assess costs against a party. Sanctions can be imposed by a court. This is discussed in chapter 16.

8) POST-AWARD ACTIONS BY ARBITRATORS

After the award has been delivered to the parties, normally the authority of the arbitrators ceases. However, under some state law and forum rules, there is a period of time during which the prevailing or defeated party can apply for a change in the award. If the application to change is made to the arbitrator or forum, it is sometimes referred to as a "change of award" or "modification of award by arbitrator" as opposed to the application to a court to modify or correct an award that is discussed in chapter 16.

A) Modification by Arbitrator

There is no authority for the arbitrators to modify an award under the Federal Arbitration Act or SRO rules. Under state law on written application of a party to the arbitrators within 20 days after delivery of the award, the arbitrators may modify the award if:

1. there was a miscalculation of figures or mistake in the description of any person, thing, or property referred to in the award;[54]
2. the arbitrators have decided a matter not submitted to them and the

award may be corrected without affecting the merits of the decision upon the issues submitted; or

3. the award is imperfect in a matter of form that does not affect the merits of the controversy.[55]

The procedure is that after the notice to the arbitrators, with copy to the other parties, an objection to modification may be made within 10 days. The arbitrators have 30 days to dispose of the application and must do so in writing, signed and acknowledged in the same manner as required for an award.[56]

Clearly the modification should be limited to these statutory grounds, and the arbitrators should not take additional evidence or reexamine the decision. Even under federal law, however, the court can remit to the arbitrators to clarify whether or not an issue has been decided in arbitration.[57] In no event should the arbitrators reexamine the grounds for the award or substantively change their decision.

B) Role of Arbitrators

THE S.I.C.A. ARBITRATOR'S MANUAL recommends that post-award matters should be conducted only under the auspices of the SRO. If an arbitrator is contacted by a party, he or she should inform the SRO, since the parties should not contact an arbitrator in any circumstances. The same is true if an arbitrator is threatened by a party with a lawsuit.

C) Liability of Arbitrators

Arbitrators are quasi-judicial officers and, as such, enjoy a high degree of immunity; they are generally exempt from civil liability for failure to exercise care or skill in performing their duties in an arbitration.[58] Under AAA Rule 47(d), neither the AAA nor any arbitrator is "liable to any party for any act or omission in connection with" the arbitration. The arbitrator is liable, however, for active misconduct, such as bribery, fraud, or corruption.[59]

In a novel case,[60] two investors sought $608,000 from the C.B.O.E. for mental anguish and the expense of defending an arbitration action where they were not given proper notice of a hearing. The panel contained no public arbitrators in violation of C.B.O.E. regulations, and a court had refused to confirm the award. The court dismissed the tort action, finding that two important policies are promoted by finding arbitrators immune from suit: first, the integrity of the decision-making process would be inhibited by the fear of reprisal from dissatisfied litigants. Second, people would be reluctant to serve as arbitrators if immunity was not granted.

9) MOTION TO VACATE, MODIFY, OR RECONSIDER

If a party has made a motion in court to confirm the award, it is proper for an application to change the award to be made in a motion to vacate or modify. The court can direct the arbitrators to answer the request. Normally this will be done by an order vacating the award and remitting the issues to arbitration to correct it. If the award has failed to dispose of certain issues and is thereby incomplete, often the court will redirect to the arbitrators. See the discussion in chapter 16.

A court is without authority to examine grounds for the award and may not take additional evidence concerning the issues,[61] reexamine or substantively change the award rendered, or compel the arbitrators to testify or produce evidence that would impeach the award.[62] This encourages the parties to present all the evidence at the arbitration, which is further supported by SRO and AAA rules that impose a waiver of the right to present further evidence after the close of the hearing.[63]

10) CONFIDENTIALITY VERSUS PUBLICITY OF AWARDS

The S.I.C.A. ARBITRATOR'S MANUAL and AAA CODE OF ETHICS FOR ARBITRATORS IN COMMERCIAL DISPUTES both indicate that all aspects of the arbitration, including the deliberations, evidence, testimony, and award, are confidential unless the forum rules, law, or the parties otherwise provide. The prior practice of SROs was to treat everything relating to the arbitration as confidential. However, as discussed above, today the SRO and AAA rules require public disclosure of some information regarding awards--specifically the award with the names of the parties redacted.[64] This confidentiality was, of course, a major advantage to arbitration and resulted in an inability to use prior awards as precedent in later cases.

Confidentiality still exists as to the record of the proceedings and other arbitration matters, except as to the parties. The public dissemination of the award information is controlled by the forum; arbitrators do not release any information in practice even to the parties, including the award itself--the forum staff does. As a practical matter, however, transcripts and other information may be released by the parties, unless subject to a confidentiality agreement.

The AAA will furnish to any party, however, at its expense, certified copies of any papers in the AAA's possession that may be required in judicial proceedings related to the arbitration.[65]

11) CONCLUSION

The arbitrator's decision is not normally a detailed statement of how the award was reached through application of the law to the facts, but rather a simple decision. The contents of an award, however, may be varied from the normal forum requirements by the parties.

As a result of SRO and AAA Rule changes, awards will be both more complete and public. The probable result of these changes will be the use of past awards as precedent in both settlement and arbitration of later disputes, as well as somewhat greater review of awards. Due to the preference for finality, however, the award is almost unassailable either in actions before the arbitrators (if any) or in court review of the award, which is discussed in chapter 16.

NOTES

1 The parties are not entitled to a hearing under SRO small claims and AAA expedited rules. They may also waive a hearing. *See* S.I.C.A. Uniform Code § 2, 3; N.A.S.D. Code of Arbitration N.A.S.D. §§ 13, 14; N.Y.S.E. Rules 601, 602; AAA Rules 38, 51-55. *See also* chapter 14 discussion.

2 AAA Rule 42(d).

3 *See* New York Arbitration Act, N.Y. CPLR 7507; Section 8 of the Uniform Arbitration Act.

4 AAA Rule 42; N.A.S.D. § 41.

5 New York CPLR 7507.

6 Normally, post-hearing briefs will be taken only if the parties agree to an extension of the time after closure of the hearing for rendering the award.

7 *See* Uniform Code § 29(d); N.A.S.D. § 41(d); N.Y.S.E. Rule 627(d).

8 The AAA adopted this same language in the 1993 Rule 42(a) changes.

9 *See* N.Y. CPLR 7507.

10 Uniform Code § 28(c); N.A.S.D. § 41(c); N.Y.S.E. Rule 627(c); AAA Rule 45.

11 N.Y. CPLR 7507.

12 Davis v. Calaway, 121 Cal. Rptr. 570 (1975), a case where one party sought to vacate an award on the grounds that he had not been properly served.

13 In fact, the SRO and AAA rules do not require arbitrators to follow the law. This would, of course, permit another grounds to challenge the award. *See* the chapter 16 discussion of manifest disregard of law as grounds for appeal.

14 Mentschikoff, *Commercial Arbitration*, 61 COLUM. L. REV. 846, 861 (1961).

15 DOMKE, COMMERCIAL ARBITRATION 391-92, (1985) citing cases.

16 Sargent v. Paine Webber Jackson & Curtis, 882 F.2d 529 (D.C. Cir. 1989). N.A.S.D. § 41(e); N.Y.S.E. Rule 627(e). A recent issue of the SEC. ARB. COMM. contained three articles all supporting a requirement of a brief statement of the reasons for the decisions. *See* 5 SEC. ARB. COMM. 2-10 (1993).

17 1993 WL 119690 (S.D.N.Y. 1993).

18 *Id.*

19 Shell, *The Role of Public Law in Private Dispute Resolution*, 26 AM. BUS. L. REV. 397 (1988).

20 As the court stated in Davis v. Chevy Chase Fin. Ltd., 667 F.2d 160, 165 (D.C. Cir. 1981) with respect to the scope of the arbitrators' powers:

> In sum, the genesis of arbitral authority is the contract, and arbitrators are permitted to decide only the issues that lie within the contractual mandate. By necessary implication, an arbitrational award regarding a matter not within the scope of the governing arbitration clause is one made in excess of authority, and a court is precluded from giving effect to such an award.

21 AAA Rules 28 and 42; N.A.S.D. § 36; N.Y.S.E. Rule 622; N.Y. CPLR 7507.

22 Allen Knitting Mills, Inc. v. Dorado Dress Shop, 39 A.D.2d 286, 333 N.Y.S. 2d 848 (1972).

23 Robbins v. Day, 954 F.2d 674 (11th Cir. 1992).

24 N.A.S.D. § 41(e); N.Y.S.E. Rule 627(e). Under both N.A.S.D. and N.Y.S.E. rules the public parties can elect to omit their names, but the industry party can not.

25 AAA Rule was amended to allow public access to awards. To protect the privacy rights of the parties, the names of all parties are to be redacted.

26 N.A.S.D. § 41(f); N.Y.S.E. Rule 627(f). There are stringent time limits to this request: the N.A.S.D. has a three day rule after notification of panel composition; remember that there are only five days to exercise a preemptory challenge.

27 *See* Federal Arbitration Act § 9 (1982); AAA Rule 47; N.Y. CPLR 7510.

28 *See* the discussion in chapters 5 and 16 regarding the finality of an award.

29 Uniform Code § 6; N.A.S.D. § 17; N.Y.S.E. Rule 605; AAA Rule 42(d).

30 N.Y. CPLR 7508.

31 Uniform Code § 28(h); AAA Rule 42(d).

32 *See* Shearson/American Express, Inc. v. McMahon, 482 U.S. 220, 238-42 (1987). *See* A LEGAL AND POLICY ANALYSIS BY THE COMPLIANCE AND LEGAL DIVISION (S.I.A. 1993), which is a memorandum compiled by the

S.I.A. regarding punitive damage issues. *See also* Sabino, *Awarding Punitive Damages in Securities Industry Arbitration: Working for a Just Result*, 27 U. RICH. L. REV. 33 (1992).

33 *See* Annotation, *Attorney's Fees or Other Expenses of Litigation as Elements in Measuring Exemplary or Punitive Damages*, 30 A.L.R. 3d 1443 (1970).

34 Garrity v. Lyle Stuart, Inc., 40 N.Y. 2d 354, 386 N.Y.S. 2d 831, 353 N.E.2d 793 (1976). *See* the discussion in chapter 11.

35 Barbier v. Shearson Lehman Hutton Inc., 948 F.2d 117 (2d Cir. 1991) (N.Y. state law prohibits punitive damages, but this is fully consistent with federal law, even if the result is that punitive damages are prohibited where they would otherwise be permitted).

36 Order Approving Proposed Rule Changes, FED. SEC. L. REP. (CCH) ¶84,414 (1989).

37 As noted, New York law does not permit arbitrators to award punitive damages. Since New York is specified as the governing law in many brokerage customer agreements, the right to punitive damages is not available unless under some statutory provision. The New York prohibition may be subject to question as a result of a recent Appellate Division case dissent and the New York County Lawyers Association Committee on Arbitration and Alternate Dispute Resolution recommending reversal by the legislature of the *Garrity* rule.

38 Kelley v. Michaels, 5 SEC. ARB. COMM. 9, 14 (N.D. Okla. 1993),

39 758 F. Supp. 638 (D. Colo. 1991).

40 This was the case in Volt Information Sciences, Inc., v. Board of Trustees of Leland Stanford Junior University, 489 U.S. 468, 109 S. Ct. 1248, 103 L. Ed. 2d 488 (1989).

41 This is opposed to labor arbitrations where arbitrators lack the power to award punitive damages absent an express provision in the contract providing for arbitration. *See* cases cited in Pyle v. Securities U.S.A., Inc., 758 F. Supp. 638 (D. Colo. 1991).

42 The Court in Raytheon Co. v. Automated Business Systems, Inc., 882 F.2d 6 (1st Cir. 1989), held that arbitrators, like courts, are empowered to award punitive damages with respect to the claims presented.

43 *See* Mastrobuono v. Shearson Lehman Hutton, Inc., 20 F.3d 713 (7th Cir. March 30, 1994), which held that if the customer's agreement is governed by state law that forbids arbitrators from awarding punitive damages, rules of a SRO forum (the N.A.S.D.) permitting such awards will not be used, even if the agreement also incorporates the SRO rules. *Cf.*, several decisions which permitted punitive awards, even when New York law was governing. *Bonar v. Dean Witter Reynolds Inc.*, 835 F.2d 1378 (11th Cir., 1988); *Raytheon Co.*

v. Automated Business Systems Inc., 882 F.2d 6 (1st Cir., 1989); *Todd Shipyards Corp. v. Cunard Line Ltd.*, 943 F.2d 1056 (9th Cir., 1991); *Lee v. Chica*, 983 F.2d 883 (8th Cir., 1993).

44 AAA Rule 42(d).

45 *See* Volt Information Sciences, Inc. v. Board of Trustees, 109 S. Ct. 1248 (1989); Cook v. Mishkin, 464 N.Y.S. 2d 761 (1983).

46 *See also* the discussion of interim relief in chapter 14.

47 N.Y. CPLR 7502(c).

48 N.Y. CPLR 7502(a).

49 Uniform Code § 20(d); N.A.S.D. § 32(d)(1); N.Y.S.E. Rule 619 (d)(1); AAA Rule 10.

50 Uniform Code §30(c). *See also* N.A.S.D. § 43 for customer claims and § 44 for industry claims; N.Y.S.E. Rule 629. AAA Rule 42(c) merely provides that the arbitrator

> shall, in the award, assess . . . [arbitration administration fees (Rule 46); travel and other expenses of the AAA representatives and arbitrator, witnesses and cost of any proof produced at the request of the arbitrator (Rule 47); and compensation of the neutral arbitrator (Rule 48)] in favor of any party and, in the event that any administrative fees or expenses are due the AAA, in favor of the AAA.

51 *See also* AAA Rule 49.

52 N.A.S.D. § 42(g); N.Y.S.E. Rule 629(g).

53 *See* First Interregional Equity Corporation v. Haughton, FED. SEC. L. REP. (CCH) ¶ 98,065 (S.D.N.Y. 1994).

54 AAA Rule 43 refers to "any clerical, typographical, technical or computational error."

55 N.Y. CPLR 7509, which refers to the quoted listing in 7511(c). The grounds are the same as Federal Arbitration Act §11, which applies in judicial modification or correction (discussed in chapter 16), but the federal provision adds: "The [Court] order may modify and correct the award, so as to effect the intent thereof and promote justice between the parties." This indicates that the federal procedure is to not approach the arbitrators for modification at all.

AAA Rule 43 was adopted specifically to authorize arbitrators to dispose of applications for correction or modification within 20 days after the date of the award, but specifically forbids a redetermination "of the merits of any claim already decided.

Under SRO rules, the arbitrators can "reopen" hearings on their own motion or application of a party only if (1) permitted by applicable law and (2) before the award is rendered. N.A.S.D. § 40; N.Y.S.E. Rule 626.

56 N.Y. CPLR 7509.

57 Galt v. Libbey-Owens-Ford Glass Co., 397 F.2d 439 (7th Cir.), *cert. denied*, 393 U.S. 925 (1968).

58 Unless they are charged with a higher duty by the law that will expressly prohibit such misconduct.

59 *See* THE S.I.C.A. ARBITRATOR'S MANUAL, Arbitrator's Immunity.

60 Austern v. Chicago Board Options Exchange Inc., 21 SEC. REG. & L. REP. (BNA) 1218 (S.D.N.Y. Aug. 11, 1989). The court found adequate remedy in defeating confirmation of the award. Further, since the C.B.O.E.'s conduct did not constitute state action, claims of violation of the fourteenth amendment and the state due process rights were rejected.

61 This included newly discovered evidence.

62 *See* THE S.I.C.A. ARBITRATOR'S MANUAL Section on Post-Award Procedure (B)(2), in Appendix C.

63 *See* the discussion in chapter 14 regarding waiver.

64 AAA Rule 42(f). N.Y.S.E. Rule 627(f) redacts the customer's name only if requested. N.A.S.D. § 41(f) redacts the arbitrators names, but not names of parties, and requires release of all awards to parties in other arbitrations having the person as an arbitrator.

65 AAA Rule 44.

Chapter 16

POST-AWARD MATTERS AND APPEAL OF ARBITRATION AWARD

The only action that can occur after the award is delivered is on the award: to confirm, to modify, or to vacate. While sometimes the arbitrators will be asked to take action within a limited time after the award has been rendered, as in a clarification or modification (see discussion in chapter 15), normally at this stage the action is in court.[1] The award is the final step in the arbitration proceeding; and, after it is delivered and no post-award actions are taken, the arbitrators are released.[2] The parties are then confronted with enforcement. This normally takes place in litigation.

If a party has died after an award is rendered, the proceedings are the same as when a party dies after a verdict.[3]

1) DEMAND LETTER

In most cases, after an award is received, the prevailing party will write a demand letter to the losing party, and the award will be recognized by meeting the demand without further action. But often the parties will request judicial action to confirm the award, or the party who did not prevail in the arbitration may contest the award under the standards established for judicial review of the arbitrators' decision.

2) ENFORCEMENT OF THE SRO AWARD

Most arbitration awards, whether in securities disputes or not, are not confirmed by court action. As noted in chapter 15, awards are usually in terms of a monetary amount. Usually the prevailing party will be paid by the defeated party a reasonable time after delivery of the award. Often the parties will be continuing in a business relationship, and this will require prompt action. Where the prior relationship is over, however, there may be reluctance to honor the award without confirmation.

A) SRO Enforcement Rules: Not Applicable to Awards Against Customers

SRO rules normally require prompt payment of the SRO awards by members or persons associated with members and empower the SRO to discipline for failure to promptly pay. For example, in N.A.S.D. arbitrations the failure of a member or a person associated with a member to honor an award where a timely motion has not been made to modify or vacate will be in violation of the N.A.S.D. Rules of Fair Practice.[4] This does not, however, apply to AAA securities arbitrations. Of course, if the customer is the losing party, SRO discipline will not be applicable and court confirmation is necessary for enforced enforcement of the award.

B) Awards Specify Time of Payment; Interest

Normally the awards will specify when payment or performance is due. Otherwise, payment is due upon receipt of the award. If the prevailing party believes that there may be delay in payment, it should seek judicial confirmation of the award. Once this is done, the award will accrue interest at the judgment rate applicable in that jurisdiction.[5] The New York Stock Exchange Rules provide for interest on arbitration awards if not paid within 30 days after receipt unless a motion to vacate has been filed with a court.[6] Awards in a dollar amount must be paid by exactly that amount. Firms may, however, credit the prevailing party's account, unless the parties otherwise consent or arbitrators order differently.[7]

The Municipal Securities Rulemaking Board requires that if a member or associated person seeks to appeal an award, they must deposit the amount of the award in a bank escrow account or provide the prevailing party an irrevocable standby letter of credit.[8]

3) COURT CONFIRMATION OF AWARD/JUDGMENT

The party wishing to confirm the arbitration award in a court action must meet statutory and procedural requirements.

A) Time Limitation

Under Federal Arbitration Act § 9 and New York Arbitration Law,[9] the parties have one year to apply for court confirmation of an arbitration award.

This period is normally calculated from the delivery of the award.[10] Notice of the application for confirmation is by the same process as service of motions in the same court.[11] Incompetency or death may extend this period in the court's discretion.[12]

The one year period in which to confirm an arbitration award under Section 9 of the Federal Arbitration Act is permissive rather than mandatory due to the use of the word "may." [R]eading Section 9 as a strict statute of limitations would be an exercise in futility. . . .[I]t would encourage, at the expense of judicial economy, the use of another analogous method of enforcing awards . . . [as individuals who prevailed and failed to confirm] would simply resort to filing actions at law."[13]

B) Confirming Court

The statutes will specify the court having the special ministerial power to confirm awards: in the Federal statute it is the district courts; in New York, the county court.[14] Of course, the court must have the requisite jurisdiction. (See chapter 2 and 5 discussion).

C) Procedure Applicable

The proceedings for summary entry of an award or contested actions where the defendant will raise defenses against confirmation, are conducted in accordance with the applicable procedural rules.

D) Confirmation as Judgment

When the court confirms the award, it does so by entering the award as a judgment of the court.[15] In effect, the confirmation pleadings will request the award be transformed into a judgment. It is treated the same as a judgment rendered in a judicial action and is entitled to the same force and effect and to be "enforced as if it had been rendered in an action in the court in which it is entered."[16]

Under state and federal law, the application for confirmation must include the following papers: the award; the arbitration agreement; copies of orders to confirm, modify, or correct the award and order of the court on such matters; information on selection of arbitrators and each extension of time within which to make the award.[17] Proof offered in support of the confirmation must conform to the issues raised; a material variance between pleading and proof is fatal.

E) Form of Application and Confirmation

The type of judicial confirmation form will vary depending on the jurisdiction. The following is a form of judgment confirming an arbitration award under New York CPLR 7510:

--- X
IN THE MATTER OF THE ARBITRATION)
BETWEEN)
[Name],) Index No.
)
Claimants,) Judgment Confirming
Award) Arbitration
-against-)
)
[Broker])
and [Registered Representative],)
)
Respondents)
--- X

The petitioner, _________, having commenced a special proceeding pursuant to CPLR 7510 to confirm the award made by the _________, as arbitrators, signed and acknowledged on the ______ day of ______, 19___, a copy of which is annexed hereto as Exhibit A and by this reference made a part hereof (the "Award"), whereby the sum of $___ was awarded the petitioner and the respondent was directed to pay the petitioner the portion of fees and expenses advanced by the petitioner to the [forum] for which the respondent was found liable, and said proceeding having regularly come on to be heard before the Hon. ______, without a jury, of this court, held at the courthouse thereof located at _____, on the ______ day of _____, 19___, and the issues in the above entitled proceeding having duly come on to be heard, and the petitioner having duly appeared by ________, [his/her] attorney, and the proofs of both parties have been adduced and their respective counsel having been heard and after due deliberation having been held thereon, and a decision of this court having been made therein and filed on the _____ day of _____, 19___, in favor of the petitioner, _______, and against the respondent, _______, and directing the entry of judgment as hereinafter provided and the costs of the petitioner having been duly taxed in the sum of _______ ($________) Dollars, it is

ORDERED, ADJUDGED AND DECREED, that judgment be entered herein confirming the Award of the arbitrators by this reference and it is further

ORDERED, ADJUDGED AND DECREED, that judgment be entered on the aforesaid Award, making said award the judgment of this court and the clerk of this court is hereby directed to enter this judgment.

____
J.S.C.

4) ENFORCEMENT OF AWARD AS JUDGMENT

Once the court has confirmed the arbitration award, it becomes a judgment and is entitled to be enforced in the same manner as any other judgment.[18] Civil contempt is an appropriate remedy for failure of a party to comply with an order of the court confirming an arbitration award.[19]

A) Common Law Enforcement

Because the parties have agreed to be bound by the arbitration result in the predispute or submission agreement, the winning party as plaintiff in a legal enforcement action is asking for contract relief. This will take the form of an action at law upon the award. The action is not based on a redetermination of the facts and law at issue in the arbitration, since they have been decided, but instead is based on the award rendered. In some cases, the defendant/losing party will raise contract defenses in the confirmation concerning the arbitration agreement from which the claimed relief emanates. These common law defenses go to the heart of the agreement itself and are discussed in chapter 3. A confirmation is not appropriate when the arbitration is a nullity.[20]

B) Statutory Enforcement

As noted above, the Federal and most state statutes provide for enforcement of the award by confirmation. The award can not be entered, however, until the time fixed by statute (usually 30 days after application),[21] unless the parties have consented to an earlier entry.

C) Levy and Execution

Once the judgment on the award has been entered in a confirmation action or in a common law action, the enforcement means are the same as for any other judgment of the court. This will normally be through levy and execution on the real and personal property of the party against whom the judgment was rendered.

The location of the property is important in state actions for confirmation, since the state judgment is limited to its jurisdiction. However, a federal judgment is entitled to nationwide enforcement through the federal courts. In addition, a state judgment is entitled to full faith and credit in the courts of other states under the U.S. Constitution.[22]

The normal procedure for levy and execution is to have the judgment entered and the local sheriff or U.S. Marshall by a legal process known as execution collect the amount of the judgment due. Once the officer identifies property (usually a bank account or other physical property) of the judgment creditor, it will be attached (levy) and sold to satisfy the judgment.

5) APPEAL OF ARBITRATION AWARD IN COURT

The arbitration award must be confirmed unless contested by a party to the arbitration. Under the statutes, the contest may be made either upon application to confirm or within three months of the award by an action to vacate or modify, which action will stay any proceedings to enforce the award.[23] A party who fails to object to an award within the time period waives the right thereafter to object to a confirmation action. Accordingly, it will be wise for the prevailing party to wait until the three month period has run before confirming, thus barring any argument that the award should be vacated. In a recent case, however, the Second Circuit found that an investor's appeal of an arbitration due to racial bias was not bound by this three month limit. It was preempted by civil rights law.[24]

As a result of the limited nature of review of arbitration awards, they are "particularly insulated from judicial review," and the scope of such review is "extraordinarily narrow."[25]

See the discussion in chapter 5 on appeal of arbitration awards.

A) Procedure

A party petitions the court to vacate or modify the award within the prescribed time after the award is rendered. Failure to so apply waives the right to seek relief.[26] In order to bring such an action in federal court, jurisdiction must exist--there is no federal question jurisdiction from just the arbitration agreement; the amount in controversy in diversity cases must also exist. Further, under federal procedural rules, the action may be subject to change in venue to the district where it might have been brought.[27]

B) Confirming an Award

Under the statutory preference for arbitration, the confirmation of an award is designed to be quick, easy, and inexpensive.

C) Grounds for Appeal of Arbitration Award

The discussion in chapter 5 set forth the statutory grounds for appeal of the award in detail.

6) APPEAL OF COURT JUDGMENT ON AWARD

If the confirmation of the award is reduced to a final judgment by the court, an appeal may be taken in the same manner as any other judicial order.

Here technical procedural rules apply. There is a split of authority as to whether the appeal of the trial court's order is *de novo* or only on the basis of an abuse of discretion by the reviewing court; the later seems to recognize the policy that arbitration results are almost sacrosanct.[28]

7) *RES JUDICATA* AND COLLATERAL ESTOPPEL EFFECT OF AWARD: LATER ACTIONS ON SAME FACTS

In accord with the principle that the arbitration award is a final determination of the issues in dispute, two doctrines preclude a party from attempting to relitigate the case.[29]

In both situations, the arbitration award will be plead as an affirmative defense under Federal Rules of Civil Procedure 8(c) which provides:

> *Affirmative Defenses.* In pleading to a preceding pleading, a party shall set forth affirmatively accord and satisfaction, arbitration and award, assumption of risk, contributory negligence, discharge in bankruptcy, duress, estoppel, failure of consideration, fraud illegality, injury by fellow servant, laches, license, payment, release, res judicata, statute of frauds, statute of limitations, waiver, and any other matter constituting an avoidance or affirmative defense. When a party has mistakenly designated a defense as a counterclaim or a counterclaim as a defense, the court on terms, if justice so requires, shall treat the pleading as if there had been a proper designation.

New York Civil Practice Law and Rules 3018(b) provides a similar defense.

A) *Res Judicata*

The term *res judicata* is issue oriented. It is a common law doctrine that precludes the readjudication of the issues already decided in a prior proceeding. While *res judicata* normally applies to prior judicial proceedings, the doctrine also precludes either judicial or arbitration resolution of the same issues. As noted in chapters 3 and 11, this is an affirmative defense that can be raised by respondent in the answer or in a judicial motion to deny arbitration.

The requirements for application of *res judicata* are:

1. There has been a final judgment on the merits;
2. The parties are identical or in privity with the parties in the earlier action; and
3. The causes of action are identical.

The real question is whether the same issues were presented in the earlier action between the same parties. In looking to the issues, the reviewer must examine if (1) the rights or interests protected in the first judgment would be altered by the second action; and (2) the actions arise from the same transactional facts.

Despite the investor's claim that certain allegations in the claim were not alleged in the previous class action, the court found there is no requirement of absolute parity in order to invoke *res judicata*,[30] as long as the claims were "similar."

B) Collateral Estoppel

Literally, collateral estoppel is another common law doctrine that will stop or prevent a party from relitigating the same facts and law. It is essentially fact oriented. Collateral estoppel looks to similar factors as *res judicata*, the same factual and legal issues, identical parties, a valid and final judgment, etc., but further requires that the party against whom the doctrine is being asserted had a "full and fair opportunity to litigate" in the prior proceeding.[31]

In *Ferreri v. First Options of Chicago, Inc.*,[32] a securities case was filed after determination by an arbitrator of damages. The Court held that arbitration provided a fair, complete and adequate substitute for a judicial trial because (1) the arbitrators had expertise in the securities industry, a specialized field; (2) the plaintiff's economic loss was resolved from the evidence[33] in a complete proceeding; (3) plaintiff was represented by his own lawyer at the arbitration and changed lawyers to pursue litigation after the arbitration was complete; and (4) the rules and procedures used in arbitration were substantially the same as at trials. The Court also noted that the damages for the violations of securities laws recoverable in arbitration were the same as in litigation. This was probably the most critical factor.

C) Law of the Case Doctrine

Under the Law of the Case Doctrine, dismissal is justified for wasteful and repetitious relitigation of the issues conclusively determined in arbitration proceedings. This is applicable when the "sole impediment to the application of the doctrines of *res judicata* and collateral estoppel to the claims was the fact that the arbitration decision was not final because final judgment had not been entered and the confirmation of the award might be subject to appellate review."[34]

D) Applicability to Arbitration Proceedings

The case law clearly indicates arbitration awards are "final decisions rendered" in order to apply both *res judicata* and collateral estoppel. This recognizes the statutory authority of arbitrators to reach a final determination of a dispute in a quasi-judicial proceeding.[35]

Under New York law, collateral estoppel can only be applied after the arbitration award has been confirmed and entered as a judgment of the court (see discussion below).[36] Prior to the new SRO arbitration rules regarding the specification of issues decided in the content of the award (see chapter 15 discussion), it was sometimes difficult to determine the grounds upon which an award was decided. This may still be the case in AAA arbitrations that do not require a statement of the issues decided, and also if the SRO award is incomplete.

E) Evidence

Obviously, the award will be submitted in favor of either doctrine's application.

If there is some question as to the scope of the award, the party seeking to dismiss on the basis of collateral estoppel or *res judicata* can provide the reviewing court with the Statement of Claim or, if one has been made, a transcript of the hearing. The hearing is taped at the N.A.S.D., and a court reporter is used at the N.Y.S.E. In AAA arbitrations, the parties can have a court reporter, but this is not usual. It may be wise to do so if liability is based on law (which the court can review) versus credibility of witnesses and evidence (which the court will not review). Under AAA Rule 46, the AAA will furnish a court with any documents in the AAA's possession regarding the proceeding.

8) SANCTIONS

In some cases, the courts have imposed sanctions on the parties or attorneys bringing a second action subject to dismissal under these principles where a case arose from the same facts as the earlier action of the same parties and the second action was determined meritless.[37]

If a party has received an award in arbitration and successfully raises the award as collateral estoppel, that party may be entitled to attorney's fees and expenses pursuant to Federal Rules of Civil Procedure 11. In *Pallante v. Paine, Webber, Jackson & Curtis, Inc.*,[38] the attorney for the plaintiff was assessed fees and costs. The court stated:

> any experienced attorney in securities law must have known that this case arouse out of the same factual predicate as plaintiff's earlier arbitration proceeding and therefore was meritless. While the plaintiffs themselves may have been unable to judge the clear impropriety of this suit, their [experienced] counsel . . . must have known not to pursue this litigation.

In a case seeking attorney fees due to "bad faith" during the arbitration discovery process, the court found that the Federal Arbitration Act, "which controls review of arbitration awards, does not grant a district court the authority to award attorney fees."[39]

9) CONCLUSION

After the award has been rendered, the winning party can hope for a voluntary payment of amounts due or performance of what is required by the award from the loser. If that is not forthcoming, in securities arbitration cases the SRO will assist in enforcement of an award rendered against a member, firm, or person associated with the SRO; in a non-SRO proceeding, however, resort to court for confirmation and execution through judicial officers may be necessary.

In the past, there has been little control over the awards resulting from arbitration, principally due to statutory restrictions on court supervision of the process. There seems little likelihood of these standards for judicial review changing, but the new SRO and AAA rules requiring the award to contain certain elements may result in somewhat greater scrutiny by the courts.

NOTES

1 *See* Corey v. New York Stock Exchange, Inc., 691 F.2d 1205 (6th Cir. 1982), holding that the exclusive remedy for challenging an arbitration award was in an action to do so; not in a collateral attack arguing that the party had not had a fair hearing in the arbitration.

2 Of course, the court can remit to the arbitrators for clarification, to determine any outstanding issues, or for other action. Normally this will be to the same panel of arbitrators. *See* the discussion of an appeal of an award below.

3 New York CPLR 7512.

4 *See* N.A.S.D. Resolution of Board of Directors ¶ 3744, referring to Article III, § 1 of the Rules of Fair Practice (effective May 1, 1973).

5 N.Y. CPLR 5004 provides that interest shall be at the rate of nine per centum per annum, except where otherwise provided by statute.

6 Interest is payable at the rate specified by the arbitrators or the judgment rate for the state where the award was rendered; and, is due from the award date if not paid within the 30 days or if the application for vacatur is denied. N.Y.S.E. Rule 627(g).

7 *Id.*

8 M.S.R.B. Rules § 31.

9 N.Y. CPLR 7510.

10 N.Y. CPLR 7510. The Federal provision is silent on the issue of delivery. Federal Arbitration Act § 9 specifies only "within one year after the award is made."

11 *See* Federal Arbitration Act § 9; in New York service of process is pursuant to CPLR, which is not part of the arbitration law.

12 N.Y. CPLR 7512.

13 Sverdrup Corp. v. WHC Constructors, Inc., 989 F.2d 148 (4th Cir. 1993).

14 Federal Arbitration Act § 9 provides that the proper court in which to apply for confirmation is either that court which the parties have agreed upon in the arbitration agreement or in the district where the award was made. New York CPLR 7502(a) specifies that the action shall be brought in the county specified in the agreement or, if none specified or there is no county, in any county, or in the county where the arbitration was held.

15 In New York it is entered on the Judgment Roll. CPLR 7514(b).

16 Federal Arbitration Act § 13.

17 *Id.*, New York CPLR 7514(b).

18 Federal Arbitration Act §§ 10, 11, and 13; Uniform Arbitration Act § 14. Parsons & Whittemore Ala. Mach. & Services Corp. v. Yeargin Const. Co., Inc., 744 F.2d 1482 (11th Cir. 1984)

19 Milano v. Hingham Sportswear Co. Inc., 366 Mass. 376, 318 N.E. 2d 827 (1974).

20 Roberto Const. Co. v. Burnham-Manning Post No. 1105 VFW, Inc., 347 Mass. 400, 198 N.E. 2d 302 (1964).

21 Federal Arbitration Act § 9 is silent on the time in which a confirmation can be granted, but does apply the one year limitation to request confirmation as discussed. New York CPLR 7511 is also silent.

22 Article IV, § 1.

23 Federal Arbitration Act §§ 10, 11, and 12. The time limitations vary from state to state. For example, New York CPLR 7511 provides 90 days.

24 Tualia Mian v. Donaldson, Lufkin & Jenrette Securities Corp., reported in THE WALL ST. J. (Oct. 19, 1993), N.Y.L.J. (Oct. 21, 1993).

25 Kupperman & Freeman, *Selected Topics in Securities Arbitration*, 65 TULANE L. REV. 1547, 1603-28 (1991), contains an excellent review of the law regarding judicial review of arbitration awards and is used in chapter 5 materials.

26 Drexel Burnham Lambert, Inc. v. Pyles, 701 F. Supp. 217 (N.D. Ga. 1988), *citing* International Bhd. of Elec. Workers Local 969 v. Babcock & Wilcox, 826 F.2d 962 (10th Cir. 1987); Cullen v. Paine, Webber, Jackson & Curtis, Inc. 863 F.2d 171 (2d Cir.), *cert. denied*, 109 S. Ct. 3159 (1989).

27 28 U.S.C. § 1404(a).

28 *See* Kupperman & Freeman, *supra* note 23, at 1604-5.

29 Grafstrom v. Bear, Stearns & Co., 1986 WL 13806 (S.D.N.Y.); No. 85 Civ. 3679 (S.D.N.Y. 1986).

30 Union Square Associates Securities Litigation, 1993 WL 513232 (De. Ch. 1993) (the claims were too similar; prior release in class actions final).

31 Index Fund, Inc. v. Hagopian, 677 F. Supp. 710 (S.D.N.Y. 1987), *citing* Gelb v. Royal Globe Insurance Co., 798 F.2d 38 (2d Cir. 1986).

32 661 F. Supp. 1186 (E.D. Pa. 1987).

33 A written transcript was referred to by the Court in determining the arbitrators had detailed evidence provided by the plaintiff. *Id.*

34 Pompano-Windy City Partners, Ltd. v. Bear, Stearns & Co., Inc., FED. SEC. L. REP. (CCH) ¶ 97,366 (S.D.N.Y. 1992).

35 *See* Shell, *Res Judicata and Collateral Estoppel Effect of Commercial Arbitration*, 35 UCLA L. REV. 632 (1988); D. ROBBINS, SECURITIES ARBITRATION PROCEDURAL MANUAL 163-164 (1991 Supp.), citing several recent New York cases.

36 Ufheil Construction Co. v. Town of New Windsor, 478 F. Supp. 766 (S.D.N.Y. 1979), *aff'd*, 636 F.2d 1204 (2d Cir. 1980).

37 *See* Gonick v. Drexel Burnham Lambert, Inc., 711 F. Supp. 981 (N.D. Cal. 1988); Robinson v. Dean Witter, 129 F.R.D. 15 (D. Mass. 1989); Pompano-Windy City Partners Ltd., v. Bear, Stearns & Co., Inc., 794 F. Supp. 1265 (S.D.N.Y. 1992).

38 Pallante v. Paine Webber, Jackson & Curtis, Inc., FED. SEC. L. REP. ¶ 92,219 (S.D.N.Y. May 14, 1985).

39 *Id.*

Chapter 17

THE FUTURE OF SECURITIES ARBITRATION

1) SOME QUESTIONS REMAIN

Rodriguez de Quijas resolved many questions regarding arbitration of 1933 Act claims. There is little doubt that investors can bind themselves through predispute arbitration clauses to give up their right to bring actions in the federal courts for violations of the securities laws of the United States. Yet, a basic question still remains: Should parties who have not knowingly done so be determined to have waived their right to a judicial hearing regarding matters of great public concern such as violations of the securities laws?[1]

While significant changes have occurred in securities arbitration since *Wilko,* and while the use of arbitration has been established not to be devastating in terms of its result, can it be said to be a "further erosion of investor protection?"[2] Is it not the case that the investor-consumer would anticipate that arbitration, even if he or she is made aware of it in opening an account, will involve contract disputes and *not* questions of violation of the laws enacted for investor protection and to enhance the integrity of the marketplace for securities? As one commentator noted, "[T]he risk of a potentially incorrect decision made by an arbitrator in a securities fraud case is simply too great to be justified by the reduction in costs."[3]

One of the first questions relates to the forums from which most broker-arbitrator agreements permit the customer to select. If the forums to resolve such disputes are located in a remote place, or in surroundings where the customer might feel intimidated, due process may not be achieved.[4]

In a logical extension of judicial preference for arbitration, it seems that ultimately the courts will be asked to review the fairness of waivers of the right to litigate rather than arbitrate in securities, antitrust, and other commercial dealings. Industries other than securities will no doubt want to include predispute arbitration provisions as a matter of course in their dealings with customers and clients. When those industries are affected with a public interest, the question remains: Is the resolution of questions by arbitration contrary to a longstanding tradition to provide complete judicial relief in these other statutorily protected areas?[5]

So will the result be development of an arbitration process more responsive to customer needs by the industry that the securities laws seek to police, and will this changing process meet the demands of the public and judicial scrutiny as providing a fair forum for the resolution of such disputes? If the SROs and regulators effectively change the arbitration process to make it more judicial-like, there will be little need to complain since the claims will be processed in a responsible manner. In reality, they must eventually meet the demands of the marketplace and instill public confidence in the process of securities arbitration.

If, on the other hand, the SROs and regulators do not continue to reform arbitration and gain this public acceptance, the legislative bodies of the federal and state governments will perhaps determine that the public good demands judicial review of all securities disputes. The burden on the courts will then increase. Is that so bad? After all, if the courts are burdened by large caseloads, should the result be to throw those who look to the judiciary for protection to the very persons against whom they seek redress--in this case, industry-sponsored and, in many cases, subsidized decisionmakers?

In fact, predispute arbitration contracts are used to reduce costs, including those relating to dispute resolution. Consequently, the customer may be realizing these cost savings through lowered commission fees. But has the customer really determined on his own that he wants these advantages, and is the price he pays this broker worth the protection he gave up?

Do *McMahon* and *Rodriguez de Quijas* really reflect congressional intent regarding the enforcement of the securities laws?[6] If not, and Congress intended investors to have free access to the federal courts, as many feel the securities laws seem to indicate, it will now take congressional action to restore to the investor the right to knowingly and freely waive that right.[7] To enforce present predispute arbitration clauses that a customer has probably not read is unfair. Also if he has read them, he may not realize their significance, and enforcement may be unfair. In an industry clothed with a national interest, regulation can protect the public who desire to buy and sell in the industry marketplace. Both Congress and the courts will have to look carefully at this question of knowing waiver. Alternatively, self regulation can also be used to foster this goal to protect the public good.

2) THE DANGER OF CHANGE

There is danger, however, in developing sophisticated arbitration procedures. Arbitration may become more and more like litigation. Its very advantages--speed and efficiency--can thereby be lost. For example, the new SRO rules require discovery and depositions and, like the courts, require a written record, written reasons for the award, and the like. These procedures all sound very desirable by protecting the investor and permitting a review of the award to be sure it has been reached fairly. But these procedures will add to delay, expense, and probably make the process of arbitration even less attractive as an alternative to litigation. It also may have the effect of precluding the small claimant from any effective forum to present his claims.

As one commentator noted regarding the absorption of equity into the law, "[w]hat had started as an alternative dispute resolution process ended up being absorbed by the law, with the result being a hybrid--an equity practice with all the procedures of the law and a legal system with equitable principles ingrained."[8]

Another commentator notes: "One of the ironies of our civil justice system is that it was derived from the English system, yet it now bears little resemblance to that system. Many of the techniques used today in securities arbitrations do bear a close resemblance to the system from which we derived our rules of law."[9]

Thus, the danger is that the SRO procedures would become too similar to litigation.[10] To make arbitration more formal would be to have it more similar to the institution it seeks to replace--the court. The result will be another legal institution. In time, the process will repeat itself as the legal system absorbs this institution as well.[11]

The question of revision of the procedures will thus draw into mind Learned Hand's observation that the parties agreeing to arbitration "must be content with its informalities; they may not hedge it about with those procedural limitations which it is precisely its purpose to avoid."[12] Arbitration should be fair, and need not be a clone of judicial litigation.

3) AREAS OF CONTINUING CONCERN IN SECURITIES ARBITRATION: WHERE WILL THE PATH TAKE US?

A) The Predispute Arbitration Agreement--Did the Customer Really Agree?

It seems crystal clear that the courts will enforce predispute arbitration agreements as a result of *McMahon* and *de Quijas*. While the states may attempt to regulate the content of contracts as part of the substantive law, if the contract has to deal with interstate commerce, as is almost always the case in the securities industry, federal preemption will occur and the clause will be enforceable anyway. It is clear that state legislatures and courts have not been able to thwart the federal policy; in fact, most state courts have embraced arbitration either on their own or due to state arbitration statutes. Perhaps the best course is for the state legislatures to be sure that the arbitration process works as well as it can through laws regarding the procedures and review of awards.

Common law defenses will still permit a party to avoid arbitration on the ground that a valid agreement was not reached by the parties, or due to waiver or other legal principles which affect the enforcement of the contract itself.

Consequently, reversal of the required arbitration of federal securities claims can occur in only three settings. First, the SROs can decide that such provisions are not appropriate in the securities business. This is very doubtful. A step in the right direction did occur, however, when the S.I.C.A. required these clauses to be highlighted in contracts so that the investor would have slightly better notice.

Second, Congress can take action to invalidate all securities arbitration agreement clauses for federal securities law violation claims. Two bills have been introduced in Congress--neither went this far. They only required that a brokerage firm could not *require* a customer to agree to predispute arbitration as a condition of opening an account in order to gain access to the investment markets,[13] or that federal rights were judicial and could not be waived[14] (a return to *Wilko*)--neither bill has been adopted.

Third, the SEC could through its power to regulate SROs rules "relating to customer disputes, including the power to mandate the adoption of any rules it deems necessary to ensure that arbitration procedures adequately protect statutory rights,"[15] perhaps more effectively regulate the arbitration process. It is apparent, however, that the SEC has taken a progressive approach and will continue to prod the SROs to take action to improve the present process. As evidenced by the SEC *amicus* brief in *de Quijas*, it is clear that the SEC supports arbitration of disputes.

Consequently, predispute arbitration agreements seem well established in the securities industry.

B) Should Private Investors Have the Right to Select Arbitral Forum?

At the present time, SRO rules require that the customer choose between several industry-sponsored forums. The AMEX window is an anachronism, but will permit non-industry AAA arbitration to the fortunate few whose brokerage agreements permit it. But today "relatively few brokerage firms

. . . include the AAA among the forum options."[16]

There seems no reason not to permit AAA arbitration. If a party is forced to arbitrate due to the clause and feels that the SRO forums are biased, he or she should be able to select a neutral body to administer the dispute resolution process. The statistics indicate the industry would perhaps pay a little more in fees due to the unsubsidized nature of AAA proceedings, but with the 1993 AAA Rules amendments, there appears little justification for this industry intransigence.

C) Should the Award be in the Form of an Opinion? Given Precedential Value?

Presently awards are being circulated among those involved in arbitration. This is a result of the new SRO and AAA rules regarding awards containing more information and public availability, even though parties or arbitrators names are redacted. But this additional information is regarding the issues presented, and no opinion is required justifying the conclusions reached by the arbitrators using the facts and law.

In securities arbitrations, the law is far more complex than in ordinary arbitrations, and errors in applying the law are likely. There should be some method of ascertaining that the arbitrators have done so correctly.[17] Other arbitration rules provide that a brief statement of the reasons for the decision, or an informal, brief discussion of the factual and legal basis for the award, be given.[18] It would be a step in the right direction to require a brief statement supporting the findings of fact and legal basis for securities arbitration awards. It would be useful as a check on the arbitrator's discretion, permitting judicial review and also a guide for others in similar situations.

At the same time, private circulation is one matter; but public filing of all awards, or a public index, would be preferable. In this way, all parties will be on an equal footing. As it now exists, some may have additional award data that others do not possess.

D) Should Judicial Review of Arbitration Awards Be Less Restricted?

At the present time, judicial review of arbitration awards is restricted by statutes as to the grounds which permit vacatur, as well as by the summary nature of the awards themselves. If it is true that securities claims are more prone to erroneous interpretation of the law than other arbitration claims, perhaps this additional reason for more complete reasons for the conclusions reached is also necessary to ensure the claimant full protection of the securities laws. This is especially true when you consider that the securities laws, both federal and state, were passed to change the legal rules and to level the information and ground rules for the capital markets.

If a record is made of arbitration proceedings and the award is more complete, judicial review can be relatively cursory. But an important safeguard would then exist for the investor as well as brokerage firm.

E) Can Nonlawyers Assist in Arbitration?

Another problem to be resolved is the use of nonlawyer firms to assist parties in arbitrations. While this is now permitted, as discussed in chapter 11, the S.I.C.A. has proposed an amendment to the Uniform Code to ban such firms from SRO arbitrations. This may result in higher costs, defeating a major attribute of arbitration. The justification for this proposal is that the rules are very complicated and such activity may be unauthorized practice of law. Whether this amendment will be adopted by the SROs and approved by the SEC is unknown, but the use of nonlawyers is one of the ways to reduce the expense of bring an action that is one of the "cornerstones of the arbitration process" and to do otherwise would make the arbitration process more difficult and complicated, justifying an argument that it might then be better to "abandon arbitration entirely and return to the court system."[19]

F) How Can Settlements Be Encouraged?

Litigation or arbitration should be the last step in dispute resolution. To have the parties rely on a third person (or panel) is unsatisfactory in a number of respects: It is more expensive and time consuming and may result in a decision made by one who does not understand industry practices and customs or the parties intent. Accordingly, there should be a maximum effort to bring the parties together to attempt to work out the problem themselves. Of course when lawyers are involved often the compromise position has evaporated, but the good attorney should explore this possibility. Unfortunately, often the lawyer's "killer instinct" will prevail (perhaps also his or her pocketbook concerns) and opportunities for conciliation and mediation will be forgotten or lost.

Possibly the biggest impediment to mediation and settlement, however, is that for most securities claims, the parties have severed their relationship. There is little to gain in compromise, unlike in business disputes when the prospect of future business between the parties may help in more give-and-take in negotiations.

4) CONCLUSIONS AND RECOMMENDATIONS

One commentator has observed that:

> The lack of evidentiary standards and, more importantly, the lack of any specification of the standard of law to be applied in arbitrations are weaknesses in the arbitration process. The lack of a written opinion, the industry-oriented background of the arbitrators, the limited availability of appellate avenues after arbitration and the involuntary nature of the arbitration agreement are also matters of concern.[20]

The securities industry can avoid review by the courts, regulators, or legislative action concerning predispute arbitration agreement easily: by making sure that their brokerage customers (whether margin, cash commodities, or options) understand what they are agreeing to when opening an account. Due to the oligopolistic nature of the securities industry, a response can come about as easily as the industry required customer contracts that almost uniformly contain non-negotiable predispute arbitration clauses. The SROs can continue and expand requirements that action be taken by all members. A new industry standard of behavior will result. Clearly, there is no place for the industry to adopt the position that if the customer does not want to give up his right to litigate claims he shouldn't open a brokerage account. This ostrich approach will work against the industry in the long run.

To ensure that an unsophisticated customer has not been abused by industry power to dictate terms of this relationship, the industry and SEC should go a step further than the most recent pronouncements. They should first require separate agreements regarding arbitration, which may not be a condition to opening an account;[21] second, undertake an affirmative disclosure[22] to be sure that the customer knows the significance of such an agreement and voluntarily agrees to it;[23] third, consider establishment of arbitration bodies independent of the exchanges or industry for securities disputes; and fourth, at the very least, continue revision of the process to ensure that the arbitration process and procedures are fair and equitable.[24] After all, knowledge in the marketplace is the purpose of the securities laws. This should apply to knowledge of the marketplace as well, and disclosure is the keystone of any informed customer. The disclosure of awards is a step in the right direction.

If the above elements exist, even in an industry-monitored investor-broker relationship, the customer should not complain. The change from judicial to arbitral forum will not mean there is a radical difference in ultimate result in such a case. He or she will have been well served by free choice and the efficient, economical, and speedy resolution of disputes in arbitration. If not, in the long run the customer should be able to avoid mandatory predispute arbitration, and probably will ultimately be allowed to do so, whether by state or SEC regulation, or court or legislative action overturning the effect of *McMahon* and *Rodriguez de Quijas*.

To paraphrase the *Wilko* Court: "'[L]et the seller also beware'--and be responsible."[25]

NOTES

1 Of course there is really no reason a customer would sign a predispute arbitration clause if he or she knew the rules--the SRO rules require arbitration of members upon customer demand anyway.

2 Wermiel, *Justices to Mull Stock Fraud Arbitration*, WALL ST. J., Nov. 15, 1988, at B12, col. 2 (remarks of Arthur Schwartzstein, a Washington lawyer representing investors). *See also* Brener v. Becker Paribas Inc., 628 F. Supp. 442, 448 (S.D.N.Y. 1985) (noting the increasing sophistication of industry arbitration).

3 Lusardi, *Enforcement of Arbitration Agreements in Securities Fraud Settlements*, 41 RUTGERS L. REV. 541, 575 (1989).

4 There is "an extreme likelihood [this] will operate against the best interests of an investor . . . against public policy--and the manifest intent of the securities acts." But see the oral argument comments of counsel for the defendant in *Rodriguez de Quijas* in response to a question raised by Justice O'Connor. The lawyer indicated that arbitration would not necessarily take place in New York City and that the practice is to hold arbitration proceedings where the plaintiffs reside. 21 FED. SEC. & L. REP. (BNA) 484 (Mar 31, 1989). This, of course, is not strictly true as the forums are usually located in central regional cities, not necessarily the locale where a claimant actually resides.

5 *Id. See also* Lusardi, *supra* note 3, at 576.

> [I]t would be incongruous for the Court to conclude that an arbitration based on a predispute agreement was incapable of dealing with the issues involved in a securities fraud case, in light of the fact that courts have routinely permitted arbitration based on post-dispute agreements, or when the parties to the agreement are members of securities self-regulatory organizations. Courts have increasingly accepted the proposition that the arbitral decision-making process is reasoned and expert.

6 Justice Blackmun did not think that Congress had abrogated the *Wilko* position in the 1975 amendments to the Exchange Act providing for SEC supervision of the arbitration proceeds of the SROs. He felt Congress was in accord with *Wilko*, as would seem to be supported by the Conference report indicating the "clear understanding of the conferees that this amendment did

not change existing law, as articulated in *Wilko v. Swan*." H.R. Conf. Rep. No. 229, 94th Cong. 1st Sess. 91, 111, reprinted in 1975 U.S. Code Cong. & Admin. News 179, 321. Blackmun certainly was correct that Congress did not take any affirmative action to overturn *Wilko*, despite that finding by the majority. *See also* Shearson/American Express, Inc. v. McMahon, 482 U.S. 220, 242-69 (1987) (Blackmun, J., concurring and dissenting). Justice Stevens in *Rodriguez de Quijas* merely restated his and Blackmun's dissenting positions from *McMahon* and was joined by Blackmun, Brennan, and Marshall. *See* Rodriguez de Quijas v. Shearson/American Express, Inc. 109 S. Ct. 1917, 1922 (1989) (Stevens, J., dissenting). Justice Stevens argued that since *Wilko*, the longstanding interpretation by the courts precluded arbitration of securities claims under the Exchange Act and any mistake in interpretation of legislative intent "is best remedied by the Legislative . . . Branch." *McMahon*, 482 U.S. *Id.* at 269 (Stevens, J., concurring and dissenting).

7 This assumes that the states will not adopt legislation requiring voluntary assent to arbitration in the securities area, or perhaps in all contracts.

8 Fletcher, *Learning to Live With the Federal Arbitration Act--Securities Litigation in a Post-McMahon World*, 37 EMORY L. J. 99, 315 (1988). Fletcher discusses a similar development in admiralty, to the point that the pattern generally shows a gradual co-opting of extralegal processes, such as arbitration, by the legal system with the result being the destruction of the alternative mode and its advantages. *Id.* at 136 (citing J. Auerbach, *Justice Without Law?* EMORY L. J. 96 [1983]).

9 Moulin, *Review of Legislative and Regulatory Issues*, SECURITIES ARBITRATION UPDATE 313, 362 (M. Fitterman and T. Krebsbach eds., 1989).

10 *See* 19 SEC. REG. & L. REP. (BNA) 1387 (Sept. 18, 1987) (describing the SEC recommendations and concluding that they result in making securities arbitration more like litigation).

11 Fletcher, *supra* note 8, at 134-35.

12 American Almond Prod. Co. v. Consolidated Pecan Sales co., 144 F.2d 448, 451 (2d Cir. 1944).

13 Securities Arbitration Reform Act of 1988, 134 CONG. REC. E2,233 (June 30, 1988).

14 Investment Advisors Disclosure and Enforcement Act of 1991, H.R. 2412, 102d Cong., 1st Sess. (1991).

15 15 U.S.C. § 78s(c).

16 Wallace, *Securities Arbitration After McMahon, Rodriguez, and the New Rules: Can Investor's Rights Really Be Protected?* 43 VAND. L. REV. 1199, 1235 (1990).

17 Gregory and Schneider, *Securities Arbitration: A Need for Continued Reform*, 17 NOVA L. REV. 1223, 1249 (1993).

18 *See* Hochman, *Reasoned Awards*, 5 SEC. ARB. COMM. 6, 9-10 (1993).

19 *See* Gilpin, *Fighting It Out Over Arbitration*, N. Y. TIMES (Oct. 31, 1993) F:17.

20 W. Herman, *Arbitration of Securities Disputes: Rodriguez and New Arbitration Rules Leave Investors Holding a Mixed Bag*, 65 IND. L. J. 697, 721 (1990).

21 Such is the practice in the commodities industry. There is a 45 day period to seek reparations under the Community Exchange Act § 14 and the CFTC regulation [17 C.F.R. § 180.5(b)(3) (1988)]. It may be that a similar period necessary for the customer to elect a resolution in all other forums other than the arbitration setting could be imposed in all securities cases. "To hold otherwise would make a mockery of the law of contracts."

22 *See* Rakoff, *Contracts of Adhesion: An Essay in Reconstruction*, 96 HARV. L. R. 1174, 1274 (1983), which states: "The carrier cannot merely recite in a form document the existence of choice and direct its agents to be silent" when the customer is signing, probably without carefully reading, the myriad of documents used to open a cash, margin and/or commodities account.

23 Two of the issues that should be disclosed to customers are the costs of litigation versus arbitration and recovery percentages of claims in each. *See* chapter 10 for a more detailed analysis indicating that arbitration may be the best way for a customer to proceed due to its lower costs, no matter what the impact of arbitration awards. Of course, there is reason why arbitration results in a higher percentage of claim recoveries--in most instances the claims themselves are limited to those with which the customer feels he is most comfortable and likely to succeed. Perhaps in litigation, attorneys will throw in every possible claim and they will measure the recovery. Nevertheless, the present state of arbitration in the securities industry is principally flawed by the take-it-or-leave-it nature of the brokerage contract as now presented to the customer. It makes more sense, this author believes, to provide election after giving information regarding the processes available for dispute resolution. Let the customer decision be made on full and fair information from which the customer can make an informed choice. If the commission rates are different, the differences should be reflected in costs to the firm, and this election can be made on a full and fair information basis as well. In this manner, the election will then be an informed choice by the consumer. With the exception of the two-tier commissions, disclosure and non-mandatory arbitration clauses seem to work well in the commodities segment of the securities industry. It may well be time for the SEC to adopt the CFTC's position and promulgate another regulation with the same result as Rule 15c2-2: protection against overreaching by the industry as it prepares form-pad contracts.

24 And the SEC should take the initiative in revising its role from reaction to action, that is, require the SROs to take action "to protect investors and public interest" as required by Exchange Act. 15 U.S.C. § 1 780-3(b)(6) (1982).

25 *See generally* Comment, *Predispute Arbitration Agreements Between Brokers and Investors: Should the Extension of Wilko Be Extended?* 50 ALB. L. REV. 339, 341 (1987).

APPENDIXES

APPENDIX A

Federal Arbitration Act
Title 9
United States Code
Arbitration
Act July 30, 1947, c. 392, § 1, 61 Stat. 669

An Act to enact title 9, United States Code, "Arbitration," codifying the general and permanent laws relating to arbitration.

Be it enacted by the Senate and House of Representatives of the United States of America in Congress assembled, That:

The general and permanent laws relating to arbitration are revised, codified, and enacted as title 9, United States Code, "Arbitration," and may be cited as "9 U.S.C. § __ ,", as follows:

TITLE 9
ARBITRATION
CHAPTER 1 - GENERAL PROVISIONS

Sec.

§ 1. "Maritime transactions" and "commerce" defined; exceptions to operation of title

"Maritime transactions," as herein defined, means charter parties, bills of lading of water carriers, agreements relating to wharfage, supplies furnished vessels or repairs to vessels, collisions, or any other matters in foreign commerce which, if the subject of controversy, would be embraced within admiralty jurisdiction; "commerce," as herein defined, means commerce among the several States or with foreign nations, or in any Territory of the United States or in the District of Columbia, or between any such territory and another, or between any such Territory and any State or foreign nation, or between the District of Columbia and any State or Territory or foreign nation, but nothing herein contained shall apply to contracts of employment of seamen, railroad employees, or any other class of workers engaged in foreign or interstate commerce.

§ 2. Validity, irrevocability, and enforcement of agreements to arbitrate

A written provision in any maritime transaction or a contract evidencing a transaction involving commerce to settle by arbitration a controversy thereafter arising out of such contract or transaction, or the refusal to perform the whole or any part thereof, or an agreement in writing to submit to arbitration an existing controversy arising out of such a contract, transaction, or refusal, shall be valid, irrevocable, and enforceable, save upon such grounds as exist at law or in equity for the revocation of any contract.

§ 3. Stay of proceedings where issue therein referable to arbitration

If any suit or proceeding be brought in any of the courts of the United States upon any issue referable to arbitration under an agreement in writing for such arbitration, the court in which such suit is pending, upon being satisfied that the issue involved in such suit or proceeding is referable to arbitration under such an agreement, shall on application of one of the parties stay the trial of the action until such arbitration has been had in accordance with the terms of the agreement, providing the applicant for the stay is not in default in proceeding with such arbitration.

§ 4. Failure to arbitrate under agreement; petition to United States court having jurisdiction for order to compel arbitration; notice and service thereof; hearing and determination

A party aggrieved by the alleged failure, neglect, or refusal of another to arbitrate under a written agreement for arbitration may petition any United States district court which, save for such agreement, would have jurisdiction under title 28, in a civil action or in admiralty of the subject matter of a suit arising out of the controversy between the parties, for an order directing that such arbitration proceed in the manner provided for in such agreement. Five days' notice in writing of such application shall be served upon the party in default. Service thereof shall be made in the manner provided by the Federal Rules of Civil Procedure. The court shall hear the parties, and upon being satisfied that the making of the agreement for arbitration or the failure to comply therewith is not in issue, the court shall make an order directing the parties to proceed to arbitration in accordance with the terms of the agreement. The hearing and proceedings, under such agreement, shall be within the district in which the petition for an order directing such arbitration is filed. If the making of the arbitration agreement or the failure, neglect, or refusal to perform the same be in issue, the court shall proceed summarily to the trial thereof. If no jury trial be demanded by the party alleged to be in default, or if the matter in dispute is within admiralty jurisdiction, the court shall hear and determine such issue. Where such an issue is raised, the party alleged to be in default may, except in cases of admiralty, on or before the return day of the notice of application, demand a jury trial of such issue, and upon such demand the court shall make an order referring the issue or issues to a jury in the manner provided by the Federal Rules of Civil Procedure, or may specially call a jury for that purpose. If the jury find that no agreement in writing for arbitration was made or that there is no default in proceeding thereunder, the proceeding shall be dismissed. If the jury find that an agreement for arbitration was made in writing and that there is a default in proceeding thereunder, the court shall make an order summarily directing the parties to proceed with arbitration in accordance with the terms thereof.

§ 5. Appointment of arbitrators or umpire

If in the agreement provision be made for a method of naming or appointing an arbitrator or arbitrators or an umpire, such method shall be followed; but if no method be provided therein, or if a method be provided and any party thereto shall fail to avail himself of such method, or if for any other reason there shall be a lapse in the naming of an arbitrator or arbitrators or umpire, or in filling a vacancy, then upon the application of either party to the controversy the court shall designate and appoint an arbitrator or arbitrators or umpire, as the case may require, who shall act under the said agreement with the same force and effect as if he or they had been specifically named therein; and unless otherwise provided in the agreement the arbitration shall be by a single arbitrator.

§ 6. Application heard as motion

Any application to the court hereunder shall be made and heard in the manner provided by law for the making and hearing of motions, except as otherwise herein expressly provided.

§ 7. Witnesses before arbitrators; fees; compelling attendance

The arbitrators selected either as prescribed in this title or otherwise, or a majority of them, may summon in writing any person to attend before them or any of them as a witness and in a proper case to bring with him or them any book, record, document, or paper which may be deemed material as evidence in the case. The fees for such attendance shall be the same as the fees of witnesses before masters of the United States courts. Said summons shall issue in the name of the arbitrator or arbitrators, or a majority of them, and shall be signed by the arbitrators, or a majority of them, and shall be directed to the said person and shall be served in the same manner as subpoenas to appear and testify before the court; if any person or persons so summoned to testify shall refuse or neglect to obey said summons, upon petition the United States district court for the district in which such arbitrators, or a majority of them, are sitting may compel the attendance of such person or persons before said arbitrator or arbitrators, or punish said person or persons for contempt in the same manner provided by law for securing the attendance of witnesses or their punishment for neglect or refusal to attend in the courts of the United States.

§ 8. Proceedings begun by libel in admiralty and seizure of vessel or property

If the basis of jurisdiction be a cause of action otherwise justiciable in admiralty, then, notwithstanding anything herein to the contrary, the party claiming to be aggrieved may begin his proceeding hereunder by libel and seizure of the vessel or other property of the other party according to the usual course of admiralty proceedings, and the court shall then have jurisdiction to direct the parties to proceed with the arbitration and shall retain jurisdiction to enter its decree upon the award.

§ 9. Award of arbitrators; confirmation; jurisdiction; procedure

If the parties in their agreement have agreed that a judgment of the court shall be entered upon the award made pursuant to the arbitration, and shall specify the court, then at any time within one year after the award is made any party to the arbitration may apply to the court so specified for an order confirming the award, and thereupon the court must grant such an order unless the award is vacated, modified, or corrected as prescribed in sections 10 and 11 of this title. If no court is specified in the agreement of the parties, then such application may be made to the United States court in and for the district within which such award was made. Notice of the application shall be served upon the adverse party, and thereupon the court shall have jurisdiction of such party as though he had appeared generally in the proceeding. If the adverse party is a resident of the district within which the award was made, such service shall be made upon the adverse party or his attorney as prescribed by law for service of notice of motion in an action in the same court. If the adverse party shall be a nonresident, then the notice of the application shall be served by the marshal of any district within which the adverse party may be found in like manner as other process of the court.

§ 10. Same; vacation; grounds; rehearing

In either of the following cases the United States court in and for the district wherein the award was made may make an order vacating the award upon the application of any party to the arbitration -

(a) Where the award was procured by corruption, fraud, or undue means.

(b) Where there was evident partiality or corruption in the arbitrators, or either of them.

(c) Where the arbitrators were guilty of misconduct in refusing to postpone the hearing, upon sufficient cause shown, or in refusing to hear evidence pertinent and material to the controversy; or of any other misbehavior by which the rights of any party have been prejudiced.

(d) Where the arbitrators exceeded their powers, or so imperfectly executed them that a mutual, final, and definite award upon the subject matter submitted was not made.

(e) Where an award is vacated and the time within which the agreement required the award to be made has not expired the court may, in its discretion, direct a rehearing by the arbitrators.

§ 11. Same; Modification or correction; grounds; order

In either of the following cases the United States court in and for the district wherein the award was made may make an order modifying or correcting the award upon the application of any party to the arbitration -

(a) Where there was an evident material miscalculation of figures or an evident material mistake in the description of any person, thing, or property referred to in the award.

(b) Where the arbitrators have awarded upon a matter not submitted to them, unless it is a matter not affecting the merits of the decision upon the matter submitted.

(c) Where the award is imperfect in matter of form not affecting the merits of the controversy.

The order may modify and correct the award, so as to effect the intent thereof and promote justice between the parties.

§ 12. Notice of motions to vacate or modify; service; stay of proceedings

Notice of a motion to vacate, modify, or correct an award must be served upon the adverse party or his attorney within three months after the award is filed or delivered. If the adverse party is a resident of the district within which the award was made, such service shall be made upon the adverse party or his attorney as prescribed by law for service of notice of motion in an action in the same court. If the adverse party shall be a nonresident then the notice of the application shall be served by the marshal of any district within which the adverse party may be found in like manner as other process of the court. For the purposes of the motion any judge who might make an order to stay the proceedings in an action brought in the same court may make an order, to be served with the notice of motion, staying the proceedings of the adverse party to enforce the award.

§ 13. Papers filed with order on Motions; judgment; docketing; force and effect; enforcement

The party moving for an order confirming, modifying, or correction an award shall, at the time such order is filed with the clerk for the entry of judgment thereon, also file the following papers with the clerk:

(a) The agreement; the selection or appointment, if any, of an additional arbitrator or umpire; and each written extension of the time, if any, within which to make the award.

(b) The award.

(c) Each notice, affidavit, or other paper used upon an application to confirm, modify, or correct the award, and a copy of each order of the court upon such an application.

The judgement shall be docketed as if it was rendered in an action.

The judgment so entered shall have the some force and effect, in all respects, as, and be subject to all the provisions of law relating to, a judgment in an action; and it may be enforced as if it had been rendered in an action in the court in which it is entered.

§ 14. Contracts not affected

This title shall not apply to contracts made prior to January 1, 1926.

§ 15. Inapplicability of the Act of State doctrine

Enforcement of arbitral agreements, confirmation of arbitral awards, and execution upon judgments based on orders confirming such awards shall not be refused on the basis of the Act of State doctrine. (Added Pub. L. 100-669, § 1, Nov. 16, 1988, 102 Stat. 3969.)

§ 16. Appeals

(a) An appeal may be taken from -

(1) an order -

(A) refusing a stay of any action under section 3 of this title,

(B) denying a petition under section 4 of this title to order arbitration to proceed,

(C) denying an application under section 206 of this title to compel arbitration,

(D) confirming or denying confirmation of an award or partial award, or

(E) modifying, correcting, or vacating an award;

(2) an interlocutory order granting, continuing, or modifying an injunction against an arbitration that is subject to this

title; or

(3) a final decision with respect to an arbitration that is subject to this title.

(b) Except as otherwise provided in section 1292(b) of title 28, an appeal may not be taken from an interlocutory order -

(1) granting a stay of any action under section 3 of this title;

(2) directing arbitration to proceed under section 4 of this title;

(3) compelling arbitration under section 206 of this title; or

(4) refusing to enjoin an arbitration that is subject to this title.

APPENDIX B

New York Arbitration Statute
Article 75--Arbitration

§ 7501. Effect of arbitration agreement

A written agreement to submit any controversy thereafter arising or any existing controversy to arbitration is enforceable without regard to the justiciable character of the controversy and confers jurisdiction on the courts of the state to enforce it and to enter judgment on an award. In determining any matter arising under this article, the court shall not consider whether the claim with respect to which arbitration is sought is tenable, or otherwise pass upon the merits of the dispute.

§ 7502. Applications to the court; venue; statutes of limitation; provisional remedies

(a) A special proceeding shall be used to bring before a court the first application arising out of an arbitrable controversy which is not made by motion in a pending action. The proceeding shall be brought in the court and county specified in the agreement; or, if none be specified, in a court in the county in which one of the parties resides or is doing business, or, if there is no such county, in a court in any county; or in a court in the county in which the arbitration was held. All subsequent applications shall be made by motion in the pending action or the special proceeding.

(b) If, at the time that a demand for arbitration was made or a notice of intention to arbitrate was served, the claim sought to be arbitrated would have been barred by limitation of time had it been asserted in a court of the state, a party may assert the limitation as a bar to the arbitration on an application to the court as provided in section 7503 or subdivision (b) of section 7511. The failure to assert such bar by such application shall not preclude its assertion before the arbitrators, who may, in their sole discretion, apply or not apply the bar. Except as provided in subdivision (b) of section 7511, such exercise of discretion by the arbitrators shall not be subject to review by a court on an application to confirm, vacate or modify the award.

(c) The supreme court in the county in which an arbitration is pending, or if not yet commenced, in a county specified in subdivision (a), may entertain an application for an order of attachment or for a preliminary injunction in connection with an arbitrable controversy, but only upon the ground that the award to which the applicant may be entitled may be rendered ineffectual without such provisional relief. The provisions of articles 62 and 63 of this chapter [CPLR] shall apply to the application, including those relating to undertakings and to the time for commencement of an action (arbitration shall be deemed an action for this purpose) if the application is made before commencement, except that the sole ground for the granting of the remedy shall be as stated above. The form of the application shall be as provided in subdivision (a).

§ 7503. Application to compel or stay arbitration; stay of action; notice of intention to arbitrate

(a) A party aggrieved by the failure of another to arbitrate may apply for an order compelling arbitration. Where there is no substantial question whether a valid agreement was made or complied with, and the claim sought to be arbitrated is not barred by limitation under subdivision (b) of section 7502, the court shall direct the parties to arbitrate. Where any such question is raised, it shall be tried forthwith in said court. If an issue claimed to be arbitrable is involved in an action pending in a court having jurisdiction to hear a motion to compel arbitration, the application shall be made by motion in that action. If the application is granted, the order shall operate to stay a pending or subsequent action, or so much of it as is referable to arbitration.

(b) Subject to the provisions of subdivision (c), a party who has not participated in the arbitration and who has not made or been served with an application to compel arbitration, may apply to stay arbitration on the ground what a valid agreement was not made or has not been complied with or that the claim sought to be arbitrated is barred by limitation under subdivision (b) of section 7502.

(c) A party may serve upon another party a demand for arbitration or a notice of intention to arbitrate, specifying the agreement pursuant to which arbitration is sought and the name and address of the party serving the notice, or of an officer or agent thereof if such party is an association or corporation, and stating that unless the party served applies to stay the arbitration within twenty days after such service he shall thereafter be precluded from objecting that a valid agreement was not made or has not been complied with and from asserting in court the bar of a limitation of time. Such notice or demand shall be served in the same manner as a summons or by registered or certified mail, return receipt requested. An application to stay arbitration must be made by the party served within twenty days after service after service upon him of the notice or demand, or he shall be so precluded. Notice of such application shall be served in the same manner as a summons or by registered or certified mail, return receipt requested. Service of the application may be made upon the adverse party, or upon his attorney if the attorney's name appears on the demand for arbitration or the notice of intention to arbitrate. Service of the application by mail shall be timely if such application is posted within the prescribed period. Any provision on an arbitration agreement or arbitration rules which waives the right to apply for a stay of arbitration is hereby declared null and void.

§ 7504. Court appointment of arbitrator

If the arbitration agreement does not provide for a method of appointment of an arbitrator, or if the agreed method fails or for any reason is not followed, or if an arbitrator fails to act and his successor has not been appointed, the court, on application of a party, shall appoint an arbitrator.

§ 7505. Powers of arbitrator

An arbitrator and any attorney of record in the arbitration proceeding has the power to issue subpoenas. An arbitrator has the power to administer oaths.

§ 7506. Hearing

(a) Before hearing any testimony, an arbitrator shall be sworn to hear and decide the controversy faithfully and fairly by an officer authorized to administer an oath.

(b) The arbitrator shall appoint a time and place for the hearing and notify the parties in writing personally or by registered or certified mail not less than eight days before the hearing. The arbitrator may adjourn or postpone the hearing. The court, upon application of any party, may direct the arbitrator to proceed promptly with the hearing and determination of the controversy.

(c) The parties are entitled to be heard, to present evidence and to cross-examine witnesses. Notwithstanding the failure of a party duly notified to appear, the arbitrator may hear and determine the controversy upon the evidence produced.

(d) A party has the right to be represented by an attorney and may claim such right at any time as to any part of the arbitration or hearings which have not taken place. This right may not be waived. If a party is represented by an attorney, papers to be served on the party shall be served upon his attorney.

(e) The hearing shall be conducted by all the arbitrators, but a majority may determine any question and render an award.

(f) Except as provided in subdivision (d), a requirement of this section may be waived by written consent of the parties and it is waived if the parties continue with the arbitration without objection.

§ 7507. Award; form; time; delivery

Except as provided in section 7508, the award shall be in writing, signed and affirmed by the arbitrator making it within the time fixed by the agreement, or, if the time is not fixed, within such time as the court orders. The parties may in writing extend the time either before or after its expiration. A party waives the objection that an award was not made within the time required unless he notifies the arbitrator in writing of his objection prior to the delivery of the award to him. The arbitrator shall deliver a copy of the award to each party in the manner provided in the agreement, or, if no provision is so made, personally or by registered or certified mail, return receipt requested.

§ 7508. Award by confession

(a) An award by confession may be made for money due or to become due at any time before an award is otherwise made. The award shall be based upon a statement, verified by each party, containing an authorization to make the award, the sum of the award or the method of ascertaining it, and the facts constituting the liability.

(b) The award may be made at any time within three months after the statement is verified.

(c) The award may be made by an arbitrator or by the agency or person named by the parties to designate the arbitrator.

§ 7509. Modification of award by arbitrator

On written application of a party to the arbitrators within twenty days after delivery of the award to the applicant, the arbitrators may modify the award upon the grounds stated in subdivision (c) of section 7511. Written notice of the application shall be given to other parties to the arbitration. Written objection to modification must be served on the arbitrators and other parties to the arbitration within ten days of receipt of the notice. The arbitrators shall dispose of any application made under this section in writing, signed and acknowledged by them, within thirty days after either written objection to modification had been served on them or the time for serving said objection has expired, which ever is earlier. The parties may in writing extend the time for such disposition either before or after its expiration.

§ 7510 Confirmation of award

The court shall confirm an award upon application of a party made within one year after its delivery to him, unless the award is vacated or modified upon a ground specified in section 7511.

§ 7511 Vacating or modifying award

(a) An application to vacate or modify an award may be made by a party within ninety days after its delivery to him.

(b) .

1. The award shall be vacated on the application of a party who either participated in the arbitration or was served with notice of intention to arbitrate if the court finds that the rights of that party were prejudiced by:

(i) corruption, fraud or misconduct in procuring the award; or

(ii) partiality of an arbitrator appointed as a neutral, except where the award was by confession; or

(iii) an arbitrator, or agency or person making the award exceeded his power or so imperfectly executed it that a final and definite award upon the subject matter submitted was not made: or

(iv) failure to follow the procedure of this article, unless the party applying to vacate the award continued with the arbitration with notice of the defect and without objection.

2. The award shall be vacated on the application of a party who neither participated in the arbitration nor was served with a notice of intention to arbitrate if the court finds that:

(i) the rights of that party were prejudiced by one of the grounds specified in paragraph one; or

(ii) a valid agreement to arbitrate was not made; or

(iii) the agreement to arbitrate had not been complied with; or

(iv) the arbitrated claim was barred by limitation under subdivision (b) of section 7502.

(c) The court shall modify the award if:

1. there was a miscalculation of figures or a mistake in the description of any person, thing or property referred to in the award; or

2. the arbitrators have awarded upon a matter not submitted to them and the award may be corrected without affecting the merits of the decision upon the issues submitted; or

3. the award is imperfect in a matter of form, not affecting the merits of the controversy.

(d) Upon vacating an award, the court may order a rehearing and determination of all or any of the issues either before the same arbitrator or before a new arbitrator appointed in accordance with this article. Time in any provision limiting the time for a hearing or award shall be measured from the date of such order or rehearing, whichever is appropriate, or a time may be specified by the court.

(e) Upon the granting of a motion to modify, the court shall confirm the award as modified; upon the denial of a motion to vacate or modify, it shall confirm the award.

§ 7512. Death or incompetency of a party

Where a party dies after making a written agreement to submit a controversy to arbitration, the proceedings may be begun or continued upon the application of, or notice to, his executor or administrator or, where it relates to real property, his distributee or devisee who has succeeded to his interest in the real property. Where a committee of the property or of the person of a party to such an agreement is appointed, the proceedings may be continued upon the application of, or notice to, the committee. Upon the death or incompetency of a party, the court may extend the time within which an application to confirm, vacate or modify the award or to stay arbitration must be made. Where a party has died since an award was delivered, the proceedings thereupon are the same as where a party dies after a verdict.

§ 7513. Fees and expenses

Unless otherwise provided in the agreement to arbitrate, the arbitrators' expenses and fees, together with other expenses, not including attorney's fees, incurred in the conduct of the arbitration, shall be paid as provided in the award, The court, on application, may reduce or disallow any fee or expense it finds excessive or allocate it as justice requires.

§ 7514. Judgement on an award

(a) A judgment shall be entered upon the confirmation of an award.

(b) The judgment-roll consists of the original or a copy of the agreement and each written extension of time within which to make an award; the statement required by section 7508 where the award was by confession; the award; each paper submitted to the court and each order of the court upon an application under sections 7510 and 7511; and a copy of the judgment.

APPENDIX C

S.I.C.A. ARBITRATION PROCEDURES

MARCH 1992

This pamphlet has been prepared by the Securities Industry Conference on Arbitration (SICA), a group composed of representatives of various self-regulatory organizations, the Securities Industry Association, and public members. SICA established a uniform system for the resolution of disputes involving investors and broker/dealers, which has been adopted by each of the self-regulatory organizations.

ARBITRATION PROCEDURES

Although most business in the securities industry is completed without a problem, disputes and controversies will occasionally arise. Such disputes and controversies can be resolved by impartial arbitration at one of the organizations listed on the last page of this pamphlet. Arbitrations are conducted in accordance with the Uniform Code of Arbitration ("Uniform Code") as developed by the Securities Industry Conference on Arbitration and the rules of the sponsoring organization where the claim is filed.

There are some differences among the rules of the sponsoring organizations, such as who may serve as public arbitrators, the availability of prior awards, and whether your name will be made publicly available. Any questions regarding arbitration may be addressed to the Directors of Arbitration or their staff at the sponsoring organizations. In addition to initiating an arbitration, investors may file their complaints with the appropriate regulatory authorities, such as the Securities and Exchange Commission, state securities commissions, or one of the self-regulatory organizations listed on the last page, when they believe there has been fraud or that other investors may be at risk. The regulatory agencies may then investigate the complaint and, if warranted, censure, fine, or suspend a wrongdoer.

This pamphlet is designed to assist prospective parties and their attorneys by explaining arbitration procedures and is not designed to give legal advice to any party or to anyone who contemplates use of these procedures. The procedures described in this pamphlet were developed for parties who represent themselves in an arbitration proceeding as well as those represented by counsel. The pamphlet explains the procedures set forth in the rules and answers questions regarding them but is not an interpretation of the rules or a substitute for the rules. We recommend that prospective parties carefully read the rules as well as this pamphlet.

WHAT IS ARBITRATION?

Arbitration is a method of having a dispute between two or more parties resolved by impartial persons who are knowledgeable in the areas in controversy. Those persons are called arbitrators. Arbitration of broker/dealer disputes has long been used as an alternative to the courts because it is a prompt and inexpensive means of resolving complicated issues. There are certain laws governing the conduct of an arbitration proceeding that must be considered by those planning to use arbitration to resolve the dispute. Most importantly, perhaps, is the fact that an arbitration award is final and binding, subject to review by a court only on a very limited basis. Parties should recognize, too, that in choosing arbitration as a means of resolving a dispute, they generally give up their right to pursue the matter through the courts.

WHAT DISPUTES ARE ELIGIBLE FOR ARBITRATION?

In considering whether to initiate arbitration, it is important to keep in mind that, generally, a public customer has a right to require a broker/dealer to submit for arbitration only disputes relating to or arising out of the business activities of the broker/dealer.

When deciding where to file your claim, you should determine which self-regulatory organization (SRO) supervises the markets where the transaction occurred or the securities are listed. The Uniform Code provides that an SRO may, with the consent of the claimant, refer a case to the appropriate forum where the transaction occurred or the securities are listed.

An additional factor to be noted is that a controversy is not eligible for submission to arbitration if six or more years have elapsed from the date of the event giving rise to the dispute. The arbitrators also may dismiss a claim barred by shorter applicable state or federal statutes of limitations. If there is a question about the statute of limitations, you should consult an attorney.

Even after a customer has signed the agreement to arbitrate, the customer may request either the sponsoring organization or the arbitrators to permit that customer to proceed with his or her claim in court. The customer should be aware, however, that in most cases the sponsoring organization and the arbitrators will retain jurisdiction and proceed with the arbitration.

A newly adopted section of the Uniform Code states that a claim submitted as a class action shall not be eligible for arbitration. The rule also sets forth the circumstances where a claim encompassed by a putative or certified class action may or may not be eligible to be filed in arbitration. For further guidance, you should refer to the rule and discuss its application to a particular case with the staff of the SRO where you intend to file your claim.

WHO ARE THE ARBITRATORS?

Arbitrators are impartial persons who are knowledgeable in the areas in controversy. Each sponsoring organization maintains a roster of individuals whose professional qualifications and experience qualify them for service as arbitrators. The arbitrators are not employees of the sponsoring organization and they, not the sponsoring organization, will decide your dispute. The arbitrators do, however, receive an honorarium from the SROs.

The Director of Arbitration will appoint a panel, usually consisting of one or three arbitrators. Unless a customer elects otherwise, the majority of the members of such panels are individuals referred to as "public arbitrators" who are neither associated with nor employed by a broker/dealer or securities industry organization.

The Director of Arbitration will inform the parties of the names and business affiliations of the selected arbitrators, their employment histories for the last ten years, as well as any conflict information disclosed pursuant to the Uniform Code. Some parties are interested in previous awards issued by prospective arbitrators. Each sponsoring organization has developed procedures to make available information on public customer awards issued since May, 1989.

CAN I BE REPRESENTED BY AN ATTORNEY?

Parties have an absolute right to be represented by an attorney and may do so at any stage of the arbitration. Parties should be aware that, even if they do not elect to be represented by counsel, the other party may have an attorney, and they can assume that broker/dealers will be represented by an attorney.

Any party represented by counsel should notify the Director of Arbitration of the counsel's name and address either in the Statement of Claim or the Statement of Answer or by a separate written notice. After such notification, communications concerning the case will be addressed to the counsel.

The sponsoring organizations cannot recommend or provide counsel in the arbitration nor can employees of that organization provide legal advice. Parties who do not have counsel and wish to be represented may want to contact the local bar association for a referral.

HOW IS ARBITRATION BEGUN?

To begin arbitration, the prospective claimant must do the following:

(1) **Statement of Claim**--File with the Director of Arbitration a typewritten or printed document stating the claim. This document should set forth the details of the dispute, including all relevant dates and names, in a clear, concise, and chronological fashion and should conclude by indicating what relief (e.g., money damages in a specific amount, performance of a particular agreement, interest, etc.) is requested. The claimant should attach copies of documents and supporting materials as exhibits to the Statement of Claim. The claimant should provide sufficient copies for each party, the arbitrators, and the self-regulatory organization.

(2) **Small-Claims Procedures**--If the amount of the claim is $ 10,000 or less, the claim will be processed under the Simplified Arbitration Procedures. In public customer disputes, unless the public customer requests a hearing, the claim will be decided solely on the basis of reading the parties' submissions. The arbitrator, however, also may request a hearing or require a party to submit additional documentation. Parties may ask to submit additional documents to an arbitrator who is deciding the case without a hearing.

(3) Service of Pleadings--After the initial Statement of Claim is served by the Director of Arbitration, it is each party's responsibility to provide every other party directly with any further pleadings, motions, or correspondence. In addition, it is each party's responsibility to simultaneously provide sufficient copies directly to the sponsoring SRO for the arbitrators and its files. Service of the filings and correspondence on the sponsoring SRO and the other parties should be made on the same date and by the same means (i.e., via overnight mail, facsimile, etc.)

(4) Counsel--State whether the claimant will be represented by an attorney and, if so, the attorney's name, address, and telephone number.

(5) Location--State where the claimant wants the case to be heard and the reasons for that choice. The actual decision as to place of hearing is made by the Director of Arbitration. Arbitrators can be empaneled in many of the major urban areas throughout the country, but consideration generally will be given to a number of factors, including the convenience of the parties, the availability of necessary records or witnesses, and the availability of qualified arbitrators. Generally, in public customer cases, the hearing location is *close to* where the customer resided when the dispute arose regardless of a predispute agreement to the contrary.

(6) Complex Cases--In appropriate cases, parties may request special services such as mediation, findings of facts and conclusions of law, expedited hearings, and the appointment of arbitrators with special qualifications. Parties seeking special or additional services should advise the sponsoring SRO at the earliest time possible. Additional fees may be charged for these services. In many complex cases, the parties may desire block scheduling of hearing dates. To the greatest extent possible, such cases will be scheduled in three-day blocks.

(7) Arbitrators--The proposed panel will be composed of a majority of persons from outside the securities industry. If a public customer would like a panel consisting of a majority of arbitrators from the securities industry, he or she should indicate that preference in writing when filing the claim.

(8) Submission Agreement--Complete and return three signed and notarized copies of the Submission Agreement provided by the sponsoring organization. By signing the Submission Agreement, the claimant agrees to submit the dispute to arbitration and to abide by the decision (the "award") of the arbitrators. The claimant also agrees to be bound by the decision of the arbitrators with regard to any counterclaim (a claim against the claimant) permitted under these procedures that may be brought by an opposing party. Once a Submission Agreement has been signed, the procedures and timing set out in the Uniform Code become operative and binding. Generally, parties may not withdraw the Submission Agreement and Claim without the consent of either the other parties or the arbitrators.

(9) Filing Fees and Deposits--Include a check or money order made payable to the sponsoring organization for the appropriate non-refundable filing fee and hearing session deposit. Where multiple hearing sessions are scheduled or conducted the arbitrators are authorized to require additional hearing session deposits by one or more parties. Additional deposits also may be required to be made for prehearing conferences with an arbitrator and for the postponement of a scheduled hearing date after the arbitrators have been selected. The arbitrators will determine in the final award if these deposits will be returned or assessed to another party. See the arbitration rules of the sponsoring SRO for the definition of a hearing session, as well as the appropriate fee and deposit.

(10) Disclosure of Arbitration Award--At some sponsoring organizations, public customers must state in writing whether they either permit or decline to permit the inclusion of their names in the public version of the award.

(11) Incomplete Filing of a Claim--A filing may be returned if it does not comport with the rules.

The Statement of Claim, including exhibits, Submission Agreement, and non-refundable filing fee and hearing session deposit should be submitted to the Director of Arbitration of the sponsoring organization at the address listed at the end of this pamphlet. All pleadings, correspondence, and exhibits after the claim is served must be sent to all parties directly with sufficient additional copies sent to the Director of Arbitration for the arbitrators and for the Arbitration Department.

WHAT HAPPENS AFTER THE CLAIM IS FILED?

Once the Statement of Claim has been received, the Director of Arbitration will send it to the opposing party (the "respondent"). Any member (e.g., brokerage houses) of an organization listed on the last page of this booklet may be a party in an arbitration proceeding. Similarly, an employee and/or representative of any such member also may be named as a party.

Following the receipt of the claim, the respondent has 20 calendar days in the case of a small-claim arbitration and 20 business days in all other arbitrations to provide an answer, unless an extension of time has been granted by the Director of Arbitration. It is within the discretion of the Director of Arbitration to grant such extensions even over the objection of a party. However, the Director of Arbitration will consider the objection when determining the length of the extension.

The respondent may assert a related counterclaim as part of its answer, or may file a claim against a third party; that is, a claim against another person who may bear responsibility for any of the alleged damages. Generally, a claim is considered to be related if it pertains to the customer's account at the broker/dealer. In support of its defense or counterclaim, the respondent should attach copies of documents and supporting materials to its answer.

The respondent also should send to each party an executed Submission Agreement and a copy of the respondent's answer and any counterclaim. The respondent's executed Submission Agreement and answer shall also be filed with the Director of Arbitration, with additional copies for the arbitrator(s) along with any deposit required under the Schedule of Fees. On receipt of an answer containing a counterclaim, the claimant has ten calendar days in the case of a small-claim arbitration and ten business days in all other arbitrations to file a reply to any counterclaim. The claimant also should send to each party a copy of the reply to a counterclaim. The reply also shall be filed with the Director of Arbitration with additional copies for the arbitrators.

Service on a party may be effected by mail or other means of delivery. Filing with the Director of Arbitration should be made on the same date and by the same means as service on a party.

APPOINTMENT OF ARBITRATORS

The Director of Arbitration will appoint, as appropriate, an arbitrator or panel of arbitrators. The Director of Arbitration will notify the parties of the names current affiliations, and ten years' business histories of the proposed arbitrators. In addition, parties will be informed of any information disclosed pursuant to the Uniform Code and the Code of Ethics for Arbitrators by any arbitrator. The arbitrators will be informed of the names of the parties to the dispute, counsel, witnesses, and the nature of the issues raised. If any arbitrator determines that he or she cannot render a fair and impartial award, the Director of Arbitration will appoint a substitute arbitrator.

In a small claim, if the arbitrator believes the controversy is such that additional expertise is needed, he or she can direct that an arbitration panel be formed with two additional arbitrators. The majority of this panel will be from the public. The arbitrator also may request that a hearing be held or that additional documentation be provided.

CAN I CHALLENGE AN ARBITRATOR?

A party has an absolute right to request that one arbitrator on the panel be replaced without giving a reason for the request. This right may be exercised by filing a written notice of a challenge with the Director of Arbitration. A party should supplement his or her written notice with a telephone call to the sponsoring organization. In addition, in all arbitrations, if any party has reason to believe that an arbitrator cannot render a fair and impartial award, he or she should immediately notify the Director of Arbitration. The arbitrator will be disqualified if the objection is based on facts that reasonably support the challenge. Each party is entitled to an unlimited number challenges for cause.

Each arbitrator must swear or affirm to render a fair and just award based on the documents and evidence presented by the parties. Also, no party should attempt to communicate directly with any of the arbitrators. Such communication may render the decision of the arbitrator invalid. Any communication for the arbitrators must be addressed through the Director of Arbitration.

HOW DO I PREPARE FOR A HEARING?

Parties must make every effort to prepare the case in advance of the hearing so that it may be resolved promptly and justly. Preparation includes arranging for witnesses and documentary evidence to be available for presentation to the arbitrators at the hearing.

The parties shall, at least ten calendar days prior to the first scheduled hearing date, serve on each other copies of documents (including graphs, charts, and recordings) they intend to present at the hearing and identify witnesses they intend to present at the hearing. Failure to comply with this requirement may result in the arbitrators excluding any document not exchanged or witnesses not identified. Arbitrators will consider such action at the request of a party. If all parties agree, they may submit exhibits in addition to those in the Statement of Claim to the Director of Arbitration for forwarding to the arbitrators prior to the hearing,.

Each party is to bring sufficient copies of any documents it intends to introduce as evidence at the hearings for each arbitrator and for the files of the SRO.

The parties should cooperate in the voluntary exchange of documents and information to expedite the arbitration. Any request for documents or other information should be specific, relate to the matter in controversy, and afford the party to whom the request is made a reasonable period of time to respond without interfering with the time set for the hearing. Document production and information exchange is to be accomplished within the time set forth in the Uniform Code.

On the written request of a party or an arbitrator or at the discretion of the Director of Arbitration, a prehearing conference will be scheduled. The Director of Arbitration will set the time and place of a prehearing conference and appoint either a staff person or an arbitrator to preside. The prehearing conference may be held by telephone, by written submission, or in person. Under the rules, there are timetables for parties either to produce requested information or to object to the production requests. If a prehearing conference without an arbitrator does not resolve the outstanding issues, those information-request disputes or issues will be referred to a single arbitrator prior to the first hearing. Where possible, each party should submit to the SRO in advance of the prehearing conference a concise outline of the outstanding issues to be resolved by the single arbitrator. The single arbitrator has the authority to issue subpoenas, direct appearances of witnesses and production of documents, set deadlines for compliance, and issue other rulings that would expedite the arbitration proceedings or enable a party to prepare its case.

To the extent possible, testimony and documentary evidence should be exchanged voluntarily by the parties without the use of subpoenas. If a subpoena is necessary, the arbitrators and any counsel of record have such power of subpoena as may be provided by the law of the state where the hearing will be held or by the Federal Arbitration Act. All parties must be given a copy of the subpoena on its issuance. If a party has an attorney, the attorney should answer all questions concerning subpoenas. Parties without attorneys may request that the Director of Arbitration ask the arbitrators to issue a subpoena. The request should be in writing, should set forth why the subpoena is necessary and what efforts the requesting party made to obtain the appearance of witnesses and the production of documents without the use of the subpoena, and should include a copy of the subpoena which the arbitrators are requested to issue. If the arbitrators issue a subpoena, the requesting party has the obligation of serving the subpoena on the opposing party and bearing the costs involved as provided by law of the state where the hearing will be held or by federal law. The requesting party may need to employ the services of a professional process server to actually serve the subpoena.

The procedures for the issuance and service of subpoenas vary. Parties may, therefore, wish to consult with an attorney to insure that legal requirements in the applicable jurisdiction are satisfied.

In addition to the subpoena process, in some instances the arbitrators have the power to direct the appearance of persons employed in the securities industry and the production of records in the possession or control of such persons. If the parties request the arbitrators to use this power, they may be required to bear all reasonable expenses in connection with such appearance or production. All such requests should be made in advance of the hearing. Parties should be aware that arbitrators may sanction a party that fails to comply with these prehearing orders.

One final thought should be kept in mind when preparing for a hearing. The arbitrators are experienced and knowledgeable individuals. They appreciate a clear presentation of the case, free from repetition and irrelevancies.

HOW ARE THE HEARINGS CONDUCTED?

The Director of Arbitration schedules the date of the hearing. The parties will be notified in writing of the date and location of the initial hearing at least eight business days in advance. A verbatim record is kept of the proceedings. A party that elects to have the record transcribed shall bear the cost of such transcript unless the arbitrators direct otherwise.

At the hearing, the parties must present their respective cases by testimony and documentary evidence to the arbitrators. Claimants should document carefully the issues involved and their proof of damages, and explain to the arbitrators how much in money damages is being claimed and how they arrived at that figure. All hearings will be conducted by the arbitrators in the manner they determine will most expeditiously permit full presentation of the evidence and arguments of the parties.

Generally, the following procedures will be observed:

(1) The arbitrators and the witnesses will be sworn.

(2) Each party will be given an opportunity to make a brief opening statement, that is, a brief outline of the issues involved and what facts that party intends to prove. A party may waive the opening statement.

(3) The claimant will present facts to the arbitrators including relevant documents and testimony to establish and prove his or her claim.

(4) The respondent will present his or her case in the same manner as the claimant. Witnesses and parties who testify will be sworn and are subject to cross examination by the opposing side and questioning by the arbitrators. The opposing party may object to any evidence prior to its receipt by the arbitrators. Parties should bring sufficient copies of documents for each of the arbitrators, other parties, and the representative of the sponsoring organization. It is inappropriate to "testify" when questioning a witness, and a party may object if another party does that. A party may offer an affidavit in lieu of the live testimony of a witness. This may or may not be allowed by the arbitrators. Parties should be prepared to explain why a witness cannot come to the hearing and to explain whether the other party had an opportunity to examine the witness. A party should be prepared to bring the witness if the affidavit is not allowed.

(5) Any counterclaim or other matter may be presented in the same way.

(6) Parties may present rebuttal evidence if appropriate.

(7) Closing statements may be presented and consist generally of final arguments by the parties and brief summations of the testimony and other evidence introduced at the hearing. A party should refer only to evidence already in the record and not use the closing statement as an opportunity to present new evidence. A party may waive a closing statement.

(8) The parties are to leave together at the end of the hearing.

(9) The arbitrators may proceed with a case even when a party does not appear and/or answer.

HOW ARE THE PARTIES NOTIFIED OF THE ARBITRATORS' DECISION?

When the arbitrators have reached their decision and have signed an award, copies will be mailed to the parties. The award shall be in writing and signed by a majority of the arbitrators. The award may be entered by the prevailing party as a judgment in any court of competent jurisdiction.

Arbitrators shall endeavor to render an award within 30 business days from the date the record is closed. The Director of Arbitration shall endeavor to serve a copy of the award: (i) by registered or certified mail upon all parties, or their counsel; or (ii) by personally serving the award upon the parties; or (iii) by filing or delivering the award as authorized by law.

The award will contain the names of the parties, the names of counsel, if any, the dates the claim was filed and the award was rendered, the number and dates of the hearing sessions, the location of the hearings, a summary of the issues including the type(s) of any security or product in controversy, the damages and other relief requested, the damages and other relief awarded, a statement of any other issues resolved, the names of the arbitrators, and the signatures of the arbitrators concurring in the award. In addition, all awards must be paid within 30 days of receipt unless a motion to vacate has been filed in court. Awards will also bear interest if they are not paid within 30 days of receipt, if the award is the subject of a motion to vacate which is denied or as specified by the arbitrators.

The awards will be made publicly available. Arbitrators are not required to write opinions or provide reasons for the award. A party, however, may request an opinion. This request should be made no later than the hearing date. Some sponsoring organizations delete from the public version of awards information that identifies either the arbitrators or the parties. The decision of the arbitrators is final; that is, the decision is subject to review by a court only on a very limited basis.

IMPORTANT: It should be kept in mind that the arbitrators' decision will be based solely and exclusively on the documents and related material provided by the parties to a dispute. In the case of a hearing, the decision will be based on both the documents and testimony presented at the hearing. It is therefore important that a party's case be carefully and thoroughly prepared. As noted, this may be done either with or without the assistance of counsel. Such preparation will ensure that all relevant facts and evidence will be presented by the parties and, thus, considered by the arbitrators. Arbitrators are not allowed to reconsider a decision because new evidence has been found after the award was rendered.

In addition, it is the responsibility of the parties to submit briefs for any novel theories of recovery and/or requests for special damages. In some cases, arbitrators may require even parties without lawyers to support their claims by reference to the relevant law.

CONCLUSION

Remember that you should carefully read the arbitration rules of the sponsoring organization you have selected. This pamphlet is not a substitute for those rules. If you have any questions regarding arbitration procedures or want a copy of those rules, contact the Director of Arbitration of the sponsoring organization.

GLOSSARY OF TERMS

Answer--A respondent's written reply to a claim.

Arbitration/Counsel or Arbitration Administrator--The person at the sponsoring organization who handles administrative matters in arbitration proceedings.

Arbitrator--A person chosen to decide disputes between parties.

Award--The written determination of the arbitrator(s).

Claim--A demand for money or other relief.

Claimant--A person making a claim.

Counsel--An attorney who advises and represents a party in an arbitration.

Counterclaim--A claim against the claimant.

Cross-Claim--A claim by a respondent against a co-respondent previously named by the claimant.

Filing--Delivery to the Director of Arbitration of the statement of claim or other pleadings, to be kept on file as a matter of record and reference.

Panel--The arbitrator(s) who decide(s) a dispute.

Party--A person or broker/dealer making or responding to a claim in an arbitration proceeding.

Pleadings--The claim, answer, counterclaim, and/or third-party and/or cross-claim filed in an arbitration.

Respondent--The person against whom a claim is made.

Service--Delivery of the statement of claim or other pleadings to those parties named in the arbitration.

Third-Party Claim--A claim by the respondent against a party not already named in the proceeding.

LIST OF SPONSORING ORGANIZATIONS

To obtain further information, contact the Director of Arbitration at one of the following organizations:

American Stock Exchange, Inc.
86 Trinity Place
New York, NY 10006
(212) 306-1000

Boston Stock Exchange, Inc.
One Boston Place
Boston, MA 02108
(617) 723-9500

Chicago Board Options Exchange, Inc.
400 LaSalle Street
Chicago, IL 60605
(312) 786-5600

Cincinnati Stock Exchange, Inc.
205 Dixie Terminal Building
Cincinnati, OH 45202
(513) 621-1410

Midwest Stock Exchange, Inc.
400 LaSalle Street
Chicago, IL 60605
(312) 663-2354

Municipal Securities Rulemaking Board
1818 N Street, NW
Washington, DC 20036
(202) 223-9347

National Association of Securities Dealers, Inc.
33 Whitehall Street
New York, NY 10004
(212) 858-4400

New York Stock Exchange, Inc.
11 Wall Street
New York, NY 10005
(212) 656-2772

Pacific Stock Exchange
301 Pine Street
San Francisco, CA 94104
(415) 393-4000

Philadelphia Stock Exchange, Inc.
1900 Market Street
Philadelphia, PA 19103
(215) 496-5000

APPENDIX D

N.Y.S.E. ARBITRATION RULES

Department of Arbitration
New York Stock Exchange, Inc.
11 Wall Street
New York, NY 10005
(212) 656-2772
Arbitration Rules
Article XI

Arbitration
Controversies Arbitrated

Sec. 1. Controversies Arbitrated. Any controversy between parties who are members, allied members or member organizations and any controversy between a member, allied member or member organization and any other person arising out of the business of such member, allied member or member organization, or the dissolution of a member organization, shall at the instance of any such party, be submitted for arbitration in accordance with the provisions of this Constitution and such rules as the Board may from time to time adopt.

Arbitration Rules

Sec. 2. Arbitration Rules. All arbitration proceedings shall be conducted in accordance with, and before arbitrators selected as provided by, such rules as the Board shall from time to time adopt.

Power to Decline Use of Arbitration Facilities

Sec. 3. Power to Decline Use of Arbitration Facilities. The Board may decline in any case to permit the use of the arbitration facilities of the Exchange and may delegate such power.

Rule 600. Arbitration

(a) Any dispute, claim or controversy between a customer or non-member and a member, allied member, member organization and/or associated person arising in connection with the business of such member, allied member, member organization and/or associated person in connection with his activities as an associated person shall be arbitrated under the Constitution and Rules of the New York Stock Exchange, Inc. as provided by any duly executed and enforceable written agreement or upon the demand of the customer or non-member.

(b) Under this Code, the New York Stock Exchange, Inc., shall have the right to decline the use of its arbitration facilities in any dispute, claim or controversy, where, having due regard for the purposes of the-New York Stock Exchange, Inc. and the intent of this Code, such dispute, claim or controversy is not a proper subject matter for arbitration.

(c) Claims which arise out of transactions in a readily identifiable market may, with the consent of the claimant, be referred to the arbitration forum for that market by the New York Stock Exchange, Inc.

(d) Class Action Claims.

(i) A claim submitted as a class action shall not be eligible for arbitration under the Rules of the New York Stock Exchange, Inc.

(ii) Any claim filed by a member or members of a putative or certified class action is also ineligible for arbitration at the New York Stock Exchange, Inc. if the claim is encompassed by a putative or certified class action filed in federal or state court, or is ordered by a court to a non SRO arbitration forum for class-wide arbitration. However, such claims shall be eligible for arbitration in accordance with Rule 600 (a) or pursuant to the parties' contractual agreement, if any, if a claimant demonstrates that it has elected not to participate in the putative or certified class action or, if applicable, has complied with any conditions for withdrawing from the class prescribed by the court.

Disputes concerning whether a particular claim is encompassed by a putative or certified class action shall be referred by the Director of Arbitration to a panel of arbitrator(s) in accordance with Rules 601 or 607, as applicable. Either party may elect instead to petition the court with jurisdiction over the putative or certified class action to resolve such disputes. Any such petition to the court must be filed within ten (10) business days of receipt of notice that the Director of Arbitration is referring the dispute to a panel of arbitrator(s).

(iii) No member, allied member, member organization and/or associated person shall seek to enforce any agreement to arbitrate against a customer that has initiated in court a putative class action or is a member of a putative or certified class with respect to any claims encompassed by the class action unless and until:

(A) the class certification is denied;

(B) the class is decertified;

(C) the customer is excluded from the class by the court; or

(D) the customer elects not to participate in the putative or certified class action or, if applicable, has compiled with any conditions for withdrawing from the class prescribed by the court.

(iv) No member, allied member, member organization and/or associated person shall be deemed to have waived any of its rights under these Rules or under any agreement to arbitrate to which it is a party except to the extent stated in this paragraph.

Rule 601. Simplified Arbitration

(a) Any dispute, claim or controversy, arising between a public customer(s) and an associated person or a member subject to arbitration under this Code involving a dollar amount not exceeding $10,000 exclusive of attendant costs and interest, shall be arbitrated as hereinafter provided.

(b) The Claimant shall file with the Director of Arbitration an executed Submission Agreement and a copy of the Statement of Claim of the controversy in dispute and the required deposit, together with the documents in support of the Claim. Sufficient copies of the Submission Agreement and the Statement of Claim and supporting documents shall be provided to the Director of Arbitration for each party and the Arbitrator. The Statement of Claim shall specify the relevant facts, the remedies sought and whether or not a hearing is demanded.

(c) The Claimant shall pay a filing fee and remit a hearing deposit as specified in Rule 629 upon the filing of the Submission Agreement. The final disposition of the sum shall be determined by the Arbitrator.

(d) The Director of Arbitration shall endeavor to serve promptly by mail or otherwise on the Respondent(s) one (1) copy of the Submission Agreement and one (1) copy of the Statement of Claim. Within twenty (20) calendar days from the receipt of the Statement of Claim, Respondent(s) shall serve each party with an executed Submission Agreement and a copy of Respondent's Answer. Respondent's executed Submission Agreement and Answer shall also be filed with the Director of Arbitration with additional copies for the Arbitrator(s) along with any deposit required under the schedule of fees. The Answer shall designate an available defenses to the Claim and may set forth any related Counterclaim and/or related Third Party Claim the Respondent(s) may have against the Claimant or any other person. If the Respondent(s) has interposed a Third Party Claim, the Respondent(s) shall serve the Third Party Respondent with an executed Submission Agreement, a copy of Respondent's answer containing the Third Party Claim, and a copy of the original Claim filed by the Claimant. The Third Party Respondent shall respond in the manner herein provided for response to the Claim. If the Respondent(s) files a related Counterclaim exceeding $10,000, the Arbitrator may refer the Claim, Counterclaim and/or Third Party Claim, if any, to a panel of three (3) arbitrators in accordance with Rule 607 of this Code, or he may dismiss the Counterclaim and/or Third Party Claim, without prejudice to the counter-claimants and/or third party claimants pursuing the Counterclaim and/or Third Party Claim in a separate proceeding. The costs to the Claimant under either proceeding shall in no event exceed the total amount specified in Rule 629.

(e) All parties shall serve promptly by mail or otherwise on all other parties and the Director of Arbitration, with sufficient additional copies for the arbitrators, a copy of the Answer, Counterclaim, Third Party Claim, amended claim or other responsive pleading, if any. The Claimant, if a Counterclaim is asserted against him, shall within ten (10) calendar days either:

(i) serve on each party and on the Director of Arbitration with sufficient additional copies for the arbitrator(s) a reply to any counterclaim, or

(ii) if the amount of the Counterclaims exceeds the Claim, have the right to file a statement withdrawing the Claim. If the Claimant withdraws the Claim, the proceedings will be discontinued without prejudice to the rights of the parties.

(f) The dispute, claim or controversy shall be submitted to a single public arbitrator knowledgeable in the securities industry selected by the Director of Arbitration. Unless the public customer demands or consents to a hearing, or the arbitrator(s) calls a hearing, the arbitrator shall decide the dispute, claim or controversy solely upon the pleadings and evidence filed by the parties. If a hearing is necessary, such hearing shall be held as soon as practicable at a locale selected by the Director of Arbitration.

(g) The Director of Arbitration may grant extensions of time to file any pleading upon a showing of good cause.

(h) (i) The arbitrator shall be authorized to require the submission of further documentary evidence as he, in his sole discretion, deems advisable.

(ii) If a hearing is demanded or consented to in accordance with section 601(f), the General Provision Governing a Pre-Hearing Proceeding under Rule 619 shall apply.

(iii) If no hearing is demanded or consented to, all requests for document production shall be submitted in writing to the Director of Arbitration within ten (10) business days of notification of the identity of the arbitrator selected to decide the case. The requesting party shall serve simultaneously its requests for document production on all parties. Any response or objection to the requested document production shall be served on all parties and filed with the Director of Arbitration within five (5) business days of receipt of the requests for production. The selected arbitrator shall resolve all requests under this section on the papers submitted.

(i) Upon the request of the arbitrator, the Director of Arbitration shall appoint two (2) additional arbitrators to the panel which shall decide the matter in controversy.

(j) In any case where there is more than one (1) arbitrator, the majority will be public arbitrators.

(k) In his discretion, the arbitrator may, at the request of any party, permit such party to submit additional documentation relating to the pleadings.

(l) Except as otherwise provided herein, the general arbitration rules of the New York Stock Exchange, Inc. shall be applicable to the proceedings instituted under this Rule.

Rule 602. Hearing Requirement - Waiver of Hearing

(a) Any dispute, claim or controversy, except as provided in Rule 601 (Simplified Arbitration), shall require a hearing unless all parties waive such hearing in writing and request that the matter be resolved solely upon the pleadings and documentary evidence.

(b) Notwithstanding a written waiver of a hearing by the parties, a majority of the arbitrators may call for and conduct a hearing. In addition, any arbitrator may request the submission of further evidence.

Rule 603. Time Limitation Upon Submission

No dispute, claim or controversy shall be eligible for submission to arbitration under this Code where six (6) years shall have elapsed from the occurrence or event giving rise to the act or the dispute, claim or controversy. This section shall not extend applicable statutes of limitations, nor shall it apply to any case which is directed to arbitration by a court of competent jurisdiction.

Rule 604. Dismissal of Proceedings

At any time during the course of an arbitration, the arbitrators may either upon their own initiative or at the request of a party, dismiss the proceeding and refer the parties to the remedies provided by law. The arbitrators shall upon the joint request of the parties dismiss the proceedings.

Rule 605. Settlements

All settlements upon any matter submitted shall be at the election of the parties.

Rule 606. Tolling of Time Limitation(s) for the Institution of Legal Proceedings and Extension of Time Limitation(s) for Submission to Arbitration

(a) Where permitted by law, the time limitation(s) which would otherwise run or accrue for the institution of legal proceedings, shall be tolled when a duly executed Submission Agreement is filed by the claimant(s). The tolling shall continue for such period as the New York Stock Exchange, Inc. shall retain jurisdiction upon the matter submitted.

(b) The six (6) year time limitation upon submission to arbitration shall not apply when the parties have submitted the dispute, claim or controversy to a court of competent jurisdiction. The six (6) year time limitation shall not run for such period as the court shall retain jurisdiction upon the matter submitted.

Rule 607. Designation of Number of Arbitrators

(a) (1) In all arbitration matters involving public customers and non-members where the matter in controversy exceeds $10,000, or where the matter in controversy does not involve or disclose a money claim, the Director of Arbitration shall appoint an arbitration panel which shall consist of no less than three (3) arbitrators, at least a majority of whom shall not be from the securities industry, unless the public customer or non-member requests a panel consisting of at least a majority from the securities industry.

(2) An arbitrator will be deemed as being from the securities industry if he or she:

i. is a person associated with a member, broker/dealer, government securities broker, government securities dealer, municipal securities dealer or registered investment adviser, or

ii. has been associated with any of the above within the past five (5) years, or

iii. is retired from or spent a substantial part of his or her business career in any of the above, or

iv. is an attorney, accountant or other professional who devoted twenty (20) percent or more of his or her professional work effort to securities industry clients within the last two (2) years.

v. Is an individual who is registered under the Commodity Exchange Act or is a member of a registered futures association or any commodity exchange or is associated with any such person(s).

(3) An arbitrator who is not from the securities industry shall be deemed a public arbitrator. A person will not be classified as a public arbitrator if he or she has a spouse or other member of the household who is a person associated with a registered broker, dealer, municipal securities dealer, government securities broker, government securities dealer or investment adviser.

(b) Composition of Panels

The individuals who shall serve on a particular arbitration panel shall be determined by the Director of Arbitration. The Director of Arbitration may name the chairman of each panel.

Rule 608. Notice of Selection of Arbitrators

The Director of Arbitration shall inform the parties of the names and employment histories of the arbitrators for the past ten (10) years, as well as information disclosed pursuant to Rule 610 at least eight (8) business days prior to the date fixed for the initial hearing session. A party may make further inquiry of the Director of Arbitration concerning an arbitrator's background. In the event that any arbitrator, after appointment and prior to the first hearing session, should resign, die, withdraw, be disqualified or otherwise be unable to perform as an arbitrator, the Director of Arbitration shall appoint a new member to the panel to if any vacancy. The Director of Arbitration shall inform the parties of the name and employment history of the replacement arbitrator for the past ten (10) years, as well as information disclosed pursuant to Rule 610, as soon as possible. A party may make further inquiry of the Director of Arbitration concerning the background of the replacement arbitrator and within the time remaining prior to the first hearing session or the five (5) day period provided under Rule 609, whichever is shorter, may exercise its right to challenge the replacement arbitrator as provided in Rule 609.

Rule 609. Peremptory Challenge

In any arbitration proceeding, each party shall have the right to one peremptory challenge. In arbitrations where there are multiple claimants, respondents and/or third party respondents, the claimants shall have one peremptory challenge, the respondents shall have one peremptory challenge and the third party respondents shall have one peremptory challenge, unless the Director of Arbitration determines that the interests of justice would be best served by awarding additional peremptory challenges. Unless extended by the Director of Arbitration, a party wishing to exercise a peremptory challenge must do so by notifying the Director of Arbitration in writing within five (5) business days of notification of the identity of the person(s) named under Rule 619(d), (e) or Rule 608 whichever comes first. There shall be unlimited challenges for cause.

Rule 610. Disclosures Required of Arbitrators

(a) Each arbitrator shall be required to disclose to the Director of Arbitration any circumstances which might preclude such arbitrator from rendering an objective and impartial determination. Each arbitrator shall disclose:

(1) Any direct or indirect financial or personal interest in the outcome of the arbitration;

(2) Any existing or past financial, business, professional, family or social relationships that are likely to affect impartiality or might reasonably create an appearance of partiality or bias. Persons requested to serve as arbitrators should disclose any such relationships which they personally have with any party or its counsel, or with any individual whom they have been told will be a witness. They should also disclose any such relationship involving members of their families or their current employers, partners or business associates.

(b) Persons who are requested to accept appointment as arbitrators should make a reasonable effort to inform themselves of any interests or relationships described in Paragraph (a) above.

(c) The obligation to disclose interests, relationships, or circumstances that might preclude arbitrator from rendering an objective and impartial determination described in subsection (a) hereof is a continuing duty that requires a person who accepts appointment as an arbitrator to disclose, at any stage of the arbitration, any such interests, relationships, or circumstances that arise, or are recalled or discovered.

(d) Prior to the commencement of the first hearing session, the Director of Arbitration may remove an arbitrator based on information disclosed pursuant to this section. The Director of Arbitration shall also inform the parties of any information disclosed pursuant to this section if the arbitrator who disclosed the information is not removed.

Rule 611. Disqualification or Other Disability of Arbitrators

In the event that any arbitrator, after the commencement of the first hearing session and prior to the rendition of the award, should resign, die, withdraw, be disqualified or otherwise be unable to perform as an arbitrator, the remaining arbitrator(s) may continue with the hearing and determination of the controversy, unless such continuation is objected to by any party within five (5) days of notification of the vacancy on the panel. Upon objection, the Director of Arbitration shall appoint a new member to the panel to fill any vacancy. The Director of Arbitration shall inform the parties as soon as possible of the name and employment history for the past ten (10) years of the replacement arbitrator, as well as information disclosed pursuant to Rule 610. A party may make further inquiry of the Director of Arbitration concerning the replacement arbitrators background and within the time remaining prior to the next scheduled hearing session on the five (5) day period under Rule 609, whichever is shorter, may exercise its right to challenge the replacement arbitrator as provided in Rule 609.

Rule 612. Initiation of Proceedings

Except as otherwise provided herein, an arbitration proceeding under this Code shall be instituted as follows:

(a) Statement of Claim.

The Claimant shall file with the Director of Arbitration an executed Submission Agreement, a Statement of Claim together with documents in support of the claim and the required deposit. Sufficient additional copies of the Submission Agreement and the Statement of Claim and supporting documents shall be provided to the Director of Arbitration for each party and each arbitrator. The Statement of Claim shall specify the relevant facts and the remedies sought. The Director of Arbitration shall endeavor to serve promptly by mail or otherwise on the Respondent(s) one (1) copy of the Submission Agreement and one (1) copy of the Statement of Claim.

(b) Service and Filing with the Director of Arbitration.

For purposes of the Code of Arbitration Procedure, service may be effected by mail or other means of delivery. Service and filing are accomplished on the date of mailing either by first-class postage prepaid or by means of overnight mail service or, in the case of other means of service, on the date of delivery. Filing with the Director of Arbitration shall be made on the same date as service.

(c) Answers, Defenses, Counterclaims and/or Cross-Claims.

(1) Within twenty (20) business days from receipt of the Statement of Claim, the Respondent(s) shall serve each party with an executed Submission Agreement and a copy of Respondent(s) Answer. An executed Submission Agreement and a copy of Respondent(s) Answer shall also be filed with the Director of Arbitration with sufficient additional copies for the arbitrator(s), along with any deposit required under the schedule of fees. The Answer shall specify all available defenses and relevant facts that will be relied upon at the hearing and may set forth any related Counterclaim the Respondent(s) may have against the Claimant, any Cross-Claim the Respondent(s) may have against any other named Respondent(s) and any Third Party Claim against any other party or person based upon any existing dispute, claim or controversy subject to arbitration under this Code.

(2) (i) A Respondent, Responding Claimant, Cross-Claimant, Cross-Respondent or Third Party Respondent who pleads only a general denial as an answer may, upon objection by a party, in the discretion of the arbitrators, be barred from presenting such facts or defenses at the time of the hearing.

(ii) A Respondent, Responding Claimant, Cross-Claimant, Cross-Respondent or Third Party Respondent who fails to specify all available defenses and relevant facts in such party's answer may, upon objection by a party, in the discretion of the arbitrators, be barred from presenting such facts or defenses not included in such party's answer at the hearing.

(iii) A Respondent, Responding Claimant, Cross-Claimant, Cross-Respondent or Third Party Respondent who fails to file an answer with twenty (20) business days from receipt of service of a claim, unless the time to answer has been extended pursuant to paragraph (5), may, in the discretion of the arbitrators, be barred from presenting any matter, arguments or defenses at the hearing.

(3) Respondent(s) shall serve each party with a copy of any Third Party Claim. The Third Party Claim shall also be filed with the Director of Arbitration with sufficient additional copies for the arbitrator(s), along with any deposit required under the schedule of fees. Third Party Respondent(s) shall answer in the manner provided for response to the Claim, as provided in paragraphs (1) and (2) above.

(4) The Claimant shall serve each party with a reply to a counterclaim within ten (10) business days of receipt of an Answer containing a Counterclaim. The reply shall also be filed with the Director of Arbitration with sufficient additional copies for the arbitrator(s).

(5) The Director of Arbitration may extend any time period in this section whether such be denominated as a Claim, Answer, Counterclaim, Cross-Claim, Reply or Third Party pleading.

(d) Joining and Consolidation - Multiple Parties.

(1) Permissive Joinder. All persons may join in one action as claimants if they assert any right to relief jointly, severally, or arising out of the same transaction, occurrence or series of transactions or occurrences and if any questions of law or fact common to all these claimants will arise in the action. All persons may be joined in one action as respondents if there is asserted against them jointly or severally, any right to relief arising out of the same transaction, occurrence, or series of transactions or occurrences and if any questions of law or fact common to all respondents will arise in the action. A claimant or respondent need not assert rights to or defend against all the relief demanded. Judgment may be given for one or more of the claimants according to their respective rights to relief, and against one or more respondents according to their respective liabilities.

(2) In arbitration where there are multiple Claimants, Respondents and/or Third Party Respondents, the Director of Arbitration shall be authorized to determine preliminary whether such parties should proceed in the same or separate arbitrations. Such determinations will be considered subsequent to the filing of all responsive pleadings.

(3) The Director of Arbitration shall be authorized to determine preliminary whether claims filed separately are related and shall be authorized to consolidate such claims for hearing and award purposes.

(4) Further determinations with respect to joining, consolidation and multiple parties under this subsection may be made by the arbitration panel and shall be deemed final.

Rule 613. Designation of Time and Place of Hearings

The time and place for the initial hearing shall be determined by the Director of Arbitration and each hearing thereafter by the arbitrators. Notice of the time and place for the initial hearing shall be given at least eight (8) business days prior to the date fixed for the hearing by personal service, registered or certified mail to each of the parties unless the parties shall, by their mutual consent, waive the notice provisions under this section. Notice for each hearing, thereafter, shall be given as the arbitrators may determine. Attendance at a hearing waives notice thereof.

Rule 614. Representation by Counsel

All parties shall have the right to representation by counsel at any stage of the proceedings.

Rule 615. Attendance at Hearings

The attendance or presence of all persons at hearings, including witnesses, shall be determined by the arbitrators. However, all parties to the arbitration and their counsel shall be entitled to attend all hearings.

Rule 616. Failure to Appear

If any of the parties, after due notice, fails to appear at a hearing or at any continuation of a hearing session, the arbitrators may, in their discretion, proceed with the arbitration of the controversy. In such cases, all awards shall be rendered as if each party had entered an appearance in the matter submitted.

Rule 617. Adjournments

(a) The arbitrators may, in their discretion, adjourn any hearing(s) either upon their own initiative or upon the request of any party to the arbitration.

(b) A party requesting an adjournment after arbitrators have been appointed shall, if an adjournment is granted, deposit a fee, equal to the initial deposit of hearing session fees for the first adjournment and twice the initial deposit of hearing session fees, not to exceed $1,000, for a second or subsequent adjournment requested by that party. The arbitrators may waive the deposit of this fee or in their awards may direct the return of the adjournment fee.

(c) Upon receiving a third request consented to by all parties for an adjournment, the arbitrators may dismiss the arbitration without prejudice to the claimant filing a new arbitration.

Rule 618. Acknowledgment of Pleadings

The arbitrators shall acknowledge to all parties present that they have read the pleadings filed by the parties.

Rule 619. General Provision Governing Subpoenas, Production of Documents, etc.

(a) Requests for Documents and Information.

The parties shall cooperate to the fullest extent practicable in the voluntary exchange of documents and information to expedite the arbitration. Any request for documents or other information should be specific, relate to the matter in controversy, and afford the party to whom the request is made a reasonable period of time to respond without interfering with the time set for the hearing.

(b) Document Production and Information Exchange.

(1) Any party may serve a written request for information or documents ("information request") upon another party twenty (20) business days or more after service of the Statement of Claim by the Director of Arbitration or upon filing of the Answer, whichever is earlier. The requesting party shall serve the information request on all parties and file a copy with the Director of Arbitration. The parties shall endeavor to resolve disputes regarding an information request prior to serving any objection to the request. Such efforts shall be set forth in the objection.

(2) Unless a greater time is allowed by the requesting party, information requests shall be satisfied or objected to within thirty (30) calendar days from the date of service. Any objection to an information request shall be served by the objecting party on all parties and filed with the Director of Arbitration.

(3) Any response to objections to an information request shall be served on all parties and filed with the Director of Arbitration within ten (10) calendar days of receipt to the objection.

(4) Upon the written request of a party whose information request is unsatisfied, the matter will be referred by the Director of Arbitration to either

a prehearing conference under paragraph (d) of this section or to a selected arbitrator under paragraph (e) of this section.

(c) Pre-Hearing Exchange.

At least ten (10) calendar days prior to the first scheduled hearing date, all parties shall serve on each other copies of documents in their possession that they intend to present at the hearing and identify witnesses they intend to present at the hearing. The arbitrator(s) may exclude from the arbitration, any documents not exchanged or witnesses not identified at that time. This paragraph does not require service of copies of documents or identification of witnesses which parties may use for cross-examination or rebuttal.

(d) Pre-Hearing Conference.

(1) Upon the written request of a party, an arbitrator, or at the discretion of the Director of Arbitration, a prehearing conference shall be scheduled. The Director of Arbitration shall set the time and place of a prehearing conference and appoint a person to preside. The prehearing conference may be held by telephone conference call. The presiding person shall seek to achieve agreement among the parties on any issues that relate to the prehearing process or to the hearing, including but not limited to, the exchange of information, exchange or production of documents, identification of witnesses, identification and exchange of hearing documents, stipulations of fact, identification and briefing of contested issues, and any other matter which will expedite the arbitration proceedings.

(2) Any issues raised at the prehearing conference that are not resolved may be referred by the Director of Arbitration to a single public member of the Arbitration Panel for decision.

(e) Decisions by Selected Arbitrator.

The Director of Arbitration may appoint a single member of the Arbitration Panel to decide all unresolved issues referred to under this Section. Such arbitrator shall be authorized to act on behalf of the panel to issue subpoenas, direct appearances of witnesses and production of documents, set deadlines and issue any other ruling which will expedite the arbitration proceeding or is necessary to permit any party to develop fully its case. Decisions under this paragraph shall be made upon the papers submitted by the parties, unless the arbitrator calls a hearing. The arbitrator may elect to refer any issue under this paragraph to the full panel. In any claim involving a public customer the selected arbitrator shall be a public arbitrator unless the public customer demands, in writing, a securities arbitrator.

(f) Subpoenas.

The arbitrator(s) and any counsel of record to the proceedings shall have the power of the subpoena process as provided by law. All parties shall be given a copy of the subpoena upon its issuance. The parties shall produce witnesses and present proofs to the fullest extent possible without resort to the subpoena process.

(g) Power to Direct Appearance and Production of Documents.

The arbitrator(s) shall be empowered without resort to the subpoena process to direct the appearance of any person employed or associated with any member or member organization of the New York Stock Exchange, Inc. and/or the production of any records in the possession or control of such persons or members. Unless the arbitrator(s) direct otherwise, the party requesting the appearance of a person or the production of documents under this section shall bear all reasonable costs of such appearance and/or production.

Rule 620. Evidence

The arbitrators shall determine the materiality and relevance of any evidence proffered and shall not be bound by the rules governing the admissibility of evidence.

Rule 621. Interpretation of the provisions of the Code and Enforcement of Arbitrator(s) Rulings.

The arbitrator(s) shall be empowered to interpret and determine the applicability of all provisions under this Code and to take appropriate action to obtain compliance with any ruling by the arbitrator(s). Such interpretations and actions to obtain compliance shall be final and binding upon the parties.

Rule 622. Determination of Arbitrators

All rulings and determinations of the panel shall be by a majority of the arbitrators.

Rule 623. Record of Proceedings

A verbatim record of all arbitration hearings shall be kept by stenographic reporter or tape recording. If a party or parties to a dispute elect to have the record transcribed, the cost of such transcription shall be borne by the party or parties making the request unless the arbitrators direct otherwise. The arbitrators may also direct that the record be transcribed. If the record is transcribed at the request of any party, a copy shall be provided to the arbitrators.

Rule 624. Oaths of the Arbitrators and Witnesses

Prior to the commencement of the first session, an oath or affirmation shall be administered to the arbitrators. All testimony shall be under oath or affirmation.

Rule 625. Amendments

(a) After the filing of any pleadings, if a party desires to file a new or different pleading, such change must be made in writing and filed with the Director of Arbitration with sufficient additional copies for each arbitrator. The party filing a new or different pleading shall serve on all other parties, a copy of the new or different pleading in accordance with the provisions set forth in Rule 612(b). The other parties may, within ten (10) business days from the receipt of service, file a response with all other parties and the Director of Arbitration in accordance with Rule 612(b).

(b) After a panel has been appointed, no new or different pleadings may be filed except for a responsive pleading as provided for in (a) above or with the consent of the panel.

Rule 626. Reopening of Hearings

Where permitted by law, the hearings may be reopened by the arbitrators on their own motion or in the discretion of the arbitrators upon application of a party at any time before the award is rendered.

Rule 627. Awards

(a) All awards shall be in writing and signed by a majority of the arbitrators or in such manner as is required by law. Such awards may be entered as a judgment in any court of competent jurisdiction.

(b) Unless the law directs otherwise, all awards rendered pursuant to this Code shall be deemed final and not subject to review or appeal.

(c) The Director of Arbitration shall endeavor to serve a copy of the award: (i) by registered or certified mail upon all parties or their counsel, at the address of record, or (ii) by personally serving the award upon the parties; or (iii) by filing or delivering the award in such a manner as may be authorized by law.

(d) The arbitrator(s) shall endeavor to render an award within thirty (30) business days from the date the record is closed.

(e) The award shall contain the names of the parties, the name(s) of counsel, if any, a summary of the issues, including the type(s) of any security or product, in controversy, the damages and/or other relief requested, the damages and/or other relief awarded, a statement of any other issues resolved, the names of arbitrators, the date the claim was filed and the award rendered, the number and dates of hearing sessions, the location of the hearing, and the signatures of the arbitrators concurring in the award.

(f) The awards shall be made publicly available, provided however, that the name of the customer party to the arbitration will not be publicly available if he or she so requests in writing.

(g) All monetary awards shall be paid within thirty (30) days of receipt unless a motion to vacate has been filed with a court of competent jurisdiction. An award shall bear interest from the date of the award: (i) if not paid within thirty (30) days of receipt, (ii) if the award is the subject of a motion to vacate which is denied, or (iii) as specified by the arbitrator(s) in the award. Interest shall be assessed at the legal rate, if any, then prevailing in the state where the award was rendered, or at a rate set by the arbitrator(s).

Rule 628. Agreement to Arbitrate

Article XI of the Constitution and Rules 600-637 shall be deemed a part of and be incorporated by reference in every agreement to arbitrate under the Constitution and Rules of the New York Stock Exchange, Inc.

Rule 629. Schedule of Fees

(a) At the time of filing a Claim, Counterclaim, Third-Party Claim or Cross-Claim, a party shall pay a non-refundable filing fee and shall remit a hearing session deposit with the Exchange in the amounts indicated in the schedules below unless such fee or deposit is specifically waived by the Director of Arbitration.

Where multiple hearing sessions are required, the arbitrator(s) may require any of the parties to make additional hearing deposits for each additional hearing session. In no event shall the amount deposited by all parties per hearing session exceed the amount of the largest initial hearing deposit made by any party under the schedule below.

(b) A hearing session is any meeting between the parties and the arbitrator(s), including a prehearing conference with an arbitrator, which lasts four (4) hours or less. The forum fee for a prehearing conference with an arbitrator shall be the amount set forth in the schedules below as a hearing session deposit for a hearing with a single arbitrator.

(c) The arbitrators, in their award, may determine the amount chargeable to the parties as forum fees and shall determine who shall pay such forum fees. Forum fees chargeable to the parties shall be assessed on a per hearing session basis and the aggregate for each hearing session may equal but shall not exceed the amount of the largest initial hearing deposit deposited by any party, except in a case where claims have been joined subsequent to filing in which cases hearing session fees shall be computed as provided in paragraph (d). The arbitrators may determine in the award that a party shall reimburse to another party any non-refundable filing fee it has paid.

If a customer is assessed forum fees in connection with an industry claim, forum fees assessed against the customer shall be based on the hearing deposit required under the industry claims schedule for the amount awarded to industry parties to be paid by the customer and not based on the size of the industry claim. No fees shall be assessed against a customer in connection with an industry claim that is dismissed; however, in cases where there is also a customer claim, the customer may be assessed forum fees based on the customer claim under the procedure set out above.

Amounts deposited by a party as hearing deposits shall be applied against forum fees, if any.

In addition to forum fees, the arbitrator(s) may determine in the award the amount of costs incurred pursuant to Rules 617, 619 and 623 and, unless applicable law directs otherwise, other costs and expenses of the parties. The arbitrator(s) shall determine by whom such costs shall be home.

If the hearing session fees are not assessed against a party who had made a hearing deposit, the hearing deposit will be refunded unless the arbitrators determine otherwise.

(d) For claims filed separately and subsequently joined or consolidated under Rule 612(d), the hearing deposit and forum fees assessable per hearing session after joinder or consolidation shall be based on the cumulative amount in dispute. The arbitrator(s) shall determine by whom such forum fees shall be borne.

(e) If the dispute, claim or controversy does not involve, disclose or specify a money claim, the non-refundable filing fee will be $250 and the hearing session deposit to be remitted by a party shall be $600 or such greater or lesser amounts as the Director of Arbitration or the panel of arbitrators may require, but shall not exceed $1,500.

(f) The Exchange shall retain the total initial amount deposited as hearing session deposits by all the parties in any matter submitted and settled or withdrawn within eight (8) business days of the first scheduled hearing session other than a prehearing conference.

(g) Any matter submitted and thereafter settled or withdrawn subsequent to the commencement of the first hearing session, including a prehearing conference with an arbitrator, shall be subject to an assessment of forum fees and costs incurred pursuant to Rules 617, 619 and 623 based on hearing sessions held and scheduled within eight (8) business days of the Exchange receiving notice that the matter has been settled or withdrawn. The arbitrator(s) shall determine by whom such forum fees and costs shall be borne.

(h) The fee for a prehearing conference with an arbitrator shall be:

SCHEDULE FOR PRE-HEARING CONFERENCE WITH ARBITRATOR(S):

AMOUNT IN CONTROVERSY	CONFERENCE FEE
$ 1,000 or less	$ 15.00
$ 1,000.01 up to $2,500	$ 25.00
$ 2,500.01 up to $5,000	$ 100.00
$ 5,000.01 up to $10,000	$ 200.00
$ 10,000.01 up to $30,000	$ 300.00
$ 30,000.01 up to $50,000	$ 300.00
$ 50,000.01 up to $100,000	$ 300.00
$100,001 up to $500,000	$ 300.00
$500,001 up to $5 million	$ 300.00
Greater than $5 million	$ 300.00

(i) Schedule of Fees

For purposes of the schedule of fees the term "claim" includes Claims, Counterclaims, Third-Party Claims or Cross-Claims. Any such claim submitted by a customer is a customer claim. Any such claim submitted by a member, allied member, registered representative, member firm or member corporation against a public customer or other non-member is an industry claim.

CUSTOMER CLAIMANT

		DEPOSIT	
Amount of Dispute (Exclusive of Interest and Expenses)	Filing Fee	Simplified	Hearing
$ 1,000 or less	$ 15	$ 15	$ 15
$ 1,001 to $2,500	$ 25	$ 25	$ 25
$ 2,501 to $5,000	$ 50	$ 75	$ 100
$ 5,001 to $10,000	$ 75	$ 75	$ 100
$ 10,001 to $30,000	$100	N/A	$ 400
$ 30,001 to $50,000	$120	N/A	$ 400
$ 50,001 to $100,000	$150	N/A	$ 500
$100,001 to $500,000	$200	N/A	$ 750
$500,001 to $5,000,000	$250	N/A	$1,000
Over $5,000,000	$300	N/A	$1,500

INDUSTRY CLAIMANT*

		HEARING DEPOSIT	
Amount of Dispute (Exclusive of Interest and Expenses)	Filing Fee	1 Arb.	3 Arbs.
$ 1,000 or less	$500	$300	$ 600
$ 1,001 to $2,500	$500	$300	$ 600
$ 2,501 to $5,000	$500	$300	$ 600
$ 5,001 to $10,000	$500	$300	$ 600
$ 10,001 to $30,000	$500	$300	$ 600
$ 30,001 to $50,000	$500	$300	$ 600
$ 50,001 to $100,000	$500	$300	$ 600
$100,001 to $500,000	$500	$300	$ 750
$500,001 to $5,000,000	$500	$300	$1,000
Over $5,000,000	$500	$300	$1,500

* This is the fee schedule for claims submitted by members, member firms, member corporations or allowed members against public customers, registered representatives or non-members other than public customers, and for claims submitted by registered representatives or non-members other than public customers against members, member firms, member corporations, allied members or non-members. The one arbitrator column is for prehearing conferences and for simplified arbitrations where the industry party is a claimant against a public customer.

Rule 630. Uniform Arbitration Code

The provisions of the Uniform Arbitration Code contained in Rules 600 to 637 shall also apply to controversies between members, allied members, member firms, member organizations and/or non-members who are not public customers except in so far as such provisions specifically apply to matters involving public customers.

Rule 631. Schedule for Member Controversies

(a) At the time of filing a Claim, Counterclaim, Third-Party Claim or Cross-Claim, a party shall pay a non-refundable filing fee and remit a hearing session deposit with the New York Stock Exchange, Inc. in the amounts indicated below:

Amount in Dispute	Filing Fee	Hearing Deposit
$5,000 or less	$100	$ 200
$5,001 to $100,000	$200	$ 750
$100,001 or more	$300	$1,000

(b) Where the claim or controversy does not involve or disclose a money claim or is unspecified, the filing fee will be $300 and the hearing session deposit shall be $1,000 per hearing session.

(c) The fee for a prehearing conference with an arbitrator in a member controversy shall be as follows:

Amount in Dispute	Conference Fee
$5,000 or less	$150
$5,001 to $100,000	$300
$100,001 or more	$500

Rule 632. Member Controversies

Any controversy between parties who are members, allied members, member firms or member corporations shall be submitted for arbitration to members of the Board Arbitration, unless non-members are also parties to the controversy. If the amount (exclusive of interest and costs) involved in the controversy is less than $10,000 the controversy shall be heard by one arbitrator. If such amount is $10,000 or more the controversy shall be heard by at least three (3) but not more than five (5) arbitrators. If non-members are also parties to such controversies, the arbitrators shall be appointed in accordance with Rule 607 unless the non-member(s) consent to arbitration before members of the Board of Arbitration.

Rule 633. Board of Arbitration

Promptly after the annual election of the Exchange, the Chairman of the Board of Directors shall appoint, subject to the approval of the Board of Directors, a Board of Arbitration to be composed of such number of present or former members, allied members and officers of member corporations of the Exchange who are not members of the Board of Directors as the Chairman of the Board of Directors shall deem necessary to serve at the pleasure of the Board of Directors or until the next annual election of the Exchange and their successors are appointed and take office.

Rule 634. Panels of Arbitrators

The Chairman of the Board of Directors shall from time to time appoint two panels of arbitrators, composed of persons who are residents of or have their places of business in the Metropolitan area of the City of New York. The first of such panels shall be composed of persons engaged in or retired from the securities business and the second of such panels shall be composed of persons not engaged in the securities business. The Chairman of the Board of Directors may likewise appoint panels similar to the panels above described to serve outside the City of New York.

Rule 635. Director of Arbitration

The Chairman of the Board, shall designate one of the officers or other employees of the Exchange as Director of Arbitration. The Director of Arbitration shall be charged with the duty of performing all ministerial duties in connection with matters submitted for arbitration pursuant to these Rules.

Rule 636. Requirements When Using Pre-Dispute Arbitration Agreements With Customers

(a) Any predispute arbitration clause shall be highlighted and shall be immediately preceded by the following disclosure language (printed in outline form as set forth herein) which shall also be highlighted:

(1) Arbitration is final and binding on the parties.

(2) The parties are waiving their right to seek remedies in court, including the right to jury trial.

(3) Pre-arbitration discovery is generally more limited than and different from court proceedings.

(4) The arbitrators' award is not required to include factual findings or legal reasoning and any party's right to appeal or to seek modification of rulings by the arbitrators is strictly limited.

(5) The panel of arbitrators will typically include a minority of arbitrators who were or are affiliated with the securities industry.

(b) Immediately preceding the signature line, there shall be a statement which shall be highlighted that the agreement contains a predispute arbitration clause. The statement shall also indicate at what page and paragraph the arbitration clause is located.

(c) A copy of the agreement containing any such clause shall be given to the customer who shall acknowledge receipt thereof on the agreement or on a separate document.

(d) No agreement shall include any condition which limits or contradicts the rules of any self-regulatory organization or limits the ability of a party to file any claim in arbitration or limits the ability of the arbitrators to make any award.

(e) All agreements shall include a statement that "No person shall bring a putative or certified class action to arbitration, nor seek to enforce any predispute arbitration agreement against any person who has initiated in court a putative class action; who is a member of a putative class who has not opted out of the class with respect to any claims encompassed by the putative class action until:

(i) the class certification is denied;

(ii) the class is decertified; or

(iii) the customer is excluded from the class by the court.

Such forbearance to enforce an agreement to arbitrate shall not constitute a waiver of any rights under this agreement except to the extent stated herein."

(f) The requirements of subsections (a) thru (d) shall apply only to new agreement, signed by an existing or a new customer of a member or member organization after September 7, 1989. The requirements of subsection (e) shall apply only to new agreements signed by an existing or new customer of a member or member organization after August 26, 1993.

Rule 637. Failure to Honor Award

Any member, allied member, registered representative or member organization who fails to honor an award of arbitrators appointed in accordance with these rules shall be subject to disciplinary proceedings in accordance with Rule 476 of Article IX of the New York Stock Exchange Constitution and Rules.

As amended and effective August 26, 1992 except as otherwise provided herein.

APPENDIX E

American Arbitration Association

SECURITIES ARBITRATION RULES

As Amended and in Effect May 1, 1993

Introduction

Each year, millions of transactions involving security and commodity futures take place. Occasionally, disagreements develop over these transactions. Many of these disputes are resolved by arbitration, the voluntary submission of a dispute to a disinterested person or persons for final and binding determination. Arbitration has proven to be an effective way to resolve these disputes privately, promptly and economically.

The American Arbitration Association (AAA) is a public-service, not-for-profit organization offering a broad range of dispute-resolution services to business executives, attorneys, individuals, trade associations, unions, management, consumers, families, communities and all levels of government. Services are available through AAA headquarters in New York City and through offices located in major cities throughout the United States. Hearings may be held at locations convenient for the parties and are not limited to cities with AAA offices. In addition, the AAA serves as a center for education and training issues specialized publications, and conducts research on all forms of out-of-court dispute settlement.

In October of 1991, the American Arbitration Association created a Securities Arbitration Task Force, comprised of representatives of various brokerage firms, customers' attorneys and others with considerable knowledge and experience in securities matters and the arbitration process. The mission of the Task Force was to consider improvements in the AAA's Securities Arbitration Rules and administrative procedures and policies that would make AAA-administered arbitration more attractive to all participants in the process. An effort was made at the same time to consider changes that would make the Securities Arbitration Rules applicable to commodity futures matters. The task force met 11 times from November 1991 through February 1993.

The report of the task force was endorsed by the AAA's Practice Committee and the rules are amended effective May 1, 1993 in response to the report.

An expedited system has been included in the rules for cases in which each party's claims involve less than $25,000, exclusive of interest and arbitration costs. This will assist parties in resolving such claims.

The rules contain procedures for the selection of arbitrators with appropriate expertise, including both those affiliated with the securities industry and those who are not. In the interest of fairness, the AAA has developed specific guidelines defining what constitutes an industry-affiliated arbitrator. Under these rules, lists of arbitrators and biographical information on each are sent to the parties for selection of the arbitrators. In addition, the arbitrators sign an oath of office and are required to disclose any relationship with the parties or their representative even if such circumstances become known after the hearing commences.

These features, as well as others contained in the rules, will assist the parties in resolving disputes fairly and promptly.

Governmental agencies have issued guidelines and regulations governing arbitration of future disputes involving securities. Consistent with such regulations, the parties can provide for the arbitration of future disputes by inserting the following clause into their contracts:

Standard Arbitration Clause

Any controversy or claim arising out of or relating to this contract, or the breach thereof, shall be settled by arbitration administered by the American Arbitration Association in accordance its Securities Arbitration Rules, and judgment on the award rendered by the arbitrator(s) may be entered in any court having jurisdiction thereof.

Arbitration of existing disputes may be accomplished by use of the following:

We, the undersigned parties, hereby agree to submit to arbitration administered by the American Arbitration Association under its Securities Arbitration Rules the following controversy: (cite briefly). We further agree that the above controversy be submitted to (one)(three) arbitrator(s). We further agree that we will faithfully observe this agreement and the rules, and that we will abide by and perform any award rendered by the arbitrator(s) and that a judgment of the court having jurisdiction may be entered on the award.

The services of the AAA are generally concluded with the transmittal of the award. Although there is voluntary compliance with the majority of awards, judgment on the award can be entered in a court having appropriate jurisdiction if necessary.

Administrative Fees

The AAA's administrative fees are based on service charges. There is a filing fee based on the amount of the claim or counterclaim, ranging from $300 on claims below $25,000 to a maximum of $4,000 for claims in excess of $5 million. In addition, there are service charges for hearings held and postponements and a processing fee for prolonged cases. This fee information, which is contained on pages 24 and 25 of this pamphlet, allows the parties to exercise control over their administrative fees. The fees cover AAA administrative services; they do not cover arbitrator compensation or expenses, reporting services, or any postaward charge incurred by the parties in enforcing the award.

MEDIATION

The parties may wish to submit their dispute to mediation prior to arbitration. In mediation, the neutral mediator assists the parties in reaching a settlement, but does not have the authority to make a binding decision or award. Mediation is administered by the AAA in accordance with its Commercial Mediation Rules. There is no additional administrative fee where parties to a pending arbitration attempt to mediate their dispute under the AAA's auspices. If the parties want to adopt mediation as a part of their contractual dispute settlement procedure, they can insert the following mediation clause into their contract in conjunction with a standard arbitration provision:

> If a dispute arises out of or relates to this contract, or the breach thereof, and if said dispute cannot be settled through negotiation, the parties agree first to try in good faith to settle the dispute by mediation administered by the American Arbitration Association under its Commercial Mediation Rules, before resorting to arbitration, litigation, or some other dispute resolution procedure.

If the parties want to use a mediator to resolve an existing dispute, they can enter into the following submission:

> The parties hereby submit the following dispute to mediation administered by the American Arbitration Association under its Commercial Mediation Rules. (The clause may also provide for the qualifications of the mediator(s), method of payment, locale of meetings and any other item of concern to the parties.)

Even if your contract does not provide for administration by the AAA, arbitration or mediation might be available through pilot projects involving various brokerage firms and securities exchanges. Your local AAA office can provide more information about these programs.

LARGE CASE PROCEDURES

Recognizing that large, complex arbitrations often present unique procedural problems, the AAA, working with attorneys, arbitrators, and industry advisory groups, has developed special Supplementary Procedures for Large, Complex Disputes as part of its Large, Complex Case Dispute Resolution Program. The overall purpose of these procedures is to provide for the efficient, economical and speedy resolution of larger disputes (i.e., cases involving claims in excess of $1,000,000). Cases are administered by senior AAA staff. The procedures provide for an early administrative conference with the AAA and a preliminary hearing with the arbitrators. Documentary exchanges and other essential exchanges of information are facilitated. The procedures also provide that a statement of reasons may accompany the award, if requested by the parties. The procedures are meant to supplement applicable rules that the parties have agreed to use. They include the possibility of the use of mediation to resolve some or all issues at an early stage.

The procedures are party driven. They will apply only where the parties agree to their use (unless a court or another entity directs their application) and the parties are free to modify any provision of the procedures. Indeed, the entire process may be tailored to suit the particular requirements of the parties to any single dispute.

Securities Arbitration Rules

1. Agreement of Parties

The parties shall be deemed to have made these rules a part of their arbitration agreement whenever they have provided for arbitration by the American Arbitration Association (hereinafter AAA) or under its Securities Arbitration Rules. These rules and any amendment of them shall apply in the form obtaining at the time the demand for arbitration or submission agreement involving a securities or commodity futures dispute is received by the AAA.

2. Name of Tribunal

Any tribunal constituted by the parties for the settlement of their dispute under these rules shall be called the Securities Arbitration Tribunal.

3. Administrator and Delegation of Duties

When parties agree to arbitrate under these rules, or when they provide for arbitration by the AAA and an arbitration is initiated under these rules, they thereby authorize the AAA to administer the arbitration. The authority and duties of the AAA are established in the agreement of the parties and in these rules, and may be carried out through such of the AAA's representatives as it may direct. The AAA may, in its discretion, assign the administration of an arbitration to any of its regional offices.

4. National Panel of Arbitrators

The AAA shall establish and maintain a National Panel of Securities Arbitrators and shall appoint arbitrators as provided in these rules.

5. Initiation under an Arbitration Provision in a Contract

Arbitration under an arbitration provision in a contract shall be initiated in the following manner:

(a) The initiating party (hereinafter claimant) shall, within the time period, if any, specified in the contract(s), give written notice to the other party (hereinafter respondent) of its intention to arbitrate (demand), which notice shall contain a statement setting forth the nature of the dispute, the amount involved, if any, the remedy sought, and the hearing locale requested, and

(b) shall file at any regional office of the AAA three copies of the notice and three copies of the arbitration provisions of the contract, together with the appropriate filing fee as provided in the schedule on page 24. The AAA shall give notice of such filing to the respondent or respondents.

6. Answers and Third-Party Claims

A respondent may file a answering statement in duplicate with the AAA within 20 days from the commencement of administration, simultaneously sending a copy of the answering statement to the claimant. A party may also file an answer to a changed or new claim, as provided in Section 8. If no answering statement is filed within the time period stated above, it will be treated as a general denial of the claim.

If a counterclaim is asserted, it shall contain a statement setting forth the nature of the counterclaim, the amount involved, if any, and the remedy sought. If a counterclaim is made, the appropriate fee provided in the schedule on page 24 shall be forwarded to the AAA with the answering statement.

If a respondent fails to file an answering statement within the time period stated above, the claimant may serve respondent with a written request for an answering statement. A respondent who fails to file an answer within 10 days of such a request may, in the discretion of the arbitrator, be barred from presenting any matter, argument or defense (other than a general denial) that could have been raised in an answering statement, but an arbitrator may not enter an award against a party without hearing evidence to support the making of an award. Arbitrators should endeavor to rule on requests to bar such matters prior to the hearing.

The demand or answer may assert a third-party claim against another party, if the third party is obliged to arbitrate the subject of that party's claim under these rules. The arbitrator is authorized to resolve an dispute over such joinder.

7. Initiation under a Submission

Parties to any existing dispute may start an arbitration under these rules by filing at any regional office of the AAA three copies of a written submission to arbitrate under these rules, signed by the parties. It shall contain a statement of the matter in dispute, the amount involved, if any, the remedy sought, and the hearing locale requested, together with the appropriate filing fee as provided in the schedule on page 24.

8. Changes of Claim

After filing of a claim, if either party desires to make any new or different claim or counterclaim, it shall be made in writing and filed with the AAA. Simultaneously, a copy must be sent to the other party, who shall have a period of 10 days from the date of such transmittal within which to file an answer with the AAA. After the arbitrator is appointed, however, no new or different claim may be submitted except with the arbitrator's consent.

9. Applicable Procedures

Unless the AAA in its discretion determines otherwise, the Expedited Procedures shall be applied in any case where no disclosed claim or counterclaim exceeds $25,000, exclusive of interest and arbitration costs. Parties may also agree to use the Expedited Procedures in cases involving claims in excess of $25,000. The Expedited Procedures shall be applied as described in Sections 51 through 55 of these rules, in addition to any other portion of these rules that is not in conflict with the Expedited Procedures.

All other cases shall be administered in accordance with Sections 1 through 50 of these rules.

10. Administrative Conference, Preliminary Hearing and Mediation Conference

At the request of any party or at the discretion of the AAA, an administrative conference with the AAA and the parties and/or their representatives will be scheduled in appropriate cases to expedite the arbitration proceedings. There is no administrative fee for this service.

At the request of any party or at the discretion of the arbitrator or the AAA, a preliminary hearing with the parties and/or their representatives and the arbitrator may be scheduled by the arbitrator to specify issues to be resolved, to stipulate to uncontested facts, to schedule hearings to resolve the dispute, and to consider other matters that will expedite the arbitration proceedings. There is no administrative fee for the first preliminary hearing. Unless tile parties agree otherwise, the AAA at any, stage of the proceeding may arrange a mediation, conference under the Commercial Mediation Rules, in order to facilitate settlement. The mediator shall not be an arbitrator appointed to the case. where the parties to a pending arbitration agree to mediate under the AAA's rules, no additional administrative fee is required to initiate the mediation.

11. Exchange of Information

Consistent with the expedited nature of arbitration, the arbitrator may establish (i) the extent of and schedule for production of documents and other information and (ii) identification of witnesses to be called. The arbitrator is authorized to resolve any dispute over this information exchange.

12. Fixing of Locale

The parties may agree on the locale where the arbitration is to be held. If any party requests that the hearing be held in a specific locale and the other party files no objection thereto within 20 days after notice of the request has been sent to it by the AAA, the locale shall be the one requested. If a party objects to the locale requested by the other party, the AAA shall have the power to determine the locale and its decision shall be final and binding.

13. Qualifications of an Arbitrator

Any neutral arbitrator appointed pursuant to Section 14, 15, 16 or 52, or selected by mutual choice of the parties or their appointees, shall be subject to disqualification for the reasons specified in Section 20. If the parties agree in writing, the arbitrator shall not be subject to disqualification for those reasons. Unless the parties agree otherwise, an arbitrator selected unilaterally by one party is a party-appointed arbitrator and is not subject to disqualification pursuant to Section 20.

The term "arbitrator" in these rules refers to the arbitration panel, whether composed of one or more arbitrators and whether the arbitrators are neutral or party appointed. An affiliated arbitrator as provided in Sections 14 and 18 is one who has or has had direct involvement in or relationship with the securities brokerage industry for a minimum of three years if now employed in that industry or for a minimum of five years if no longer so employed. Involvement in or relationship with would include (a) employment at a brokerage firm in a professional capacity, whether employed in sales, management, support or trading, or (b) employed as counsel, accountant or other professional who devotes a majority of his or her efforts to brokerage or brokerage-related matters. Persons out of the industry for more than 10 years are not affiliated. Persons whose firms or direct family members derive significant income from securities brokerage or brokerage-related matters, but who do not qualify as affiliated arbitrators as defined above, may not serve as arbitrators.

14. Appointment from Panel

If the parties have not appointed an arbitrator and have not provided any other method of appointment, the arbitrator shall be appointed in the following manner: immediately after the filing of the demand or submission, the AAA shall send simultaneously to each party to the dispute two lists of names and biographical information of persons chosen from the panel. The first list, from which one arbitrator will be appointed, will contain names of arbitrators affiliated with the securities industry. The second list, from which two arbitrators will be appointed, will contain names of arbitrators not affiliated with the securities industry. Additional biographical information on proposed arbitrators may be available from the AAA and will be furnished to a party upon request. Each party to the dispute has 20 days from the transmittal date in which to strike any names objected to, number the remaining names in order of preference, and return the list to the AAA. If a party does not return the list within the time specified, all persons shall be deemed acceptable. From among the persons who have been approved on both lists and in accordance with the designated order of mutual preference, the AAA shall invite the arbitrator(s) who will serve.

If appointments cannot be made from the submitted list, the AAA will submit to the parties a final list of proposed arbitrators, consisting of a limited number of names. Each separately appearing party may strike on a peremptory basis one name for each arbitrator to be appointed, and return the list to the AAA within 10 days from the date of the AAA's transmittal to the parties. The AAA shall make the appointment(s) from the name(s) remaining on the list.

15. Direct Appointment by a Party

If the agreement of the parties names an arbitrator of specifies a method of appointing an arbitrator, that designation or method shall be followed. The notice of appointment, with the name and address of the arbitrator, shall be filed with the AAA by the appointing party. Upon the request of any appointing party, the AAA shall submit a list of members of the panel from which the party may, if it so desires, make the appointment.

If the agreement specifies a period of time within which an arbitrator shall be appointed and any party fails to make the appointment within that period, the AAA shall make the appointment.

If no period of time is specified in the agreement, the AAA shall notify the party to make the appointment. If, within 2 days, an arbitrator has not been appointed by a party within the specified period, the AAA shall make the appointment.

16. Appointment of Neutral Arbitrator by Party Appointed Arbitrators or Parties

If the parties have selected party-appointed arbitrators, or if such arbitrators have been appointed as provided in Section 15, and the parties have authorized them to appoint a neutral arbitrator within a specified time and no appointment is made within that time or any agreed extension, the AAA may appoint a neutral arbitrator, who shall act as chairperson.

If no period of time is specified for appointment of the neutral arbitrator and the party-appointed arbitrators or the parties do not make the appointment within 10 days from of the last party-appointed arbitrator, the AAA may appoint the neutral arbitrator, who shall act as chairperson.

If the parties have agreed that their party-appointed arbitrators shall appoint the neutral arbitrator from the panel, the AAA shall furnish to the party-appointed arbitrators a list selected from the panel, and the appointment of the neutral arbitrator shall be made as provided in Section 14.

17. Nationality of Arbitrator in International Arbitration

Where the parties are nationals or residents of different countries, any neutral arbitrator shall, upon the request of any party be appointed from among the nationals of a country other than that of any of the parties. The request must be made prior to the time set for the appointment of the arbitrator as agreed by the parties or set by these rules.

18. Number of Arbitrators

Where the claim of any party exceeds $25,000, the dispute shall be heard and determined by three arbitrators. Unless the parties otherwise agree, the majority shall be arbitrators not affiliated with the securities industry. All other disputes shall be heard and determined by one arbitrator not affiliated with the securities industry, as provided in Section 52.

19. Notice to Arbitrator of Appointment

Notice of the appointment of the neutral arbitrator, whether appointed by agreement of the parties or by the AAA, shall be sent to the arbitrator by the AAA, together with a copy of these rules. The signed acceptance of the arbitrator shall be filed with the AAA prior to the opening of the first hearing.

20. Disclosure and Challenge Procedure

Any person appointed as neutral arbitrator shall disclose to the AAA any circumstance likely to affect impartiality, including any bias or any financial or personal interest in the result of the arbitration or any past or present relationship with the parties or their representatives. Upon receipt of such information from the arbitrator or another source, the AAA shall communicate the information to the parties and, if it deems it appropriate to do so, to the arbitrator and others. Upon objection of a party to the continued service of a neutral arbitrator, the AAA shall determine whether the arbitrator should be disqualified and shall inform the parties of its decision, which shall be conclusive.

21. Vacancies

If for an reason an arbitrator is unable to perform the duties of the office, the AAA may, on proof satisfactory to it, declare the office vacant. Vacancies shall be filled in accordance with the applicable provisions of these rules. In the event of a vacancy in a panel of arbitrators after the hearings have commenced, unless the vacancy shall be filled as provided above, and the newly constituted panel shall determine all or part of any prior hearing shall be repeated.

22. Date, Time and Place of Hearing

The arbitrator shall set the date, time and place for each hearing. The AAA shall send a notice of hearing to the parties at least 10 days in advance of the hearing date, unless otherwise agreed by the parties.

23. Representation

Any party may be represented by counsel or other authorized representative. A party intending to be represented shall notify the other party and the AAA of the name, address and telephone number of the representative at least three days prior to the date set for the hearing at which that person is first to appear. When a representative initiates an arbitration or responds for a party, notice of representation is deemed to have been given.

24. Stenographic Record

Any party desiring a stenographic record shall make arrangements directly with a stenographer and shall notify the other parties of these arrangements in advance of the hearing. The requesting party or parties shall pay the cost of the record.

If the transcript is agreed by the parties to be, or determined by the arbitrator to be, the official record of the proceeding, it must be made available to the arbitrator and to the other parties for inspection, at a date, time and place determined by the arbitrator.

25. Interpreters

Any party wishing an interpreter shall make all arrangements directly with the interpreter and shall assume the costs of the service.

26. Attendance at Hearings; Experts

The arbitrator shall maintain the privacy of the hearings unless the law provides to the contrary. Any person having a direct interest in the arbitration is entitled to attend hearings. Although expert witnesses are generally permitted to attend the hearing, the arbitrator shall have the power to require the exclusion of any witness, other than a party or other essential person, during the testimony of any other witness. It shall be discretionary with the arbitrator to determine the propriety of the attendance of any other person.

27. Postponements

The arbitrator for good cause shown may postpone any hearing upon the request of a party or upon the arbitrator's own initiative, and shall grant a postponement when all of the parties agree.

28. Oaths

Before proceeding with the first hearing, each arbitrator may take an oath of office and, if required by law, shall do so. The arbitrator may require witnesses to testify under oath administered by any duly qualified person and, if it is required by law or requested by any party, shall do so.

29. Majority Decision

All decisions of the arbitrators must be by a majority. The award must also be made by a majority unless the concurrence of all is expressly required by the arbitration agreement or by law.

30. Order of Proceedings and Communication with Arbitrator

A hearing shall be opened by the filing of the oath of the arbitrator, where required; by the recording of the date, time and place of the hearing, and the presence of the arbitrator, the parties and their representatives, if any; and by the receipt by the arbitrator of the statement of the claim and the answering statement, if any.

The arbitrator may, at the beginning of the hearing, ask for statements clarifying the issues involved. In some cases, part or all of the above will have been accomplished at the preliminary hearing conducted by the arbitrator pursuant to Section 10.

The complaining party shall then present evidence to support its claim. The defending party shall then present evidence supporting its defense. Witnesses for each party shall submit to questions or other examination. The arbitrator has the discretion to vary this procedure but shall afford a full and equal opportunity to all parties for the presentation of any material and relevant evidence.

Exhibits, when offered by either party, may be received in evidence by the arbitrator.

The names and addresses of all witnesses and a description of the exhibits in the order received shall be made a part of the record.

There shall be no direct communication between the parties and a neutral arbitrator other than at oral hearing, unless the parties and the arbitrator agree otherwise. Any other oral or written communication from the parties to the neutral arbitrator shall be directed to the AAA for transmittal to the arbitrator.

31. Arbitration in the Absence of a Party or Representative

Unless the law provides to the contrary, the arbitration may proceed in the absence of any party or representative who, after due notice, fails to be present or fails to obtain a postponement. An award shall not be made solely on the default of a party. The arbitrator shall require the party who is present to submit such evidence as the arbitrator may require for the making of an award.

32. Evidence

The parties may offer evidence that is relevant and material to dispute, and shall produce such evidence as the arbitrator deems necessary to an understanding and determination of the dispute. An arbitrator or other person authorized by law to subpoena witnesses or documents may do so upon the request of any party of independently.

The arbitrator shall be the judge of the relevance and materialization of the evidence offered, and conformity to legal rules of evidence shall not be necessary. All evidence shall be taken in the presence of all the arbitrators and all of the parties, except where any of the parties is absent in default or has waived the right to be present.

33. Evidence by Affidavit and Posthearing Filing of Documents or other Evidence

The arbitrator may receive and consider the evidence of witnesses by affidavit, but shall give it only such weight as the arbitrator deems it entitled to after consideration of any objection made to its admission.

If the parties agree or the arbitrator directs that documents or other evidence be submitted to the arbitrator after the hearing, the documents or other evidence shall be filed with the AAA for transmission to the arbitrator. All parties shall be afforded an opportunity to examine such documents or other evidence.

34. Inspection or Investigation

An arbitrator finding it necessary to make an inspection or investigation in connection with the arbitration shall direct the AAA to so advise the parties. The arbitrator shall set the date and time and the AAA shall notify the parties. Any party who so desires may be present at such an inspection or investigation. In the event that one or all parties are not present at the inspection or investgation, the arbitrator shall make a verbal or written report to the parties and afford them an opportunity to comment.

35. Interim Measures

The arbitrator may direct whatever interim measures are deemed necessary with respect to the dispute, including measures for the conservation of property, without prejudice to the rights of the parties or to the final determination of the dispute. Such interim measures may be taken in the form of an interim award and the arbitrator may require security for the costs of such measures.

36. Closing of Hearing

The arbitrator shall specifically inquire of all parties whether they have any further proofs to offer or witnesses to be heard. Upon receiving negative replies or if satisfied that the record is complete, the arbitrator shall declare the hearing closed.

If briefs are to be filed, the hearing shall be declared closed as of the final date set by the arbitrator for the receipt of briefs. If documents are to be filed as provided in Section 33 and the date set for their receipt is later than that set for the receipt of briefs, the later date shall be the date of closing the hearing. The time limit within which the arbitrator shall endeavor to make the award shall start to run, in the absence of other agreements by the parties, upon the closing of the hearing.

37. Reopening of Hearing

The hearing may be reopened on the arbitrator's initiative, or upon application of a party, at any time before the award is made. If reopening the hearing would prevent the making of the award within the specific time agreed on by the parties in the contract(s) out of which the controversy has arisen, the matter may not be reopened unless the parties agree on an extension of time.

When no specific date is fixed in the contract, the arbitrator may reopen the hearing and shall have thirty days from the closing of the reopened hearing within which to make an award.

38. Waiver of Oral Hearing

Where each party's claim does not exceed $5,000, exclusive of interest and costs, the dispute shall be resolved by submission of documents, unless any party requests an oral hearing, or the arbitrator determines that an oral hearing is necessary. The parties may also provide, by written agreement, for if the part the waiver of oral hearings in any case. If the parties are unable to agree as to the procedure, the AAA shall specify a fair and equitable procedure.

39. Waiver of Rules

Any party who proceeds with the arbitration after knowledge that any provision or requirement of these rules has not been complied with and who fails to state an objection in writing shall be deemed to have waived the right to object.

40. Extensions of Time

The parties may modify any period of time by mutual agreement. The AAA or the arbitrator may for good cause extend any period of time established by these rules, except the time for making the award. The AAA shall notify the parties of any extension.

41. Serving of Notice

Each party shall be deemed to have consented that any papers, notices, or process necessary or proper for the initiation or continuation of an arbitration under these rules; for any court action in connection therewith; or for the entry of judgment on any award made under these rules may be served on a party by mail addressed to the party or its representative at the last known address or by personal service, in or outside the state where the arbitration is to be held, provided that reasonable opportunity to be heard with regard thereto has been granted to the party.

The AAA and the parties may also use facsimile transmission, telex, telegram or other written forms of electronic communication to give the notices required by these rules.

42. The Award

(a) The arbitrator shall endeavor to issue the award promptly and, unless otherwise agreed by the parties, within 30 days from the date of closing of the hearing or, if oral hearings have been waived, from the date of the AAA's transmittal of the final statements and proofs to the arbitrator.

(b) The award shall be in writing, shall be signed by a majority of the arbitrators, and shall be executed in the manner required by law. The award shall contain the names of the parties and representatives, if any, a summary of the issues, including type(s) of any security or product in controversy, the damages and/or other relief requested and awarded, a statement of any other issues resolved, a statement regarding the disposition of any statutory claim, the names of arbitrators, the date when the case was filed, the date of the award, the number and dates of hearings, the location of the hearings, and the signatures of the arbitrators concurring in or dissenting from the award.

(c) The arbitrator may grant any remedy or relief that the arbitrator deems just and equitable and within the scope of the agreement of the parties, including, but not limited to, specific performance of a contract. The arbitrator shall, in the award, assess arbitration fees, expenses, and compensation as provided in Sections 46, 47 and 48 in favor of any party and, in the event that any administrative fees or expenses are due the AAA, in favor of the AAA.

(d) If the parties settle their dispute during the course of the arbitration, the arbitrator may, upon the written agreement of those parties, set forth the terms of the agreed settlement in an award. Such an award is called a consent award.

(e) Parties shall accept as legal delivery of the award the placing of the award or a true copy thereof in the mail addressed to a party or its representative at the last known address, personal service of the award, or the filing of the award in any other manner that is permitted by law.

(f) An award issued under these rules shall be publicly available provided that the names of the parties will be not publicly available.

43. Correction of Award

Within 20 days after the transmittal of an award, any party, upon notice to the other parties, may request that the arbitrator correct any clerical, typographical, technical or computational error in the award. The arbitrator is not empowered to redetermine the merits of any claim already decided.

The other parties shall be given 10 days to respond to the request. The arbitrator shall dispose of the request within 20 days after transmittal by the AAA to the arbitrator of the request and any response thereto.

44. Release of Documents for judicial Proceedings

The AAA shall, upon the written request of a party, furnish to the party, at its expense, certified copies of any papers in the AAA's possession that may be required in judicial proceedings relating to the arbitration.

45. Applications to Court and Exclusion of Liability

(a) No judicial proceeding by a party relating to the subject matter of the arbitration shall be deemed a waiver of the party's right to arbitrate.

(b) Neither the AAA nor any arbitrator in a proceeding under these rules is a necessary party in judicial proceedings relating to the arbitration.

(c) Parties to these rules shall be deemed to have consented that judgment upon the arbitration award may be entered in any federal or state court having jurisdiction thereof.

(d) Neither the AAA nor any arbitrator shall be liable to any party for any act or omission in connection with any arbitration conducted under these rules.

46. Administrative Fees

As a not-for-profit organization, the AAA shall prescribe filing and other administrative fees to compensate it for the cost of providing administrative services. The fees in effect when the demand for arbitration or submission agreement is received shall be applicable.

The filing fee shall be advanced by the initiating party or parties, subject to final apportionment by the arbitrator in the award.

The AAA may, in the event of extreme hardship on the part of any party, defer or reduce the administrative fees.

47. Expenses

Unless the parties agree otherwise, all expenses of the arbitration, including required travel and other expenses of the arbitrator and AAA representatives, and the cost of any proof produced at the direct request of the arbitrator, shall be borne equally by the parties, subject to final allocation by the arbitrator as provided in Section 42(c).

48. Neutral Arbitrator's

Compensation Unless the parties agree otherwise, members of the National Panel of Securities Arbitrators will receive compensation for the first and second days of service at the rate of $400 per day per arbitrator, advanced equally by the parties.

For service thereafter, an appropriate daily rate and other arrangements will be discussed by the administrator with the parties prior to the appointment of the arbitrator. If the parties fail to agree to the terms of compensation, an appropriate rate will be established by the AAA and communicated in writing to the parties.

49. Deposits

The AAA may require the parties to deposit in advance of any hearings such sums of money as it deems necessary to cover the expense of the arbitration, including the arbitrator's fees, if any, and shall render an accounting tothe parties and return any unexpected balance at the conclusion of the case.

50. Interpretation and Application of Rules

The arbitrator shall interpret and apply these rules insofar as they relate to the arbitrator's powers and duties. When there is more than one arbitrator and a difference arises amon them concerning the meaning or application of these rules, it shall be decided by a majority vote. If that is not possible, either an arbitrator or a party may refer the question to the AAA for final decision. All other rules shall be interpreted and applied by the AAA.

Expedited Procedures

51. Notice by Telephone

The parties still accept all notices from the AAA by, telephone. Such notices by the AAA shall subsequently be, confirmed in writing to the parties. Should there be a failure to confirm in writing any notice here under, the proceeding shall nonetheless be valid if notice has, in fact, been given by telephone.

52. Appointment and Qualifications of Arbitrator

The AAA shall submit simultaneously to each party an identical list of five proposed arbitrators drawn from the National Panel of Securities Arbitrators, from which one arbitrator shall be appointed. The arbitrators contained on the list will not be affiliated with the securities industry.

Each party may strike two names from the list on a peremptory basis. The list is returnable to the AAA within 20 days from the date of the AAA's transmittal to the parties.

If for any reason the appointment of an arbitrator cannot be made from the list, the AAA may make the appointment from among other members of the panel without the submission of additional lists.

The parties will be given notice by telephone by the AAA of the appointment of the arbitrator, who shall be subject to disqualification for the reasons specified in Section 20. Within seven days, the parties shall notify the AAA, by telephone, of any objection to the arbitrator appointed. Any objection by a party to the arbitrator shall be confirmed in writing to the AAA with a copy to the other party or parties.

53. Date, Time and Place of Hearing

The arbitrator shall set the date, time and place of the hearing. The AAA will notify the parties by telephone, at least seven days in advance of the hearing date. A formal notice of hearing will also be sent by the AAA to the parties.

54. The Hearing

Generally, the hearing shall be completed within one day, unless the dispute is resolved by submission of documents under Section 38. The arbitrator, for good cause shown, may schedule an additional hearing to be held within seven days.

55. Time of Award

Unless otherwise agreed by the parties, the arbitrator shall endeavor to render the award not later than 14 days from the date of the closing of the hearing.

Administrative Fees

The AAA's administrative charges are based on filing and service fees. Arbitrator compensation, if any, is not included. Unless the parties agree otherwise, arbitrator compensation and administrative fees are subject to allocation by the arbitrator in the award.

Filing Fees

A nonrefundable filing fee is payable in full by a filing party when a claim, counterclaim, or additional claim is filed, as provided below.

Amount of Claim	Filing Fee
Up to $25,000	$300
Above $25,000 to $50,000	$500
Above $50,000 to $250,00	$1,000
Above $250,000 to $500,000	$2,000
Above $500,000 to $5,000,000	$3,000
Above $5,000,000	$4,000

When no amount can be stated at the time of filing, the filing fee is $1,000, subject to adjustment when the claim or counterclaim is disclosed.

When a claim or counterclaim is not for a monetary amount, an appropriate filing fee will be determined by the AAA.

HEARING FEES

For each day of hearing held before a single arbitrator, an administrative fee of $100 is payable by each party.

For each day of hearing held before a multi-arbitrator panel, an administrative fee of $150 is payable by each party.

POSTPONEMENT FEES

A fee of $100 is payable by a party causing a postponement of any hearing scheduled before a single arbitrator. A fee of $150 is payable by a party causing a postponement of any hearing scheduled before a multi-arbitrator panel.

PROCESSING FEES

No processing fee is payable until 180 days after a case is initiated.

On single-arbitrator cases, a processing fee of $150 per party is payable 180 days after the case is initiated, and every 90 days thereafter, until the case is withdrawn or settled or the hearings are closed by the arbitrator.

On multiarbitrator cases, a processing fee of $200 per party is payable 180 days after the case is initiated, and every 90 days thereafter, until the case is withdrawn or settled or the hearings are closed by the arbitrators.

SUSPENSION FOR NONPAYMENT

If arbitrator compensation or administrative charges have not been paid in full, the AAA may so inform the parties in order that one of them may make the required payment. If such payments are not made, the arbitrator may order the suspension or termination of the proceedings. If no arbitrator has yet been appointed, the AAA may suspend the proceedings in such a situation.

HEARING ROOM RENTAL

Rooms for hearings are available on a rental basis. Check with our local office for availability and rates.

AAA OFFICES

AZ Phoenix (85012-2365) - Harry Kaminsky
333 East Osborn Road, Suite 310 - (602) 234-0950/230-2151 (Fax)

CA Irvine (92714-6220) - Lori S. Markowicz
2601 Main Street, Suite 240 - (714) 474 5090/474-5087 (Fax)
Los Angeles (90010-1108) - Rocco M. Scanza
3055 Wilshire Boulevard, Floor 7 - (213) 383-6516/386-2251 (Fax)
San Diego (92101-5278) Dennis Sharp
525 C Street, Suite 400 (619) 239-3051/239-3807 (Fax)
San Francisco (94104-1113) - Charles A. Cooper
417 Montgomery Street - (415) 981-3901/781-8426 (Fax)

CO Denver (80264-2101) - Mark Appel
1660 Lincoln Street, Suite 2150 - (303) 831-0823/832-3626 (Fax)

CT East Hartford (06108-3240) - Karen M. Jalkut
111 Founders Plaza, Floor 17 - (203) 289-3993/282-0459 (Fax)

DC Washington (20036-4104) - Garylee Cox
1150 Connecticut Avenue, NW, Floor 6 - (202) 296-8510/872-9574 (Fax)
***Office of National Affairs - Thomas R. Colosi**
1730 Rhode Island Avenue, NW, Suite 512 - (202) 331-7073/331-3356

FL Miami (33131-2501) - Reni Grafals
99 SE Fifth Street, Suite 200 - (305) 358-7777/358-4931 (Fax)
Orlando (32801-2742) - Mark Sholander
201 East Pine Street, Suite 800 - (407) 648-1185/649-8668 (Fax)

GA Atlanta (30345-3203) - India Johnson
1975 Century Boulevard, NE, Suite I - (404) 325-0101/325-8034 (Fax)
*Does not administer cases

HI Honolulu (96813-4714) - Keith W. Hunter
810 Richards Street, Suite 641 - (808) 531-0541/533-2306 (Fax)
In Guam, (671) 477-1845/477-3178 (Fax)

IL Chicago (60601-7601) - David Scott Carfello
225 North Michigan Avenue, Suite 2527 - (312) 616-6560/819-0404 (Fax)

LA New Orleans (70130-6101) - Deann Gladwell
650 Poydras Street, Suite 1535 - (504) 522-8781/561-8041 (Fax)

MA Boston (02110-1703) - Richard M. Reilly
133 Federal Street - (617) 451-6600/451-0763 (Fax)

MI Southfield (48076-3728) - Mary A. Bedikian
One Towne Square, Suite 1600 - (313) 352-5500/352-3147 (Fax)

MN Minneapolis (55402-1092) - James R. Deye
514 Nicollet Mall, Suite 670 - (612) 332-6545/342-2334 (Fax)

MO Kansas City (64106,-2110) - Lori A. Madden
1101 Walnut Street, Suite 903 - (816) 221-6401/471-5264 (Fax)

St. Louis (63101-1614) - Neil Moldenhauer
One Mercantile Center, Suite 2512 - (314) 621-7175/621-3730 (Fax)

NV Las Vegas (89102-8719) - Kelvin Chin
4425 Spring Mountain Road, Suite 310 - (702) 364-8009/364-8084 (Fax)

NJ Somerset (08873-4120) - Richard Naimark
265 Davidson Avenue, Suite 140 - (908) 560-9560/560-8850 (Fax)

NY Garden City (11530-2004) - Mark A. Resnick
666 Old Country Road, Suite 603 - (516) 222-1660/745-6447 (Fax)

New York (10020-1203) - Florence M. Peterson
140 West 51st Street - (212) 484-4000/307-4387 (Fax)

Syracuse (13202-1376) - Deborah A. Brown
205 South Salina Street - (315) 472-5483/472-0966 (Fax)

White Plains (10601-4485) - Marion J. Zinman
34 South Broadway - (914) 946-1119/946-2661 (Fax)

NC Charlotte (28202-2431) - Neil Carmichael
428 East Fourth Street, Suite 300 - (704) 347-0200/347-2804 (Fax)

OH Cincinnati (45202-2809) - Philip S. Thompson
441 Vine Street, Suite 3308 - (513) 241-8434/241-8437 (Fax)

Middleburg Heights (44130-3490) - Eileen B. Vernon
17900 Jefferson Road, Suite 101 - (216) 891-4741/891-4740 (Fax)

PA Philadelphia (19102-4106) - Kenneth Egger
230 South Broad Street, Floor 6 - (215) 732-5260/732-5002 (Fax)

Pittsburgh (15222-1207) - John F. Schano
Four Gateway Center, Room 419 - (412) 261-3617/261-6055 (Fax)

RI Providence (02903-1082) - Mark Bayliss
115 Cedar Street - (401) 453-3250/453-6194 (Fax)

TN Nashville (37219-2111) - Sheila R. Davy
221 Fourth Avenue North - (615) 256-5857/244-8570 (Fax)

TX Dallas (75240-6620) - Helmut O. Wolff
13455 Noel Road, Suite 1440 - (214) 702-8222/490-9008 (Fax)

Houston (77002-6708) - Therese Tilley
1001 Fannin Street, Suite 1005 - (713) 739-1302/739-1702 (Fax)

UT Salt Lake City (84111-3834) - Diane Abegglen
645 South 200 East, Suite 203 - (801) 531-9748/531-0660 (Fax)

WA Seattle (98101-2511) - Neal M. Blacker
1325 Fourth Avenue, Suite 1414 (206) 622-6435/343-5679 (Fax)

AAA164-20M-4/93

INDEX

About the Author

J. KIRKLAND GRANT, Professor of Law, Touro College of Law, Huntington, New York, has taught securities and business law courses at many universities, and was dean at the Delaware Law School. He received his law and business degrees from the University of Michigan and is a member of the Bars of Michigan, New York, South Carolina and federal courts including the U.S. Supreme Court. Grant was in general corporate and securities practice with the Wall Street firm of Sullivan & Cromwell and the Boston firm of Bingham, Dana & Gould. He is a member of the American Law Institute, American Bar Association, Scribes and other legal societies. He serves on the arbitration panels of the American Arbitration Association, New York Stock Exchange, N.A.S.D. and other groups. He authored *New York Corporation Law Handbook* (1993), and other books and articles in periodicals and law reviews.

www.ingramcontent.com/pod-product-compliance
Ingram Content Group UK Ltd.
Pitfield, Milton Keynes, MK11 3LW, UK
UKHW020228290926
15470UKWH00001B/414

9 780899 306827